THE BIOPOLITICS
OF FEELING

Race, Sex, and Science

in the Nineteenth Century

KYLA SCHULLER

Duke University Press   Durham and London   2018

Designed by Amy Ruth Buchanan
Typeset in Arno Pro and League Gothic by Westchester
Publishing Services

Library of Congress Cataloging-in-Publication Data
Names: Schuller, Kyla, [date] author.
Title: The biopolitics of feeling : race, sex, and science in the
    nineteenth century / Kyla Schuller.
Description: Durham : Duke University Press, 2017. | Series:
    Anima | Includes bibliographical references and index.
Identifiers: LCCN 2017025273 (print)
LCCN 2017043095 (ebook)
ISBN 9780822372356 (ebook)
ISBN 9780822369233 (hardcover : alk. paper)
ISBN 9780822369530 (pbk. : alk. paper)
Subjects: LCSH: Sentimentalism in literature—History—
    19th century. | Emotions in literature—History—
    19th century. | Eugenics in literature—History—
    19th century. | Sex role—History—19th century. | Literature
    and science—United States—History—19th century.
Classification: LCC PN56.S475 (ebook) | LCC PN56.S475 S385
    2017 (print) | DDC 303.3/72—dc23
LC record available at https://lccn.loc.gov/2017025273

Cover art: Photo of Dr. Mary Walker, 1890. Legacy
Center Archives, Drexel University College of Medicine,
Philadelphia.

Duke University Press gratefully acknowledges the support
of the Rutgers University Research Council, which provided
funds toward the publication of this book.

Vivre, c'est sentir

—PIERRE-JEAN-GEORGES CABANIS

CONTENTS

....

ACKNOWLEDGMENTS

....

In the early spring of 2013, I became suddenly and extravagantly ill. Each day I lost another basic faculty: the strength to lift a fork, the concentration to find and attach a file to an email, the short-term memory and physical stamina to speak with a friend. I thought I was dying, and that if I could hold on another three months, it would be more than enough time to finish this book—as clear a sign of impaired cognition as could be. While I had previously been feeling overwhelmed by the enormity of the task of completing *The Biopolitics of Feeling*, when late-stage, neurological Lyme Disease struck it was this project, and the community which has made it possible, that first reminded me there was work I desperately wanted to continue.

I am deeply grateful to the many people who have helped this project become something to be proud of and who have helped me stabilize, and restabilize, during what is now a chronic, enduring illness. I thank Abena Busia and the Rutgers–New Brunswick Department of Women's and Gender Studies for arranging leave and for covering my courses during weeks and semesters I have been unable to teach: thanks in particular to Marisa Fuentes, Jasbir Puar, Brittney Cooper, Sylvia Chan-Malik, Maya Mikdashi, and Nikol Alexander-Floyd. I thank the Rutgers AAUP-AFT chapter for negotiating spectacular healthcare benefits that everyone should have; without the generous terms of this union healthcare plan I do not know if I would currently be well enough to work, let alone to have completed this book. I am grateful to my medical care team for seeing me through many periods of crisis, including osteopaths, integrative internists, neurologists, acupuncturists, psychotherapists, physical therapists, nurses, and ER teams: Dr. Kevin Weiss, Dr. Linda Tao, Dr. Carolyn Britton, Dr. Alan Pollock, Dr. Maurice Beer, Dr. Pamela Yee, Dr. Jess Armine, Dr. Raphael Kellman, Selma Rondon, Monica Vitenson, Lisa Sottung, Katherine Hudson Tan, Lauren Bernard, Meghan Frederick, and others.

Many friends have helped to feed me, house me, and escort me to appointments when I lacked the physical and cognitive capacity to leave the house alone, friends to whom I owe everything: Ingrid Dudek, Marisa Fuentes, Beth Ryan, Bill Ryan, Andrea Lounibos, Brandon Best, Maureen Healy, Kent Bassett, Marta Zarzycka, William Verheul, El Glasberg, Genevieve Yue, Catherine Zimmer, Nick Gaskill, Judy Gerson, Cristina Gallo, Tia Koonse, Aimee Bahng, Gus Stadler, Raul Fernandez, Todd Huffman, Diana Lee, William Oliphant, Janet Neary, Maxe Crandall, Diana Cage, Sam Feder, Jinah Kim, Mel Chen, Elizabeth Steeby, Andy Urban, Rossi Kirilova, Nicole Fleetwood, Jordan Stein, Robyn Overstreet, Max Hantel, Jessica Ree, Sarah Blackwood, Lauren Klein, Karen Weingarten, Greta LaFleur, Jacob Hodes, Robert Chang, Jenny Hall, Cookie Woolner, Cassie Wagler, Sarah Klevan, Timothy Stewart-Winter, and others. I thank all my families for their care and concern that have helped me through these last four years, including Karen and Paul Schuller and Lisanne and Emily Dinges.

This project began in calmer times in the UC San Diego Department of Literature, a wonderful place to explore the cultural politics of racial and gender formation. Deep thanks to my dissertation committee: Shelley Streeby, Lisa Lowe, Nayan Shah, Michael Davidson, and Rosaura Sánchez, as well as Winnie Woodhull for providing such rigorous models of ethical scholarship and practices of professional care. This book would never have come to be without the freedom to be undisciplined offered first by my dissertation committee and then by my wonderful colleagues at Rutgers–New Brunswick Women's and Gender Studies, a fantastic home for work that investigates the imbrication of materiality and power. Jasbir Puar, Judy Gerson, Marisa Fuentes, Mary Hawkesworth, Brittney Cooper, Sylvia Chan-Malik, Maya Mikdashi, Carlos Decena, Ed Cohen, Harriet Davidson, and Radhika Balakrishnan in particular have provided key engagement with this book's ideas and support for its completion. And at the beginning, Clare Lees, Barbara Welke, Katya Hokanson, and Roland Greene at the University of Oregon were kind and attentive mentors who inspired me, and enabled me, to pursue a future in academia.

I have been beyond lucky to belong to several writing groups, thinking with Neel Ahuja, Aimee Bahng, Sarah Schulman, Elizabeth Steeby, Maxe Crandall, Greta LaFleur, GerShun Avilez, Andy Urban, and Jamie Pietruska, all of whom offered crucial insights into this manuscript. With Sarah Blackwood, Lauren Klein, and Karen Weingarten I have been granted the gift of visionary readers who see arguments that don't yet exist. Our writing group of six years and counting has been among the most enjoyable and functional parts of my career to date.

Many people read or heard all or parts of this manuscript and offered vital encouragement and advice: Mel Chen, Harriet Davidson, Ed Cohen, Kyla Wazana Tompkins, Peter Coviello, Dana Luciano, Gus Stadler, Arev Pivazyan,

Jordan Stein, Mia Bay, Ann Fabian, Benjy Kahan, Nick Gaskill, Cori Hayden, Marianne Noble, Jack Halberstam, Carla Freccero, Tamara Ho, Claire Jean Kim, Tonglin Lu, Banu Subramaniam, Erica Fretwell, Justin Rogers-Cooper, Neil Meyer, Christian Haines, Jason Berger, Lara Langer Cohen, Allegra McLeod, and Chase Smith, among others, and audiences at Pomona College, Rutgers–Newark, UC Berkeley, Yale University, and Haverford College. I thank my undergraduate and graduate students at Rutgers for lively discussions about many of the materials I explore in this book and for making the classroom such an enjoyable and productive space.

During archive trips and writing retreats, Aimee Bahng and Bill Bahng Boyer; Benita Brambhatt and Denise Khor; Brad Borevitz and Joe Clement; David Serlin and Brian Selznick; Johanna Fateman and Sini Anderson; and Libby Schaefer have provided a welcome mix of focus and distraction. Special collections librarians and archivists at the Bancroft Library at UC Berkeley, the Beinecke Rare Book and Manuscript Library at Yale University, the library at the American Museum of Natural History, the Patricia D. Klingenstein Library at the New-York Historical Society, the Sophia Smith Collection at Smith College, the New York Public Library, and the New York Foundling furnished crucial materials that made this book's arguments much richer. For research assistance, keen insight, moral support, general wizardry, and fierce commitment to this project, I thank Lindsey Whitmore.

Courtney Berger at Duke University Press has been a steady and patient hand at the helm, and I am grateful for her unflagging attention and support, as well as for the work of Duke's production and marketing teams. I am deeply and happily indebted to the two reviewers for the press who saw what was working in the text that was, saw what the text could become, and gave me the focus I needed to get there.

For teaching me how to write with more pleasure and less anxiety, I am grateful to Wendy Belcher for her book *Revising Your Journal Article in Twelve Weeks* and Eric Hayot for *The Elements of Academic Style: Writing for the Humanities*. I thank the American Council of Learned Societies New Faculty Fellows Program and the UC Humanities Research Institute residential research group "Species Spectacles," organized by Mel Chen, for generous fellowship terms that enabled me to work on this project, as well as the Margaret Storrs Grierson Travel-to-Collections Grant of the Sophia Smith Collection for research support. The UC Berkeley Science, Technology, and Society Center provided a much needed home during early stages of revision. Portions of an earlier version of chapter 1 appeared as "Taxonomies of Feeling: The Epistemology of Sentimentalism in Late-Nineteenth-Century Racial and Sexual Science," *American Quarterly* 64, no. 2 (2012).

INTRODUCTION

....

Sentimental Biopower

[Mothers] have the charge of immortal beings, whose physical, mental, and moral temperament, are for a long period, exclusively in their hands. Nothing save the finger of God has written on the tablet, when it is committed to them. It is important that they secure time to form deep and lasting impressions.

LYDIA HOWARD SIGOURNEY, *Letters to Mothers* (1838)

The task before us [at Carlisle Indian Industrial School] was not only that of accepting new ideas and adopting new manners, but actual physical changes and discomfort had to be borne uncomplainingly until the body adjusted itself to new tastes and habits.

LUTHER STANDING BEAR, *Land of the Spotted Eagle* (1933)

In the long, hot month of August 2015, a meme circulated on social media affirming that, contrary to recent events, "Black lives > white feelings." Police shot and killed sixty-one African Americans that summer with impunity. These murders were sometimes captured in videos that themselves became viral, merging violence and spectacle in a manner uncomfortably reminiscent of the popularity of lynching postcards a century prior. Meanwhile, the Black Lives Matter movement began directly challenging 2016 presidential hopefuls in the midst of public speeches to elucidate their commitment to racial justice. The media widely accused movement participants of incivility and jeopardizing democracy. Activists responded in part by further theorizing whiteness studies scholar Robin DiAngelo's notion of white fragility, an affective state that can result from lifelong protection from race-based stress: when such protection momentarily recedes from those who have enjoyed it, they can erupt in highly defensive behavior and outbursts of anger and rage.[1] The "Black lives > white feelings" meme captures the interdependence of two seemingly disparate dynamics driving racial formation that the summer of 2015 brought into cruel relief: white emotional well-being is produced in part by the ritualized entertainments of the security state, which hinge on the regularized death of black people.

What analytics is needed to understand a form of power that brokers black lives, in the national imaginary, as an acceptable price to pay for white affective security and national norms of political civility? "Black lives > white feelings" provides a good start: it identifies and reverses the sentimental affective economy long at the heart of U.S. power. Sentimentalism posits that the needs of the individuated subject can be reconciled to those of other individuated subjects through the guiding moral philosophy of sympathetic feeling. The Black Lives Matter meme rejects a basic premise of the domain of the political: the sentimental state, which identifies the feelings of the civilized individual— and only the civilized individual—as the kernel of liberal democracy.[2] Literary and cultural scholars have long parsed the asymmetry of sentimental sympathy, particularly as it functioned in its nineteenth-century heyday.[3] Sentimentalism stimulates the moral virtuosity and emotional release of the sympathizer and her affective attachment to the nation-state at the expense of the needs of the chosen targets of her sympathy, typically those barred from the status of the individuated Human: often the impoverished, the racialized, the conquered, the orphaned, and/or the animalized. Yet the meme crystallizes a dynamic at the core of sentimental power that has barely been addressed, let alone theorized.[4] White feelings, in the context of the United States, are the fertile products of racialized vulnerability, disposability, and death. Sentimentalism, in the midst of its feminized ethic of emotional identification, operates as a fundamental mechanism of biopower.

The Biopolitics of Feeling historicizes and theorizes this perhaps unexpected phenomenon: sentimentalism's role as a foundational technology of biopower.[5] In biopower regimes, the general trend of liberal democracy in the West since the late eighteenth century, biological existence forms the key domain of the political. State and nonstate actors govern by fostering the health and vitality of some members of the nation, while designating others for dispossession and death. At first glance, the administration of physiological "life itself," which currently includes the engineering, marketizing, and redistribution of the subcellular capacities of living bodies, lies seemingly far afield from the aesthetics and ethics of sympathy and the stock sentimental figures of the dying child and suffering slave.[6] Yet by 1978, in her study that launched sentimentalism as an academic market in its own right, Ann Douglas had already identified the recurrent biological themes running throughout nineteenth-century mass literature and their authors' floral pseudonyms.[7] However, she positioned this engagement with the living world as key evidence of her argument that sentimental culture entails a flight from the political. What Douglas acknowledges only to dismiss is that sentimentalism's interest in nonhuman life and "organic markers" like birth, illness, and death, rather than the traditional machinations of sovereign power, was part of a larger intellectual and political upheaval in the nineteenth century in which the biological emerged as the key subject and agent of history.[8] Scholars have long since reassessed Douglas's thesis, analyzing the effects of sentimental power. "In all its narrative manifestations, sentimentality is more than an exchange of ideas and emotions," Glenn Hendler writes. "It is a form of embodiment, a 'bodily bond' that links character and reader to each other and the social body."[9] Yet very few have taken up the project of assessing the integral involvement of sentimentalism—a discourse of emotional *and* physiological feeling, temporality *and* materiality—in the politics of life.[10] Given the flourishing scholarly interest in ontology in the contemporary moment, the time is ripe to reconsider sentimentalism's function as a biological discourse.

Sentimentalism's organic nature offers a bountiful yield, transforming how we think of biopower and its key agents, tactics, realms, knowledges, and social effects. In this book, I uncover how biopower materialized through the deployment of a vast and varied discourse that determined the vitality or unresponsiveness of a living body, and therefore its political claims to life, on the basis of its relative impressibility, or the energetic accumulation of sensory impressions and its capacity to regulate its engagement with the world outside the self. Sentimental discourse elaborated finely wrought rankings of the disparate corporeal capacity to receive, incorporate, and transmit sensory impressions, and for the mind to direct appropriately nonimpulsive, emotional responses to sensations—named "sentiments"—that would benefit the individual, race, and species.[11] Excavating sentimental biopower disrupts some of our most cherished scholarly and popular narratives, including binary oppositions between: social and organic processes; sentimental and scientific accounts of ontology and reason; biological and cultural interpretations of racial status; hegemonic and feminist versions of sex difference; and determinist and vitalist accounts of the capacities of matter. The biopolitical work of feeling continues into the present, and the Black Lives Matter meme directly confronts its ongoing ramifications.

The notion of the nervous system as a differentially pliable and agential entity in continuous interplay with its environment lies at the heart of nineteenth-century U.S. culture and politics. Delineating and managing the varied impressibility of the national population functioned as a key strategy of biopower, a mode I call the *sentimental politics of life*. Sentimentalism, in its function as an aesthetic mode, epistemology, and ontology, was deployed to intercede in the impressibility of the civilized body by cultivating the ability to respond to sensory stimulations on the basis of emotional reflection, rather than instinctive reflex.[12] Together, impressibility and sentimentalism distinguished civilized bodies as receptive to their milieu and able to discipline their sensory susceptibility and as such in possession of life and vitality that required protection from the threat posed by primitive bodies deemed to be impulsive and insensate, incapable of evolutionary change, whose existence was very close to running out of time. The tension between bodily vulnerability and pliability, a microcosm of the larger antinomy between the individual and the collective enshrined in liberalism, was stabilized by sentimentalism. Sentimentalism served to explain how an originally separate individual could be affectively and politically reconciled to its material coexistence with the external environment it depended on for self-constitution.[13]

Sentimental biopower emerges as the answer to the fundamental question guiding my research: How did bodies come to be understood as capable of binding together into the biopolitical phenomenon of population, an entity conceived at the biological level of species-being, in which the actions of one person, animal, or object affect the potential of the rest, even at a spatial and temporal distance? I further ask: What other technologies of power unfolded along with the new idea that sensory stimulations and heritable tendencies constitute the individual and species body? How does this overlooked history of vital matter impact our understanding of race and sex difference, particularly the paradigm that sees race in the nineteenth century as a framework of determinist and immutable divergence? These questions reexamining discourses of the body's interaction with its environment from the era prior to genetics have particular purchase given that we are currently in an era *after* the "century of the gene," in which the idea of the gene "is in considerable disarray."[14] Today, models of human and nonhuman materiality that emphasize the impact of experience on hereditary material are once again accepted by the scientific mainstream, and a range of critical theories have reopened the idea of lively matter. How does recognizing the legacy of impressibility discourse impact contemporary feminist theories that claim that plasticity, porosity, and vitality are "new" notions of matter that can overthrow liberal humanism's lingering rationalist paradigms?

The sentimental politics of life played out across scientific, medical, literary, and reform spheres in the last two-thirds of the nineteenth century, and I follow its lead across this range of sources. I uncover how scientists, reformers, and writers alike saw themselves as working in concert with a neurobiological substrate that they conceived of, in its ideal form, as in dynamic exchange with the surrounding bodies, objects, and forces that press on it, especially during the tender years of youth. I bring together accounts of the divergent dynamism of the body and the stabilizing effects of sentimentalism from a variety of genres and contexts, including: Lamarckian and Darwinian evolutionary science, abolitionist poetry, black feminist notions of sexuality, the gynecological work of the earliest women physicians, large-scale efforts to remove Irish and Native American children from their families and communities, popular and now-canonical novels and short stories, black uplift novels, and early sociology.[15] Matter responsive to all its stimulations is matter in continually erotic and fertile relations with its milieu. This book is accordingly a story of plant orgasms, internal penises, thrilling touch, race-building caresses, fragile anuses, enfolded vaginas, the "husband inheritance," hermaphrodites, masturbating children, Sapphic geese, and child prostitutes, among other phenomena.

Throughout, I examine the intertwined movements of the two most prominent discourses that consolidated political power at the site of the feeling body: science and sentimentalism.[16] This multidisciplinary approach emphasizing the politics of plasticity, rather than determinism, in nineteenth-century culture displaces many of the best-known figures in the politics of race, sex, and the human sciences in the period, and brings a more diverse cast to the fore. Lamarck, rather than Darwin, emerges as the most prominent evolutionary theorist in the American scene; the scientific cohort of the American School of Evolution, instead of the American School of Ethnology, takes center stage; Elizabeth Blackwell and Mary Walker overshadow J. Marion Sims as a major innovator in gynecology; and black feminist intellectual-activists such as Frances Harper, rather than researchers such as Richard Dugdale, figure as significant theorists of heredity and its familial legacies. With this shift, both relational ontologies and the foundational contributions of African American and white female theorists become salient to the modern concepts of racial and sexual difference.

Overall, I argue that nineteenth-century biopower consolidated in a sentimental mode that regulated the circulation of feeling throughout the population and delineated differential relational capacities of matter, and therefore the potential for evolutionary progress, as the modern concepts of race, sex, and species. Racial and sexual difference were not assigned the role of immutable, static qualities of the individual body in the nineteenth century, as has been frequently claimed. Rather, race and sex functioned as biopolitical capacities of impressibility and relationality that rendered the body the gradual product of its habit and environment, differentially positioning the claims of individuals and races for belonging in the nation-state. The notion of impressibility developed in the nineteenth century in conjunction with the emergent framework of the population, an entity governed by the processes of contagion, probability, and risk. Within the consolidating framework of biopower, bodies signify not singularly, but within a collective in which the health and vitality of the individual functions as an element of the prospects of the population, linked as it were across space and over time through the network of sympathetic nerves. Race, sex, and species difference, I assert, defined a body's relative claims to life on the basis of the perceived proportional vitality and inertia of the sensory and emotional faculties. The long, unrecognized history of sentimental biopower is necessary to our current efforts to assess and negotiate the political work done by hierarchies of bodily and emotional difference as well as to tease out the political implications of the contemporary theoretical turn toward vital materiality.

IMPRESSIBILITY AND POPULATION

I unpack the hierarchies of feeling at the heart of sentimental biopower through theorizing two new keywords that have been hiding in plain sight: *impression* and *impressibility*. Despite the central role of the "impression" in the discourse of reason from Plato to Immanuel Kant, the term is infrequently examined in its own right. It typically does not appear as an entry in philosophy or critical theory reference books, or as an indexed word in monographs that nonetheless depend on the notion, such as scholarship on John Locke, histories of neuroscience, or the philosophy of mind. As one of the strongest books in affect theory puts it, amid a careful introduction rigorously defining a range of related concepts: *impression* needs no definition, for it is simply "a word that means what it says."[17] Taking this term and the related concept of impressibility for granted, however, leaves us unable to fully reckon with the key role of the sensory body in Western epistemology and political practice.

Related to sensation, sentiment, and affect, yet not a subset of them, the *impression* characterizes how a living body is acted on by the animate and inanimate objects of its environment. The *Oxford English Dictionary* describes an impression as "the pressure of one thing upon or into the surface of another."[18] The act of touching a surface and the resulting indentation are thoroughly confounded in the noun *impression*; the act of objects coming into contact with one another necessarily leaves a "mark, trace, or indication."[19] As used by Enlightenment thinkers such as Locke and David Hume, an impression describes the movement in which an object presses on a sensory organ, creating sensation, as well as the resulting copy of the feeling registered by the brain in the form of an idea. Impressions thereby refer both to a causal action and its effects, particularly "a change produced in some *passive* subject by the operation of an external cause."[20] Objects have tangible influence on the subject by the mere act of contact, yet the independent status of each remains undisturbed. Throughout Western philosophy, sensory impressions are the means through which the individual acquires knowledge, develops ideas, and retains memory. Impressions denote the trace an object or idea leaves on the passive nervous system at the precise locations of their juncture, a marking that reinforces the ontological distinctness of each. The individual's self-transparency depends on the material world that nevertheless remains fundamentally external.

By contrast, *impressibility* denotes the capacity of a substance to receive impressions from external objects that thereby change its characteristics. Impressibility signals the capacity of matter to be alive to movements made on it, to retain and incorporate changes rendered in its material over time. Impressibility thus has a distinctly different register from the more familiar term *impressionability*, although the two registers do overlap. Sensory impressions were understood to be the trace left by contact with another, and impressionability accordingly signals suggestibility and susceptibility in the immediate time of the present, the often-racialized quality of being easily moved. However, impressibility indexed the agential responsiveness of the nervous system to external stimuli, the results of which over time would metonymically transform the body as a whole. Impressibility was understood to be an acquired quality of the refined nervous system that accrues over evolutionary time through the habits of civilization that transform animal substrate into the cultural grounds of self-constitution.[21] One of impressibility's chief theorists, psychometrist and eclectic physician Joseph Rodes Buchanan, put it bluntly: "Impressibility in its general sense, or the power of being affected by external agents[,] is proportional to the development of life."[22] The impressible nervous system rendered the civilized body the gradual outcome of its habit and surroundings, accumulating over the life span of individuals and the evolutionary time of the race.[23]

While sensibility refers to the capacity of the mind to register a sensory impression made on a nerve ending, impressibility connotes the agency of the sensorium, including its capacity to create its own attachments independent of the cerebrospinal axis. Buchanan explained in 1850: "It is nervous impressibility that binds man to the universe and establishes active relations between every element of his constitution and every element of the surrounding world."[24] The more layers the cultural practices of civilization had impressed on the familial substrate over time, the more the individual possessed impressibility and the potential for further change—or rapid degeneration. It thereby characterizes matter possessing simultaneous vitality and vulnerability. Multiethnic reformers, scientists, and writers debated the degree to which the allegedly uncivilized races maintained a degree of impressibility that would spur further development. They also discussed the possibility that the uncivilized had maxed out their evolutionary potential long ago and been left to fester in bodies that were insensate and impermeable, incapable of the phenomenon of being affected and moving through time, thereby remaining imprisoned in the present-tense mode of impulsive reaction. Impressibility came to prominence as a key measure for racially and sexually differentiating the refined, sensitive, and civilized subject who was embedded in time and capable of progress, and in need of protection, from the coarse, rigid, and savage elements of the population suspended in the eternal state of flesh and lingering on as unwanted remnants of prehistory.[25]

The notion of impressibility fills a crucial gap in theories of biopower: how bodies were understood to bind together into the organic phenomenon of population. Foucault elaborated the spatial concept of the milieu, marking the environment in which a population forms. He built on the notion of milieu proposed by Jean-Baptiste Lamarck, founder of evolutionary theory, who proposed that individual and species growth depends on environmental context. For Lamarck, a milieu denotes the "circumstances" through which an organism develops.[26] Foucault explained that the concept provides "what is needed to account for action at a distance of one body on another. It is therefore the medium of an action and the element in which it circulates."[27] Yet the ontological concept, the corporeal framework in which a body is understood as capable of being acted on by its environment as an individual or as an element of a biological phenomenon, has not yet been fully addressed. Biopower, in this molar and pregenetic era, requires a somatic interface at the level of the organ or bodily system through which the individual body links to a larger species-being that materializes over time.[28] How does the milieu act on the soma? The answer, I show, is found in Lamarck's work itself. His *Zoological Philosophy* (1809) translates the theory of sensory impressions into the groundbreaking idea that not only the mind, but the entire nervous system, acquires its structure from the sensations an organism habitually pursues and that the organism retains these adaptations throughout its life and transmits them to offspring. In extrapolating the impression into an account of species change, Lamarck built on T. R. Malthus's earlier political theory of population in which witnessing the suffering of the starving impresses the well-off with the experiences necessary to cultivate their capacity of benevolent sympathy, therefore refining civilization as a whole.[29] Impressibility discourse was born, transforming the individuals who comprise a nation into the biological phenomenon of population forged through the impressions bodies leave on one another.

Scientists, reformers, religious leaders, writers, and domestic ideologues elaborated sentimental discourse into an account of the broad circulation of feeling throughout a milieu.[30] Connecticut theologian Horace Bushnell represents a key element of a tradition consolidating in the nineteenth century, in the wake of Malthus and Lamarck: the impressibility theory of population, in which the flow of unconscious influences forges individuals, in Bushnell's words, "into a general mass."[31] Bushnell's 1852 tract *Unconscious Influence* represents a pivotal flashpoint in the sentimental ontology of population. The impressible body is an "open door," Bushnell explained to his readers, and "on this open side you all adhere together as parts of a larger nature, in which there is a common circulation of want, impulse, and law" (*UI*, 17). For Bushnell, human bodies have "two inlets of impression," one in the sensory organs that receive sensations and communicate them to the mind through the powers of reason, and another rooted in the nervous system's "sympathetic powers" (*UI*, 14), which receive nonverbal communication via a series of "inlets, open on all sides" to the "common reservoir of influence" (*UI*, 13) and which thus circumvent the cerebral-spinal axis. Influences continually "flow" throughout the population; when they enter the receptacle of the impressible body, they initiate nonsensory impressions (*UI*, 13). Yet impressibility is not merely the capacity to passively receive; even in the child it denotes the active capacity of the body to "dra[w] from [adults] impressions and moulds of habit" that never cease to shape its growth (*UI*, 20). Following Bushnell, impressibility signifies a body endowed with "the capacity to receive impressions," of incorporating them into the body, and finally of "diffusing" these elements throughout the body of the host and "among the thoughts as long as we live" (*UI*, 15). Bodies not only flow into each other via their inlets; impressibility also adheres each body to the population, such that common influences forge common desires and instincts. "While you are a man," Bushnell explained, "you are also a fractional element of a larger and more comprehensive being, called society—be it the family, the church, the state," and society shapes individual feeling in the likeness of the collective (*UI*, 15). The impressible body—and the sentimental body—is a biopolitical effect, constituted by its affective linkages to the other bodies within its milieu. Sentimentalism, as we shall see, is a broad regulatory technology in which neurological and emotional tendencies play important roles in reconciling the impressible body to its role in a biological population, rather than a narrower aesthetics and politics of the moral aptness of emotional identification.

For Bushnell, the expressions of one body circulate throughout society and become impressions on others, affecting all in its wake. In one sense, Bushnell articulates the familiar ideal of sympathetic identification as explored in the robust scholarly literature on sentiment, which entails both the imaginative work of deliberate emotional investment in another and the affective shuttling of sentiments directly between bodies themselves, circumventing the mind. Yet Bushnell's rhapsodizing reveals that sympathy functions not only as the sharing of conscious and unconscious emotions, but also as the neurological linking of individual bodies together, as he puts it, into "one mass, one consolidated social body, animated by one life" (*UI*, 17). Impressibility functioned as the nineteenth-century precursor of the notion of affect, or the circulation of energy throughout a milieu in a manner that binds bodies together through common stimulation. The physiological dimension of sympathy has been overlooked. This has precluded understanding how affect has a genealogy rooted in the historical formation of the biopolitical entity of population and how sentimentalism was elaborated in the nineteenth century as a central biopolitical technology to regulate the vulnerability of the civilized body.

THE MATERIALITY OF RACE

Over the last two-thirds of the nineteenth century, an epoch bounded by the emergence of heredity as a biological concept in the 1830s and the debut of genetics after 1900, impressions and impressibility did complex and highly influential work as the mechanisms of sensory activity, cognitive function, emotional feeling, vital capacity, affective connection, erotic contact, individual growth, hereditary transmission, species change, racial development, sexual difference, and population formation. Impressibility discourse built on the imperial discourse of sensibility outlined in the sciences and literary cultures of the eighteenth century, which predicated civilization on refined capacities of emotional and physiological feeling.[32] Its progenitors also include the eighteenth-century Anglo-American logic of environmentalism in which race marked an exterior effect of climate that shifted in accordance with the body's geographic location.[33] Yet impressibility brought these older ideas of bodily mutability into concert with the new geological and evolutionary theories of time and the new concept that reproduction involves the transfer of heredity, an innate but not immutable biological substance.[34] For example, early medical practitioner Harriot Hunt argued in the 1850s that the body took shape as the gradual accumulation of "hereditary qualities, tendencies, and impressibilities" that must be "cultivated."[35] The nineteenth century was a period of transition between the "transformable race" of the eighteenth century and the rigid, interior genetic logics of the twentieth, and biopower consolidated amid this shifting terrain, turning humans into a species and making biology their history.[36]

Pliability, rather than rigidity, has recently come to characterize the materiality of the body as it was understood in the nineteenth century.[37] The nature of race in the nineteenth century is of particular import, as scholarly consensus has long agreed that the modern notion of race as a biological concept determining a body's relative value was an invention of this period.[38] Current scholarship seeks to overturn the extremely influential argument that the nineteenth century was an epoch committed to biological determinism, the notion that the body's biological material is a discrete, immutable, and dissimilar substance, meted out by capricious nature in wildly unequal fashion, that locks the individual into a predetermined set of aptitudes and behaviors. In the words of Tavia Nyong'o, "Race was mobilized in this period as itself a mutable and even volatile category."[39] Yet despite this newer account of the dynamic ontology of race, a variety of texts and fields nonetheless remain quite attached to the social constructionist–era interpretation that the body, and the idea of race more generally, in the period was understood as innate, fixed, and "brute" biology that stands guard against any encroachments of culture. Racism, in this dominant view, equals biological determinism, and vice versa.

Taking recourse in the logic of binary opposition, social constructionist accounts of race generally conceive of social frameworks of flexibility, mutability, relationality, and dynamism to counteract what they see as the determinist, individualizing political effects of liberal humanism and its social and scientific practices of corporeal differentiation. This approach can involve the telling move of privileging the mobility of the body as resistance to racism, even in the midst of important disability critique.[40] Yet accounts claiming that the liberatory potential of mobility and plasticity can redress what they see as the fixed taxonomies of nineteenth-century racial personhood misrecognize one of biopolitics' most pervasive effects. Biopower works by situating individuals in dynamic relation and calculating and regulating how their bodies affect one another within a milieu. It governs through a pervasive animacy hierarchy that unevenly apportions the capacities of plasticity and determinism among a population.[41] Contemporary frameworks that seek to contest biological determinisms with flexible materiality do not escape the political legacies of liberal humanism—rather, they unwittingly recapitulate the conceptual apparatus of the biopolitics of feeling.

The ongoing purchase of the biological determinist paradigm in American studies is partly due to the lack of an existing theoretical frame that explains how the uneven distribution of somatic dynamism was central to the materialization of modern ideas of racial and sexual difference. In chapter 1, I propose that sentimental biopower provides this missing framework. The prison of biology can seem self-evident given that black bodies *were* overwhelmingly dismissed as animalistic savages, Asian bodies as "enervated" and "stagnant" remnants of the past, and Native bodies as animated fossils destined to go the way of the dinosaurs—all of which, at best, fitted a body to labor on behalf of the capital accumulation of the civilized and disqualified the person from political rights.[42] Yet white bodies, and the wealthier classes of African Americans, Latinx, and Native Americans in resistant discourse, were ascribed with material agency and forward-moving temporality that had evolved the arts of civilization.[43] Race did not name a fixed, interior quality of individualized matter and did not function primarily to limit the perceived potential of some bodies. Rather, it helped produce hierarchies of somatic capacity, the biological phenomenon of the population, and the corresponding central goal of power to measure and manage the uneven distribution of vital potential throughout national territory, including overseas colonies.

I propose a palimpsestic model of race before genetics, in which racial status indexes the impressions that accumulate over the life span of individuals and the evolutionary time of races. Developed by colonial anthropology and other life sciences, race demarcated the accumulated physical effect of a group's relative achievement of the seven cultural traits defined as determinant of civilization: sexual differentiation, monogamous marriage, Christian faith, arts and literacy, domestic architecture, capitalist accumulation, and democratic government.[44] According to its Lamarckian model, the habits of civilization were thought to impress on physicality and transmit across time as physical inheritance. The embodiment of the civilized races gradually materializes through the accumulation of layers of impressions over the individual time of the body and the phylogenetic temporality of generations. The civilized body figures as a repository of cultural value, an outcome of racial capital. Civilization emerged after layers and layers of beneficial impressions that propelled impressible bodies forward through time, yet their animal and savage substrate ever threatened to reemerge. Sigmund Freud investigated the somnambulant return of the repressed "permanent memory-trace" of one's own animal nature impressed on the bottom layer of the mind's wax-like "mystic writing-pad": such repressed memories erupted, most famously, in the canine dreams of his aristocratic patient "Wolf Man."[45] In the hands of black feminist intellectuals such as Frances Harper, Pauline Hopkins, and Anna Julia Cooper, on the other hand—the subject of chapter 2—the palimpsestic accumulation of impressions enabled a notion of embodiment in which the history of white men's sexual abuse of black women always seeps through, shaping present circumstance. Above all, civilization "extend[ed] out to the capacity for capacity" that Jasbir Puar locates at the heart of the biopolitical "ascendancy of whiteness": "the capacity to give life, sustain life, and promote life" within "forward-looking, regenerative bodies."[46] The nineteenth century circumscribed this state of enduring potentiality within the material condition of impressibility.

Impressibility discourse unveils a genealogy of affect that reveals that affect's common formulation as the "capacity to affect and be affected," as well as "felt-aliveness," functions itself as an animacy hierarchy.[47] The contemporary notion of affect is chimerical, suturing two distinct capacities—that of emitting impressions and that of absorbing impressions—into one apparently seamless whole. Yet impressibility reveals that affect has a forgotten twin that has been swallowed up within its definitional reach: the state of affecting, but being unable to be affected in turn. Affect, in other words, depends on the notion of impaired relationality as its constitutive outside. Affective capacity depends on its definitional opposite, debility, for theoretical solidity, a reliance that suggests that affect materializes across the multitemporal reach of populations, rather than individual bodies.[48] Within biopower, racialization and sex difference do the work of unevenly assigning affective capacity throughout a population.[49] In effect, the common use of the affect concept, which conflates the capacities of affecting and being affected into one phenomenon, reifies, rather than interrogates, the historical ontology of whiteness.

The racialized were assigned the condition of unimpressibility, or the impaired state of throwing off affects but being incapable of being affected by impressions themselves. Leading evolutionary scientist E. D. Cope contrasted the "susceptibility" of youthful tissue—a category that includes the most recently evolved group, the civilized race—with the primitive condition of "unimpressibility," or "resistance on the part of tissue to the usual stimuli."[50] At best, unimpressible bodies merely react to sensory impressions, rather than absorbing them, reflecting on them, and incorporating their effects. The uncivilized races were consigned to the immediacy of childlike sensation and instinctive response, captive to whatever stimulations crossed their paths.[51] Positioned as the worn-out antecedents of the civilized, people of color were accused of torpidity, sluggishness, impulsiveness, and mimicry, evaluations of nerve force that denounced the racialized body as unable to move forward through time. To be unimpressible was to be assigned the unsexed state of "flesh," Hortense Spillers's term for the ontology of antiblackness in which the black body is suspended outside the movements of time, lingering in a raw organic state useful only for resource extraction.[52] The racialized body was a disabled body (and vice versa), deemed unfit for social life due to its reduced cognitive and corporeal capacities, which rendered it incapable of self-constitution. The unimpressible are figured themselves *as* history, rather than its subjects, *as* energy that can be set in motion to produce for others but remains incapable of accumulating anything in return.

To possess a nervous system characterized as responsive only to external motion and incapable of internal response was to be frequently accused of being benumbed to both progress and pain. The advantages of such a presumption for settler capital accumulation are clear, as the racialized could be recruited from across the Americas, Africa, and Asia for multiple forms of unfree and free labor, forced reproduction, and/or coerced experimentation on the grounds that they lacked the nervous capacity to feel any harm. The most widely read turn-of-the-century account of China, Arthur Smith's *Chinese Characteristics* (1894), echoed a common refrain when it assured readers that the "absence of nerves" and "a capacity to wait without complaint and to bear with calm endurance" rendered the coolie an ideal laborer.[53] For literary critic Eric Hayot, "the coolie's biologically impossible body was the displaced ground for an awareness of the transformation of the laboring body into a machine" within modernity, such that the body of the coolie became a site of projection for the anxieties of capitalism.[54] Indeed, Cope likens unimpressibility to "automatism," signaling the suitedness of the racialized body more generally for the highly orchestrated and repetitive movements of industrializing labor.[55] Unimpressibility connotes much of the meaning cultural theorist Sianne Ngai captures in the fitting concept of "animatedness," a racialized affect in popular culture in which the body of an Asian or African American character is portrayed as incapable of independent action, only made to move by the will of others.[56] As Ngai emphasizes, this perceived lack of agential vitality renders figures not inert but "mechanical," overly malleable, and emotionally explosive.[57] This fantasy of the racialized body, she illuminates, suits an industrial economy in which bodies of color are set into motion like the commodities they produce, and their individual feeling serves only as unmarketizable excess.

Biopower functions as an umbrella term combining two different yet overlapping instruments of postsovereign power deployed within the regime of civilization: the discipline of the individual body, which worked to "integrate the body into a system of economic productivity"; and the "regulatory controls" of biopolitics, which "aim to adjust population to economic processes."[58] The sentimental politics of life illuminates how biopower consolidated around the impressible body/unimpressible flesh dynamic in both dimensions throughout the nineteenth century. Biopower functioned through the diagnosis, surveillance, and subjectivization of the docile body and the transformation of a multiplicity of individuals from a congregation of persons into a biological phenomenon existing in evolutionary time that could be measured, administered, and regulated over generations through the same processes governing the natural world.[59] Biopolitics does not seek to directly control the population, for population is a "natural" corpus that preexists the social. Rather, the regulatory functions of security power seek to allow the population to maintain homeostasis over time through the processes inherent to it.[60] In order for the national population to maintain its equilibrium, biopolitics fosters the life of the population as a whole by identifying those groups whose continued existence would threaten its economic and biological stability and who thus must be allowed to die. I follow Puar and Neel Ahuja in conceiving of the interlocking function of the necropolitical "subjugation of life to the power of death" and the biopolitical governance of life, and see the concept of civilization as the early stages of the security regime that distribute death for the economic stability of the imperial center.[61] As Achille Mbembe writes in his seminal account of necropolitics: "What one witnesses in World War II is the extension to the 'civilized' peoples of Europe of the methods previously reserved for the savages.'"[62] The uneven distribution of death, in other words, is a key function of biopower's efforts to maintain life.

Biopower works by delineating differential capacities of organic matter based on the division of flesh and culture. The biopolitical imagination posits binary oppositions between dynamism and determinism, vitality and mechanics, affecting and being affected, and culture and biology that produce distinct claims to life. Contemporary analytic frames that echo these oppositions, whether social constructionist notions of race that privilege notions of malleable embodiment over fixed biologies or affect theories that fail to interrogate how representations of affective capacity function as a key vector of racialization, therefore remain within the biopolitical imaginary.

SEXUAL DIFFERENTIATION

The subject is constructed in Western philosophy as a highly vulnerable entity, for it is wholly dependent on sensory impressions from the environment for its own self-development and acquisition of knowledge. Scientists, writers, reformers, and others located the pliability, vitality, and penetrability of the subject in the capacity of the impressible nervous system. Impressibility connotes qualities of both dynamic vitalism and susceptibility that render the body in need of careful guardianship. Impressibility discourse crystallizes what theorist Denise Ferreira da Silva posits as the internal "threat posed by universal reason, that it necessarily produces modern subjects as coexisting and relational beings."[63] Recurring descriptors capturing the nervousness of the civilized, especially during the more malleable stage of youth, include elasticity, springiness, responsiveness, sensibility, impressionability, and sentimentality. The latter two terms hint at a problem: one could certainly be *overly* sensitive, too easily moved by external objects, as well as overly guided by emotional identification rather than abstract justice. Indeed, impressibility was deemed to be heightened among the feminine: ladies, children, artists, and homosexuals, among others.[64] The impressible body and the regulatory faculty of sentiment, which were cause and effect of civilization, required a ballast.

The new concept of sex difference was deployed to stabilize the precarity of the impressible body. The discourse of thorough divergence in the character, physiology, mentality, and emotion of men and women emerged in both conservative and feminist discourse of the nineteenth century and served to diagnose a specialized trait that allegedly only the civilized had developed.[65] A flurry of new and long-lasting tactics of sex difference emerged in this period, including policed dress; sex- and race-segregated bathrooms; restrictions on abortion and contraception; sex- and race-based admissions policies to newly established educational and professional institutions; the gradual consolidation of modern sexuality; and feminist claims for women's political rights.[66] Across this varied terrain, a common paradigm emerges: race stabilizes the economic and biological health of the population, which enables the development of civilization, while sex difference stabilizes civilization. Sex served to balance the somatic vulnerability of the impressible races by dividing the civilized body into two halves: the sentimental woman, who possessed both a heightened faculty of feeling and a more transparent animal nature, and the less susceptible and more rational man, thereby relieved from the burdens of embodiment. The two halves of male and female reunited through the organ delineating and containing the threat of penetrability: the vagina. The vagina served as a biopolitical instrument, as chapter 3 reveals through readings of the work of early women physicians who positioned the vagina of the white woman as the apex of nervous impressibility and therefore the basis of her claim to political rights. In dominant discourse, however, the permeability of woman secures the disembodiment of rational man. That is, the achievement of rationality—a key component of civilization—is made possible only through the sex difference allegedly lacking in the racialized.[67] Binary sex is both cause and effect of reason.

A short story published anonymously in 1857 evokes the pain of being caught in the interstices of the newly solidifying biological and hereditarian logic of sex. "The Man Who Thought Himself a Woman" details a protagonist raised as male who begins designing and sewing clothing "with all the ardor of a young mother shaping a dress for her first-born" to self-birth as a woman.[68] The first time she wears her clothing, both sewn and borrowed, in front of her family, she is dead: the startlingly modern-sounding suicide note explains, "As I have passed so long, falsely, for a man, I am ashamed to show myself in my true colors."[69] The note leaves the exact cause of shame ambiguous: for passing in the past, or for revealing herself now. The tale situates her "oddities" in relation to a hereditary predilection for "singularities, queerities, quips, quirks, and oddities" common to all her immediate male ancestors.[70] In this story, newly consolidating biological ideas of self ultimately defeat the white subject's act of self-formation that counters the seeming naturalness of the biological paradigm. Heredity can be seen to structure an emergent, but not yet fully solidified, biological account of differential sex, giving rise to new binaristic accounts of body morphology, identity, and relationality that make some lives impossible, even in the midst of their own self-constitution. In other words, sex difference was elaborated as a biopolitical security strategy in which power maintains the homeostasis of the population through material givens inherent to its biological existence, a process that sacrifices the existence of the aberrant for the cohesion of the whole.

I stress that binary sex does not exist in a parallel or intersecting dimension with race. Rather, the rhetoric of distinct sexes of male and female consolidated as a *function* of race. Yet my formulation does not relegate sex difference to the role of secondary or analogical effect of racial formation.[71] Rather, I name sex, sexuality, and, in the post–World War II era, gender as key ways that race fragments the domain of the biological.[72] The sentimental politics of life framework draws on and extends the tremendous insight of Roderick Ferguson's queer of color critique that "racist practice articulates itself generally as gender and sexual regulation, and that gender and sexual differences variegate racial formations."[73] Finding sympathy between queer of color theory and Michel Foucault's account of race as the primary means by which biopower differentiates those who will live from those who will die, I suggest that nineteenth-century biopower provides the backstory that illuminates how binary sex has come to accomplish the work of racial differentiation.[74] In other words, not only gender but also the physiological category of sex are variegations of race and effects of racial biopower. Accordingly, as I explore throughout the first three chapters, this throws open the category of woman—not only the now-dismissed concept of Victorian "true womanhood"—as an instrument of racial thought.[75] This has profound consequences for women of color and for feminism. As the struggle for the rights of woman coincident with the category's new ontological status, feminism derives its political purchase from and within the larger framework of biopolitics. If woman is the product of racial thought, nineteenth-century feminism itself becomes a civilizational and biopolitical strategy, and not only in its explicitly imperial variants.

THE SENTIMENTAL POLITICS OF LIFE

The impressible body is a volatile body, subject to the objects, people, and forces pressing on it for its own self-constitution. In order to avoid bodily disaggregation and racial degeneration, the impressible body required a corollary: a corresponding capacity for regulating sensory experience, at the individual and populational level.[76] Dana Luciano illuminates that sentimentalism was figured in the nineteenth century as a temporal capacity that freed the civilized from the impulses dictated by immediate sensation, enabling them to reflect on their stimulations and to orient themselves within the forward movements of time.[77] Throughout this book, I argue that sentimentalism took shape as a technology to circulate and regulate feeling throughout a milieu, a political praxis that consolidated the modern hierarchies of race, sex, and species. Sentimentalism became a broad technology of power, the mechanism through which impressible bodies could be cultivated and populations secured, despite the unequal vital capacities of which the latter were composed. I offer the term *sensorial discipline* to capture the imperative placed on the civilized races, especially its female members and those aspiring to civilization and citizenship, to learn to master their sensory impulses and thus direct the development of themselves and their descendants. The "experiences" that "make their proper impression," Dr. Elizabeth Blackwell cautioned, are those that enable the civilized "to understand and direct our daily life, instead of being carried away by it."[78] Such discipline was transmitted via a flurry of new mechanisms: the gradual deployment of sexuality; the aesthetic discourse of taste, understood as "a faculty dependent on permeability to impressions and the habit of reflecting upon them"; sex-segregated factory labor; public health campaigns; household manuals, including advice on the training of domestic labor; architecture and interior design; women's moral reform societies; institutions for free black southerners, especially after the Civil War; vice squads; public and parochial educational facilities; the mass domestic novel, which not only narrated in a didactic mode but also was understood to actively make new impressions on its readers as it elicited sensory and emotional response; the ideal of the bourgeois woman who could mute the very presence of her body; new social movements and print cultures to regulate the gustatory appetites of the population, including temperance and dietetic reform and the new genre of cookbooks; and religious revivals and imperial missionary efforts, among many other reform efforts, cultural traditions, and political tactics.[79] Sentiment was the special provenance of woman, but common to civilized man.

Sensorial discipline regulates the accumulation of the civilized self and of the phylogenetic palimpsest, forging a racial common sense over time. The sentimental orchestration of the habits of perception and interaction worked, along the Lamarckian model, to racially differentiate the civilized and uncivilized in terms of shared cultural traditions, nervous capacity, and physicality. Residents of San Francisco's Chinatown in the second half of the nineteenth century, for example, were castigated as posing threats of "infection, domestic chaos, [and] moral danger" that would contaminate the rest of the booming city. The housing of the bachelor-dominant neighborhood was accused of lacking the "intimacy, gender roles, or rights of privacy" afforded by the reproductive, rather than productive, bourgeois household allegedly removed from the public sphere.[80] Historian Nayan Shah explains that "respectable domesticity enabled the proper moral and biological cultivation of citizen-subjects necessary for American public life to flourish," while the lifeways of Chinese laborers were understood as contagions that threatened civilization.[81] Indeed, nineteenth-century biopolitical strategies precede the twentieth-century division between culture and biology. Mechanisms such as the domestic home were understood to work at the level of the organic body, cultivating a common sensorial repertoire and moral life over the time of individuals and of generations. Common sense, for film theorist Kara Keeling, marks "a shared set of memory-images and a set of commonly habituated sensory-movements . . . in which shared conceptions of the world are inseparable from motor functions."[82] A century earlier, social scientists understood sensory-motor repertoires and the memories they imprint to be the mechanism of cultural life as well as the substrate of hereditary material. The habits of civilization—a framework which its key theorists, such as Adam Smith and Lewis Henry Morgan, outline as the transmission of cultural effects and embodied memory over time—were understood to forge a racial common sense.[83]

The sentimental politics of life helps illuminate how biopower is so effective at creating atmospheres in which people come to identify with the needs of the state and capitalism as their own best interests. Biopower works not only at the level of regulating reason and desire, but also in choreographing a repertoire of sensory stimulations that exceeds the ways that modern sexuality, in Foucault's words, came to gradually subsume "the sensations of the body, the quality of pleasures, and the nature of impressions, however tenuous or imperceptible these may be" into the apparatus of sexual identification.[84] Lauren Berlant argues that the general organization of politics in the United States over the last 150 years increasingly depends on sentimental structures of attachment and identification, in which a "world of private thoughts, leanings, and gestures [is] projected out as an intimate public of private individuals inhabiting their own affective changes."[85] Sentimentalism worked to position the body's differential capacity of feeling as the object and method of state power and capitalist development, a project that works not only through the rehearsal of emotional experience and consumer gratification, but also through the stimulation and regulation of the body's vital capacities. The discourse of sentimentalism stabilizes the inherent susceptibility of the "advanced" body, orchestrates affective relations with the larger species and object worlds in which it is enmeshed, and helps produce some bodies as vulnerable and others as projects to be saved or persons to be expelled.

The rubric of sentimentalism illuminates how biopower, affect, and privatization go hand in hand, and not only in the neoliberal era. Recent work on biopower, necropower, and the plantation, in particular, encourages us to refuse the public/private, metropole/colony divide that liberalism enshrines.[86] The "family" currently has an important place in studies of biopower as the site of psychosocial discipline, but less so the components of the institution itself: women, children, domesticated pets, and the home.[87] Yet the domestic deserves broad recognition as a technology of biopower, functioning as the site of the deployment of sexuality in particular, as well as women's paid and unpaid labor, the discipline of children, the geographic interface between the individual and the population, and the grounds of proscription from entering the space of the nation, as in the case of the Chinese Exclusion Act of 1882.[88] Thus key institutions of nineteenth-century U.S. biopower include not only the state-run entities of concentration camps, schools, hospitals, military facilities, colonial outposts, and prisons, but also private sector sites such as the plantation, slave ship, church, orphanage, domestic home, domestic novel, factory, women's auxiliary societies, reform movements, and extranational settlements, in the expanding settler state and its colonial sites in the Caribbean and Pacific.[89] Ann Laura Stoler has been at the forefront of uncovering the biopolitical functions of domesticity and analyzing sentiment and affect as sites of imperial control.[90] In the words of Stoler, one of sentimentalism's key victories was that children "became the subjects of legislative attention and were at the center of social policy as they had never been before" during the mid- to late nineteenth century in North America and Europe.[91] This included both the children removed from their homelands and those raised in homes imagined to serve as the microcosm of the nation.

Foucault named the process of population management that produces citizens who constitute themselves according to the needs of the state *governmentality*.[92] Governmentality did not yet fully transpire in the nineteenth-century United States, however. In this period, nonstate actors such as churches, domestic homes, private reform societies, slave auctions, health movements, synagogues, and club societies inaugurated sentimental technologies of biopower that combined atomizing measures of disciplinary castigation and/or redemption and populational tactics of managing risk and economic productivity. In other words, the tasks of the biopolitical state evolved out of the private institutions of sentiment.

The sentimental politics of life frequently deployed the new domestic instrument of "biophilanthropy," or the middle-class project of uplifting uncivilized youth by placing them in the Christian institutions of school and home that would press new sensations into their somewhat pliable forms. In this mode of incremental life, racialized youth were gradually made to live and enter the capitalist economy. The alleged constitutional rigidity of the uncivilized did not solidify until adulthood. Youthfulness, Cope explained, was a stage of heightened impressibility, "the period of growth . . . much more susceptible to modifying influences and . . . likely to exhibit structural change in consequence."[93] A number of reform movements accordingly argued that the nervous systems of uncivilized youth could be impressed with beneficial sensations, and sought to mutate their bodies and their heritable material into assets, rather than threats, to capital and land accumulation. According to this schema, a childhood spent barefoot in a Plains tipi impressed savage propensities on the body and mind that the child would never unlearn and would transmit to offspring, whereas the customs of leather shoes, wool and cotton clothing, and a stick-frame house served as both the cause and effect of civilization. Off-reservation boarding schools, which removed Native youth hundreds of miles from their families and subjected them to severe discipline, are among the most drastic implementations of this belief that regulating the sensory experience of primitive children would transform the racial body. Chapter 4 explores a less widely known example of the deliberate attempt to evolve a people by orphaning their children—the Children's Aid Society's emigration of one hundred thousand European immigrant youth from New York City from the 1850s through the 1920s to farm families across the nation. Biophilanthropy suggests that eugenics comes in many forms, including the deliberate molding of hereditary material that was deemed susceptible and malleable.

Reformers eagerly extrapolated the theory of impressibility into a theory and practice of eugenic breeding. For some readers, this claim will immediately generate suspicion. Eugenics is best known as the early twentieth-century move-ment to encourage "fit" women to increase their birthrate and to rob "unfit" women of the capacity to conceive, an agenda that reached its nadir in Nazi Germany. In literary, cultural, and ethnic studies scholarship, eugenics is often taken to be synonymous with biological determinism. Yet in these characteriza-tions, the almighty power of the twentieth-century gene has cast its shadow backward, gathering radically different, non-Mendelian notions of heredity and environment under its pall. According to this dominant logic, the notion of mutable heredity is precisely the inverse of eugenics programs—and rac-ist thinking as well. However, eugenic sciences and policies are rooted in the application of the sciences of heredity to improve racial groups, not in deter-minist versions of genetics specifically.[94] As feminist science studies scholar Banu Subramaniam clarifies, eugenics denotes a broad-based and multispe-cies discourse and practice of evaluating the fitness of biological variation and assessing the relative influence of heredity versus environment, a practice that encompasses a wide range of scientific, social, and agricultural agendas.[95]

The notion of impressible heredity that prevailed in the nineteenth-century United States looks markedly different from classical geneticists' view that life unfolds according to the predetermined plan of the internal genetic code, and eugenic efforts differed accordingly. Francis Galton coined the term *eugenics* by adapting the Greek words for "well" and "born," giving a name, twenty-five years before the "gene," to the already-popular belief that social progress required manipulating hereditary material. Galton defined eugenics as "the cultiva-tion of the race" and "the science of improving stock, which is by no means confined to questions of judicious mating, but which . . . takes cognisance of all influences that tend in however remote a degree to give to the more suitable races or strains of blood a better chance of prevailing speedily over the less suitable than they otherwise would have had."[96] Eugenics as a term is agnos-tic, however, about which approach to heredity must prevail in service of race building through the regulation of "influences."[97] Granted, early twentieth-century eugenicists *did* frequently identify sentimental reformers, who be-lieved that hereditary material could be transformed through experience, as their principal opponents, as I explore in chapter 5. Yet in important ways, the sentimental politics of life represented less a radical threat to eugenicists' goals than an antecedent. Far from an emotional logic of political remediation, sen-timent functioned as a technology to regulate the hereditary quality of the population and thereby enacted one of biopower's chief tactics. More broadly, projects to "improve" the hereditary material of the individual and the popu-lation are a constitutive element of biopower, not only its twentieth-century flowering.

To date, most work on biopower emphasizes either nineteenth-century Europe or the contemporary period in Europe and the United States. Yet the era of U.S. national consolidation and imperial expansion across the nineteenth century witnessed a number of key developments that expand and nuance our theories of biopower. This book reconsiders biopower in light of political phenomena key to the nineteenth-century United States: slavery; race science; Jim Crow; European immigration; and settler colonialism and expansionism. Chief among the resultant insights is that contrary to the claims of many theorists, the notion of optimizing and marketizing the biological substrate is fundamental to the practice of biopower and is not unique to the contemporary molecular era. Recently proposed terms to periodize the contemporary era of biopolitics, such as *control, the politics of life itself,* and *pharmacopornopower,* tend to exaggerate scalar differences in the operation of power, overstating the novelty of networked lives that operate within economies that modulate the global flow of physiological material and bodily capacities.[98]

In a highly influential analysis, Nikolas Rose argues that in contrast to an earlier period largely focused on eliminating contagions from the population, contemporary power "is concerned with our growing capacities to control, manage, engineer, reshape, and modulate the very vital capacities of human beings as living creatures," particularly through intervention at the molecular level.[99] Rose is careful to stress that what he names an emergent "politics of life itself," marked by an ethos of organic optimization in which the management and improvement of health becomes a citizen's key responsibility and form of subjectivity, builds on and extends earlier forms of "vital politics," rather than represents an epochal shift.[100] Nonetheless, he identifies the rise of technologies of "susceptibility" and "enhancement," such as prenatal tests to identify genetic mutations and pharmaceuticals that act directly on sexual capacity or sexed attributes, as specific to the molecular era. His criteria is that they work not to eliminate disease from the organism, but to alter biological function. He contrasts the contemporary belief in biological plasticity and the ability to act directly on somatic potential with the belief in "inherited predispositions" of the latter half of the nineteenth century, which, while attuned to the assessment of risk in the population, lacked the present ethos of "bring[ing] potential futures into the present and tr[ying] to make them the subject of calculation and the object of remedial intervention."[101] For Rose, mechanisms such as cloning and medical treatments available subsequent to the sequencing of the human genome establish new "technologies of optimization" that form natural-cultural assemblages.[102] The health of the individual is now produced as the site of the imperative for biological maximization in a way that sharply differs from the often "coercive" national eugenic regimes of the first half of the twentieth century, which conflated "population, quality, territory, nation, and race" in pursuit of racial fitness at the scale of population.[103] Yet the conception of organic material as dynamic, flexible, and augmentable is by no means particular to life in the genetic era. Biotechnology has indeed shrunk the key vector of the body from its sensory acuity to its molecular and atomic components while simultaneously magnifying by many times the market share of biological manipulation, changing the nature of capitalism in the process.[104] But from the beginning, biopower has functioned through technologies of biological optimization that rely on ideas of corporeal mutability and plasticity as the interface between the individual and the population that predate genetic-era divisions between the political and natural world. In fact, one of biopower's key innovations is the very determinist/plasticity binary itself.

In a similar but less nuanced grain, Paul B. Preciado writes that "whereas the disciplinary system of the nineteenth century considered sex to be natural, definitive, unchangeable, and transcendental, pharmacopornographic gender seems to be synthetic, malleable, variable, open to transformation, and imitable, as well as produced and reproduced technically."[105] While the phenomenon of molecular gender may indeed be specific to the hormonal and sexological sciences of the chemical revolution era, the sexed body of the nineteenth century was far from a "transcendental" phenomenon. On the contrary, sex was understood as the accumulative result of matter made "malleable" over generations by the technologies of civilization, and as open to "transformation" and technological production as any other capacity of whiteness. The overwhelming critical emphasis on the influence of Darwin and Galton has come at the expense of attending to Lamarck's outsized impact in the nineteenth century and reflects a historical positivism that privileges the "winners" of competing scientific paradigms and ignores those who lose. The lack of theoretical attention to the nineteenth-century Americas, where the myths of the vitalizing potential of contact with the primitive on the frontier and the blank, ready-to-be-written history invoked by settler colonialist ideology made Lamarckian-based programs of plasticity, enhancement, and optimization particularly appealing to elites, exacerbates the problem. A resulting chronobiopolitics of matter emerges in the literature in which the nineteenth century becomes defined by a belief in the determinism of the organism, and the present by a commitment to a disaggregated body newly open to fine-grained manipulation and decomposition. But the Lamarckian world developed a range of mechanisms to ameliorate and recirculate hereditary particles, particularly through the varied institutions of sex difference, labor, and sentiment.

Contemporary biotechnology, like affective labor, builds on long-standing frameworks of imperial biopower in which vital potential can be cultivated, accumulated, marketed, and redistributed.[106] Comparative ethnic studies scholar Kalindi Vora analyzes the extraction and transfer of "vital energy," or "the substance of activity that produces life" from the Global South to the North through the colonial and postcolonial labor market, a continuum she sees as stretching from nineteenth-century industrial production to the affective labor of call centers in South Asia.[107] Reframing labor power in terms of the transfer of vital force, Vora shows how the exploitation of the vital capacities of the body is not a new phenomenon. The extrication and transfer of vital force, such as in dominant nineteenth-century frameworks in which the racialized and proletarian body was unimpressible, capable of being automated for the movements of labor yet incapable of self-directing its own energies, structure capitalist economies. The very distinction between molar and granular, vital and inert matter is not a recent historical development. Rather, the plasticity/determinism dualism reflects the productive work of the colonial paradigm of civilization reverberating throughout our contemporary paradigms.

Impressibility haunts highly influential theoretical models of vital materiality. Feminist "new" materialisms generally insist that they are overturning long-standing Cartesian dualisms that contrasted active mind with inert matter, a framework in which materiality registers as passive, nonconsequential substance that lacks any capacity of relationality or action. In many new materialist arguments, social construction theory represents the most recent flowering of the romance of matter as mere surface on which the human world acts; nature has meaning only to the extent in which it is "imprinted by cultural beliefs."[108] Yet the cultural scripts of social construction theory are not the only critical tradition that has kept the frameworks of the imprint and impressibility alive in feminist thought.

New materialist thinkers such as Jane Bennett and Diana Coole seek to challenge the enduring triumph of reason through drawing on a range of contemporary physical and life sciences and twentieth-century philosophy to conceive of innovative ontological frameworks that can newly capture the porosity, malleability, and vitality of matter. However, science studies scholar Angela Willey cautions that "new materialist storytelling seems to celebrate as a feature of scientific progress the 'discovery' of the principles of agency and plasticity."[109] Taking scientific paradigms to be self-evident, such "storytelling" ignores decades of feminist and postcolonial science studies that situate epistemologies of science within their larger social arena, including the history of science itself.[110] In fact, the teleological view of scientific discovery Willey observes, which positions inertia as an outdated conceptual trapping of reason and liveliness as the insight of a posthuman future, echoes the temporal logic of race.

New materialisms generally animate racial thought in three ways. First, they often carve a trajectory of critical thought that takes shape as an animacy teleology moving from ideas of inert matter (the past) to vital materiality (the future) that mirrors, rather than contests, civilizationist ontologies of the nineteenth century. Second, their sweeping historical narrative regularly fails to recognize the structuring role of the intertwined ideas of vital matter and inert material in the deployment of biopower over the last two centuries. As Victoria Pitts-Taylor observes, "Since its earliest modern elaboration, in fact, plasticity has been envisioned and enacted through the modification and preemptive governance of individuals and groups."[111] For Pitts-Taylor, the recognition of the dynamic capacities of matter is not in and of itself counterhegemonic; rather, its political implications depend on how plasticity is deployed within scientific discourse and the work of its interpreters.[112] Contemporary thinkers have not been the first to break through the Cartesian wall and portray matter as plastic and agential. Rather, notions of dynamic matter were alive and well in the nineteenth century and served as the ontological basis of race. This recent history in which agential matter was figured as the sedimentary effects of cultural difference needs to be a key site of new materialist engagement—rather than celebration—so as not to unwittingly reproduce racial hierarchies.[113] For example, in sketching out the idea that an object is not merely the passive site of human action, but rather that an object "leaves its impression" on the bodies that use it and orients their habitual tendencies, Sara Ahmed turns to the turn-of-the-nineteenth-century interior design theories of leading white feminist Charlotte Perkins Gilman.[114] For Ahmed, Gilman "speaks of the shaping of women's bodies through the way they inhabit domestic interiors," such that furnishings "create certain bodily positions."[115] Yet Gilman is no easily recruited ally for contemporary feminist theory. Gilman's notion of the impressions the material world carves into the bodies with which it engages was a fundamental component of her civilizationist feminism. For Gilman, white bodies and white bodies alone were impressible. It was their duty to train their aesthetic sensibilities for the sake of national progress as well as to remain vigilant against the degenerating effects of the coarse trappings of barbarism, such as ornate decoration and brightly colored clothing.[116] The racial logic of impressibility lies within the concepts of vitalism, material agency, and intersubjectivity with the external world which current theories, in the absence of critical interrogation of the concepts they inherit, risk reanimating.

Finally and most problematically, new materialisms often unwittingly reproduce the colonial logics of impressibility, or the idea of self-constituted matter, in their account of the agency and force of the material world. For example, Diana Coole queries: "Is it not possible to imagine matter quite differently [than inert] . . . as perhaps a lively materiality that is self-transformative and already saturated with the agentic capacities and existential significance that are typically located in a separate, ideal, and subjectivist, realm?"[117] Coole's framework is in fact all too easy to imagine, for it is reminiscent of the very idea of impressible corporeality: matter that accumulates agency over time, becoming "already saturated with the agentic capacities"; matter possessing potential for action and the transformational work of self-constitution; matter that enables interior transparency and self-determination.[118] Coole's account echoes the biopolitical logic of whiteness, implanting it as the key measure of all matter.

Theorists of lively matter may seek to depart from the land of reason, but they nonetheless carry its epistemic baggage. The "realm" of subjectivity did not emerge as a foreign landscape from the realm of matter.[119] Rather, reason—as the logic in which the individual is constituted by its own impressions—itself depends on the racially determined capacity of self-affecting matter, qualities it reserved for civilization.[120] Analyzing the ubiquity of ideas of plasticity to new materialisms, Willey continues: "Rather than challenging our sense of nature as predictably law-governed, agency—or plasticity—runs the risk of becoming another natural law."[121] Seemingly outside the rational worldview, new materialisms nonetheless conceive of a natural world governed by something like reason, if we follow Denise da Silva's insight that one of reason's greatest achievements was the conception that the natural world is governed by law and that nature itself is identifiable as the law of how things affect each other.[122] In fact, agential matter is a central achievement of biopower's racializing effects. Porosity and vitality are biopolitical tactics of racialization and demand interrogation as such, rather than masquerading as neutral qualities of life itself that are discovered by science and exist before the political. The idea of porous, plastic, vital matter is not in itself an alternative to liberal humanism; it is one of the unnamed effects of the biopolitical ontology in which humanism was enlisted. Biopower itself lies at the foundation of agential/mechanical and culture/matter binaries. What we need is theories that account for the coconstitution of material and cultural processes over time.

So how do we periodize the internal shifts and modulations of biopower since its late seventeenth-century debut? From the perspective of the sentimental politics of life, what is distinct about the post–World War II era is the very idea that organic and social life are delineable and divergent processes; one shapes the biological body, and the other forms the interior space of identity. In this new agenda Francis Galton once more serves as a towering and precocious figure: in the late nineteenth century he coined the phrase *nature versus nurture*.[123] However, biopower analyses often reproduce, rather than interrogate, Galton's dichotomous division between nature and culture. Key among these approaches reigns Giorgio Agamben's extremely influential notion of "bare life," or the biological substrate of the body to which an individual is reducible by state power in order to disqualify the subject from political recognition.[124] The common refrain that biopower addresses "life itself" similarly reifies the delineation between the organic and political worlds.[125] Yet this split between the organic and the social, in which the efforts of the latter have no impact on the former except in the case of contemporary biotechnologies and related nano-interventions and in which liberation politics is equivalent to opposing biological determinisms, came about in the 1930s and 1940s. In the most common account, the horrors of Nazi concentration camps caused governments and nongovernmental organizations to flee from the terrain of biology into the more egalitarian arms of culture. But there is a larger frame here, in which state cleansing played a gruesome part: that biopower regimes mutate in response to shifts in the notion of heredity. Heredity has been pressed into service as the biological mechanism that explains how the species-being of population interacts with the world around it. Its conceptualization is key to the operation of biopolitics.

The heyday of the sentimental politics of life falls between the emergence of heredity as a biological concept and the inauguration of genetic heredity in the early twentieth century. Whereas heredity previously had been used strictly in an adjectival mode to refer to the transmission of property and titles within families, French physiologists and physicians in the 1830s adapted this legal term to mark differences between human and animal populations across Europe and its colonies and began referring to "hérédité" in noun form.[126] This nominalization heralded the rise of "a structured set of meanings that outlined and unified an emerging biological conceptual space," the new notion that reproduction involved the transmission of a discrete—but not necessarily immutable—part of the body to progeny.[127] Theories of the substance of heredity emerged in the mid-nineteenth century, particularly in the work of Darwin, Prosper Lucas, and Galton.[128] Historians of science Staffan Müller-Wille and Hans-Jörg Rheinberger argue that the notion of heredity appeared so late as the 1830s because it served the newer biopolitical goal of differentiating within a population, rather than simply tracing familial commonality and descent.[129] Heredity enabled colonial powers to assert, calculate, and adjudicate biological difference across territories and within species. Heredity posits tension between the environment and the individual body, figuring the organism as ontologically distinct from the world in which it is immersed, forged of diachronic relationships of descent that lie in contradistinction from synchronic ecologies.

Heredity marks a key interface that differentiates and conjoins the milieu, individual, and population. Foucault emphasizes the work of sexuality as the junction between the organism and the species; we might broaden the frame of sexuality—which scholars have shown to be a racialized phenomenon—to include the phenomenon of heredity.[130] In fact, the trajectories of sexuality, race, and heredity track closely together. Sex in the nineteenth century does not necessarily fit the criteria of what we today recognize within the domain of the sexual and may be unrecognizable as such.[131] For Peter Coviello, sex was not yet understood to be a property of the self. It took shape as "a mode of relation, a style of affiliation," rather than as an aspect of individual identity.[132] Similarly, heredity was understood to transpire through the expansive dynamics of relation characterizing the sexual in the nineteenth century and thus often looks unrecognizable today. In the nineteenth century, the belief in the impressibility of the civilized body and the Lamarckian inheritance of acquired traits legitimated a range of sexual, childless, and professional relationships to fall within the folds of hereditary transmission. As Jasbir K. Puar has argued, queer theory has mistakenly privileged "the always already implicit heterosexual frame" assumed in critiques such as Lee Edelman's influential notion that the reproductive imperative lies at the heart of modern power, which takes shape in the form of the innocent child figuring as the preeminent subject of futurity.[133] If the assemblages of "race and sex are to be increasingly thought outside the parameters of identity," she suggests, "what is at stake in terms of biopolitical capacity is therefore not the ability to *reproduce*, but the capacity to *regenerate*, the terms of which are found in all sorts of registers beyond heteronormative reproduction." In the nineteenth century, heredity, the mechanism that enables the species being, modulated the broad phenomenon of populational regeneration—including maintaining "health, vitality, capacity, fertility, 'market fertility' and so on"; it did not belong exclusively to the more narrow act of gestational reproduction.[134] In this light, analyses that see biological plasticity, the manipulation of vitality, and other mechanisms of regeneration as specific only to the contemporary era fall within the heteronormative paradigm Puar notes.

Furthermore, the impressibility of the civilized body held the potential to render queer relations fertile. This suggests the existence of an immediate prehistory to the epoch covered in Siobhan Somerville's important account of the emergence of ideas of the homosexual through biologically determinist race science at the turn of the century.[135] In this earlier period, it was precisely the "biological indeterminism" of the body, the as-yet-undifferentiated roles of the social and biological, that enabled reformers to conceive of same-sex relations as generative.[136] Impressibility discourse exposes the long roots of homonationalism, Puar's apt term for the ranking of civilization and savagery on the basis of the inclusion of same-sex erotic relations in the national agenda.[137] Same-sex relations consolidated as formations within the larger biopolitical project that tied sexual difference, heredity, and vitality into interwoven strands. Furthermore, the emergent nineteenth-century logic of same-sex sexuality necessarily depended on the civilizationist hierarchy that produces sex difference as a racial attribute. From the beginning, queer legitimacy emerges within the frame of civilization—a legacy still reverberating loudly today.

Modern sexual discourse materialized not only in the form of the intertwined emergence of the heterosexual/homosexual dyad and racial determinism increasingly visible by the last decade of the nineteenth century, but also through the inauguration of modern heredity. The two criteria of modern heredity, as proposed by Evelyn Fox Keller, are the notion that inheritance transpires through "the passing on of an internal substance" belonging to the body itself and the belief that hereditary particles are "fixed entities that were passed on from generation to generation without change," immutable in the face of diverse environmental conditions.[138] In this framework, nature and nurture become "disjoint," figured as processes that are not only distinct from one another, but belong to different spheres entirely and have no overlap.[139] Modern heredity brings to fruition a fundamental shift: that the body and milieu contain distinct chronologies.[140] Toward the end of the nineteenth century, experimental and theoretical investigations into the sciences of heredity on both sides of the Atlantic, including the work of Galton and August Weismann, began to test the degree to which impressions were transmitted from one generation to the next as physical adaptations, instinct, or racial memory.[141] This work increasingly showed that acquired characteristics could not be transmitted, suggesting that heredity was an immutable substance. No longer a diffuse index of relational experience, heredity gradually became a biopolitical category of speciation that differentiated sexes, races, sexualities, and family lines.[142] As Keller argues, modern heredity only speaks to the populational level: it cannot quantify which elements of an individual organism are due to physical inheritance and which are due to environmental conditions.[143] The term *gene* was coined in 1908 to denote the basic unit of immutable inheritance in the wake of the 1900 rediscovery of Austrian monk Gregor Mendel's experiments hybridizing pea plants. The body soon became a blueprint, not a malleable wax tablet, and its key substance was the microscopic gene, not the tangible nervous system. Alongside the emergence of modern sexuality, which identified discrete properties of the body rather than modes of relation, modern heredity theory restricted hereditary transmission from all manner of impressions to the union of male and female sex cells.

Heredity had become, like sexuality, an innate and discrete property of the body. The emergent solidification of modern sexual discourse picked up speed in the 1890s, and sexuality came to be deemed an inherent aspect of interiority, a property of the liberal individualist self that sexologists now identified as either heterosexual or homosexual. Sex before sexuality manifested as a proliferating dynamic between bodies, whereas sexual discourse taxonomizes discrete individual qualities, including the gene.[144] By 1915, determinist notions of sexuality, race, and heredity were increasingly prominent, and both sexuality and race were classified as discrete, identifiable, and innate properties of the biological body itself. In chapter 5, I illuminate how W. E. B. Du Bois reached backward to sentimental models of impressibility to challenge the solidification of genetic racisms, a move that brought along with it the notion that race is a cultural, rather than physiological, phenomenon. While the impressible body rendered reproduction a social act, classical genetics restricted transmission to male and female. Breeding efforts quickly shifted from determining who was most fit to raise the children of the civilizing, to regulating who was the most fit to conceive. In fact, one of the many victories of twentieth-century eugenicists was the conceptual restriction of reproduction to the emergent notion of heterosexuality.

Within biology, the reconciliation of population genetics with natural selection in the modern Darwinian synthesis of the 1930s completed the consolidation of modern hereditary theory and signaled the rapidly dwindling influence of the idea that experience shapes hereditary material—though neo-Lamarckian interpretations lingered in French-influenced settings, such as Mexico.[145] In this modern take on Darwin, environment does not act directly on the body itself, but shapes outcomes at the broad level of population.[146] Evolution, in other words, transformed from a site of disciplinary action that emphasized the molding of the individual and familial body in spaces of "enclosure," to the broader work of populational stabilization.[147] At the same time, the larger political economic structures in which the biological sciences are immersed similarly came to prioritize the tasks of populational homeostasis and the open-ended "modulation" of markets and people in techniques that Foucault called security and Deleuze referred to as "societies of control," to accomplish the tasks originally outlined by disciplinary mechanisms.[148] The modern Darwinian synthesis marks a large shift in biopolitics in which organic and political processes were now seen as fundamentally distinct. One of the most fruitful outcomes of this division, consolidated by the 1940s and 1950s, has been discourses that identify gender and race as cultural, not biological, phenomena. Yet these newer apparatuses have revitalized, rather than dismantled, the function of racial and sexual differentiation as sites of social control.[149] In this contemporary framework, the task of power—in repressive governments or liberation movements—becomes the conjoining and/or separation of the social and biological at the site of the molecule, the individual, and the population.

At the close of the twentieth century, however, life scientists began insisting once again on the possibility that experience affects the expression of genetic heredity. Epigenetics lessens the cleave between biology and culture dominant since the modern Darwinian synthesis, suggesting that new forms of biopower may indeed be emergent that proliferate novel kinds of racial and sexual differentiation and novel kinds of resistant practices. From the perspective of the twentieth century, the vital politics of the twenty-first century indeed look new. Yet we need to consider new biological technologies and markets in the nuanced terms of scale and effect that contextualize notions of epigenetic imprinting within the history of inherited impressions of the pregenetic age. Promising existing theoretical models that emerge from this broader frame include models of race, sex, and affect as assemblages that combine cultural and biological elements and conceptions that the vital capacities of organisms shape the forms that power assumes, and not only the reverse.[150] These theoretical models exist in relation to earlier biocultural forms, such that the assemblage succeeds the palimpsest and affect updates impressibility. To disentangle radical politics from biopower, we must examine the various ways that power has long managed the circulation of vital energies and the differing ends to which such energies are conceived and enlisted.

CHAPTER OVERVIEW

Chapter 1 analyzes the function of sentimentalism as a technology of species, race, and sex differentiation by turning to the once prominent but now forgotten work of the American School of Evolution. I argue that these scientists translated the era's deeply entrenched beliefs about the sentimental nature of knowledge formation as judicious reflection on sensory impressions into a vitalist theory of species, race, and sex formation. They reassured anxious Anglo-Saxons of their ability to direct evolutionary change on the grounds of their unique capacity of sexual differentiation. Chapter 2 explores the work of black feminists, particularly Frances Harper, in developing the palimpsestic notion of race as an accumulative process over evolutionary time. Harper forges a tactile method of racial uplift in which both the erotic and eugenic aspects of the palpable impression play a central role in civilizing the race. In chapter 3, I show how the sentimental politics of life enabled defenses of women's sexual self-determination and women's same-sex domesticity by turning to the medical theories of the vagina of two early women physicians. I argue that Dr. Elizabeth Blackwell and Dr. Mary Walker's conceptualization of the corporeality of white women as impressible, adaptable, and ultimately the incarnation of growth itself opened up space for white women's same-sex affiliations, sexual agency, and professional pursuits to be folded within the normative biopolitical operations of civilization. Chapter 4 turns to the effects of sentimental biopower on children subject to biophilanthropic measures to improve hereditary material through schooling and rural and domestic labor, particularly the two hundred thousand kids sent west on "orphan trains." In this method of incremental life, reformers rehabilitate those deemed primitive and marked for expiration into a useful population of wage laborers that will raise the standard of living of the population as a whole. The final chapter moves into the early twentieth century to track how theories and strategies of progress via impressibility gradually gave way to theories of immutable heredity that explicitly overthrew sentimental paradigms of heredity. I show that antiracist figures like W. E. B. Du Bois, in response, adapted impressibility to reconceive of efforts to shape the biological quality of the population through reproductive means in the years leading up to the modern Darwinian synthesis. A brief epilogue considers the ongoing legacy of impressibility within social construction theory and epigenetics.

....

In the sentimental politics of life, vital forces unleashed by sex and other forms of sensory excitement circulate among a milieu, adhering bodies to one another in promiscuous relation. Impressibility forges a population through shared vital material, even in the absence of reproduction and parentage. Yet biopower works through a zero-sum game that turns the social sphere into a competitive arena composed of bodies continually shaped through and against each other over time. Responsivity, relationality, and adaptability become technologies of administrative power. In this context, race and sex emerge not as interior genetic or psychosocial attributes of fixed organisms, but as biopoliti-cal categories ranking the degree to which each body is acted on and/or acts on the larger population—which reaches backward into evolutionary time. The ongoing insidiousness of race and sex lies in their precipitation from intimacy, care, friendship, and alliance. They are calculations of relational capacity, and indeed, biopower governs at the level of basic interactions between friends and lovers, laborers and bosses, and neighbors and families, as well as the state-determined categories of nation and population. Sentimen-talism represents a prime example of liberal individualism's transformation of feeling, relationality, and care into an asymmetrical dynamic—a market of feelings. Biopower seeks to transform the very capacity of feeling into mecha-nisms of population security and biological optimization.

CHAPTER 1

Taxonomies of Feeling

Sensation and Sentiment

in Evolutionary Race Science

If it be true that reason must direct the course of human evolution, and if it be also true that selection of the fittest is the only method available for that purpose; then, if we are to have any race-improvement at all, the dreadful law of destruction of the weak and helpless must with Spartan firmness be carried out. . . . The use of the Lamarckian factors, on the contrary, is not attended with any such revolting consequences. All that we call education, culture, training, is by use of these. Our hopes of race-improvement therefore are strictly conditioned on the fact that . . . changes in the individual, if in useful direction, are to some extent inherited and accumulated in the race.

JOSEPH LE CONTE, "The Factors of Evolution" (1891)

Charles Darwin's theory of evolution, the story often goes, shot into history with the force of truth and transformed the course of science and politics on both sides of the Atlantic. Yet a host of U.S.-based evolutionary scientists stridently disagreed with the principles of natural selection on the theory's 1859 debut, preferring other models of species change. Leading paleontologist Edward Drinker Cope and his cohort of zoologists, herpetologists, anatomists, and others who made up the self-described "American School of Evolution" challenged Darwin's theory that species change occurs through random variation and the struggle for existence.[1] They championed instead the early nineteenth-century work of the French naturalist Jean-Baptiste Lamarck, in which organisms' pursuit of pleasure and avoidance of pain determines the course of evolution.[2] In American School affiliate Joseph Le Conte's Lamarckian view, displayed in this chapter's epigraph, habitual behavior, rather than "the dreadful law of destruction of the weak and helpless," is the mechanism of evolutionary modification. Yet Le Conte was both a slave owner and slavery apologist who obtained his post as the University of California's first professor of natural history, botany, and geology in order to avoid teaching black students back home in South Carolina.[3] His colleague Cope loudly insisted that woman suffrage and the presence of Africans and their descendants in the United States signaled the "two perils of the Indo-European."[4] In what limited scope, then, is Le Conte committed to education as a strategy of evolutionary progress? And how does Cope's attack on the expansion of the suffrage and a multiethnic citizenry align with his oft-stated belief that sentiment, rather than struggle, guides species change?

In this chapter, I show how the Lamarckian belief in the progressive power of habit was bound up in what I am calling the sentimental politics of life, a dominant mode of nineteenth-century biopower in which the regulation of feeling qualifies members of a population for life. Our understanding of nineteenth-century sentimentalism ought to take into account not only Harriet Beecher Stowe's imperative that "feeling right" is the best guide to political action, but also Cope's notion of "right feeling," in which he locates the "source" of the supremacy of U.S. civilization in its ability to restrain animalistic impulses and maintain the sexual differentiation of the civilized.[5] Dominant frameworks of nineteenth-century biopower too often portray its racial logics as built on determinist notions of the biological. In fact, biopower consolidated in the era through technologies of feeling that managed bodies understood to be differentially plastic and malleable.

From the late 1860s until his death on the eve of the twentieth century, Cope, the zoologist Alpheus Hyatt, the invertebrate paleontologist Alpheus Spring Packard Jr., Le Conte, and others developed a prominent theory of evolution built on a Lamarckian understanding of the interplay of sensation and sentiment. These "neo-Lamarckians," and most of all Cope, argued that the mechanism of species change was not the "promiscuous" variation of natural selection but the "self-control" of "intelligent selection," in which an organism chooses its repeated impressions and its body develops according to these habitual movements.[6] In this vitalist process, an organism's "impressibility"— which Cope saw as its "capacity for response" to its environment—shapes its physical form and that of its descendants.[7] Eighteenth- and nineteenth-century scientists understood the capacity to mount an emotional response to a physical impression as "sentiment."[8] Over time, the American School argued, the faculty of sentiment appeared in the most advanced species and races. They followed David Hume in arguing that emotional response to these physical sensations simultaneously impresses the brain with ideas, creating memory and mental development. "Natural benevolence of and generosity of character, and sympathy for other persons," in Cope's words, guides the pursuit of and response to sensations and thus the evolution of allegedly advanced groups.[9] In short, sentimental feeling encompasses both physical sensation and emotional expression and can regulate the body's growth. Cope's work was "taken seriously by all late-nineteenth-century naturalists," according to a notable historian of evolutionary science, suggesting that the scientific community considered his theory of self-regulating evolution plausible rather than far-fetched.[10]

The work of the American School of Evolution illuminates the significant, yet overlooked, role that discourses of impressibility and sentiment played in consolidating nineteenth-century U.S. biopower. I argue that the American School translated the era's empiricist epistemology, or the idea that knowledge derives from sensory experience, into a theory of species, race, and sex formation. In their view, species originated in sensory stimulation, and civilization originated in the faculty of sentiment, granting individuals, and especially the civilized, control over their own evolution. Impressibility and sentiment became the material basis of race, the criteria by which members of the population were determined to be an asset to the whole whose life should be enhanced, or a threat to its flourishing who must be disposed. Yet discourses of sensibility and sentimentalism present their own instabilities, even as they were enlisted to secure control over biological processes. Sensitivity connotes both the capacity for growth and the possession of nervous "susceptibility," a characteristic allegedly overdeveloped among wealthier women. Impressibility posed both the potential for progress and an unwelcome vulnerability to degenerating influence, while sentimentality frequently verged on hysteria.

I show how sexual and racial differentiation works out some of the contradictions inherent in pregenetic theories of organic development. To resolve the paradox of feeling, the American School bifurcated the civilized body into a two-part unit, reunited in reproduction. The Anglo-Saxon female absorbs the instability of impressibility and its tendency to excess, leaving her male counterpart to enjoy the benefits of *sentiment* while relieving him of the liabilities of *sentimentality*. To these leading evolutionists, restricting the suffrage and deporting African Americans were necessary measures to maintain the dynamic attraction between civilized feminine sensitivity and masculine justice that propelled racial advance and to remove contaminating influences from impressible flesh. I emphasize that uncovering the central role of feeling in the practice of biopower reveals the key role of sexual difference, not only racial difference, in the effort to stabilize the health of the nation as a whole. In this period, the notion of male and female emerge as a function of the larger effort to maintain homeostasis of the species by carving the population up into racial groups with differing claims to life.

The American School of Evolution's extended use of the sentimental rhetoric of feeling points to several ways scholars might rethink the politics and practices of sentimentalism. These scientists' work reveals the continued and surprising presence of sentimental discourse in U.S. science well into its postbellum period of professionalization and illuminates how sentimentalism's epistemological function appealed to a wide range of nineteenth-century writers and readers. Additionally, the American School's research provides a new angle on the politics of the sentimental account of the embodied nature of emotion. These scientists understood sentimental feeling, when expressed through a sexually differentiated couple, as a subjugation of the organic body to the allegedly higher faculty of sentiment. Their work illuminates how sentimentalism involves not only an epistemology and aesthetics of feeling, but also a mode of discipline and species regulation rooted in the impressibility of the body. The sentimental politics of life fashioned physiological and emotional feeling into the basis of national belonging and species formation, a widespread and varied strategy of power that suggests the foundational role of impressibility in crafting the biopolitical divisions of race *and* sex.

RACE SCIENCE AND SENTIMENTALISM

Until recently, literary and historical scholarship positioned scientific practice and sentimental discourse as polar opposites according to most meaningful categories of distinction. One principal exception proves the rule. For example, some historians of science dismissed midcentury naturalists as "sentimental amateurs" who befriended their animal specimens at the expense of developing objective quantitative and qualitative research methods, thereby simultaneously muddying their trousers and their claims to objectivity.[11] While this charge seemingly acknowledges the historical presence of sentimentalism in the practice of science, more often such thinking creates an epistemological divide that distinguishes professionalizing postbellum science from its emotional and therefore idiosyncratic predecessor. By this logic, science became science the moment it ceased to be sentimental. More recently, scholars such as Dana Nelson and Thomas Hallock have shown how sentiment sustained networks of scientists in the days before and during professionalization, creating bonds between researchers that enabled a scientific community to form.[12] As science studies scholars have shown for decades, scientific meaning is deeply embedded in larger cultural narratives. To that end, it is little surprise that one of the most prominent intellectual and cultural traditions of the late eighteenth and nineteenth century shaped scientific as well as literary output.

Empiricism depends on embodied, sensory knowledge. Sentimentalism not only sustained a network of affiliation between gentlemen naturalists but also provided an epistemology. The discourse of sensibility, which arose partly from physiologists' efforts to understand the nervous system and its relation to perception, represented an epistemological bedrock of scientific empiricism.[13] Scholars often point to the role of Louis Agassiz, the most prominent scientist working in the nineteenth-century United States and mentor to many members of the American School of Evolution (although not Cope), in ushering in the professionalization of science and the development of empirical research methods. Yet a brief examination of an infamous passage from Agassiz's writings suggests how discourses of sensibility and sentimentalism informed his scientific method. Soon after emigrating from Switzerland to the United States in 1846, Agassiz wrote to his mother that he had experienced his first "prolonged *contact* with negroes." Until that moment, he had opposed the burgeoning theory of polygenesis, which considers each "race" to be a distinct species descended from unique ancestors. His encounter with African American waiters in the dining room of his Philadelphia hotel, however, compelled him to revoke his commitment to the theory of the unity of human origin in a single Edenic pair. Despite professing "pity" for "this degraded and degenerate race" that "fills me with compassion in thinking of them as really men," Agassiz related that it was "impossible for me to *repress the feeling* that they are not of the same blood as us." Proclaiming the necessity of "truth before all," he confesses that he "can scarcely dare tell . . . the painful *impression* that I received, so contrary was the *sentiment* they inspired in me to our ideas of the fraternity of humankind." The scientist reported that this "impression" was a direct result of his corporeal exposure to the "advanc[e]" of the waiter's "hideous hand toward my plate." Registering his sensibility of the waiter's presence as a penetration of his bodily space, Agassiz pivoted to the threat he feels a multiethnic society poses "for the white race," apostrophizing, "God protect us from such *contact*!"[14]

Stephen Jay Gould, who first translated and published this passage in its entirety, cites the excerpt's ghastly racism as an indication that the naturalist converted to polygenesis on account of the superficialities of "immediate visceral judgment" and professional pressure, rather than the "deeper" evidence of Agassiz's own scientific research.[15] Yet Agassiz's language of "sentiment," "feeling," "impression," and "contact" were constitutive elements of nineteenth-century science, structuring methodological approach, analytic object, and professional strategy.[16] By relating an impressibility at once emotional and physical, Agassiz formulates an embodied epistemology as the basis of his empirical observation. He was far from alone. Jessica Riskin's groundbreaking *Science in the Age of Sensibility* reveals what she calls the "sentimental empiricism" of French Enlightenment physics, mathematics, and chemistry by showing how scientists argued that knowledge of the natural world both stemmed from an "openness" to "physical sensation" and "originate[d] equally in emotion" that such sensations provoked. Riskin argues that, overall, "sentimentalism was integral to the method of Enlightenment science as a whole."[17] In the U.S. context, the broad purchase of sentimental discourse enabled sentiment to persist as a structure of empiricism well into the nineteenth century.

The role of sensation and sentiment in scientific empiricism suggests the utility of analyzing sentimentalism as an epistemology, in addition to a politics, discourse, and mode. Clarifying the overlapping meanings of the terms *sensibility* and *sentiment*, which refer at once to a theory of knowledge in which sensory experience is the most reliable indicator of truth and to an individual's sensory and emotional capacity, helps illuminate their epistemological function. Fiction writers and physiologists alike theorized "sensibility" as the faculty of receiving impressions, or "an organic sensitivity dependent on brain and nerves."[18] In this "impression theory of sensation," the more refined and delicate the tissue, and by association the individual, the greater the organism's capacity for impressibility.[19] Heightened impressibility enabled growth and the acquisition of knowledge. Yet to be impressible is to be vulnerable. Those of the wealthiest classes, especially women, were thought to have highly responsive natures and a correlated delicacy that frequently threatened weakness.[20] "Sentiment," in turn, marks an emotional response to a physical impression and connotes a refined rather than impulsive quality. As scholars have widely recognized, sentiment describes a phenomenon at once mental and corporeal. Like sensibility, sentiment can signify a delicacy of feeling, prone to excess. Sentimentalism emerged as an epistemological, aesthetic, and political mode of regulating the volatility of the impressible body by subjecting sensory feelings to the reflective capacity of emotion. Sentimental epistemologies both grounded knowledge in the capacity for feeling and meted out this capacity according to the hierarchical rankings of civilization and were thus particularly appealing to race scientists.

Rethinking sentimentalism as an epistemology that informed race science also demands rethinking the ontology of the nineteenth-century body. What matters to the nineteenth-century body is how it responds to what is external to it, not what fixed material allegedly dwells within. Agassiz was in good company in his belief that his somatic sensibility posed both great promise (his impressibility denotes a providential capacity to arrive at new knowledge) and peril (his impressibility denotes an unwelcome vulnerability to negative influence). As the historian of anthropology George Stocking Jr. has shown, the operative notion of race and the body in the nineteenth century was not the biological determinism of innate difference, as scholars frequently assert, but a Lamarckian "sociobiological *indeterminism*." The body was understood as a "biocultural" formation, he explains, in which culture impresses itself directly on its material and produces inheritable traits. Conversely, physicality shapes behavior.[21] Affective experiences mold the plastic body of the civilized races over time, guided by the self-regulating faculty of sentiment. Many insisted with Cope that coarse, "unimpressible, and little sensitive" constitutions characterized the capacious category of the "primitive."[22] As such, familial and cultural traditions were deemed to produce corporeal changes at a rate relative to the individual's degree of impressibility. Racial status thus indexed a hierarchy of impressibility.

In the sections that follow, I explore how Cope and the American School of Evolution drew on the long tradition of sensory impressions, a discourse that first comes into focus in the work of Plato and Aristotle and that Lamarck later extended into the species-notion of impressibility. The American School drew on this legacy to posit that self-control and reflective feeling could manage the mutability of the civilized body over time, thereby moderating the vulnerabilities of impressibility by enlisting the regulatory function of sentiment and the classifying power of the biological sciences. The American School divided the population into the impressible civilized who must be protected from the stagnant primitive who must be disposed of. And among the civilized, they similarly split the liabilities of impressibility across the two sexes, a bisexual organization which they argued the civilized alone had attained. To stabilize the impressible body and thus the evolution of the race, the American School enlisted the emergent logic of sex difference and the modulating powers of sentiment.

FIRST IMPRESSIONS

The function of sentimentalism as a technology of race science specifically, and biopower more generally, comes into view when we understand how the body was understood to be differentially mutable and adaptable in the nineteenth century. The body's relative capacity for receiving and regulating impressions—for sensibility and sentiment—became the criteria of race and sex. In this section, I investigate the key antecedents of sentimental biopower in the nineteenth-century United States by tracing the trajectory of the notion of the impression from its use in antiquity as a metaphor for memory to the Enlightenment as an explanation for individual development and the idea of the self. The notion of the impression at the core of pregenetic theories of development has played a prominent role in epistemology since antiquity and yet is woefully underaddressed in critical theory. Over the course of Western epistemology, the body's relational capacity is the means through which it comes to matter.

From the beginning, the metaphor of the impression denoted the process of mental activity and signaled that such potential was distributed unevenly. Plato was the first to offer the "wax block" image of the mind, enlisting as metaphor a writing surface in which several narrow boards were bound together and sealed with wax.[23] Plato recounts that for Socrates, to form a memory is to "hold the wax under our perceptions and thoughts and take a stamp from them, in the way that we take imprints of signet rings. Whatever is impressed upon the wax we remember and know so long as the image remains in the wax; whatever is obliterated or cannot be impressed, we forget and do not know."[24] The materiality of the substrate, which for Plato dwells in the soul, determines whether the mind will absorb the perception or thought stamped on it. A waxen surface that is "deep and abundant, smooth and worked to the proper consistency," will harbor indelible memories, whereas a block that is "'shaggy' and rugged, a stony thing with earth or filth mixed all through it" results in "indistinct impressions."[25] Similarly, impressions slide right off wax that has hardened, for it lacks sufficient "depth," while they become "blurred" and "indistinct" in wax overly "soft" or as yet too thoroughly imprinted for its dimension.[26] Already, for Plato, the impression metaphor for memory depends on a seemingly indexical logic in which experience stamps itself directly on the mind. Yet the capacity for memory is wrapped up within the properties of matter. The temporality of memory depends on the spatial qualities of density, malleability, depth, and texture.

Plato's student Aristotle expanded the impression from a metaphor of memory into an image of sensory perception, thereby inaugurating a millennium-long tradition of empiricist philosophy. Whereas for Plato the wax block receives impressions of perceptions that have already occurred and then crystallizes them as memory, for Aristotle and many in his wake, sensation itself occurs through the act of impression. Sensation, Aristotle explained, is "the power of receiving into itself the sensible forms of things without the matter," of being physically open to and impacted by the shape and spirit of an object without incorporating the object itself into the body.[27] He continued Plato's image of the stamp, analogizing sensation to "the way in which a piece of wax takes on the impress of a signet-ring without the iron or gold."[28] Absorbing the pressure of the signet, the surface of the wax seal continues to bear the trace of its encounter for long thereafter, an ever-present testimony to its past. This framework maintains a sharp ontological distinction between the objects that act and the surface that is impressed.

While impressions describe sensations, impressibility for Aristotle was more generally a property of matter that gave it the capacity to be affected. He explained: "The process of being impressed is the sinking of a part of the surface of a thing in response to pressure or a blow, in general to contact."[29] He classified substances such as copper and wax as "impressible," meaning that physical touch affects the "part of the surface" that come directly into contact with another object.[30] In turn, impressibility can be broken down further into two subcategories: objects that easily receive and retain a new shape are "plastic," whereas those that do not yield as easily are "squeezable." Importantly, squeezable substances retain their internal coherence and integrity in the face of grasping contact, for instead of disintegrating they "contract into themselves under pressure, their surface sinking in without being broken and without the parts interchanging position." By contrast, "non-impressible" materials are either so "hard" that contact cannot change its structure, or so "liquid" that "there is a reciprocal change of place of all its parts."[31] Impressibility, as outlined by Aristotle, describes a quality of a stable, unified object subject to change whose clearly defined boundaries nonetheless remain steady over time, both despite and because of matter continually pressing on it. By contrast, in a dynamic interactionism, bodies would dissolve into one another through the course of their codevelopment.

The impression became a central metaphor in Enlightenment epistemology, capturing the capacity of the mind to experience the crush of tastes, noises, aromas, and caresses as building blocks in the gradual aggregation of a self that persists over time, rather than as invasions that effect the subject's dissolution. Most famously, John Locke positioned the sense impression at the center of his political philosophy, a body of work now regarded as a key origin of empiricism and liberalism. Disagreeing with innatists such as René Descartes, who argued that much of human knowledge was acquired a priori, Locke insisted that the newborn baby came into this world with a mind akin to a blank sheet of paper.[32] The unmarked mind gradually acquired ideas through impressions on the sensory organs that stimulated thoughts, such that "*Ideas* in the Understanding are coeval with *Sensation*; which is such an Impression or Motion, made in some part of the Body, as produces some Perception in the Understanding."[33] More or less akin to sensation in Locke's treatment, the impression describes the movement of matter on matter, as well as the mind's subsequent reflection on this sensory stimulation, a two-step process that enables cognitive development and self-awareness.

In minds with the material capacity of intellect, a capacity understood as belonging to both the mind and the larger culture in which it is nurtured, impressions accumulate as the grounds of the self. Ideas perform the dual role of the product of the interaction between the self and the external world as well as a potential mediating boundary at its interface. Through the process of contributing mental labor to the originating sensory stimulation, idea formation ensures that the individual possesses its experience and is not merely set into motion by the object world. The key quality of matter for Locke is its "solidity," a term he finds less "vulgar" than the synonymous "impenetrability."[34] Solidity describes matter's condition of "repletion," or a fullness that prevents another object from occupying its own space, even when one object bears down on another, creating sensation.[35] We might think of Locke's civilized body as having achieved solidity, such that it can be affected, but not penetrated, by its experiences. In the apt words of Monique Allewaert, Locke's thought "produces the body as a single, self-identical, and particular consciousness that persists despite the diverse materials, things, temporalities, and places that press upon and pass through it."[36] I would add only that the stable, civilized self achieves singularity not despite, but on account of, this range of impressions. Indeed, the dependence of mental development on the movements of the material world was a source of great consternation to Locke and the many who followed in his footsteps. As Allewaert argues, Locke is at the heart of the Enlightenment construction of personhood as a self-continuous formation rooted in the stable body, a coherent whole that subsumes all the qualities and capacities of its parts. Allewaert contrasts this hegemonic conception with the radical potential of what she calls "minoritarian" materialisms in the Caribbean, which celebrated the propensity of bodies to disaggregate within the material world in which they are immersed.[37]

The condition of primitivity, in contrast, becomes the state of penetrability, a heightened affectability in which sensations pass right through the body, failing to stick. While all minds commenced as a stark sheet of paper, Locke followed his predecessors in antiquity in underscoring the differential capacity of matter to absorb touch, stimulate ideas, and therefore develop over time. Locke relied on the hierarchies of colonialism to delineate which minds were "fitted to receive" mental impressions stimulated by sensations, finding "amongst *Children, Ideots, Savages,* and the grossly *Illiterate,*" only "notions [that] are few and narrow, borrowed only from those Objects, they have had most to do with, and which have made upon their Senses the frequent-est and strongest Impressions."[38] This colonial roll call of alleged equivalents served Locke as evidence of the inexistence of innate principles; in the absence of culture or the capacity to engage with it, the primitive mind lacked abstract ideas and reverberated only the body's most fundamental occupations. Indeed, Locke, who himself had a leadership position in British settler colonial ventures, excluded Native Americans from his notion of the right to property.[39] Only labor or another means of contributing to property "something that is his own" renders lands a private possession.[40] He deemed the indigenous devoid of proper relations to objects that subordinate matter to the development of mind, insisting that they instead merely "borrowed" from the qualities of matter. The indigenous thus lacked ideas, labor, and the right to ownership. In rendering the emergence of mind dependent on its relations with the material world in which it was immersed, Locke's notion of the impression was a central concept in suturing the notion of the liberal individual to material conditions of political economy and culture.

The impression establishes a relation of dependence between the civilized self and its environment that philosophers attempted to manage through the labor of mediating mental activity. Building on Allewaert's helpful distinction between the Lockean concept of self-identical personhood and Caribbean models of corporeal dissolution, I want here to emphasize the degree to which the subject of reason relies on objects that remain external to it for its own self-constitution. Even the most abstract of thoughts results from the movement of matter on matter. Locke worried: "As the Bodies that surround us, do diversely affect our Organs, the mind is forced to receive the Impressions; and cannot avoid the Perception of those *Ideas* that are annexed to them."[41] Individuation transpires through the vulnerable process of object relations. The relational, rather than autonomous, development of the individual in which all external to the self serves primarily to further its own development is a notion suited to colonial economies, in which value is extracted through the subjugation of lives, lands, and resources figured at geographic and/or temporal remove. In Locke's thought, the constant regulation of sensation produces the boundaries of the coherent yet highly vulnerable self. Civilization becomes imperative for subordinating the immediate gratification of sensation to the reflection of sentiment.

But as this book explores, during the dawn and organization of the discipline of biology, the impression was refigured as the biopolitical concept of impressibility. In the regime of impressibility, the matter of the body could engage directly with the material world, potentially carrying the mind along for the ride. And the key political construct becomes not only the individual, but also the aggregated mass of the population.

What is the life span of an impression? Nineteenth-century earth and life sciences raised the temporal stakes of the impression theory of mental development and lengthened its account of individual maturity into the mechanism of the organic growth of species more generally. Charles Lyell and others in the 1830s supplanted the biblical chronology that determined that creation had occurred five thousand years prior with a new sense of the vastness of terrestrial time, declaring that the earth was millions of years old. The sciences of geology illustrated the new notion of prehistory by pointing to the impressions long ago left by matter within the earth itself. "Who would think that the yielding sand in which the footstep of the passerby leaves its impression," posed an article Frederick Douglass reprinted in *North Star*, "should reveal that foot-print a thousand years afterwards to the men of a remote generation?"[42] Yet such claims did not necessarily challenge Christian faith, and in fact were often found compatible with natural theology and Protestant belief by geologists and the general public alike. One response, pervasive in the United States, was a sentimental-Protestant interpretation of evolution premised on Anglo-Saxons' ability to discipline the body's impressibility, and thus evolutionary development, through self-control. A wide variety of U.S. thinkers and cultural producers considered both Lamarck's and Darwin's work to offer a blueprint of how species change occurred through the transmission, from one generation to the next, of physical modifications resulting from impressions. As domestic ideologue Catharine Beecher enthused, "[Children's] plastic nature will receive and retain every impression you make; [and] will transmit what they receive from you to their children, to pass again to the next generation, and then the next, until a *whole nation* may possibly receive its character and destiny from your hands!"[43] The language of impressibility linked domestic morality, natural science, and Protestantism into complementary accounts of nation building through intimate contact.

While the majority of Darwin's enthusiasts saw natural selection as outlining a teleological plan for biological improvement, life scientists often made a more rigorous distinction between Lamarckian evolution through the pursuit of pleasure and avoidance of pain and Darwinian evolution through competition. No researcher staked his career on mounting an opposition to Darwin as fiercely as Edward Drinker Cope, who waged rhetorical war against the struggle for existence.[44] Hoping to discredit random variation as a plausible account of evolution, Cope and his American School adapted the impression account of development into an explanation of species and race modification via conscious feeling. They doubled back on the epistemology of sensibility and sentiment by drawing on the French naturalist Jean-Baptiste Lamarck's (1744–1829) account of evolution, which transformed sensory impressions into dynamic impressibility.[45] Lamarck had inaugurated a new discipline he called "biology" and developed the notion that species change transpired through natural processes, rather than, in Darwin's rendering of the then-current belief, "miraculous interposition."[46] He did so by extrapolating from the discourses of sensation and sensibility.

Lamarck made two paradigm-shifting contributions to impression theory, and to intellectual history more broadly, in his landmark *Zoological Philosophy* (1809). First, he argued that repeated sensations create not only the substance of memory, but also the shape of organisms that possess nervous systems. According to the late eighteenth-century "impression theory of sensation," on receiving a stimulating impression, the affected body part contracts as nervous fluid rushes toward the brain to communicate that impression.[47] The brain then dispatches a returning flush of fluid, which swells the affected part and results in action. "Animal orgasms," Lamarck explained, not only denote "the special affection" most commonly associated with the term but also describe select animals' capacity to receive impressions.[48] If an "exciting cause" habitually re-curs, repeated waves of "an invisible, expansive, penetrating fluid" enlarge the stimulated part of an animal's body.[49] In this model of internal orgasm, penile stimulation serves as the apotheosis of stimulation.[50] Conversely, a protracted absence of stimulating activity induces atrophy. For Lamarck, an animal's form is the result of its habitual pleasures. To be affected means to be stimu-lated, potentially to satisfaction, an erotic dynamic that remains at the heart of impressibility discourse.

In his second major contribution to the emergent discourse of impress-ibility, Lamarck proposed that sexual reproduction transmitted these physical adaptations—such as a lengthened finger or a shortened thigh—to progeny. Repeated impressions, for Lamarck, transmit across generations. Activities of ancestors become the morphological and instinctual character of descendants. His most famous example of this principle of the inheritance of acquired char-acteristics, now known as Lamarckism, contends that giraffes possess long necks as a result of centuries of reaching upward to tall treetops to graze. Add-ing the element of time to the Lockean notion of the development of the nervous system, Lamarck transformed impressions from the mechanism of individual mental development to the mechanism enabling the emergent no-tion of species and evolution. Individual organisms were now linked to one another as a species, in which the growth of one generation could affect the growth of the whole. Impression was becoming impressibility, a concept in which the development of the individual *and* the species depended on "the influence of the environment," which was "in all times and places operative on living bodies."[51] In other words, the development of the individual and the species proceeded from the impressions the individual received from its milieu.

As impression theory was intertwined with colonial and other labor hierarchies, so was its successor, impressibility. Sensibility, in which the organism possesses the "faculty of feeling" that enables it to avoid harmful sensation and pursue pleasant feelings, guides the development of the species among most life-forms.[52] Among the most advanced species, however, an emotional response to a physical sensation—what others called sentiment—motivates the body's movement and subsequent development. Building on the distinction between fine and coarse sensibilities developed by naturalists including Comte de Buffon and Pierre-Jean-Georges Cabanis, Lamarck theorized a hierarchy of feeling in which morality and interior sentiment guide the growth of the most advanced animals. The "most perfect animals," those on the uppermost tier, possess highly sensitive nervous systems. Lamarck proposed they were capable of an "intimate feeling of existence" that pertained to the nervous system as a whole (rather than a vitalism attributed to the affected body part).[53] This "inner feeling" enables animals to act according to instinct, or the inherited habitual actions of their ancestors, and according to emotion, or "moral sensibility."[54] Emotion enables the most evolved to guide their behavior and thus their physical changes according to their awareness of themselves, not only in response to external sensation. Lamarck's schematic safely places the agency of evolutionary change under the control of the individual organism's relationship with its milieu—especially among those allegedly higher animals that possessed the advanced faculty of sentiment to regulate their impressions. This is a striking difference from Darwin's later theory of natural selection, in which environmental pressure determines the survival rates of random adaptations at the level of the species.

With Lamarck, we see key elements of sentimental biopower taking shape. Lamarck transformed the capacity for absorbing impressions from its function, within the Lockean framework, as the basis of individual development, into a process that links individual bodies to each other over time. Impressions became an early notion of heredity, understood as the precipitate of experience that bodied forth the feelings of the past in the bodies yet to come. The inherited results of habitual feelings are transmitted as morphology and instinct down the generations. Individual experience radiated across time, linking the organism's history of self-discipline to the generational outcome of the species. Impressions, in other words, were central to the new notion of population, which conceives of organic bodies at the level of species. Sentiment accumulates among the most evolved animals as the faculty of reflective emotion, which enables the active regulation of growth, of the individual and by extension the species. Sentiment regulates the relentless pursuit of stimulation that evolution directed by the habitual pleasures of internal penises might require.

TAXONOMIES OF FEELING

The new Lamarckian notion that the growth of organisms over time depended on the capacity of their bodies to be affected by the milieu provided one of the key elements in the consolidation of biopolitics. Since the late seventeenth century, strategies of charity, governing, and sociality at the local and national level had turned toward conceiving of the field of power to be biological life itself, in a material and temporal sense.[55] Biopower began first with disciplinary technologies—of which sentiment was an important one—that addressed the corporeality of the individual, of establishing institutions that work toward producing tractable and productive social members. In the late eighteenth century, new technologies of security power gradually superseded—but did not supplant—disciplinary power. Security was deployed to manage the nation as if it were a biological phenomenon, subject to processes of organic development en masse, via its own natural processes: rates of birth, death, disease, economic vitality, and so on. Security functioned as the instrument of the emergent regime of biopolitics, which was directed at the condition of humanity as a population, or what Foucault calls "man-as-species," that evolves over time.[56] Security mechanisms endeavor to protect the health of humanity as living being by regulating the biological processes inherent to it, of predicting and therefore regularizing the random events that affect the population's stability and growth. Rather than defending from the perceived enemy without, in the era of biopolitics power would now materialize as the decentralized process of the "purification" of the national body, in Foucault's words, within. Biopower maintains the best life chances for the biological entity of the population by identifying and eliminating threats to its health and survival.[57]

To do this securitizing work, biopolitics required a criteria for determining the relative biological value of the features of the population. For Foucault, "race" becomes the primary "way of fragmenting the field of the biological that power controls," of identifying which characteristics of the population were beneficial to its growth and which threatened its ongoing survival and would best be eliminated.[58] Mid-nineteenth-century theories of polygenesis are a clear manifestation of the new racial logic of man-as-species, deployed in this case according to a rule of multiplicity in which race and species become identical. Foucault argues that the perceived evolutionary exigency to determine which traits of the species were harmful to the health of the whole inaugurated the notion of race in its modern iteration and that during the emergence of evolutionary theory "racism is inscribed as the basic mechanism of power, as it is exercised in modern states."[59] Foucault's analysis is particularly useful here to stress my argument that *race* is not conceived to be innate difference, at the level of the individual body, in the nineteenth century or the present. Rather, race demarcates an allegedly differential capacity to be affected over time. As such, *racism* as a structural feature of modern power does not proceed by ranking the inherent and fixed qualities of groups. Rather, racism is far more insidious: it entails managing the variability of the species as it evolves by regulating the interactions among the species' members. Cope thereby hailed fellow racist readers with a probing question about the nation's black population: "Is our own race on a plane sufficiently high, to render it safe for us to carry eight millions of dead material in the very center of our vital organism?"[60] Modern race and racism come into being as relational phenomena, as the predictors and precipitates of social life.

Cope and the rest of the American School of Evolution's chief innovation was to explicitly cast impressibility as the origin of species and race variation and to position the flourishing discourse of sentimentality as its moral guide. Calling themselves the "neo-Lamarckians," they expanded Lamarck's principles of the transmission of acquired characteristics and the role of emotion in stimulating action into a theory of development that could displace Darwinian competition and chance as the most compelling account of species change. Cope conceded that natural selection did occur, functioning as a kind of "tribunal" that determined which randomly generated adaptations would persist in future generations.[61] But Cope insisted that he, and not Darwin, had accounted for the "origin" of species variation in the first place by identifying habit as the engine of change. To be fair, this claim is less outrageous than it may sound, given that a principal critique of Darwin to this day remains that natural selection describes the process of species change, but not how life came to be in the first place.[62] For Cope, "intelligent selection," rather than natural selection, best describes the origin of new adaptations and new species. Making a "plea" on "behalf" of Lamarckian principles of evolution, he explained that Lamarck's theory of use and disuse accounted for the origin of new variations.[63] Repeated use enlarges a body characteristic, whereas lessened activity causes it to diminish, and the next generation inherits these modifications. Yet the neo-Lamarckians extended Lamarck's theory to meet their own exigencies as white men threatened by the increasing political power of white women and African Americans in the 1870s through 1890s. Lamarck had outlined the evolution of species through repeated and inherited impressions; the U.S. neo-Lamarckians outlined the evolution of the civilized race through the varied capacity of impressibility, or receptivity to impressions, and the regulatory faculty of feeling.

Impressibility massed individuals together into the biological phenomenon of the species and ensured its capacity for continual growth. Cope underscored Lamarck's idea that sensation drove evolution and could function as the motivator of species change. He explained that all organisms, including "even the lowest *Protozoön*," have sensibility, or some degree of will and consciousness that directs their desires and habits.[64] Feeling thus guides the organism's conscious pursuit of pleasure and avoidance of pain, such that "the movements and habits of animals . . . lie at the foundation of the principal characters of species." "Ornamental" characteristics, however, do not arise from function and "are the direct result of the physical impress of the environment" on the nervous system.[65] In other words, environmental influence was responsible for decoration alone and worked directly on the organism's body, rather than through the secondary effect of population pressure, as Darwin had it. Over the time of generations, conscious acts become instinctual behaviors, such that "all life-processes which are now automatic and mechanical were originated in sensation."[66] Overturning Darwin's rejection of agency, the American School conditioned the origins of life itself on individual feeling. Cope's idea of evolution was strictly teleological: he believed that evolution could be directed toward the pursuit of perfection. This view differs sharply from current understandings of natural selection, in which evolution means adaptation to environments, not growth or improvement. But it more than suited Cope's contemporaries, who nearly universally interpreted Darwin to similarly outline a plan for progressive growth.

Belief in animal consciousness—the process by which an animal registers whether something is painful or pleasurable and acts accordingly—was a widespread nineteenth-century phenomenon and fueled a host of studies on animal cognition and emotion and the popular literary genre of animal autobiography. Neo-Lamarckian work represents an apex of these beliefs in the universality of will, memory, and desire. Bureau of Ethnology director John Wesley Powell went so far as to claim that the repeated exercise of the capacity of sensation developed "the endeavor to secure happiness," evident in the ways that "the cubs of the bear dance on the greensward; the swallow floats on

FIG. 1.1. "Edward Drinker Cope in His Study." Image #104670,
American Museum of Natural History Library.

the air with lilting wings of joy; the trout plays in the brook as if sunlight were elysium."[67] If evolution is the consequence of pursuing pleasure and avoiding pain, then animals necessarily have demonstrably developed consciousness and desire, and the pages of the *American Naturalist*, which was run by neo-Lamarckians, were accordingly filled with reports of friendly snails, sensitive horses, sympathetic bulls, highly cognizant cats, and same-sex pairs of geese throughout the last two and a half decades of the nineteenth century.

In the hands of the American School, impressibility became the mechanism of species and racial differentiation. Impressions drive not only the changing morphology of the body, but also mental and social development over ontogenetic and phylogenetic time. The neo-Lamarckians put forth the idea that physical sensibility was a nearly universal trait, whereas impressibility was the provenance of the advanced. Differential impressibility accounts for the differential development of mental and emotional faculties among and within species and racial groups and, accordingly, whether a race has an evolutionary future or merely lingers as a preserved remnant of the past. Individual variation within these parameters drove species change. "Those in which these impressibilities are most highly developed will accumulate mental acquisitions most rapidly; in other words, they will be the most *intelligent* of their species. . . . Those in whom consciousness most frequently recognizes events will *originate* new acts and habits," Cope contended.[68] Whereas Darwin insisted that organisms inherit a bodily structure directly from their parents, the vitalist neo-Lamarckians asserted that organisms inherit the *energy* to make a structure. This energy dwells in the nervous system and varies in intensity according to ancestral levels of development.[69] Lamarck had stressed that physical and mental sensations resulting from impressions were due to the function of an organism's nervous system as a whole, not to a "faculty of feeling" distributed throughout the body: "It is not matter that feels," he clarified.[70] But for Cope and his cohort, each part of the body was imbued with a vitalist life force. Drawing on impression theory, they forged a causal relationship between emotional and intellectual development and bodily form. Cope's work in comparative anatomy advanced the Lamarckian assumption that behavior determines physical shape to assert that anatomical features express a race's level of mental evolution. Mental activities "impress themselves on the external as well as the internal organization," Cope explained.[71] Among the civilized races, a sensitive face manifests the sensitive nerves underneath the skin. Among the less developed, however, a turgid "unimpressibility," or "resistance on the part of tissue to the usual stimuli," meant that the basic act of maturation used up each individual's finite quantity of growth force.[72] Cope's work in comparative anatomy offered alleged proof that the primitive races directed an overabundance of growth force toward bodily development; his illustrations compared gross racial caricatures of African Americans with idealized Greek statues. He surmised that black mental development had "stagnated" as a result and that the race was firmly lodged in the past.[73]

Impressibility linked the corporeal and the self into singular personhood as sensation traveled the distance between the external sensory organ and the mind within. The self developed relationally, dependent on its sensory experience for its self-constitution. In contrast, sensations merely reverberated throughout matter in a body deemed to lack impressibility. In the flesh alone, there was no mind to register the feelings of pain or pleasure. The denial of sensitivity and the capacity for pain and suffering consigned the racialized to, in the apt words of the feminist historian of science Rebecca Herzig, "the absence of selfhood," a status of pure corporeality that prevents the self-possession necessary for legal rights in the Lockean framework. Herzig usefully emphasizes the logic of private property underlying the Lockean liberal individual, the "proprietal constitution of the self," which splits the subject from the fleshy material that it is said to own. An opposing discourse of "dispossession," in Herzig's words, stripped the enslaved, captive, and other racialized subjects of not only the right to their own bodies but also the capacity for pain.[74]

Impressibility became one of the key technologies of biopower, because it delineated those whose vitality should be cultivated for they would flower increased sentiment and sympathy from those whose only possible contribution to continual growth could be their own death. For the race scientists in the American School of Evolution, impressibility not only determined whether a body should be removed from the nation for the health of the whole but also signified bodies whose inner essence was already dead. "Only certain types have been susceptible of evolution," Cope hissed, and blackness represented "dead material" that rendered the race unable "to properly direct the force of animal desire" and thus to advance.[75] The matter of the black body itself, for Cope, had long ago exhausted its vitality, yet it lingered on as a contagion within the national milieu. Given the impossibility of preventing sexual relationships between African Americans and Anglo-Saxons that would "cloud or extinguish the fine nervous susceptibility, and the mental force" of the Indo-European with "the fleshy instincts and dark mind of the African," he concluded that forced colonization schemes were the only way to ensure the continued sensitivity and progress of the civilized.[76] His view clarifies that an animacy hierarchy in which the plastic body of the civilized and the static flesh of blackness stand at opposite poles lies at the heart of sentimental biopower.

The concept of race, for these scientists and the second half of the nineteenth century more broadly, crystallized as a relative index of the body's degree of impressibility. Even the most primitive bodies were generally not thought to be composed of fixed biological material impervious to its environment, contrary to what decades of scholarship on biological determinisms in the nineteenth century has stressed. Rather, racialized bodies were seen as overly excitable and functionally dead, due to the absence of the regulatory capacity to respond appropriately to their stimulations. While black and white stood at the poles of the racial hierarchy, Natives and Asian laborers occupied intermediary rungs of evolutionary development representatives of the past. Indigenous peoples were frequently positioned as the evolutionary origins of the civilized races that could be nudged out of stasis and into the forward movement of time by whites; this idea underwrote the reservation system as well as the century-long off-reservation boarding school movement.[77] As Kim TallBear writes, Native racialization "enabled a scientific narrative in which whites did not colonize and displace Native peoples but, rather, represented a more evolved form of the same people, 'Americans.' "[78] Asian peoples were frequently cast as overly mechanical and lacking in emotional development, qualities that rendered them too easily moved by others, particularly employers. Most visibly, Western white workers mobilized fears of Asian unimpressibility in their struggles against monopoly capital. Races were ranked according to their perceived potential of developing the capacity to absorb the impacts of their impressions and to self-regulate through the emotional faculty of sentiment.

THE EVOLUTION OF SENTIMENT

The volatility of the impressible body, which depended on its impressions from the external world for its own development, required a strict disciplinary technology. Sentiment was enlisted for this purpose. The alleged supple impressibility of the civilized races ensured that they continuously developed new, hopefully advantageous, physical and mental characteristics. Most important among these was the capacity for sentiment. Cope argued that the advanced "social life and the family relation" of civilization "have developed the benevolent sentiments and the affections," as the effects of evolution became the stimuli themselves.[79] Sentiment, in these scientists' work, involves the ability to make an appropriate and sympathetic reaction to an impression, rather than an impulsive and self-serving one. Cope and his cohort posited that racial progress stems from the ability of the civilized to control the impulses of their body through the faculty of sentiment. Le Conte surmised that "sympathy, pity, [and] love" thus drive species change among the most advanced races, freeing them from the indignity of struggle.[80] Hence for Cope "evolution is . . . the long process of learning how to bring matter into subserviency to the uses of mind," or the sublimation of the body to "self-control, from the material as well as from the mental standpoint."[81] Sentiment thus functions as an epistemology, an ontology, and a discipline.

Scientific articulations of sentimentalism clarify that sympathy has an intercessory and teleological function, in that it ensures that civilized responses to stimuli benefit racial progress. In her recent analysis of the role of sympathy in late nineteenth-century sciences of the mind, Susan Lanzoni argues that late nineteenth-century psychologists and philosophers believed sympathy to increase with evolutionary advance. For Herbert Spencer, sympathy is the "awareness of consequences," or an access to the future as opposed to the primitive "impulsivity" of "reflex-oriented" responses, which are mired in the eternal present.[82] Primitive bodies, Spencer maintained, were capable only of reflexes, not of reflection; they kicked experience off rather than absorbing it over time. In his view, social experience reverberates off black bodies in artful mimicry entertaining to their racial superiors, but arguably useless to themselves. Other scientists proposed that a "savage would throw a crying baby to the ground because of 'torpid sympathy.' "[83] For Cope, sympathy enables the civilized to transform basic impulses of pleasure or pain into a moral feeling that considers the social good, yet still ensures individual development. Cope characterized sympathy as an advanced faculty evolving from sentiment that acts as a gatekeeper between the impressible civilized body—especially the more delicate female constitution—and its environment. This mediating capacity ensures that those who possessed it could overcome the threats inherent to the impressible body, for sympathy allowed them to transform others' suffering into opportunities for personal growth rather than for degeneration. On account of its developmental function, Cope declared that sympathy is ultimately in one's own self-interest: "The affections or sympathies should be developed sufficiently to produce a desire for the happiness of others, through the pleasure the happiness of others gives us."[84] Presenting the formula of the domestic novel as evolutionary doctrine—that making others feel good, especially those beneath you in social stature, brings its own reward—Cope lays bare the function of sympathy as building the actor's body and character.

Cope's emphasis on the asymmetrical relations of sympathy illustrates the aptness of Glenn Hendler and Elizabeth Barnes's analysis that sentimental sympathy functions as an "act of imagining oneself in another's position" that ultimately works to constitute the self.[85] Sympathy both increases and regulates the body's affective experiences. Abolitionists famously drew on the sentimental discourse of shared feeling. Yet sentimental taxonomies of feeling broadly denied a common intensity of feeling and self-possession. As Saidiya Hartman has argued, the sentimental principle that a shared capacity for pain renders all life worthy of political recognition was a process that cut two ways, one that subjected blacks *to* power far more than it granted liberal individualist subjectivity to the enslaved.[86]

The American School's emphasis on the reflective quality of sentiment, as opposed to the immediate and impulsive acts of sensation, suggests a final way in which these scientists drew on sentimentalism in their account of species change. As Dana Luciano has argued, nineteenth-century U.S. sentimentalism marks "a way of using deployments of mixed feeling (pleasure and pain) to negotiate problems in time."[87] For these evolutionists, fundamentally concerned with the narration of temporality, sentimentalism proved a rich resource through which to challenge Darwin's account of evolutionary time as a ruthless, senseless process. In the first half of the century, Luciano argues, a wide variety of writers and lecturers understood grief as a way to access sacred, affective time that connected the grieving subject to the repetitive cycles of the organic and to offer protection from the linear, relentless, forward-moving temporality of national progress as well as from the impetuousness of sensation. Sensation "signals a mode of intensified embodiment in which all times but the present fall away—a condition simultaneously desired, in its recollection of the infantile state, and feared, in its negation of social agency"; by contrast, "a morally regulated sentimentality," manifested particularly in the capacity of reflection, "properly disperses feeling across time."[88] Cope and the American School adapted sentimentalism's function as a measured, reflective orientation of the civilized subject in time into an evolutionary discourse that gave the civilized the ability to manage the future development of the race. In keeping with their political paradigm, this entailed reworking affective feeling as a sacred time *outside* the linear time line of national development into the *means by which* the organic body could be brought in synchrony with national and imperial progress. The American School drew on sentimentalism to assert Anglo-Saxons' capacity to subjugate the recursive rhythms of organic time to the service of the linear progress of national development. In the post-Darwinian context, the sentimental premise that refined feeling enables the transcendence of the physical body promised Anglo-Saxons a correlated control over natural time both cyclical and linear.[89]

Denied the status of fellow subjects of the nineteenth century, racialized peoples were understood to be animated fossils of the evolutionary past. The "great chain of feeling," in historian Martin Pernick's apt phrase, hierarchized human groups on the basis of their assumed sensibility and extended spatially to the expanding borders of the nation and temporally from the past to the future yet to come.[90] The American School championed the cyclical theory of recapitulation, in which fetuses literally retrace the development of their ancestors in the womb, only fully reaching the evolutionary plane of their parents at puberty. Recapitulationists rearranged the spatial distinctions that polygenesis, as articulated by Agassiz and others in the American School of Ethnology, relied on to conceive of racial difference. Cope and Hyatt interpreted their collections of fossilized dinosaurs and cephalopods as evidence that different species exhibit parallel development, such that evolutionary change is best depicted not as a branching tree but as a common trunk that divides into multiple parallel lines of differing length. Frozen somewhere near the dawn of civilization, blacks, Native Americans, Asians, and other racial groups formed different stages of "the infancy of civilized man," which nonetheless persisted into the present.[91] They were the roots of humanity, the base from which the civilized had branched off and surpassed.[92] The primitive would retrace the evolution of lizards and other animals in the womb: they would become human at birth but remain frozen in the same developmental state as their parents, even as their body seemingly matured.

Biopolitics entails the racialization of temporality. In Foucault's words, it is the nineteenth-century "recasting of the theme of racial confrontations . . . [within] the theory of evolutionism and the struggle for existence," in which some peoples now represent "the past of [the] race" that consolidates modern "biologico-social racism" as well as modern political power.[93] As opposed to earlier understandings of human difference in which races were unequivocally distinct entities with diverse origins and were thus fundamentally at odds with one another, evolutionary perspectives conceived of racial difference as "permanently, ceaselessly infiltrating the social body," and as the lingering prehistory of the individual body.[94] To be racialized in biopower is not to be figured as an innately distinct species, as the American School of Ethnology infamously had it several decades prior, but to be located within the past of civilization itself. Population management aimed to harness the enemy lurking within the very borders of the settler colonial nation and the matter of the civilized body. Sentiment, in turn, functioned as one of the key technologies to contain the threat of the biological past that haunted the settler colonial nation-state.

MEN'S SENTIMENT, WOMEN'S SENTIMENTALITY

Yet sentimental sympathy exacerbates the vulnerability inherent to impressibility even as it suggests a blueprint for individual and racial development. In fact, Cope's premise that the civilized races could discipline the growth of the organic body through the capacity of sentiment was far from water-tight, according to the logic of sentiment itself. The long-standing Western idea of delicacy as signifying both "refinement and debility" captures the fundamental instability at the core of the intertwined discourses of impress-ibility and sentimentalism.[95] The hydraulic model of the body common to both sentimental discourse and materialist science implies that the harmonic balance of the sentiments is continually on the verge of destabilization. The capacity for delicate feeling can easily swell into an outlandish susceptibility to impressions—this very fear lies at the heart of Edgar Allan Poe's corpus. And indeed, many intellectuals of the Gilded Age fretted that the dependence of progress on an increasing amount of impressibility and sentimentality and a decreasing level of manliness would result in an effete "overcivilization" un-prepared for the responsibilities of empire.[96] They offered a variety of pro-tective measures ranging from confining middle-class women to roughing up middle-class boys. Whereas domestic novelists tended to work out sentimen-talism's categorical volatility by depicting their heroines' ability to achieve the upper hand over their vulnerable corporeality, race scientists did what they do best: they taxonomized. Late nineteenth-century evolutionists, especially those affiliated with the American School, stabilized the paradox of impress-ibility by dividing the civilized body into two interdependent units, male and female. In this dimorphic pair, the adult female absorbs the instability of im-pressibility and its tendency to hysteria, absolving her male counterpart of the excesses inherent to delicate feeling.

Within the logic of civilization, the two sexes represented a unique achieve-ment of the civilized race. Evolutionists, anthropologists, and many others from across the life sciences and beyond determined that only the civilized had reached the stage of sexual dimorphism and that all other peoples had only one sex.[97] While some physical "diversity of sex is of very ancient origin," a differentiated "mental sex character" distinguishes humankind from the rest of the animal kingdom, as Cope put it.[98] Analogously, while physical sex was a universal feature of humanity, only the civilized had achieved mental sex characteristics—which, in turn, had created additional physical adaptations. Accounts of Native women performing the work of drudges and elaborate caricatures of the androgyny of nonwhite and poor peoples are but two examples of the relentless evidence offered of the lack of sex differentiation among the less evolved. Anglo-Saxons, at the top of the evolutionary ladder, possessed the most highly differentiated physical, mental, and psychological profiles. For the great majority of the consolidating white middle class over the course of the second half of the nineteenth century, sex difference represented racial attainment. Male and female were racial achievements born of the feed-back loop between the material and cultural aspects of civilization. As we will see throughout this book, recognizing this overlooked genealogy of sex both supports and adds nuance to analyses of biopower that see racial difference as fundamental to the function of modern power.

In effect, civilizationists placed civilized women at an evolutionary level halfway below that of their male counterparts, suspended between civi-lized men and the racial group below them in the hierarchy. The bodies and minds of civilized women were more childlike than those of men and thus retained heightened plasticity throughout their life span; correspondingly, their hyperimpressibility triggered responses exceeding the stimulating impression. Cope, Hyatt, Le Conte, and others made clear that the "bisexual organization" of civilization consisted of one distinctly superior and one inferior component.[99] In a widely read essay, Cope explained that woman, yoked to family life through her inheritance of the "disability" of reproduction, became "a being of affec-tions," while man, on account of his "muscular strength" and "active life," became "the master of the two."[100] Women's heightened impressibility ensured that they could make new adaptations and transmit them to offspring, as long as their male partners carefully disciplined their excesses and the state regulated their access to political power.

In short, race scientists assigned the Anglo-Saxon male *sentiment* and con-signed his female counterpart to *sentimentality*. They transferred onto women the pejorative connotations of the adjective *sentimental*, which according to Janet Todd refers to "the display of emotion for its own sake beyond the stimulus and beyond propriety."[101] In other words, while impressibility of *tissue* provides the conditions of growth, impressibility of *character* connotes emotional excitability, or the tendency to an emotional response above and beyond its stimulating impression. In its excess, for Cope, sympathy took the form of "physical vices, superstitions, and selfish ambitions," traits that lead first to the degeneration of an individual and eventually to the downfall of a society.[102] When Charles Guiteau fatally shot President James A. Garfield in 1881, Cope and Packard wrote two editorials diagnosing the assassin as insane, meaning that "the emotional or sentimental elements of character have so far overcome the rational as to cause the commission of self-destructive acts."[103] Guiteau had become, in other words, overly feminized, as his overindulgence in feeling vitiated his capacity for temporal reflection.

Civilization regulated the constitutional vulnerability it depended on through biological sex difference that pressed women into the service of their male counterparts. Cope argued that the adult male, matured past the ten-dency to excess but tempered from cruelty by the *"indirect* influence" of his wife's delicate feelings, enjoys a life of rationality and altruism at the head of the family and the imperial state.[104] Poised in counterbalance to sympathy, the rational faculty of justice "enable[s] the possessor to dispose of his sentiments in the proper manner," for he enjoys a synchronicity of reason and sentiment.[105] The harmony of civilization depends on white men's use of women "in the proper manner"—that is, as sentimental helpmates who absorb the volatility and permeability of sensibility. While necessary for racial advance, sympathetic identification functions as an "escape from" the pressures of empire building and only furthers Anglo-Saxon supremacy when it represents "the function of a special class or sex."[106] Since women's place was far removed from the public sphere, the vigor of the race remained unthreatened by their sentimentality. As the weaker sex, women's stimulation of men's love also ensured their own survival. In fact, Cope argued, a civilization's level of ethical development can be measured by men's treatment of women, for civilized men would reenslave women were it not for their own refined yet tempered feeling.[107] "There is absolutely no reason why men should expend their energies on women, excepting as an expression of personal affection," Cope maintained.[108] Rather more bluntly, he wrote to his daughter, Julia, who nonetheless served as one of her father's key interlocutors, that "in fact women have no standing with men excepting through the bonds of affection. Outside of these they 'don't count.' "[109] Cope elsewhere clarified that if women were a nation, men would have invaded them long ago.[110]

The two-bodied subject sticks together through a heterosexual attraction that has been transformed from the instinctive sexuality of animals and savages into the reflective faculties of sentiment and sympathy. For Le Conte, "the only natural relation between the sexes is that of being *mated*."[111] Cope and Hyatt maintained that civilization itself depends on the reunion of the dimorphic body. They recommended that social institutions compel heterosexual behavior and guard against "gender confusion."[112] Cope advocated for both higher education for women to increase their attractiveness to men and easy access to divorce if a particular marriage proved unproductive or harmful. For those men possessing exceptional energy, he even proposed "voluntary polygamy" so that their abundant affection would produce even more civilized offspring, in a kind of eugenic hyperheterosexuality.[113] Yet while Cope and his cohort positioned what was soon to be named heterosexual attraction as both the method and the goal of civilization, the neo-Lamarckians acknowledged that such desire did not always transpire. "Women of *feminine type, with developed intelligence*, have *never failed* of response from the other sex," Cope insisted, implicitly letting on to the existence of different, "not normal types" of women with other kinds of responses, such as those "who are forbidden by some sinister destiny from conforming" to bisexual mating.[114]

The very viability of sexually deviant subjects proved to be one of the neo-Lamarckians' principal pieces of evidence that civilized individuals must stave off inappropriate behaviors that would rapidly erode the psycho-physical differentiation of the sexes. Above all, the growing campaign for woman suffrage most threatened to masculinize women. As Hyatt explained, civilized women seemed far too eager and able to "become virified."[115] The impressions resulting from women's electoral participation would stimulate the growth of masculine traits and atrophy feminine characteristics, causing women and the civilized race to slide down the evolutionary timeline back to primitivism. Cope shrieked that women's political activity catalyzes "the effeminization of men and the masculinization of women," a condition that finds "counterfeits of both sexes, each a fraud to the other, and both together frauds before the world and the universe!"[116] Hyatt was forced to admit that such physical transformation—that is, a physical modification resulting from a repeated impression—follows the basic neo-Lamarckian principle of species change. It is thus "perfectly natural and not in a common sense degenerative." Nevertheless, such sexual deassignment "would not belong to the progressive stages of the evolution of mankind."[117] The evolutionary account of sexual difference thus opened the door to the possibility that queer behaviors precipitate queer bodies, a naturalistic explanation for sexual deviance rooted in the plastic capacities of whiteness that later identity models of sexuality foreclosed.

Racial progress depended on the ability of white men to maintain a dimorphic body and to regulate their other half. Both sex and race difference were elaborated as hierarchies of impressibility. Among the civilized, the highly impressible female half undertakes the emotional labors of civilization and the animalistic labors of the reproductive cycle, while the masculine half enjoys the sentiments of justice, altruism, and self-control. For the U.S. neo-Lamarckians, men, rather than women, achieve the sentimental ideal of transcending the encumbrances of embodiment. Sex difference thus secures the stability of civilization and is itself a key aspect of biopower's racializing force.

SENTIMENTAL SCIENCE

The work of the American School of Evolution has attracted limited attention in the history of science, a field that has traditionally favored proponents of theories that stand the test of time. Cope has a distinguished scientific record—he published more than any scientist in U.S. history, authoring more than thirteen hundred articles and two monographs, and identified (and often unearthed himself) more than six hundred species of extinct vertebrates, including fifty-six new dinosaur species, such as the *Coelophysis*. He is best known to posterity, however, for his extravagant and even violent attempts to sabotage O. C. Marsh, his rival dinosaur-hunting paleontologist.[118] (Their "Bone Wars" rivalry to unearth and name new prehistoric species was indeed spectacular: it included stealing train cars of specimens, blowing up fossil collection sites, and outlandishly attacking each other's scientific credibility, as well as at least one fistfight.)[119] Yet Cope's belief that function determines form, and that these adaptations are transmissible to descendants, was widely embraced by late nineteenth-century paleontology.[120] Similarly, the cultural politics of evolution in the second half of the nineteenth century echoed the teleological narratives of Cope and his cohort far more than they indicated an embrace of the population pressures of natural selection, an element of Darwinism that population geneticists and others brought to the forefront when they synthesized Darwinism with Mendelian genetics in the 1920s and 1930s.[121]

In turning to the epistemology of sentimentalism to manage the lengthening temporalities of the post-Darwinian organic body—linear growth now extended back into deep time as well as forward to eternal harmony on earth—Cope and his cohort were in the company of a wide variety of U.S. authors, scientists, and reformers. Allied colleagues such as the philosopher Charles Peirce "willingly confess[ed] to having some tincture of sentimentalism in [them], God be thanked!" and heralded the powers of love as evolutionary forces.[122] Many Anglo-Saxons looked forward not just to ongoing biosocial evolution but also to a millennial ascent into perfection in which the kingdom of heaven would be realized on earth. Reformers drew on sentimentalism and evolutionary theory (usually a Lamarckian interpretation of Darwinism that granted ample agency to human intervention) to postulate that the civilized races could shape the growth of primitive peoples by managing their sensations and thus the impressions absorbed by the body. The abolitionism of Harriet Beecher Stowe and Lydia Maria Child pivots on their belief that African American imitation of the habits of the civilized would trigger gradual physiological and cultural development. Approaches to evolutionary progress emphasizing the role of sensibility and sentiment were also attractive to African American feminists such as Frances Harper and Pauline Hopkins, who were eager to interpret racial thinking in ways that might promote the economic and social justice aspirations of the emerging black middle class, as I explore in the next chapter. Combined efforts of white abolitionists and African American feminists suggest the broad political appeal of sentimental evolutionary theories that emphasized the agency of the civilized over species change. The popularity of ideas like these led Julian Huxley to believe that the late nineteenth century marked "the eclipse of Darwinism" in the United States.[123]

While sentimentalism continued to represent a viable scientific discourse during the professionalization of U.S. science, the American School's vitriol toward women and their sentimentality nonetheless suggests the changes under way in scientific practice by the close of the nineteenth century. Cope's location outside formal research institutions and in intimate publics of print befits the larger organizational trends of sentimental biopower, when private settings inaugurated the biopolitical work that was later managed by the state. In presenting their arguments to the public, Cope and Packard cast the value of scientific knowledge in the natural theological terms of an affective bond between the researcher and the beauty of the world. "The cultivation of pure science," they instructed, "has a sentimental as well as an intellectual origin."[124] While Cope framed public appeals for increased funding for science in Protestant-sentimental terms in the 1880s, by the 1890s he praised political critique approached "from a rational, instead of from a sentimental standpoint."[125] Cope's writings in the 1890s increasingly suggest that just as civilized men tempered sentiment with rationality, science had outgrown its sentimental nature and deserved a commensurate professional stature. Cope joined many of his contemporaries in advocating for the professionalization of the sciences through increased funding, the creation of research appointments free from the responsibilities of teaching, the foundation of research centers, legal protection of the availability of "insane, idiotic, or deformed person[s]" for study and public exhibition despite the ethical objections of nonspecialists, and other means.[126] He was eager for the difficulty he experienced in obtaining funds for full-time research to go the way of the dinosaurs he unearthed. Cope's work echoes the larger process of scientific professionalization in the last quarter of the nineteenth century, when the standardization process at the core of the concept of scientific objectivity emerged partly through its differentiation from sentimental practices of knowledge that drew on individual feeling.[127]

The American School of Evolution drew on the epistemology of sentimentalism to promise the ability of Anglo-Saxons to discipline their sensation and thus their evolution. Turning to Lamarck rather than Darwin and elaborating on the sentimental premise that the civilized can mediate their sensibility, they granted well-off Anglo-Saxons command over evolutionary development and cast everyone else as captives of the present tense, without a future and without a past. Cope and his cohort reciprocally linked physiological and psychological feeling such that a body's degree of impressibility indexed its racial and sexual status and vice versa. To reconcile the unstable affectivity of the impressible body at the heart of biopower, I have argued, scientists of the American School split the civilized body in two. Women suffered from the vulnerability and excess of sentimentality but were allocated increased sympathy to both capitalize on and mediate their extreme impressibility; men enjoyed rationality and altruism on account of the synchronicity of their organic and political development. The ideal that sentiment would discipline the impressibility of the civilized nervous system makes apparent that biopower works to protect the health of the population as a whole not only by carving up its members into distinct races with distinct claims to life, as has been widely analyzed beginning with Foucault, but also by dividing the population according to sex. Sex difference represents one of the key mechanisms through which race fragments the biological into governable units.

The American School's most immediate legacy—as measured by the work of their scientific students—suggests the biopolitical outcome of the sentimental account of desire and its regulation determining the body's form. Cope and his cohort, guided by the belief in the individual's (relative) permeability, advocated social policies such as the deportation of African Americans and restriction of the suffrage to remove harmful stimuli from the tender bodies of the civilized. The work of the American School of Evolution suggests the fluidity between the sentimental regulation of bodily impressibility and later eugenics movements, which promoters touted as the "self direction of human evolution."[128] The school's emphasis on civilization as a process of subsuming the malleable organic body to conscious will through self-control and sympathy asserted the eugenic imperative of manipulating the individual body to advance the nation's racial stock. For Cope, the notion of human rights itself entailed "*the right to pursue a course of progressive evolution without obstruction by unnecessary obstacles.*"[129] Their method was distinct from early twentieth-century eugenicists, who developed harder notions of heredity in which the sex cells were impervious to experience. Thus twentieth-century eugenicists sought to prevent the fertility of unfit women and promote the productivity of the civilized. Despite the difference in approach, these two generations of race scientists shared a common belief that the civilized could, and should, direct the evolution of the national population. In fact, Cope's protégé and biographer, Henry Fairfield Osborn, the paleontologist and longtime head of the American Museum of Natural History, played a leading role in U.S. eugenics movements in the 1920s and 1930s.

The U.S. neo-Lamarckians' extended use of the sentimental rhetoric of feeling points to several ways scholars might begin to conceptualize biopower in the nineteenth-century United States, a project just now under way. The promise sentimentalism offered to the middle classes was not only a politics premised on the rightness of individual emotion, but also an epistemology and ontology in which such emotions would continually improve their own bodies. Literary and cultural scholars have long wanted theories of bodily mutability, including Lamarckism, to function as a more progressive approach to midcentury debates about slavery, Indian removal, and empire than racial determinisms or natural selection, which championed bodily fixity and competition between groups as the natural order, respectively. Yet this celebratory view of abolitionists, friends of the Indian, novelists, and others' wide use of the notion of the reciprocal link between experience and corporeal development overlooks the biocultural nature of the nineteenth-century concept of race and as such misconstrues the consolidation of biopower as an antiracist strategy.[130] Rather, the discourse of nervous impressibility represents the full flowering of an ancient and empiricist tradition in which individual development transpires through impressions from the outside world, a process in which the self is formed through the subjugation of all that is external to it. The relational, rather than determinist, nature of growth was accordingly understood to require the careful regulation of the individual and social body. Rather than construed to be the quality of interior character, difference was born of social relations themselves.

Race emerged as a hierarchy of relative impressibility, which denoted the capacity for further change. Racial difference in the nineteenth century connotes the degree to which a body has been impressed by civilization in its ancestral past and will continue to be receptive to external influences into the future. Race and sex comprise a spatiotemporal account of the body's affective, emotional, and regulatory capacity, serving as an index of impressibility that extends beyond the frame of the present generation to recursively pronounce the possibilities of the future on account of the incarnation of the past. The relative sense and sentiment of one's ancestors and descendants layer on each other in ways that promise increasing mobility, paralyzing stasis, or sudden atavism that renders the past legible once more. This palimpsestic body confounds any contemporary attempt to retroactively impose twentieth-century biological determinisms on the decades prior to genetics or to distinguish between the emotional and physiological dimensions of feeling in nineteenth-century thought. Rather, race materialized as a hierarchy of impressibility in which whiteness and blackness served as its limits and indigeneity as the ancestral past.

Far from an emotional salve, the sentimental account of feeling and the women placed at its helm were deployed to promise that the civilized could manage their constitutional vulnerability through the emotional faculty. White women, in the service of the population, did the work of managing the animal body. Sentimentalism functions as a technology to submit the impressible body of the civilized to the workings of the mind, and the racial phenomenon of sex difference is its chief instrument.

CHAPTER 2

Body as Text, Race as Palimpsest

Frances E. W. Harper and

Black Feminist Biopolitics

A race in such a stage of growth is peculiarly sensitive to impressions. Not the photographer's sensitized plate is more delicately impressionable to outer influences than is this high strung people here on the threshold of a career. What a responsibility then to have the sole management of the primal lights and shadows! Such is the colored woman's office. She must stamp weal or woe on the coming history of this people.
ANNA JULIA COOPER, *A Voice from the South* (1892)

Can there be a black feminist biopolitics, or is such a position a contradiction in terms? I take up the possibility that black feminists may be considered among biopower's strategic agents—that they do not simply number among its victims—by turning to one of the most widely, yet incompletely, read black women writers of the nineteenth century: the abolitionist feminist Frances E. W. Harper (1825–1911). Harper's prolific writing is frequently seen as repressed and overly sentimental, both prudish in its restraint and saccharine in its excess.[1] In response, feminist scholars have defended Harper and other black women writers' use of the sentimental genre, clarifying that it represents a political decision rather than a lack of aesthetic innovation.[2] However, they have tended to do so in terms that suggest sentimental discourse is primarily useful as a sartorial charade that cloaks authors' true ambitions, rather than as a valid avenue of intellectual and artistic inquiry in its own right. Yet Harper's interest in sentimentalism was not only on account of what it could disguise. Harper's engagement with sentimentalism is not a stylistic shortcoming or subterfuge but a window onto the vastness of her epistemological and political project and onto the consolidation of biopower. We need not apologize for Harper's sentimentalism; rather, we should continue to plumb its depths.

Consider the following charge Harper issued at the 1893 World's Colum-bian Exhibition: "Through weary, wasting years men have destroyed, dashed in pieces, and overthrown but today we stand on the threshold of woman's era, and woman's work is grandly constructive. In her hand are possibilities whose use or abuse must tell upon the political life of the nation, and send their influ-ence for good or evil across the track of unborn ages."[3] Harper's line is justly one of the most famous propositions in women's literary and political history. The flurry of black feminist production in the 1890s has, in the wake of Hazel Carby's recovery work nearly a century later, indeed come to be known as the "woman's era." Yet Harper also made a set of bold declarations in the same address that has received scant attention: "What we need today is not simply more voters, but better voters. . . . I do not believe in unrestricted and uni-versal suffrage for either men or women. I believe in moral and educational tests. I do not believe that the most ignorant and brutal man is better pre-pared to add value to the strength and durability of the government than the most cultured, upright, and intelligent woman."[4] In her most famous speech, Harper articulates a biopolitics of sexual difference. She contrasts a masculine world of deterioration, destruction, and death with a feminine politics rooted in productivity, regeneration, and fertility, adjudicated through standardizing instruments such as poll exams that stem from the moral "hand" of women.

Harper's use of the encompassing rubric of civilization to differentiate the "better" voters from those who should be denied suffrage reveals how black feminists worked *within* the larger field of biopower to contest a nation that de-nied them access to the rights of citizenship and the domain of the human. In its most general form, power was increasingly consolidating in the late nineteenth century in diffuse, dispersed forms as the regulation and optimization of the population through the primary category of race and the secondary category of sex, itself understood to be a racial attribute. In the hegemonic view, such as that espoused by Edward Drinker Cope examined in the last chapter, liberal freedom depended on the removal and disposal of the sexually undifferentiated and unimpressible black race, along with all other contagious material, from the (white) population. Black women themselves were most frequently identified as the eternal remainders of the animal past lurking within the human race, so primitive that they lacked the capacity of sensory self-management and were mentally indistinguishable from black men. Yet it is precisely because of the abject status outside time to which they were assigned that black feminists had to contend directly with power's function as the production and "prac-tical manipulation of discrete, racially and nationally calculable and codifiable population units."[5] Prominent women race leaders, activists, and writers such as Harper, Anna Julia Cooper, Ida B. Wells, and Pauline Hopkins were forced to work, at least partially, within the terms set by race scientists, white women ideologues of domesticity, black and white promoters of black colonization schemes, elected and unelected officials legalizing slavery and its reinvention in the form of sharecropping and mass imprisonment, and others who racially differentiated the population through calculations of the body's relative dynamism or fixity. Resistance from the emergent black middle class took the form of inhabiting the structures of power differently, of interrogating the practice of stabilizing the health of the population as a whole through sexualized racial difference and of consigning to each group different claims to life. Harper's work offers a crucial example of biopolitics articulated from the position of those cast into death.[6]

The framework of the sentimental politics of life helps us come to grips with the emergence, over the second half of the nineteenth century, of a black feminist biopolitics. The significant contributions of black feminists to conceptualizing and modifying the framework of biopower comes into relief when sensation and sentiment are understood to be themselves biopolitical technologies, rather than external reform strategies for its remediation. I focus in particular on the prolific fiction, poetry, and speeches of Harper, the bestselling black author in the nineteenth century. Sentimentalism was a popular and, yes, often sickly sweet aesthetic mode, but it was also a technology that provided the very scaffolding for the production of the modern self, state governance, and scientific knowledge. Consequently, Harper's use of sensation and sentiment did not serve primarily as "camouflage" or accommodation.[7] Rather, the epistemology and practice of sentiment is part of the substance of her work as a significant public intellectual. Recognizing sentimental biopower resituates Harper as an innovative participant in the broadest structures of politics and knowledge of her age. Far from merely reacting to a political framework consolidated elsewhere, Harper and other black feminists were active producers of modern theories and practices of power, albeit with significantly different goals.

Harper articulated a *negotiated* biopolitics, one that worked within and modified structures of sentiment and sexualized racial difference to move the mass of African Americans toward civilization and thus toward life. Her black feminist biopolitics sought to maximize the potential that African Americans would civilize, or learn to regulate physical impressions through the disciplinary faculty of sentiment, by underscoring the role of the tactile embedded in the ubiquitous impression framework of development. Among the civilized, women were assigned the role of guarding and appropriately inscribing the individual body and the collective racial text. Harper insisted that the emergent black middle class had attained the necessary level of civilization to undertake this work on behalf of the race as a whole, to liberate those who remained "steeped in sensuous gratifications" into the habits of self-respect.[8] Harper outlined a relational framework for black uplift in which the individual and racial body slowly evolved over generation upon generation of impressions rendered through individual touch and the careful regulation of such contact at the level of the race. Yet Harper engaged with biopower, and its politics of respectability and sciences of heredity, with a significant twist, one that located sensual and emotional pleasure at the heart of civilization.[9] I argue that Harper seized the interdependence of human development and the act of touch to conceive of a biopolitics of racial uplift in which the act of impressing one another—with all the erotic, aesthetic, and eugenic resonances of a self that accumulates and a population that coheres primarily through physical contact—evolves blacks into civilization.

Harper's biopolitics of touch makes tangible that the nineteenth-century notion of race far exceeded the rubric of inherent, or even mutable, biological difference that today we most commonly identify in that period, the pivotal precursor to our own.[10] Divergent physicality, mental and emotional capacity, and labor activity were not understood to make up the substance of racial difference. Rather, they function as symptoms of race's all-encompassing diagnosis, in which the individual body represented only one part.[11] Race and sex were deployed as teleological measurements of the degree to which hereditary material was embedded in time and retained the capacity to be affected in the future—in other words, their impressibility. Civilization linked newer evolutionary logics with the preexisting colonial hierarchies of civilization and savagery to indicate a palimpsestic process in which impressions layer on one another over the life span of the individual and the evolutionary time of the race. I propose the term *racial palimpsest* to signal how the concept of racial difference far exceeded the delineation of a body's relative biological quality and instead indexed the compound inheritance of physiological capacity, political economy, aesthetic taste, cultural habit, religious practice, erotic relations, and sexual difference impressed into the flesh. Layer by layer, sensory impressions were understood to gradually transform animal carnality into human rationality. In Harper's emphasis on the regulation of touch, we can see how sentimentalism functioned as a technology to discipline and regularize the flow of tactile pressures on the impressible body—a technology administered at the level of individual self making as well as at the populational level of racial formation.

Frances Ellen Watkins Harper published in a variety of genres and on a variety of topics, including slavery, Christianity, aesthetics, uplift, heredity, epistemology, motherhood, temperance, and childhood. Arguably the first black woman public intellectual in the United States, she also maintained an extraordinary lecturing career.[12] The success of Harper's endeavors—she delivered thirty-three lectures in twenty-one different towns in the span of a mere six weeks during 1854, her first year on the speaking circuit,[13] and sold more than fifty thousand books by 1871[14]—suggests that she found an audience receptive to her ambitious work.[15] She was eager for other African Americans to similarly engage in broad political and intellectual debates, insisting, "If our talents are to be recognized we must write less of issues that are particular and more of feelings that are general. We are blessed with hearts and brains that encompass more than ourselves in our present plight. . . . We must . . . delve into the heart of the world."[16] Today critics read Harper primarily through the crucial lenses of abolitionism, feminism, and sentimentalism. Yet the scholarship sometimes runs the risk of overlooking how she entered these political debates in a manner that drew on and furthered multiple traditions of nineteenth-century thought.[17] A focus on Harper's engagement with impression theory reveals how she made an ontological defense of black viability by extrapolating from this central concept of political theory.

Harper broadly reinterpreted the doctrine of impressibility, understanding it to be a quality of youthfulness—of either an individual body or a race—rather than an achievement of whiteness alone. Like other black intellectuals of the era, Harper emphasized the youthfulness of the African American race to stress their ongoing plasticity. This appropriation of accusations of the "child-like" behavior of the primitive emphasized that blacks had retained the state of impressibility and were poised "look[ing] hopefully towards the future."[18] She contrasted this state of receptivity to the retrograde and unimpressible nature of aging races such as Native Americans, who orient themselves "gloomily back to the past."[19] Anna Julia Cooper similarly differentiated the "effete and immobile" nature of Turkish and Arabian cultures and other "washed out and worn out races" from the potential of African Americans, a race that "is young and full of the elasticity and hopefulness of youth."[20] Cooper and Harper decouple impressibility from its function as a synecdoche of whiteness. Experience, for Harper, inscribed all youthful races and their transmissible material as a stylus marks a text; these impressions, as we shall see, script racial destiny. "As a matter of political economy it is better to have the colored race a living force animated and strengthened by self-reliance and self-respect, than a stagnant mass, degraded and self-condemned," she insisted.[21] For Harper, cultivating the potential of African Americans had a biopolitical payout for the nation as a whole, implicitly as opposed to attending to those peoples who lingered on as artifacts of the past.

Harper engaged extensively with the impressibility hierarchy at the heart of biopower that differentially distributes the capacity for vitality, agency, and affectability over time. She maintained that dynamic bodies continually impress on other animate and inanimate objects and are impressed by them in return, for good or evil. As a character from her 1873 story "Fancy Etchings" would have it, "I think sometimes the physical objects of a place impress themselves on a people's character, and help to mould it."[22] The speaker echoes a widely held belief among Harper's contemporaries in the power of household effects to stamp themselves on human inhabitants, a theory that informs bourgeois texts as divergent as Stowe's *Uncle Tom's Cabin* and Edith Wharton's *The Decoration of Houses* (1898), one of the first interior design manuals published in the United States.[23] Whereas Wharton was primarily concerned with the evolutionary effects of heavy curtains and ornate woodwork on white middle-class home dwellers, Harper drew on objects' capacity to form and receive impressions on the bodies of those who use them in order to trace the pall which slavery cast throughout its milieu, even at a distance. Object relations of the nineteenth century were understood to be crucial not only to character formation but also, through the inheritance of acquired characteristics, to the uneven development of racial groups. Functioning as a conduit of human relations, objects were understood to be able to retain impressions but not to self-transform through the act of their use. Movements made on them reinforced the distinctness of the two entities coming into contact. Objects—a category that for many included the enslaved—were thus impressionable but not impressible.

Commodities are formed through repeated impressions made on them by laborers that the objects retain and reflect. Harper's antebellum ballad "Free Labor" (1857) describes how garments produced by enslaved versus free labor make different kinds of sensory impressions on the bodies they clothe:

> I wear an easy garment,
>   O'er it no toiling slave
> Wept tears of hopeless anguish,
>   In his passage to the grave.
>
> And from its ample folds
>   Shall rise no cry to God,

Upon its warp and woof shall be
    No stain of tears and blood . . .

This fabric is too light to bear
    The weight of bondsmen's tears,
I shall not in its texture trace
    The agony of years . . . [24]

Political economy takes sensory form in the poem. The speaker explains her choice to wear clothing made from free-labor cotton by referring to the register of touch and the impressions made in the cloth. Marx famously decried the marketplace's mystification of the conditions of production of commodities, in which relations among humans are subordinated to the alchemistic appeal of relations among objects. For Harper, there can be no such distinction between the circulation of human labor and the circulation of goods. She characterizes wage labor as producing "easy" garments that "lightly . . . press the form" of the wearer, for they have not soaked up the "sad despairing cry" of plantation slaves. Slave products, by contrast, are heavy with burdens. "The agony of years" becomes part of the "texture" of the garments slaves produce. Clothing becomes a multilayered text, a kind of palimpsest in which enslaved workers first make impressions on fabric that later jumble together with the impressions made by the body of the wearer. Slave-produced commodities are inscribed with the misery of their makers' plight and affectively transmit this pain to the sensing body of the wearer, as well as to the divine witness. Rather than a fetish abstracted from its means of production, the "warp and woof" of the garment's cotton fabric is engraved with the dense sensual trauma of enslavement itself. For Harper, impressions link producers and consumers across space and time through the mediating role of inanimate objects that are nonetheless heavy with human experience.

Throughout her work, Harper drew on impressibility to figure enslavement itself to include, among other physical abuses, a lack of jurisdiction over the function of one's own senses. In keeping with abolitionist positions, Harper frames the black body as sensate and impressible. Yet she went much further than white allies such as Lydia Maria Child and Harriet Beecher Stowe, who tended to emphasize black malleability that would enable the imitation of white superiors, rather than insist upon the bodily agency of impressibility. For Harper, the enslaved lack command over their own power of touch and are instead at the receiving end of slavery's cruel hand. She emphasizes the tactile pressure the oppressor (literally, the one who presses down) must wield to shackle the slave, a physical restraint on the responsive, vibrant body underneath. Her poetry details fetters that restrict the movement of slaves' hands and slave mothers who are denied the ability to embrace their own children. "The Slave Mother" famously observes that "cruel hands / May rudely tear apart" a mother's "circling arms" that clutch her child in a "last and fond embrace."[25] The "hand of oppression" holds the enslaved in its grasp, committing "bondage and torture" and wielding "scourges and chains" on their bodies.[26] Harper employs the feeling body that dwells at the heart of nineteenth-century biopolitics to render the anguish of slavery into concrete, material relationships of physical and emotional pain. Harper's imagery underscores the animation and vitality of the black body and demonstrates that political economy, rather than an inability to feel the emotional bonds of motherhood, is what prevents many African Americans from exercising the full capacity of their senses.

Rendering black pain in concrete detail is of particular importance: the racial logic that the black body couldn't absorb sensory impressions led to the conclusion that blacks were insensible to pain. Their reproductive and productive labor and corporeal organism could thus be extracted and experimented on with the sole aim of benefits for the civilized.[27] Abolitionists, in response, sought to portray black pain as "true feeling," in Lauren Berlant's phrase, in which the "culturally privileged humanize those subjects who have been excluded" by cultivating affective connection with the suffering.[28] In this reform dynamic, black pain nonetheless remains instrumentalized for white progress, as Berlant, Saidiya Hartman, and others detail. Pain represents one of the most explicit junctures where the logics of biopower and sentimentalism reveal their interdependence, in which "the discursive mobilization of pain" at the heart of sentimental reform genres simultaneously categorizes, hierarchizes, and affectively binds vastly differently positioned bodies.[29] For black activists like Harper, pain also represented a significant claim of impressibility. Pain denotes the capacity of absorbing and integrating impressions over time, as opposed to unimpressible objects and bodies, which merely store impressions and reflexively bounce them off again into an affectable body. In Harper's writing, we can see how impression theory could illuminate both the sensory and emotional trauma of enslavement and the vital potential of blackness.

THE BIOPOLITICS OF TOUCH

In the nineteenth century, the body's sensory capacities became the grounds of its affective link to the national political sphere. Literary theorist Erica Fretwell names this synaesthetic mode of attachment "sensitive citizenship," or a notion of belonging that capitalized upon "the material and emotional vulnerability that national affiliation demands."[30] Impressibility discourses extrapolated sensitive citizenship into a paradigm for the evolutionary age, in which the development of the individual and the species transpired through habitual stimulation of the senses. The self and social body that proceeds *relationally*— rather than through the individualist narratives of self-making and psychological interiority that came to dominate in the twentieth century—required careful management. Sentimentalism helped constitute modern governance as both the discipline of contact between individual bodies and the regulation of the domain of the population. From this angle, sentimentalism's function as an aesthetic mode emphasizing the proper regulation of feeling becomes legible within a larger context in which the management of feeling formed the primary field of the political.

While for Harper impressibility is a quality of youthfulness, the sentimental capacity to manage this absorptive capacity over time pertains only to the civilizationist criteria of class, faith, comport, and sexual difference. Her intervention into impression theory doubled down on sentimentalism rather than sidelining it. Within Harper's framework, the *regulation* of impressions maintained a crucial function in the development of the physiology of the individual and the accumulation of the hereditary legacy of the race. "The true strength of a race means purity in women and uprightness in men," a model character in *Iola Leroy* instructs in one of Harper's characteristic formulations.[31] Throughout Harper's poems, novels, essays, and speeches, she elaborated on the rubric of sensorial discipline she first learned from her uncle and childhood teacher William Watkins: that impressions mold the race, and teaching their regulation, especially during the most highly plastic stage of childhood, can move a people away from suspension in the immediacy of grasping sensation and toward the forward movements of reflective feeling. Given the indelible impact of youthful impressions, Watkins maintained that it was the duty of parents and formal educational institutions to protect children from "false impressions" that create "early associations" and "inveterate habits" and thus result in a "*pernicious*" education.[32] In contemporary literary criticism, Harper is infamous for her advocacy of individual restraint and self-discipline. Yet her aim was evolutionary in nature, a rarely noted aspect of her work. Harper cast motherhood as a creative act analogous to literary work, and literary work as a maternal force. "Every mother should endeavor to be a true artist," she advised, "the artist who will write on the tablet of childish innocence thoughts she will not blush to see read in the light of eternity and printed amid the archives of heaven."[33] She advocated that blacks undertake artistic projects that would benefit the young and attest to the maturity of the race. Harper embraced women's role as engraving "innocent and impressible childhood" to ensure the race's ongoing evolution.[34] Analogizing reproductive and artistic creation as similarly tactile acts, she celebrated the expressive didacticism of "earnest, self-sacrificing" adults who learn to "stamp themselves not only on the present but [also on] the future" through motherhood and literary and artistic work.[35] Her evolutionary aesthetics posited that maternal care and artistic production benefit not only growing youth but also future descendants to come.

Her stories explore the physical and emotional repercussions of impulsive sensibility run rampant. Harper frequently contrasts characters who dwell in the present gratification of desire, and thus commonly expire before their time, with upwardly mobile Christian adults who discipline present-oriented impulses with the promises of the eternal. Novels like *Sowing and Reaping* (1876–1877) chart the consequences of parents' behavior in the form of the inherited proclivities of the next generation. Repeated metaphors of somnolence subtly challenge evolutionary discourse by framing the black poor as merely abstracted from, rather than altogether lacking, a still-dormant vitality. Yet she positioned the middle class on a different evolutionary plane than the poor, radiant with "life force," whereas their brethren are sleeping the years away. Both challenging and contributing to social evolutionary discourse, she transformed accusations of African Americans' impulsivity of sensation into the promise of sensorial discipline. All the same, for Harper, progress depended on mastering sensorial discipline in a surprising way: by harnessing the uplifting and pleasurable power of touch.

Uncovering the role of the impression at the heart of nineteenth-century culture and politics makes salient that the body that develops relationally, through its sensory stimulations, takes shape specifically through the haptic. While sight has frequently been assigned the mantle of the privileged sense of modernity, touch—particularly given the synaesthetic framework, which saw touch as the basis of all sensory reception—has played an important part. For Aristotle, touch was the basic sense, the "common sense" from which sight, taste, hearing, and sound emanated.[36] Centuries later, touch plays a submerged role in Locke's impression theory. Ann Jessie Van Sant has shown how Locke's natural philosophy intersects with research into the senses undertaken by natural scientists and physiologists of the period. She stresses that while Locke avoids analyzing the corporeal dimensions of sensation in his emphasis on the development of mind, "he cannot do without its vocabulary." She notes that the traditional epistolary terms of experience as *impressing, imprinting,* or *stamping* the mind fuse in his work with new scientific understandings of sensation as "the impact of imperceptible bodies on the senses and the corresponding motion of nerves and animal spirits."[37] Accordingly, Lockean empiricism articulates the process of knowledge acquisition within a physiological framework, particularly in the domain of touch.[38] Van Sant clarifies that eighteenth-century sensibility discourse, in both its scientific and literary dimensions, concerned "both the subjective awareness of experience and the organic sensitivity through which that awareness occurs" and that both of these mechanisms depended on touch to set them in motion.[39] For example, late eighteenth-century physiologists such as the Abbé de Condillac asserted that all five senses operate as tactile impressions on the nerves of the affected organ.[40] In this schematic, sight depends on touch; the eye is understood to literally come into contact with the objects in its vision. Van Sant shows that both empiricist epistemology and literary explorations of feeling were dramatically reshaped by physiological research positing the foundational role of touch in the function of the sensing body. The overlap between the emotional and somatic senses of being "touched" became central to the indexical relationship between physiology and psychological interiority. "The language of touch—in scientific terms, *contact and motion*; in experiential terms, *feeling*—gained centrality, and the structures of *feeling* (nerves and delicate fibers) became the location of experience."[41] Sensibility depends on physical and emotional touch as the mechanism that links the body with its environment at the molar level of that which can be felt, palpated, and caressed.[42]

In the nineteenth-century United States, racial discourse elaborated on the somatic and the psychological dimensions of sensibility discourse. Different individuals were thought to touch and feel in different ways, depending on the degree of civilization the person had attained. Naturalists and anthropologists often remanded touch, along with the other "lower" senses of taste and smell, to an early developmental stage characteristic of the primitive races. Leading German naturalist Lorenz Oken, for example, rated the sensual capacity of five major races and identified the African "skin-man" as the least developed race, having mastered only the register of touch, the basest of sensations.[43] Historian Mark Smith contends that in the United States, "slaveholders maintain[ed] that blackness was not simply a color but also a tactile condition" and viewed their slaves as thick-skinned, impervious, and suited to hard labor, conditions that rendered them relatively insensitive to pain and thus requiring excessive force when punished.[44] Work with the hands—whether tilling a field, scrubbing a blackened cast-iron stove, or even, to some degree, stitching delicate embroidery—was thought to bring the worker "'in constant contact with the inertia of matter,'" a transference that dragged the individual down into the immediacy of sensation.[45] By contrast, Immanuel Kant praised sight as "detached, distanced, and inherently reflective," a sense that allowed the subject to maintain an appropriate physical and temporal distance from stimuli.[46] In Constance Classen's summation, the hierarchy of the senses echoed the gendered division of labor. "The supposedly lower, feminine senses of touch, taste and smell" were associated with domestic work, whereas "men used their eyes and ears outside in the world."[47] Touch could represent the immediate grasping characteristic of the primitive, whereas sight enabled reflective consideration that strengthens, rather than compromises, the perceiver. Given that race marked the allegedly differential accumulation of impressions within the population, touch became an important vector of racialization.

Sentimental self-discipline thereby stressed the regulation of touch. As a historian of the senses in eighteenth- and nineteenth-century France argues, " 'What was decisive was the degree of delicacy of the hand' . . . the ability to resist direct contact, to pause and keep a distance versus the submission to tactile impulse, the grasp, the clumsy lunge, the heavy-handedness of handling."[48] The heavy, superficial, sexual, and immediate tactility of labor stands opposed to the delicate, absorbent, refined, and enduring stroke of leisure. The touch of the laborer was particularly associated with sexuality. The overwhelmingly discreet genre of Christian midcentury fiction, for example, nonetheless abounded in indirect discussions of sexuality when the reform genre turned to the working classes. Writers such as Elizabeth Stuart Phelps penned reform tracts noting the unbecoming indulgence in sexual pleasure among female workers who spent their days palpating "the dirty products of the mills, factories, and sweatshops."[49] In contrast, elite women whose bodies created small ripples in their surroundings received high praise for their delicacy of touch and what Marianne Noble has termed their "corporeal abjection," or the ideal that "a woman could minimize the impression created by her body."[50] After attending one of Frances Harper's lectures in 1866, white abolitionist writer Grace Greenwood praised Harper's capacity to be "impressive," to adopt a manner capable of "touching" her audience. Yet Greenwood emphasizes that her effectiveness is due in part to the delicate claims her body makes on the audience. Greenwood approvingly notes that Harper's face displays "a nature most femininely sensitive" and that "her form is delicate, her hands daintily small. She stands quietly beside her desk . . . with gestures few and fitting."[51] For Greenwood, Harper's skill as an orator lies within the feminine stillness of her body, her capacity to subdue her bodily touch. The regulation of touch was central to biopower's management of feeling.

In keeping with this frame, Harper's notion of progress depends on the senses, especially the haptic. Yet for Harper, the prominent role of touch at the heart of racial formation opened up new avenues for black uplift *and* new avenues for black pleasure. Nowhere are Harper's biopolitics of touch more clear than in her serialized novel *Trial and Triumph* (1888–1889), which tells of the maturing, yet troubled, orphan Annette. In a key scene, Annette's spiritual guardian, Mrs. Lasette, tells Annette of her reaction to meeting Annette's father, Frank Miller. Years before, Frank had abandoned Annette's mother Lucy after Lucy's "lack of self-control" resulted in her impregnation.[52] Following Lucy's death, Frank returned to the town to open a profitable and allegedly respectable saloon. Mrs. Lasette encounters Frank at a social gathering during which youthful attendees "occasionally clasped hands together" and engaged in "romping and promiscuous kissing." Mrs. Lasette emphasizes to Annette how much she "heartily disliked" the profligacy of the evening's activities and how "instinctively" her body fought against Frank's caress: "During the play Frank Miller's hand came in contact with mine and he pressed it. I can hardly describe my feelings. It seemed as if my veins were on fire, and that every nerve was thrilling with repulsion and indignation. Had I seen him murder Lucy and then turn with blood dripping hands to grasp mine, I do not think that I should have felt more loathing than I did when his hand clasped mine. I felt that his very touch was pollution; I immediately left the play, tore off my glove, and threw it in the fire."[53]

When she relates the event to Annette, Mrs. Lasette regrets the dramatics of her disgust. Her future husband—who was intently watching her reaction—nonetheless had "gloried in her courage" when he "saw her shrink instinctively from his touch" and emphasizes that "from that hour I learned to love her."[54] That "every nerve" burned with "repulsion" testified to the strength of her self-discipline. The exertion of nerve force has directionality: to impress is to dispatch force from one body into another; to express is to body forth interior feeling outwardly, in the form of gesture and animation. To depress is to dampen and stifle nerve force. To repress, as Freud elaborated, is to relegate nerve force to a prior stage in life, sending it back in time by burying the experience in the mind's sedimentary layers. Mrs. Lasette's refusal of Frank's touch activates another option—the repulse.

An affect necessary for the faithful, repulsion indicates a pleasurable moral and physical fighting back against a sensory impression. Repulsion marks the capacity to exert nerve force of equivalent pressure that pushes an intruding stimulation away. Both Mr. Lasette and his future wife understand that the materiality of an impression in the civilized is inveterate rather than transient: it is as if Frank's hands are still "dripping" with Lucy's "blood" years later. Fortunately, Mrs. Lasette's ability to protect her sensual affectivity from harmful impact was so developed as to become instinctual. Accordingly vigilant in her supervision of attempted breaches of her body's borders, she "tore off [her] glove" and incinerated it, its matter transformed forever as the hearth metonymically manifests the internal "fire" of her senses.[55] Yet Mrs. Lasette's stimulation suggests a "thrilling" excitement, a "fire" not altogether unpleasant. Her repulsive acuity delights both her and her husband: sensory discipline is its own pleasurable stimulation. Harper exposes the erotics of impressible embodiment and sentimental regulation, in which development is activated by touch.

Repulsion bears similarity with shame: an affect that hegemonic discourses of race denied to African Americans and that discourses of respectability seem to double down on as a path to social legitimacy.[56] Performance studies theorist Tavia Nyong'o complicates dominant understandings of respectability politics, finding the display of shame by antebellum black authors, activists, and performers to be a deliberate staging of affect's function as a vector of racialization. For Nyong'o, black performance of shame throws the affect back on white offenders, offers its own erotic stimulations, and rouses unpolitical blacks into sympathy with the cause of antislavery. Repulsion, too, can function as a strategic "deployment of affect as a technology of the racial self," in Nyong'o's apt phrase.[57] Repulsion is the affective—in both its nervous and emotional dimensions—movement of blocking a violating impression, of rebounding nerve force off the body and sending it back into the milieu.

The rigors of respectability involve the erotic nuances of subjectification, in which the process of submitting to a disciplinary regime creates self-meaning and stimulating attachments to structural systems of control.[58] The union of her mind and body in repelling an unwanted stimulation with equivalent force "thrill[s]" the soon-to-be Mrs. Lasette. Her titillation evokes another expression of praise by one of Harper's characters: that an acquaintance is dedicated to "wearing sobriety as a crown and righteousness as the girdle of her loins," protecting the body from harmful touch.[59] As the image of righteous undergarments attests, the tactility inherent to sociality promises its own sacred stimulations. While Harper certainly should be viewed within the larger attempt of the black aspiring class to craft the politics of respectability, we should keep in mind that she did so in part by stressing the sensual physicality of the Western philosophical tradition itself. Far from foreclosing the desiring body altogether, Harper underscores the reliance of liberal thought on stimulating contact between bodies.

Given the number of scholars who have agreed with Hazel Carby's assessment that in Harper's texts "female and male sexuality were repressed and replaced by mental and spiritual kinship," in her efforts to defend black women's capacity for civilization and womanhood, the prominence of the pleasures of the sensate body in Harper's work comes as something of a surprise.[60] My reading builds on recent scholarship such as Nyong'o's that nuances this older work, illuminating how pleasure—including erotic pleasure—features prominently in nineteenth-century black feminism, even right in the midst of respectability politics.[61] Geoffrey Sanborn provocatively argues that "Harper represents race work as a mode of sexual experience," drawing our attention to the raw passion coursing throughout Harper's fictional characters, rendered most frequently in the form of throbbing, pulsing blood.[62] African American sensuality is embedded in Harper's emphasis on the "cardiovascular arousal" and life force she sees inherent in blackness, Sanborn proposes. He underscores the courageousness of her equation of "flushing" with vibrancy, struggle, and protest in the midst of an environment in which fantasies of black women's acute and unregulated sensation functioned as key technologies of racialization.[63] Harper's writing celebrates the internal force possessed by black reformers while also exploring how development, progress, and epistemology transpire relationally, through touch and other forms of bodily contact.

Harper's sentimental account of the disciplining of the body's sensuality does not so much preclude the importance of sensation as rely on it. The affective connections at the heart of sensationist ideologies of progress are profoundly physical. As Mrs. Lasette "instinctively" knew, the tactility of sensation results in a blending of the self and other as the body incorporates the trace of another's.[64] While impressions on objects leave indentations, impressions in the impressible are absorbed deep within the body, where they stimulate a provoking response. The sentimental body is penetrable rather than impermeable; external touch reaches deep inside its contours. Thus the imperative to transcend impulsivity does not imply the foreclosure of sexual pleasure altogether.[65] When Annette meets her future beau at a dinner party, an honest, "quite wealthy" man dedicated to racial uplift through Christian virtue, her body absorbs the pleasure of their contact. Aroused to erotic sensation for the first time, Annette yields to "a sense of deep enjoyment flooding her soul . . . He had loosened her lips and awakened within her a dawning sense of her own ability, which others had chilled and *depressed*. He had fingered the keys of her soul and they had vibrated in music to his touch. Do not smile, gentle reader, and say that she was very easily *impressed*, it may be that you have never known what it is to be hungry, not for bread, but for human sympathy."[66]

It is not that Annette's sensibilities had never been touched; rather, she had yet to be "fingered" in the right way. She "had lived in an atmosphere of coldness and *repression*," a clamping down of her sensibilities that "*depressed*" her life force rather than "vibrated" it.[67] Emphasizing the tactile physicality of the impression, Harper engages the erotics of racial progress embedded in sensationist epistemology. "Sympathy," in this passage, retains its seventeenth- and eighteenth-century physiological meaning as simultaneity and affinity between bodily organs. It functions as an affective and physical vulnerability, an open-ness to the parts of one's own or another's body. In a direct appeal to the reader, Harper preempts any knowing grins at Annette's naïveté, stressing that she is not "very easily *impressed*."[68] Rather, Annette's hunger has attuned her to the ministrations of one who plays her like a piano, provoking vibrations that re-spond in sympathy to his touch.

To be sure, the eroticism of a body that draws touch deep within its folds is never far from the surface. Indeed, impressibility served as one of the key bodily relations gradually bound together into the discourse of sexuality over the course of the U.S. nineteenth century. One of the clearest expressions of how erotic experience provides key sedimentary strata in the impress-ible body appears in a satire of scientific experimentation, Nathaniel Haw-thorne's "The Birth-Mark" (1843).[69] In this story, the esteemed alchemist Aylmer marries the "nearly perfect" Georgiana, a woman whose beauty he nonetheless soon comes to see as gravely marred by a birthmark on her face (37). This "earthly imperfection" (37), formed in the shape of a "human hand" (39), taunts Aylmer as if it were a living remnant of Geor-giana's tactile pleasures. Aspiring suitors had been fond of declaring it the "impress" (38) of a fairy's hand that had caressed her infant cheek, but her newlywed husband sees "the crimson stain" (39) as a pulsating reminder of her "liability to sin, sorrow, decay, and death" (39). When Georgiana is aroused, the red mark disappears amid the general flush of her countenance. At all other times its "glimmering" on the otherwise virginal "snow" of her skin conspicuously flags her prior episodes of stimulation (38). The ethereal bride has become a sexualized wife, and the "crimson hand" becomes ever more apparent to her husband as evidence of her appalling materiality (39). Yet this emblem of creation, akin to the signet's press in a letter's waxen seal, doesn't merely decorate the surface of her skin. It not only bears testament to surface stimulations, but also renders visible her sexualized mind. Facial redness emblazons private thoughts on a public text, as Darwin attested. An expert in the physiology of emotion, Darwin explained that the oft-noted mental confusion that accompanies blushing is due to "the intimate sympa-thy which exists between the capillary circulation of the surface of the head and face, and that of the brain."[70] Thus Georgiana's flesh is impressible, not merely impressed; the stamp shines forth "deeply interwoven . . . with the texture and substance of her face" (37). Faced with this prominent display of their sexual contact—and Georgiana's premarital sensory pleasures—in her very substrate, Aylmer designs an experiment to carve the mark from her cheek. Its successful execution kills her, a death she welcomes as redemption of her husband's legacy of scientific failure: he has succeeded at last in creating perfection, a state untenable on earth. The story brilliantly illuminates the eroticism at the core of empirical epistemology in which all bodily vitality, cognitive function, and interpersonal relations transpire through penetrating contact.

Yet Harper's reclamation of the senses for the sake of personal pleasure and collective uplift represents a bold move in the dangerous political climate in which she lived. From a critical position that works to grasp the connections between ideas of temporality, touch, and racial formation in the nineteenth century, sexual restraint emerges as an overdetermined criterion of civilization. Sexual desire, in the evolutionary view, represents a primitive inability to temper impulses to touch with reflective thought. The trope of black sexual voraciousness precisely captures the immersion in the impulsive grasp allegedly characteristic of the less evolved. The civilized, by contrast, were portrayed as masters of managing both time and touch, and their mating promised emotional fulfillment rather than physical gratification. Such beliefs in black primitivism provided ideological fuel for one of the most violent periods African Americans have endured in the history of the United States. Myths of black hypersexuality and perverse desire provided cover for lynch laws that, in the words of Ida B. Wells, were "an excuse to get rid of Negroes who were acquiring wealth and property."[71] While such discourses targeted both women and men, narratives of sexual forthrightness and promiscuity were far more publicly damaging to black women who were denied the biopolitical category of womanhood. In fact, this was the very purpose these bifurcating narratives served: black women's alleged promiscuity underwrote white women's sensorial discipline. Sexual relations between black women and white men, whether consensual or nonconsensual, were often pinned on black women's voracious desire, thus relieving men from responsibility for actions unbefitting the civilized. The response of many black strivers to the central role sexual and moral deviancy played in racial thought was to demonstrate the race's ability to master the sexual restraint characteristic of civilization. As Claudia Tate has argued, building on Barbara Moses, many black activists concluded "that the acquisition of their full citizenship would result as much or more from demonstrating their adoption of the 'genteel standard of Victorian sexual conduct' as from protesting racial injustice."[72]

Recent scholarship, however, has considerably complicated our idea of what genteel standards of sexuality looked like in the mid-nineteenth century. Frances Harper, who for decades was deemed the most prudish and sentimental of nineteenth-century black writers, emerges as a more nuanced figure when we don't take for granted that we know in advance the contours of the erotic in the decades before the consolidation of modern sexual discourse.[73]

Her repeated incantation of the need to maintain "self-control, self-reliance, and self-respect" does not so much shut down the possibility of erotic pleasure among the upright as direct her audience to what she understands to be its most lasting source: the satisfaction of sensuality deeply felt and integrated within the body and mind.[74] The pleasures of the biopolitics of touch, of the process of self and racial formation through the capacity to be affected, lie at the heart of Harper's notion of freedom.

Harper's complex engagement with sentimentalism thus has queer implications, in addition to feminist meaning. Sentimentalism, I show throughout this book, functions as a regulatory technology that transpires at the level of the senses. Harper explores the erotic attachments that maintain any disciplinary regime, especially one that elevates touch to the status of the prime instigator of individual and social development. Writing of the erotics of suffering in sentimental literature, Marianne Noble argues that "sentimentalism . . . is shot through with sadomasochistic pleasures that complicate its overtly humanitarian motives."[75] For Noble, (white) women's erotic attachment to pain brings about a kind of agency, a way to counteract the bodily suppressing dictates of white womanhood by working "*within* the ideological constraints of the culture."[76] Noble's analysis of the sexual stimulation Ellen Montgomery feels watching her brother / father figure / future husband whip her horse into submission is particularly striking; the aptness of highlighting the eroticism of the scene is borne out even more explicitly in a similar passage in Elizabeth Stoddard's overlooked 1862 novel *The Morgensens*. There's a similar, but distinct, process of stimulating self-discipline at work in the writing of Harper and other promoters of black respectability politics in the era, a kind of biopolitical erotics for bourgeois black women. The erotics of respectability represents a form of resistance to hegemonic arrangements of sex that denied the very capacity of feelings deeply felt to African Americans, regardless of class or economic standing. Yet the self-directed black female subject who takes pleasure in her own command of sensuality, in the delayed gratification of submitting sensation to measured reflection, and in the knowledge that her own record of tactile contact will accumulate gradually not only in her own maturation, but in the uplift of the race yet to come, also materializes through a deeply eroticized, bourgeois attachment to disciplinary biopower.

RACIAL INHERITANCE

The erotics of a form of power, and an organic ontology, that depends on the regulation of sensation underscores the function of sentimentalism as a disciplinary technology throughout the nineteenth century. But what of the other vast realm of biopower, the administration of the health of a population at the level of the species, the process alternately understood as biopolitics, security, or control? Here, too, coming to grips with the discourse of impressibility unlocks new aspects of the political and intellectual breadth of black women reformers. Black feminists interceded in hegemonic biopower not only at the level of disciplinary institutions targeting individuals, but also at the populational level that conceived of the members of a nation on the basis of their collective organic processes. At this level of species-being, race consolidated as a means to delineate the chosen from the disposable among a given population.[77] The technology of sentimentalism functioned to discipline individual feelings, as well as to regulate the accumulation of impressions over time through hereditary transmission. As we saw in the prior chapter, the relative capacity of the body to be affected by its sensation, to indelibly absorb and transmit its impressions to progeny, formed a central component of the logic of racial difference. Harper and other black feminists recognized the potential of the new sciences of heredity emerging in the second half of the nineteenth century to interrupt the national order that cast racialized bodies as sexually undifferentiated fossils whose bodies were suitable only as sites of extraction. Impressible bodies, layered with records of past pleasures and traumas, preserve a record of their stimulations throughout their life and pass them on to any offspring as physical inheritance. Black feminists deployed sentimentalism to regulate the impressible body at the level of the individual and the race.

Harper advocated for black women's role in the uplift of the race, her right to education, as well as her rights to personhood *as a woman* in part by emphasizing the impact of pregnancy on the development of the population. Mothers could direct the future evolution of the race, she urged, by dedicating themselves to "putting the right stamp on an antenatal life."[78] Impression theory placed a heavy burden on the pregnant woman, for her hidden desires and public contacts were thought to materialize in the flesh of her fetus. "The sensitive embryo receives the impressions made upon the mind of the mother," Tuskegee's first librarian, Adella Hunt Logan, explained to an Atlanta audience of black women, such that a woman who wished she were not pregnant could produce "in very truth a murderer!"[79] The early modern theory of maternal imagination became the nineteenth-century notion of maternal impression, in which the sight of rodents, monkeys, the disabled, and other bodies perceived to be out of place in modernity would imprint the embryo with their very shape. The persistent influence of the notion of maternal impression within newer eugenic regimes is visible in Francis Galton's inclusion of "any strong mental impression" on the mother during pregnancy among the necessary descriptions of a newborn infant in the new practice of baby books he inaugurated in the 1880s (see figure 2.1).

Description of Child at Birth.

Name ....

Date of Birth ....

Previous health of Mother＊ ....

Birth at full time, or premature ....

Labour natural, or instrumental..

Physical peculiarities, if any (including "Mother's marks") ....

Weight at birth (naked) ....

Length ....

Girth round nipples ....

Colour of eyes†..

Colour of hair, if any...

Child healthy, or ailing...

  „   quiet, or active...

  „   feeble, or vigorous ....

  „   good-tempered, or fretful ....

＊ Any strong mental impression, fright, shock, or fancy, occurring to the mother previous to
the birth of the child, should be recorded if possible *before* the birth.

† The eyes of infants at birth are always dark blue; but it should be observed at what period
after birth their colour begins to change. This generally occurs within a few days.

FIG. 2.1. "Description of Child at Birth." From Francis Galton,
The Life History Album (London: Macmillan, 1884).

Each layer of impressions absorbed by the body would impact the future development of the individual organism and the race as a whole, especially those stimulations affecting the highly malleable phases of embryonic development and infancy.

The work of motherhood ensured that the future was in good hands and demonstrated that bourgeois urban African Americans had in fact attained sexual differentiation. To deny black womanhood was to deny that even the wealthiest members of the race had achieved civilization; black feminists insisted on their status as *women* and consequently on the past gains and future potential of the race. I echo here Hazel Carby's and Hortense Spiller's famous argument, but with a difference, for black feminists were not making a gendered analysis (a biopolitical category that did not yet exist as such). Rather, they were participating in consolidating the significance of sexual difference itself as an attribute of civilization while expanding who could be counted among its elite ranks.[80]

For Harper, erotic contact was an opportunity for black women of the aspiring class to shape the race's future with their own hands. She was in good company. As Michele Mitchell has argued, "Afro-American thought was dominated by debates about racial destiny" from the post-Reconstruction era until the early 1930s.[81] These discourses emphasized motherhood as a site of racial "regeneration," in the words of Anna Julia Cooper.[82] Like other black intellectuals committed to racial uplift, Harper both drew on and advanced the emergent eugenic logic that the manipulation of children's impressibility (before and after birth) would stimulate racial progress. In her work, marriage and sexual reproduction presented a palpable opportunity for racial improvement in which parents could actively construct their children's biological development prior to and following birth. "Marriage," for Harper, is best regarded as an institution that "not only . . . affect[s] our own welfare but that of others, a relation which may throw its sunshine or shadow over the track of unborn ages."[83] The results of a sexual partnership make themselves felt by the trace of time. To best impress their children, Harper encouraged mothers to pay "attention to the laws of heredity and environment" through private study and participation in book clubs.[84] Her fiction breaks the mold of sentimental-domestic novels, which typically end with the marriage of the orphaned heroine, decorously gesturing toward rather than explicating the sexuality on which the genre's chronobiopolitical frame depends.[85] In contrast, Harper's novels such as *Trial and Triumph* explore the formation of the next generation resulting from the nuptial bond, a reproduction that transpires through physical and social transmission. Through her emphasis on the futurity of the marriage relation, Harper encourages her readers—which, according to Frances Smith Foster, appear to be increasingly from the black middle class—to see themselves as subjects of time, with a future within their control.[86]

The possibility of transmitting impressions from one generation to the next saturate and in fact structure the work of Frances Harper and other leading black feminists of the era, such as Pauline Hopkins and Anna Julia Cooper. Hopkins published four domestic novels emplotting the impact of heredity on African Americans and an ethnological essay on the racial potential of African descendants. All three figures demonstrate a working familiarity with hereditarian science.[87] More broadly, information about hereditarian science and how it might be used against the grain to demonstrate black capacities for progress shaped such staples of middle-class black life of the period as conduct books, mothers' meetings, baby books, the women's club movement, the black press, and Better Baby contests at segregated state fairs.[88] Heredity theory as an applied science of motherhood represents a key feminine arena of what African American studies scholar Britt Rusert has termed "fugitive science," or nineteenth-century black engagement with the natural sciences, in this case in a "practical" bent, that advances and draws on scientific knowledge as a strategy of racial liberation.[89] Fugitive science often materialized among the unassuming folds of sentimental motherhood.

In particular, heredity theory enabled Harper to point her finger at what she felt was the true origin of primitive tendencies lurking among African Americans: sexual abuse by white men, whose conduct violated the basic tenets of civilization. Like Hopkins and Cooper, she cast sexually licentious and exploitative white men (often working class, and therefore uncivilized) as the true progenitors of the impulsive sensibility for which black women were widely condemned. She defends black women and implicates men's culpability in abusive power relations for which social approbation fails to hold them responsible, such as condemning their own children to slavery. Harper emphasizes that men transmit a faulty inheritance through both physical reproduction and the affective dimensions of their deeds and character. "A wicked man, intellectual and gifted, may send his influence for evil across the track of unborn ages, and hurl with mortmain hand a legacy of maledictions to future generations," she poses in an 1885 lecture.[90] Her emphasis on the tactile dimensions of progress is particularly suggestive in this context, as an abusive man's deathly stroke highlights the physical nature of his transgressions. In so many words, Harper embeds a critique of men's sexual abuse of black women in and out of slavery in the decorous language of sentimentality.

In common with other political deployments of heredity in the period, Harper's use of inheritance to conceptualize black uplift works through the biopolitical logic of differentiating among the biological quality of members of the population in order to determine which families' reproduction should be encouraged and which curtailed. "I think the laws of transmission and heredity are very little understood," a character in one of Harper's short stories muses, "and in dealing with the dangerous and the perishing classes, these laws should largely be taken into consideration."[91] Men who condemn their children to slavery commit a double crime of inheritance against their offspring, "robb[ing] them not simply of liberty but of the right of being well born."[92] Harper frequently draws on the emergent science of eugenics to posit a crime of transmission, echoing Francis Galton's term *eugenics*, developed from a combination of Greek phrases to signify "well born." In the late nineteenth-century framework of malleable heredity, hereditarian science blended easily into eugenic practice. Scholars have begun to demonstrate the emergent black aspiring classes' wide interest in eugenic methods of racial uplift, a topic that is the subject of the last chapter of this book.[93] The motivations for their engagement in what Gregory Michael Dorr and Angela Logan have called "assimilationist eugenics," or an interest in human breeding that maintained "distinctions between 'fit' and 'unfit' people" but dismissed the role of race in determining such fitness, were multiple.[94] Particularly by the 1890s, eugenic arguments became a large component of black feminist biopolitics, just as was true among white feminists, male-led black uplift campaigns, and other Progressive movements at the turn of the century. Feminist eugenic arguments like Harper's attempted to transform sexuality from an alleged site of black savagery into a source of racial modernization led by women. With so-called "better breeding" strategies, black women could demonstrate their capacity to reproduce with science, sentiment, and civilization, thereby affirming their own achievement of womanhood. The management of impressions figured as a key tactic of black women's efforts to contribute to racial destiny through engaging with the proliferating sciences of heredity.

EVOLUTIONARY AESTHETICS

Recognizing the palimpsestic nature of race as it was understood in the nineteenth century highlights another significant aspect of Frances Harper's work, as well as that of sentimental culture more generally: its evolutionary aesthetics and the textual nature of embodiment. The pivotal role assigned to reading, listening, speaking, and other acts of aesthetic expression and impression stemmed in part from the wide belief that representation not only reflected civilization, but stimulated it. A body formed through layered impressions is a textual body in a double sense, as itself a writing surface, and one whose very development depends on other texts. For decades, literary critics have underscored how the sentimental genre orchestrates a logic of embodiment in which "the sobs of character and reader work to blur the distinction between them." Furthermore, the bodies that sentimental texts affect are multiple. Ideas that reading is "an experience affecting more than a single, discrete, individual body are ideas central to sentimentalism's self-understanding," Glenn Hendler writes, pointing us toward sentimentalism's function as a public structure of feeling.[95] Yet sentimental reading captures not only the shared emotion bonding the reader in the flesh to the character on the page, but also how imaginative work creates impressions in the reader's mind that accumulate over time. The distinction between embodied and discursive experience blurs as the reader's brain functions as a text that writers inscribe. The earnest didacticism of the sentimental mode thus involves more than the intent to model moral behavior for impressionable readers; it aims to directly engrave impressible readers with scenes of self-control, measured reflection, and Christian sacrifice. Sentimentalism's dynamic is as much material as representational.

Harper's notion of aesthetics underscores that in the late nineteenth century, representation was thought to have broad material effects. Literary culture was particularly important to black uplift projects, given attempts to curtail the literacy of the enslaved earlier in the century. As Elizabeth McHenry has argued, the promotion and circulation of black literature "was considered fundamental to the agenda of racial uplift and social reform and one potential avenue to the assertion of political agency."[96] Several schools of anthropological thought believed that a society's climb up the evolutionary ladder existed in dynamic relationship with its literary production.[97] Artistic expression not only made impressions on readers that would catalyze future development; it also demonstrated the heights the civilization had already attained. For this reason, evolutionary theorists considered the appearance of literary arts to indicate that a civilization had reached an apex. The paleontologist Cope, for one, went so far as to rank the genres of literature according to the level of racial development they allegedly reflected. He asserted that realist representation far surpassed the relatively immature efforts of romantic novelists, who lacked the discipline of rationality.[98] Borrowing from evolutionary discourse, Harper saw aesthetic production as proof of an advanced society. "We cannot tell what a race can do till it utters and *expresses* itself," Annette's future husband affirms.[99] Her own prolific body of poetry, novels, and lectures both testifies to this capacity of expression and performs as agents of impression. Harper's evolutionary aesthetics responds to these pressures by underscoring that artistic effectiveness is reciprocally linked to the faithfulness of prose to Christian truth.[100] In the late nineteenth-century genres of sentiment, literary characters catalyze evolutionary characteristics within readers and thus, regardless of the fanciful nature of their tales, also serve as realist production.

Sensory studies and material theories of culture are opening up new questions about how aesthetics constitute social relations. A text's format, means of transmission, intended audience, and genre all contribute to the meanings that it coheres and circulates. Along these lines, recent critics highlight the public functions of Harper's work—how the materiality of her genres, including inexpensive poetry chapbooks, lectures bound as leaflets, poems printed in abolitionist newspapers, and spoken performances that filled the room with her memorable rhymes, are key to her impact. Meredith McGill argues that in the first half of Harper's career, before the Civil War, she primarily strove to create a political community through her work, rather than to establish a successful literary persona. Her highly distributable ephemeral formats, McGill contends, effectively "helped strengthen opposition to slavery and knit together scattered communities of activists."[101] Ivy Wilson attends to the sonic politics of Harper's writing, highlighting that her frequent use of the rhyming quatrain sequence "allowed her poems to be not only consumed and internalized but recalled and reiterated. . . . [Its] conceit sought to ventriloquize her voice through other bodies and form a cadre of interlocutors."[102] For Wilson, "the sensory modalities of literature and art might also unveil early theories about African American art," in particular its antebellum function as a "shadow" realm where democratic politics could be constituted and social bonds forged, despite its producers' utter lack of formal and informal rights.[103] Both critics emphasize that Harper's circulation of literary work was a means of democratic and abolitionist political action.

There is a larger political dimension of this shared textual public, however, one that the functional significance of *circulation* highlights: how shared sensations over time, in nineteenth-century epistemology, forge not only a public, but also a population. A poem is a vector of impression, writing itself onto the brain, occupying the throats of others, and leaving potentially indelible auditory and visual memories that will transmit to future generations. A poem, in this era a key form of the vernacular, contributes a tiny amount of text to the palimpsest of the civilized body as a whole. Kirsten Silva Gruesz writes of the nineteenth-century poetic vernacular that "its aim is not to outdo previous achievements or to establish new standards of taste, but to make a new impression from a known template."[104] Poetry's very familiarity ensures its repeatability and consequently its potential as a vector of population formation, forged through the circulation and transmission of hereditary material.

Harper's evolutionary aesthetics thus suggest a useful corollary to the idea that the political entity of the public arises from textual literacy and networks of print culture and other media. Print has been credited with helping to constitute the notion of the nation beginning in the late eighteenth century, for its vast and simultaneous distribution across a territory helped audiences "becom[e] part of an arena of the national . . . that cannot be realized except through such mediating imaginings."[105] Print, the argument goes, enabled the dispersed peoples of a nation to share common experience over space and time and thereby forged the possibility of national identity. Taking up the function of circulation as a means of producing the "imagined community" of the nation complicates the primarily discursive notion of the public, which is "a social space created by the reflexive circulation of discourse."[106] Print also helped consolidate the material and biological dimension of population, not only the mediated notion of the public. If the public is forged through discourse, then the population is forged through organic impressions. Bodies themselves become the most prominent texts within biopolitical regimes.[107] The body is impressed by culture; textual publics have a corporeal dimension, one in which the sensations and memories they create take hold within the body of the individual and circulate and gradually accumulate among the milieu. Population, rather than public, captures how synchronic textual circulation and diachronic textual accumulation were conceived of as the material substrate of civilization. Sentimental aesthetics, in turn, cultivates responses to sensory impressions and is ultimately concerned with the nature of the population, itself an inscribable text, layered over time. Across nineteenth-century regulatory technologies and the associated ontological notions of race, textuality represents a key method and goal of civilization.

THE RACIAL PALIMPSEST

Harper's notion that the body and the race precipitate through tactile impressions on the flesh accumulating over generations offers an important corrective to the contemporary scholarly frame of nineteenth-century race that understands it as a deterministic phenomenon denoting individual interiority. Harper's work suggests how race took shape in the period before genetics as a populational phenomenon on the dimension of the species. I build on Harper's representation to propose a theory of racial formation, as it was understood in the nineteenth century, as a palimpsestic process in which impressions layer upon one another over the life span of the individual and the evolutionary time of the race. The palimpsest metaphor of race captures how the Lockean notion of the infant mind as a tabula rasa transformed, over the course of the nineteenth century, into the idea of the body as the accumulation of organic impressions over generations, as Freud would later argue.[108] In the pre-evolutionary epoch, Locke deemed mental, emotional, and physiological development to transpire solely through repeated impressions of culture and environment on the living body, such that the earliest of traces date only to the individual's own first days. In contrast, the nineteenth-century body came to be understood as palimpsestic, in which impressions slowly accumulated in the forms of instinct, inherited tendencies, and relative impressibility. In the decades following the emergence of the new notion of heredity as a biologically transmissible substance in the 1830s, impressibility did complex conceptual work as the mechanism of hereditary transmission. Early "irregular" physician Harriot Hunt of Boston, for example, advised in her 1856 memoir that "impressibility is not a law of caste. It has nothing to do with streets, wealth, or social position; but it has to do with maternity and paternity."[109] For Hunt, the indelible imprint forms the substance of biological inheritance. In conjunction with concurrently developing evolutionary theories, impressibility discourse expanded the timeline of the individual body beyond the frame of the human life span. In this pregenetic framework, the body is first constituted by the impressions it inherits and, subsequently, by the impressions it obtains according to its relative degree of impressibility. Crucially, this text can never efface the markings that came before. The body, now a spatiotemporal phenomenon, becomes the inheritor of the written record of its own variably alterable genealogy it carries into the future.

A central figure in the emergence of the racial palimpsest is the same writer who first thoroughly outlined the biopolitical notion of a nation as a population whose very organic needs threatened its own existence. It is also a writer rarely, if ever, included among the ranks of sentimentalists, despite his deep indebtedness to sentimental paradigms of individual and racial development: Thomas Robert Malthus. Malthus's *Essay on the Principle of Population* (1798) works from the premise that the people of England do not comprise the abstract political entities of subjects or citizens who are best administered through civic measures, but maintain a biological existence contingent on its organic nature for its own survival. For Malthus, the biological nature of its being subjected the population above all to two primary natural laws that governed its own continuance. These were the ceaseless need for food and the phenomenon of sexual reproduction that, over time, will increase the number of mouths to feed exponentially, in excess of available foodstuffs. Malthus hastily penned his now-classic tract to give voice to his outrage over William Godwin's doctrine of perfectability (1797), which proposed that civilization could gradually eradicate vice and even, potentially, the appetites of the flesh, if youth received only virtuous impressions. This would be achievable for Godwin through measures such as eliminating private property.[110] In response, Malthus thunders that not only will the English people never be able to supersede their organic nature, but also the very "principle of population"—the idea that a population's fertility rate will always exceed its rate of agricultural production—ensures that the dictates of biological being will continually function as limits to human potential. A population is not an aggregation of individual organisms, but a biological phenomenon unto itself best governed through its own natural processes, such as maintaining optimal rates of birth, death, disease, and agricultural and economic production.[111] The regulation of these indexes attempts to achieve homeostasis for the population as a whole, despite roiling competition for resources within. With Malthus, the biopolitical notion of population emerges distinctly: his solution to the dilemma of the exponential growth of the population and the merely geometric increase in agricultural production was to sacrifice the poor to starvation, disease, and death so that the population as a whole could continue to advance. Yet Malthus arrives at his conclusion that a given population must experience ceaseless competition for survival—a proposition that famously inspired Darwin to conceive of natural selection—through a different interpretation of the same doctrine of impressibility than Godwin depended on.

Impressibility discourse enables Malthus's idea of population and its biopolitical governance. Human development, for Malthus, involves transforming the "torpor and corruption of the chaotic matter" the body is composed of into an active mind, a process that transpires through "the various impressions that man receives through life."[112] The greatest impression-inducing experiences that "awaken" torpid flesh are those that stem from want of subsistence.[113] "Had population and food increased in the same ratio," he opines, "it is probable that man might never have emerged from the savage state."[114] As it happened, however, the desperate struggle for survival stimulated over time the gradual development of reason among those populations who learned to discipline their desires and consequently received many layers of beneficial impressions. Yet a child born of civilized parents in full possession of reason could not merely ride on those coattails: the nature of maturation required that each individual also receive their own impressions. Evil exists so that some members of each generation learn to avoid it, a process that induces new layers of beneficial impressions into their text.[115]

Witnessing suffering was necessary for a population to develop the highest class of faculties: the sentimentalism characteristic of civilization. Malthus explained that high rates of death and disease among the poor directly benefit the advance of the English population—and that the government should *not* attempt to alleviate the misery of the poor—for "the sorrows and distresses of life form another class of excitements which seem to be necessary, by a peculiar train of impressions, to soften and humanize the heart, to awaken social sympathy, to generate all the Christian virtues, and to afford scope for the ample exertion of benevolence."[116] Bound together into an organic whole through impressibility, a population must sacrifice its poor members for the wealthier's evolution of higher emotional faculties on account of witnessing, and sympathizing with, such suffering. Malthus thereby makes the civilizing process of the whole reliant on the suffering and death of its "redundant" members.[117] In this biopolitical framework, civilization is not a salve for brutality, but rather is forged out of the competitive dynamics of population itself.

Malthus plays a pivotal role in elaborating the biopolitical function of sentiment, wherein the widespread misery and death inherent to the unequal distribution of resources in capitalism furthers the sympathetic faculties of the population as a whole. Malthus is not only a biopolitical writer, he is also a sentimental one, a conjunction that reveals the operative roles of discourses of impressibility and sentimentalism in population governance. Similarly, the hereditarian logic of impressibility illuminates the biopolitical dimensions of Harper's investment in sentimental rhetoric. Across the work of both writers, despite their enormous political differences, the progress of civilization accumulates over time through layers of beneficial sensory impressions engraved in the flesh. Both Malthus's and Harper's idea of the civilized body that compiles stratum after stratum of impressions over time helped inaugurate palimpsestic metaphors of racial development.

Race in the nineteenth century didn't evoke determinist prisons of fixed biological material or thoroughly plastic spaces of becoming, but figured unstable palimpsests built of generations of sensory impressions. Race, in the context of Malthus, Lamarck, Bushnell, Cope, and others, served to measure the relative degree to which civilization was worked into animal flesh over time. Yet this process was never absolute. The body that accumulates through generations of impressions forms an unstable palimpsest in which any prior mark always threatened to reappear. A palimpsest, as its first theorist, Thomas De Quincey, explained in 1845, "is a membrane or roll cleansed of its manuscript by reiterated successions." Due to the scarcity of parchment, vellum, and other materials suitable for "receiving such impressions" in the centuries before industrialization, writing surfaces regularly had to be scraped or washed clean before they could be reinscribed with new text. These subsequent impressions would erase, yet not entirely efface, prior impressions, resulting in a multilayered document that preserves traces of the past even as it bodies forth a new present. Every experience leaves an impression, resulting in a haphazard text, full of seemingly "incongruous" events. Yet in the "deep memorial palimpsest of the brain," they become "fused into harmony."[118] Every contact—or the feeling resulting from its refusal—leaves an indelible imprint and casts its shadow over all subsequent events, coloring them in its own hue.

A new organic whole is continually produced through each haphazard contact. A palimpsest is a heterogeneous archive in which discrete impressions from years past integrate with sensations of the moment. Temporality registers in the material form of textuality, yet it maintains an ethereal quality in which the past is at once legible to the senses of touch and sight, and yet not fully tangible. The present becomes a semiopaque vantage onto its own antecedents, which remain in tantalizingly close proximity. Piling up experience on experience, the palimpsest becomes a site of contestation, forged of disparate and competing cultural events that nonetheless cohere as one.[119] Drawing on Julia Kristeva's work on intertexuality, Sarah Dillon refers to the ways that temporalities collide in material form in the palimpsest as its "productive violence," directing attention to the process of "involvement, entanglement, interruption and inhibition" waged between multiple texts as they fuse into singular form.[120] A single text contains temporal multitudes that must vie for transparency. For this reason, in palimpsestic models of race any impression can play an important role in individual, familial, and racial destiny, particularly if it becomes habitual.

The palimpsest metaphor captures how past, present, and future contact made up the civilized body. Civilization was understood to be a repository of cultural value pressed into the flesh over time, the juncture of temporality and materiality. Anna Julia Cooper explained: "Whatever notions we may indulge on the theory of evolution and the laws of atavism or heredity, all concede that . . . no life is bound up in the period of its conscious existence. . . . The materials that go to make the man . . . are the resultant of forces that have been accumulating and gathering momentum for generations."[121] Its temporal nature renders a palimpsest inherently unstable. Layers do not accrue in a linear fashion. Rather, the most recent record of contact coheres with even the oldest. This malleability opened the door to withering degeneration, should the nature of new impressions be deleterious, and atavism, in which a largely effaced stratum of impressions from an earlier, more primitive stage of racial development suddenly resurfaces. Each new impression paradoxically modifies the inherited—and transmissible—text, yet does not fundamentally alter the earlier layers, which remain somewhat discernible. Civilization thus marks only the tenuous triumph of culture over the material.

THE BIOPOLITICS OF SENSATION

"I may venture to affirm," David Hume reflected in the mid-eighteenth century, "that we are nothing but a bundle or collection of different sensations, which succeed each other with an inconceivable rapidity, and are in a perpetual flux and movement."[122] Taking exception to Hume's mechanistic empiricism more than two hundred years later, Oliver Sacks laments that a patient entirely lacking the ability to lay down new memories has realized the stark Humean ideal. For Sacks, his patient has experienced the "reduction of a man to mere disconnected, incoherent flux and change . . . a meaningless fluttering on the surface of life."[123] Both Hume's and Sacks's perspectives are distinct from the meanings attributed to sensory impressions in the nineteenth century. In this period, new theories of population, hereditary transmission, and evolutionary change conceived of the impressible body in which sensations layer on top of one another in a palimpsestic fashion. Such impressions are deeply felt and integrated to some degree with each other and the body's substrate. Far from a "meaningless" collection of brief bursts, sensations build the organism and the species over time, a compendium of profound sensory relation to the environment and to those who came before. Over time, impressions construct the ontology of civilization.

In sensationist accounts of the permeability of the civilized body, cultural expression registers as physical impression. Throughout Frances Harper's work, she both elaborates on the specifically tactile nature of the nineteenth-century framework of human development and demonstrates the discourse's receptivity to black manipulation. Her literal fleshing out of humanist discourse by means of elaborating on the physicality of the impression suggests that progress has a materiality reformers can hold in their "moulding hands."[124] Frances Harper has been the target of substantial critical scorn on account of her overt sentimentality and her perceived relinquishing of black pleasure in the pursuit of bourgeois respectability. Yet a reading of her politics of sensation reveals her emphasis on the centrality of stimulating touch to political and social reform. Her work capitalized on the erotic dimensions embedded in the notion of impression at the heart of Western epistemology, and she adapted the sentimental politics of life into a defense of black potential and a blueprint for class-based social uplift. Engaging in the nineteenth-century discourses of race and sex, she transforms accusations of black impulsive sensibility and lack of reflective sentimentality into evidence of their very potential and of the needed leadership of black women. For Harper, self-discipline stimulates inner reserves of impressibility.

Harper's poems labor in the service of a black feminist biopolitics, one that works through the sensory discipline, pleasure, and inscription of the individual body as well as by regulating the hereditary transmission of impressions throughout a population. Within Harper's evolutionary aesthetics, both motherhood and artistic work have evolutionary effects, for the circulation of impressions contribute layers to the palimpsestic racial body that is resistant, striving, and pointing steadily toward the future. By expanding on the concept of the sentimental touch, Harper's work demonstrates that black people can have a modern sexuality that is deeply felt, reflective, chaste, pleasurable, delicate, and regenerative. Harper grabs hold of the material effects of the sentimental account of time, the unmistakable trace culture leaves on the body. For Harper, progress is a corporeal state that the capable hands of black women could maneuver, manipulate, and massage. Her textual theory of racial progress fingers the palimpsestic nature of civilization, in which aesthetic stimulations arouse the cultivated mind and dispatch the animal body within to slumber.

....

CHAPTER 3

Vaginal Impressions

Gyno-neurology and the Racial Origins
of Sexual Difference

There are women that love women, Mr. Yorke, care for 'em, grieve over
'em, worry about 'em, feel a fellow feeling and a kind of duty to 'em, and
never forget they're one of 'em, misery and all.

ELIZABETH STUART PHELPS, *Doctor Zay* (1882)

For two of the earliest women physicians in the English-speaking world, the
apex of the refined nervous system—the intricately folded organ that exemplified the civilized body's powers of memory, sensitivity, plasticity, and
communication—was not the brain, but was rather, the vagina. Dr. Elizabeth
Blackwell (1821–1910) thereby cautioned the public that the vagina is "endowed with the elasticity necessary for the passage of a child, rich in secreting
glands, in folds, in power of absorption," and "cannot be treated as a plane surface, to be washed out."[1] What's more, "the sexual act is a physiological nerve-
storm."[2] For Blackwell, the heightened impressibility of the vagina required
that women, not men, should direct the timing and frequency of the marital
sex act. Sensory impressions on the highly responsive vaginal nerves of white
women created intense feelings of pleasure, but also stimulated deep and lasting changes in neurological structure and function that had repercussions
throughout longevity. In Blackwell's Lamarckian perspective, impressions on
the vaginal nerves of the civilized races—and only the civilized races—make
"modifications" to "the nervous system" itself and these changes are transmitted to any future offspring.[3] Racial health thus hinged on vaginal experience,
even in the absence of immediate pregnancy. Although fluid, the vagina's sins
of experience could not be washed away.

Dr. Mary Walker (1832–1919), who graduated from medical school six years
after Blackwell had become the first woman to receive a medical degree in the

Western world in 1849, similarly portrayed the vagina as a crucial neurological structure. Walker and Blackwell both positioned anatomy and physiology as partners in enforcing white women's rights of sexual self-determination and the sexual law of racial purity. Yet Walker was considerably more bold, as captured in her 1878 sex advice book *Unmasked*, addressed "to gentlemen."[4] Describing a woman born of "marital rape," Walker explained that "when man uses force to compel against the desire of woman, a poison is sent forth from the walls of the vagina that injures his whole system, and shortens his days" (*UM*, 142). Impressions forcibly made during the violation of the mother later manifest in the function of the daughter's vagina. The daughter will have "inherited such a power of vagina resistance that the coition grasp in orgasm" results in "excruciating pain" for male partners, regardless of her own arousal and intent (*UM*, 82). The responsiveness and malleability of vaginal nerves, for Walker, affectively records, disseminates, and punishes men's proclivities for philandering and rape. To avoid these dire consequences for civilization, she urged white men to learn to decipher and obey the genital "language of the nerves" (*UM*, 142).

These early women physicians offer an overlooked account of the vital and affective materiality of the vaginal nerves. In their medical texts, the vagina exemplifies the civilized nervous system, which is imbued with a life force that is wholly irreducible to its biochemical substrate and is capable of forms of transformation, communication, attachment, and transmission that eclipse the will and awareness of the individual. Blackwell's and Walker's vaginal vitalisms have received little attention either in their own time or in ours.[5] Their writings on sexuality and medicine more generally in the 1850s–1880s have received scant consideration from scholars, who have overwhelmingly preferred to focus on their compelling biographies, rather than their seemingly outlandish physiological theories.[6] Nonetheless, their attention to the anatomy and physiology of the vaginal structure is all the more remarkable in light of the vast gaps in this knowledge that persist today, nearly 150 years later, in both scientific and popular spheres.[7] Walker's portrayal of the retributive and lingual vagina that communicates directly with the peripheral nerves and cerebrospinal axis of sexual partners bears all the marks of unscientific premodern medical theory. Scholars have thus dismissed her medical knowledge as replete with "archaic myths" and "sexual superstition."[8] Both Blackwell and Walker conjure a sentimental universe in which feelings, rather than genes or germs, govern growth and health, and their intellectual contributions have been marginalized accordingly.[9] Yet for this very reason, their work crystallizes how hierarchies of impressibility, or the relative capacity to affect and be affected, played a key role in medical knowledge and modern ideas of sexual and racial difference.

Drs. Blackwell and Walker transformed accusations of the overly height-ened impressibility of civilized women into evidence that white women's sexual and social self-determination was a biological and political imperative. In this chapter, I tell a racial history of sex that builds on the analysis in the book's first chapter of the emergence of modern notions of sex difference out of biopolitical imperatives for population stabilization, such as those articu-lated in dominant neo-Lamarckian evolutionary frameworks that ballasted the highly unstable impressible body by shunting its liabilities onto women. This excavation complements the discussion of black feminist biopolitics in chapter 2, showing how white women similarly worked within the available framework in which impressibility and sentimentality were understood to be racial criteria of civilization and touch its key mechanism. I consider Black-well and Walker's work in the context of their personal lives, especially the groundbreaking career choices and same-sex relationships in which Walker and a majority of other nineteenth-century women doctors, including Eliza-beth's sister Dr. Emily Blackwell, were engaged.[10] For example, a San Francisco medical journal praised Walker as "the most distinguished sexual invert in the United States" at the turn of the century.[11] Overall, I argue that impressibility discourse so thoroughly endowed the civilized body with the qualities of vi-tality and adaptability that space emerged for white women's sexual and social self-determination to fall within the purview of civilized sexuality, whether or not they birthed children themselves. The unconventional medical careers, domestic lives, and, in the case of Walker, sexed presentation of these early women physicians were thus interdependent with and even enabled by their commitments to improving the health of the national population in the con-texts of U.S. settler colonialism and British imperialism. Their work and lives reveal how normative biopolitical operations of whiteness expanded life op-tions for white women.

This argument has two central stakes. First, the notion of "woman" as a polit-icized category of identity, the identity at the core of feminist politics of the last two centuries, is revealed to be a biopolitical subjectivity. Nineteenth-century U.S. women who conceived of womanhood as a political category, including Frances Harper and Anna Julia Cooper, were working within the racial hierar-chy of civilization, a genealogy that is woefully underrecognized in feminist and sexuality studies. Womanhood, like manhood, was understood as an advanced state of mental, physiological, emotional, and anatomical specialization only achieved by the civilized.[12] In other words, white woman suffrage leaders such as Susan B. Anthony and Elizabeth Cady Stanton's Reconstruction-era sabotage of their black allies, including Frederick Douglass, is only part of the picture of the racial priorities of early women's rights. The larger issue still remains to be depicted in full: how the very category of woman is itself a racialized concept, one born of the impulses to differentiation and hierarchization of affective capacity characteristic of nineteenth-century biopower. "Woman" marks neither an interiority nor an individuated, independent subject—indeed, there is no discrete identity in impressibility regimes, only the folding inward of the sensations resultant from coming into contact with the external world. Rather, "woman" represents a tactic of risk management grounded in ideas of relative bodily feeling, responsiveness, and malleability that correlate with the perceived properties of genitalia. Feminism may be a liberation project for many, but it works within biopolitical priorities to administer bodies according to distinct physiological types that protect the normatively sexed bodies of whiteness, root womanhood in the possession of a penetrable vagina, and condemn the bodies of everyone else.

Second, distinct but intertwined ideas about the affectivity, vitality, and plasticity of matter have emerged within biopower and do not trouble liberal humanism's explanatory frame as much as they enable it. Scholars have claimed that affect, as a body's independent and autonomic intensity that transcends rationality, names "forces that exceed the classical liberal thematics of self sovereignty" and therefore offers the possibility of an oppositional ontology and politics.[13] Yet the individualist subject was never as contained, stable, or rational as liberalism promised, forged, as it were, through repeated sensory impressions from the outside world. Indeed, the entire project of sexual difference is to manage the inherent instability and porosity of the liberal subject, which it accomplishes, as we shall see, through an ontology of holes, or the demarcation of appropriate and inappropriate avenues of interpersonal penetration and linkage. Impressibility names the animacy hierarchy that lies at the heart of the ontology of affect.[14] It is a hierarchy of liveliness that differentiates between those malleable bodies that can affect as well as be affected, from those intractable bodies that can only affect, that fail to absorb the impressions incurred by their own experience and thereby continually recirculate the contagions of prehistory. Affectivity, plasticity, and vitality function as the grounds of biopower's deployment of racial and sexual difference, an ontology that long-standing attachment to determinist frames of race has precluded from view.

THE SENTIMENTAL POLITICS OF LIFE

The consolidating logic of sex difference may be profitably understood through the rubric I am calling *the sentimental politics of life*, a mode of nineteenth-century U.S. imperial biopower that governed its population by regulating the circulation of affect throughout its expanding milieu. The sentimental politics of life characterizes a style of governmentality that disciplines the nervous system's response to sensory impressions, privileging sympathy, susceptibility, and self-control as prime instruments of subjects' willing self-regulation, and domesticity and womanhood as key technologies of political power. Its methods of individual discipline and populational regulation work at the site of the body's present sensations, but with an eye toward future generations yet to come. The sentimental politics of life works to accumulate in the civilized, along the Lamarckian model, hereditary traits deemed beneficial for the nation as a whole. Writing against the still-pervasive view that determinisms characterized the nineteenth-century vantage on embodiment, literary critic Justine Murison emphasizes that the rise of neurology in the period resulted in "the open body" of the nineteenth century, or the idea that corporeality "was not a stable unit precisely because the nervous system governed it."[15] Capable of independent intention, attachment, and communication, the civilized nervous system rendered the nation in need of a system of governance that reached inward. Woman, a biological and political category forged within the racial logic of civilization, emerged as the bearer of this task. Her technologies include a surprisingly literal and corporeal interpretation of the sentimental politics of life's internal purview: the vaginal biopolitics of Blackwell and Walker.

The sentimental politics of life provides a particularly useful framework for reform projects that emphasize women's agency, yet fit uncomfortably within contemporary feminist paradigms. While Elizabeth Blackwell's status as the first woman in the modern world to receive a medical degree has made her the subject of several generations of academic scholarship and lay historical work, this research has been overwhelmingly restricted to women's history and popular biography.[16] The reticence of scholars to explore her significance more broadly can be linked to Blackwell's uneasy relationship to women's rights and her strident moralism: she dismissed the campaign for woman suffrage (in which many of her family members were very much involved) as "an anti-man movement"; decried the promotion of contraception by feminists in the United Kingdom and United States; and devoted much of her career to spreading the gospel of sexual hygiene.[17] Even her sister Dr. Emily Blackwell called her "dull."[18] The important "sympathy and science" frame that historian Regina Morantz-Sanchez developed to analyze the work of early women doctors can be pushed further: these professionals not only combined the two practices in unique ways, but also positioned their trailblazing work precisely at the juncture of these interlocking methods, epistemologically and politically. Furthermore, Walker and Blackwell's turn to medicine falls within recently offered literary and cultural paradigms for the work of mid- to late nineteenth-century white women activists who turned to the life sciences. Terms such as *evolutionary feminism* and *biological feminism*, however, are typically meant to signal a problematic grounding of feminist agency within the biological body itself.[19] These constructions position nineteenth-century feminisms' links with biological discourse as primarily restricting the reach and legacy of its political work, rather than enabling it. Feminist histories of nineteenth-century science offer limited opposition, often tending to emphasize the marginalization—or agency—of women within larger structures of scientific power and authority.[20]

Yet biopower is feminism's enabling condition. Feminist scholarship has been slow to come to terms with this uncomfortable genealogy. A recent historical intervention that does insist on the productive function of the biological sciences for nineteenth-century feminism argues that "evolutionary science was an unwitting and unlikely ally in the struggle for women's rights." Kimberly Hamlin claims that while the racial hierarchies of Darwinian evolution "severely limited" the political work of (white) feminists including Antoinette Blackwell, Charlotte Perkins Gilman, and Margaret Sanger, racial hierarchies "are not the only aspect of this story. . . . While modern readers recognize the connections between gendered and racial oppression and the ways in which racial ideologies structure gendered ones, and vice versa, it would be ahistorical to discount the contributions of Darwinian feminists because they did not."[21] The claim that race is an "aspect" of evolutionary feminisms, one of its discrete components that rigorous historical methods would best relegate to the side as particular to our own vantage in order to properly assess the contributions of white women reading Darwin, manages to miss the significance of its own topic. The evolutionary notion of the distinct sexes of male and female, understood as specialized divergences in physiology, anatomy, and mental function that only the most civilized had achieved, was itself a racial hierarchy.[22] I stress in this book that the very idea of sex as a biological and political subjectivity is a product of the biopolitical logics unfolding hand in hand with the sciences of species change. Indeed, racial and sexual difference are currently understood to intersect *because* we live in the ongoing legacy of biopolitical regimes in which sex difference is understood to be a function of racial status. Movements for gender equality have materialized amid a field of power in which, at least since Malthus, the interdependence of reproduction and economics forms the primary field of the political. As Michelle Murphy reasons, "Historicizing feminisms as a biopolitics that has taken 'sex,' and its subsidiary, 'reproduction,' as central concerns requires that we understand feminisms in all their variety and contradiction as animated within—and not escaping from—dominant configurations of governance and technoscience."[23] Feminisms necessarily form part of the contours, however uneven at times, of biopower.

Drs. Elizabeth Blackwell and Mary Walker offer particularly compelling examples of how the articulation of womanhood as a political subjectivity was imbricated specifically with the deployment of biopower in the sentimental mode, for their medical knowledge was in concert with their prominent political work. After years of negotiating for a formal assignment during the Civil War—even though she was already serving in such a capacity, wearing a uniform she adapted herself, bloomer-style—Walker occupied a formally approved Union army post as acting assistant surgeon. Her quest for the first female medical appointment in the Civil War gained her national fame, and she made sure all who saw her in person realized her significance: "I let my curls grow while I was in the army so that everybody would know that I was a woman," she later wrote.[24] Walker also served as a spy for the Union. She was held as a prisoner of war for four months in Castle Thunder, a notorious Confederate jail that left her with partial muscular atrophy, ending her surgical career—but not her medical practice. For her war service, she was awarded the only congressional Medal of Honor ever bestowed on a woman, which she wore proudly every day thereafter.[25] Blackwell's career was considerably more staid, but no less in support of national government. (Her own hopes for a surgical career were dashed when an infection acquired while receiving postgraduate training in the Parisian hospital La Maternité resulted in the removal of her left eye.) Blackwell dedicated the last thirty years of her career to campaigning for sexual hygiene. Her belief that moral rectitude would free humankind from disease, a position termed *Christian physiology*, motivated her to launch several prominent social purity societies, publish over fifteen books, and advocate for the repeal of the British Contagious Diseases Act. She joined feminists objecting to the legislation on the grounds that Britain's continued sponsorship of prostitution in its colonies, particularly India, was resulting in the "gravest form of racial injury"—disease spread as the result of interracial sex.[26] Both doctors understood their medical training to enable their work as agents of the growth and progress of the nation-state, in acts of consolidation and imperial expansion. Exploring their studies of vaginal impressibility sheds light not only on the function of sexual difference as a political and biological subjectivity, but also on the field of power in which movements for women's professional and sexual self-determination take shape.

FIG. 3.1. "Dr. Mary Walker, circa 1865." Legacy Center Archives, Drexel University College of Medicine, Philadelphia.

By the nineteenth century, nerves had long been the carriers of a prominent colonial discourse that differentiated the delicate, precise, and sensitive faculties of the civilized from the coarse, unrefined, and overly reactive bodies of the savage races. Yet impressibility renders the civilized body highly vulnerable to its external conditions, even as it enables further progress. In light of the increasing importance of nervous impressibility to modes of political power, two interlocking discourses were mobilized throughout the second half of the nineteenth century to address the problem of the susceptible civilized body: binary sexual differentiation and civilized sexuality. As we saw in the first chapter, sex dimorphism generally stabilizes the precarity inherent to impressibility for white men, for women's bodies were generally assigned the liabilities of the "nervous self."[27] The overly nervous female was sacrificed for the homeostasis of civilization. Her very openness ensured that she could function as the subunit of her male counterpart, at once corporeally distinct from him, yet capable of being reattached at his will. Sex difference allowed men to enjoy the capacity for progress that impressibility enables all but unencumbered by its risks. Civilized sexuality, when properly deployed, reunited the two halves under strict conditions of reproductive monogamy.[28] As Elizabeth Blackwell's sister-in-law Antoinette Brown Blackwell put it, "The diverging lines, male and female, converg[e] again in the child. It is not each added to the other, but the one balancing the other."[29]

Yet Antoinette studied the evolutionary achievement of sex specialization in order to insist, contra Charles Darwin and Herbert Spencer, that "average males and females, in every species, always have been approximately equals, both physically and mentally."[30] For her, the logic of sex differentiation was total—"even to every hair of the head"—yet the specialized nervous powers of each, when balanced in a common reproductive whole, were equivalent in energy of development and capacity of force.[31] Blackwell and Walker made similar arguments in defense of women's physiology. More unusually, they explicitly located women's physiological difference in the vagina and deemed the vagina the only orifice suitable for the reunion of the bifurcated body. Their work contributed to the deployment of vaginal sexuality as one of the key criteria that distinguished civilized from primitive sexual practices, a practice of continual delineation in settler colonial societies that for Scott Lauria Morgensen inaugurates "modern sexuality."[32] Walker and Blackwell are key figures in articulating the emergent biopolitics of heterosexuality and cisnormativity, but with a vaginal twist. Given that the vagina serves as the literal linkage between the body and the race, it became the basis of their feminist claims for (white) women's political rights and their anatomical understanding of female subjectivity that located womanhood in the vaginal structure.

Whereas Lamarck had positioned the ejaculating penis as the metaphor of the refined nervous system's response to sensory contact, Blackwell and Walker extended the logic of binary sexual differentiation to incarnate the racialized capacity of openness and responsiveness in the vagina of the white woman. As opposed to the primitive inertia of "such a vestige as the clitoris," Blackwell stressed that the vagina is constituted by "a vast amount of erectile tissue" as well as "contractile" muscular tissue that manifests a highly energetic response to impressions.[33] This "most highly sensitive ganglion of nerves" condensed what they saw as the qualities of the fine nervous system of the civilized races: the vagina possessed tremendous impressibility, implying sensitivity, malleability, transmissibility, and the ability to form its own affiliations, independent of the individual's consciousness (UM, 141). The vagina was penetrable, pliable, responsive, and absorptive, its internal depths folded within yet nonetheless readily accessible. The vagina was the singular achievement of evolutionary sex differentiation, itself understood along a capitalist model in which specialization inexorably led to progress. In this precursor to contemporary neuroplasticity discourses, the vagina, rather than the brain, was the apex of neurological dynamism.

The open, responsive physiology of the vagina, in Blackwell and Walker's view, afforded white women greater capacities of stimulation and therefore development in both body and brain than their male counterparts or the sexually undifferentiated primitive. Blackwell explained that "the savage nation gains health and strength by their untutored activity, but they remain brutal and degraded—they gain no mental refinement by their exercises."[34] Lacking the absorptive capacity of impressibility, in which physical sensations trigger neural development, activity only strengthens the brute, unsexed matter of the racialized. In contrast, among the civilized, "physical passion possesses that distinctive human characteristic—receptivity to mental impressions," such that sexual stimulation cultivates intellectual capacity. The highly sensitive nexus of the vagina thereby rendered women capable "of a stronger power of human sexual passion" than that of men, for the stimulation of vaginal nerves occasions profound sexual pleasure *and* mental and emotional advance.[35] A long-standing medical trope had positioned the orgasm as an autonomic reflex, like a sneeze, and thus a body's independent and ungovernable act.[36] Blackwell and Walker made the opposite move, in a century that widely doubted women's autonomic capacity for orgasm, and rendered sexual satisfaction the apex of the mind/body link.[37] Their use of the impressibility framework overturns Cartesian dualisms between mind and body. In a circuitous pattern, additional layers of cognitive development result in white women's "increasing physical satisfaction" and increased ardor that guides civilization toward ever greater harmony (*UM*, 10).[38] Sociologist Kate Krug observes that for Blackwell, "sexuality is that capacity through which the highest human development is made possible."[39] Sex among the civilized becomes a largely mental phenomenon, transformed from primitive instinct to abiding love through the direct neurological link between the vagina and the brain. Layer by layer, the white woman's vagina had become the greatest achievement of the civilizational palimpsest.

And therein lay the problem: there was no custom or right for women to regulate their own sexual activity. While Blackwell and Walker may seem to displace physical passion in favor of the "higher" capacities of emotional regulation, in their framework, the civilizing process depends on white women's sexual satisfaction as well as their sexual agency. As in Frances Harper's accounts of the stimulations inherent to the emotional regulation of physical sensation, the disciplinary function of the sentimental politics of life may not necessarily be wholly repressive, with regard, exclusively, to women of their own class and race. Rather, the writings of all three suggest a pleasure in the act of self-regulation, of meeting sensory excitement with an equivalent emotional force, of wielding a union of mind and body deemed unique to women's sympathetic faculty. In what we might think of as a precursor to contemporary sex-positive feminism, the political possibility of women's sexual satisfaction emerges through white women's adaptation of the biopolitical logic of sex difference as racial advance.

Sexual stimulation left deep impressions on white women's vulnerable bodies and brains that would come to make up hereditary material. Dr. Mary Walker explained: "As the sexual relation calls for the most intense nerve excitement, and the strongest and most powerful and concentrated emotions, so does it as surely call forth and receive the brain impressions, that in spite of all other considerations, are lasting and transmissible. And those who associate in the sexual relation with the low, the ignorant, the vile, the fickle, the unmethodical in thought, the undeveloped in mind, cannot avert the law of effects upon themselves that they are powerless to throw off" (*UM*, 28–29). Impressibility is a biological condition of the population, as much as a capacity of the individual organic body. In contrast to the "savage," Blackwell specified, a member of the civilized race "approaches more nearly to the true type of man, and has acquired the capacity of transmitting increased capacities to his children."[40] The vagina, for Blackwell and Walker, realizes the full potential of the impressible nervous system of the civilized, granting each act of sexual stimulation a role in the gradual development or degeneration of the population as a whole.

Walker and Blackwell stress that improper vaginal impressions could permanently damage highly responsive vaginal nerves, preventing the reproductive reunion of the civilized body. Walker attributes cases of infertility to "the harshness of husbands on wedding nights," such that "the nerves of the vagina" have been so "shocked and partially paralyzed" that they fail to ever recover their magnetic power of attracting sperm (UM, 65). Diseases acquired through sexual contact were particularly damaging to the vagina, for infection set about "gnawing [its] intricate folds" (UM, 123). Among rich women, dildos and corsets present the main threats to civilized sexuality. "Rubber male organs" sold in graduated dimensions under the name of "Ladies' Companion" accustomed elastic tissues to increasingly expansive sexual excitement. "When one size is outgrown, another is purchased," Walker fretted. Masturbation with dildos results in damage to the brain, "elongation of the clitoris, and a formation of warty excrescences on the vulva" (UM, 115–116). The corset numbered among the harmful sexual apparatuses available to the civilized for Walker, an ardent dress reformer. It dislodged the uterus from its proper positioning in the body cavity and thereby proliferated disease throughout, for "there can be no restraints without injury, not only to the particular part, but to every part, through the law of sympathy" (UM, 96). Furthermore, the wearing of corsets continually stimulates the sex organs, resulting in "inherited irritability" in offspring (UM, 123). The structure of the individual soma and the palimpsestic civilized body as a whole are transformed via habitual sensory stimulations.

Among the poor, too-frequent sexual impressions ran the risk of overstimulating vaginal tissue. In "the unnatural parchment-like condition," characteristic of the "vaginal mucous membrane of the harlot," Blackwell contends, "tissue is so disorganized that it cannot absorb virus into the system of the individual, but only transmit it to the vicious companion."[41] The repetitive stimulations of the prostitute overwhelm her absorptive powers, transforming a living palimpsest into a desiccated relic. Her vagina is now an unimpressible space that can only affect but cannot be affected, having been rendered a stagnant reservoir of contagion. Blackwell also strove to illuminate the role new medical technologies played in impressing vaginal nerves, particularly those of the poor, whom she argued possessed an inferior capacity of self-regulation and self-knowledge. "The use of the speculum" as standard gynecological procedure "is a serious national injury," she warned readers, for its insertion in poor patients thwarts the development of the key behaviors of civilization, "personal modesty and self-respect."[42] It was incumbent on physicians to

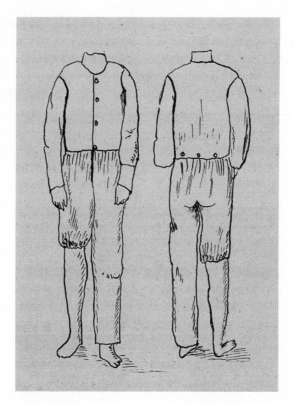

FIG. 3.2. "Reform Undersuit. Renders rape 'impossible.'"
From Mary Walker, *Unmasked, or, The Science of Immorality.*
To Gentlemen (New York: Wm. H. Boyd, 1878).

guard the nation's sexual morality, not to undermine it through unnecessary vaginal stimulation.[43] She inveighed against the poor's use of contraceptive devices on the grounds that they lacked the knowledge to manually navigate labyrinthine vaginal terrain and position them appropriately. The vagina's "soft, irregular . . . passage," she explained, is of a "length . . . often apparently greater than the ordinary finger" and difficult for even medical professionals to traverse without error.[44] The intricate folds of the vaginal archive require carefully regulated use to keep them elastic and nubile.

Maintaining civilized sexuality required that each individual's sexual impressibility unfold in accordance with the normative time lines of racial evolution. Elizabeth Blackwell used her prominent position to lecture on what we might call, following Dana Luciano, the chronobiopolitics of civilization, or the idea that racial development must abide by the temporal dictates of civilized sexuality.[45] Soon after Blackwell established the first women's medical college, as well as the first teaching hospital associated with a medical school in the United States, she relocated back to England and became increasingly devoted to disseminating the rules of sexual health for the success of the British empire. She particularly emphasized that children must acquire the capacities of self-control before experiencing the intoxicating pleasures of sexual stimulation. In order to successfully navigate childhood—a stage of heightened impressibility in which the civilized, according to the principles of recapitulation, must retrace the evolution of their race from savagery to civilization—youth male and female alike must be protected from the lure of sex.

Blackwell warned that should the children of the civilized races experience "precocity of physical sensation" before their time, such stimulation would arrest the civilized child in this "primitive elementary instinct."[46] Mothers must therefore prevent their children from masturbation, an act that saturates the supple nerves of youth with the viscous attachments of sex. Masturbation poses "injury to the mind through the nervous system," impressing the child's extra-malleable brain with deep etchings that result in a pronounced nervous "irritability," in which the slightest of sensory provocations arouses the individual.[47] Such an agitated physical state threatens to erode the achievement of chastity, which "Christian civilization" alone has attained as a "physiological habit."[48] Self-pleasure posed the risk of regressing the individual back into the condition of primitivity, a lower evolutionary stage marked by sexual profligacy whether in "semibarbarous countries" or "the slums of all great towns."[49] The physiological basis of civilization lay in the capacity to match nervous sensation with the "force of will," an achievement that sexual impressions during the malleable stage of youth could prevent.[50] The regulation of sexual sensation, rather than reproduction more narrowly, divided the civilized from the primitive races. Civilization depended on confining sexual stimulation to vaginal sex among married couples.

By contrast, primitive sexuality is overdetermined by unimpressibility and marks a population for disposability and death. Many scientists agreed that just as the genitals and pelvis typified the sexual difference achieved by the civilized races, so did the pelvis, including genitalia and buttocks, of the racialized exemplify primitivity.[51] Extensive research and public display of African women alleged that their bodies retained animalized characteristics and failed to fully differentiate from men. Such accusations were grounded in hierarchies of sensation in which black women's genitalia were highly reactive, yet barely receptive, easily aroused but unable to absorb the effects of their impressions. Gynecology as a field and the obstetrics procedure known as the Cesarean section originated in unanaesthetized surgical experimentation on enslaved and free African American women and impoverished urban immigrants.[52] As one surgeon proclaimed, black women's "failure to receive impressions upon the nervous system which would seriously effect [sic] a more delicate organization" rendered them insensate to pain and thus available as experimental material.[53] J. Marion Sims, heralded as the founder of gynecology (and inventor of the speculum), purchased fourteen enslaved women for the purposes of experimental gynecological surgery. Anarcha endured thirty surgeries in just five years, all without recently available anesthetics.[54] Sims "reported in his autobiography that the slave women on whom he operated begged him to repeat his attempts. 'They were clamorous,'" he wrote.[55] Sims's work was directly productive for Walker and Blackwell's gyno-neurology, given his prominent, though wavering, and somewhat unique support of white women physicians, especially Emily and Elizabeth Blackwell's hospital and medical school for women, the New York Infirmary for Women and Children.[56] One of the vectors of modern sexuality—the ceaseless differentiation of civilized from primitive erotic practices—was the careers of white women physicians.

Blackwell argued that whereas civilized sexuality could surpass the need for physical expression and flower into abiding love, the "Mohammedan and other Eastern races" lacked not only chastity, but also the attendant capacities of sympathy, charity, truth, and honesty that result from impressibility. Accordingly, for Blackwell "the special danger of specific diseases also arriving from the congress of different races, is a well-known fact."[57] Illness signals moral failure and renders an individual an unfit guardian of the race's future.[58] She warned working-class women "that it is a cruelty and a crime to bring sickly children into the world."[59] As for how poor women could contribute to the vitality of the nation, Blackwell's advice was starkly Malthusian: "The greatest good that working women can now do to their country, is to leave it."[60] The task of the medical expert, Blackwell insisted, was to educate the civilized about the "two great forces of Habit and Heredity," which rendered repeated indulgence in sensation not merely momentary dalliances, but race-degenerating acts.[61] As with many of her nineteenth-century contemporaries, the biopolitical criteria Blackwell relies on to determine which groups' vitality the nation depends on and those whose removal or death it requires is not strictly class or race, but the compound inheritance of sensory, emotional, and affective capacity; race; class; sexuality; religion; and political organization that fell under the rubric of civilization.

The cost of violating the harmonic balance between the bifurcated roles of male and female in civilization was severe. For Blackwell, violating civilized sexuality foretold the death of not just individuals, but entire populations. "Race after race has perished," she admonished, "from blind or willful ignorance, or neglect of the inexorable moral law bound up with our physiological structure."[62] Among the British, sexually transmitted diseases presented the "gravest form of racial injury" and resulted in "enfeebled offspring" and "national degeneracy."[63] The imperative to manage the affectivity and transmissibility of the impressible body through the responsive vagina thus required that "woman assumes her due place as the regulator of sexual intercourse."[64] Judicious experience of vaginal sensations determines whether an individual and couple belongs among the population of the civilized, and thus deserving of life, or among the barbarous whose continued existence jeopardizes national prosperity. Sexed anatomy linked the genitals with the brain, culture with biology, and the two-bodied individual with the population, a framework that Blackwell and Walker adapted to articulate women's political and sexual identity and agency.

The vagina consequently serves as a biopolitical instrument. Whereas binary sexual differentiation generally saddled women with the risks inherent to an impressible nervous system and made them responsible for the labors of racial reproduction, Blackwell and especially Walker understood civilized sexuality to sympathetically link the male and female body in reciprocal nervous relation. As Walker put it, "Women cannot suffer without men being sufferers also" (UM, 134). In their view, male and female are, "if not identical . . . strictly parallel."[65] Yet the otherwise parallel lines intersect at one key point. As the axis of the civilized body, the vagina was properly the executor of sexuality, regulating national destiny. Blackwell explained, "The man joins himself to woman in loving companionship, and her constitution henceforward, must determine the times of the special act of physical union."[66] While national law did not grant white women, or any women, rights to their own person, vaginal neurology ensured that the organ would execute retribution for its misuse, as in the hereditary transmission of "vagina resistance" to penetration in the cases of girls born of rape (UM, 82). Walker argued that it was the state's responsibility to "*castrate*" rapists to ensure they could no longer abuse and contaminate girls and women (UM, 89). Yet since spousal rape was not prosecuted—and indeed it wouldn't be for another century—it was up to the sensorium to punish offenders, a graphic and surprising example of sentimental biopower. The ubiquity of rape—Walker asserted that most children were born of marital sex by force and that men were known to rape girls as young as two or three—worked to keep both men and women restricted to a lower stage of civilization (UM, 88–90). Walker took the lack of legal protection against rape into her own hands, instructing fathers that it was their duty to teach daughters how to defend themselves from rape "by grabbing the testicles" of would-be offenders. For these physicians, the neurology of the vagina dictated that true civilization was marked by the recognition of women's rights—an uncommon application of an increasingly common argument over the second half of the nineteenth century. In Walker and Blackwell's hands, the role of the vagina as the crossroads of the bifurcated white body and the population rendered women's sexual agency a racial imperative. They elaborated the physiology of sex difference as a condition grounded in genitalia and requiring women's sexual self-determination, working toward a notion of white womanhood as a biopolitical subjectivity deserving of rights that was fundamentally tied to sex organs.

THE VAGINAL FOLD

These early women physicians literalized their belief that civilized women incarnated the highest potential of the impressible, open body by writing extensively on the enfolded, absorptive, and communicative properties of the vagina. Blackwell explained that the vagina was "marked by longitudinal and transverse folds" that create "inequalities and hiding places" among "innumerable little furrows," perfect conduits for biological material to pass through the highly "absorbent" tissue of the vaginal "membrane."[67] The highly impressible, enfolded space of the vaginal canal retains the traces of all that entered, whether human or object, within its flesh. The qualities of a first lover could be transmitted to children fathered by a different man years or decades later (UM, 24). Vaginal impressions sympathetically linked the brains and bodies of lovers, the folds synthesizing the distinct bodies of male and female into one. Should death sunder the relationship, "the severe and compound suffering," of the widow, Blackwell mused, is due not only to "mental loss," but also "an immense physical deprivation."[68] Walker reported, with her characteristic attraction to sexual scandal, that consequently "some widows resort to all measures to gratify the sexual passions," yet nonetheless somehow manage to "retain the respect of people by a chaste appearance" (UM, 73). Bodies merge into one in the vaginal fold, such that sexual acts are never completely in the past and the circulation of vital forces within its many furrows never comes to rest. The vaginal fold opens up a perspective onto how Blackwell and Walker's vaginal biopolitics not only posits the political justification of rights but also grounds white women's subjectivity in the genitalia.

Gilles Deleuze's fold metaphor captures how the constitution and awareness of the self proceeds through the incorporation of what is external to it, the folding inward of what the subject encounters in its milieu. For Deleuze, the phenomenon of the fold is marked by the condition of material doubling onto itself that obviates any distinction between exterior and interior, for the shape itself is constituted by the incorporation of dynamics external to it.[69] In this space of becoming, relations forge the matter of the self. "The interior is only a selected interior," he explains, in that it originates from dynamics outside the individual, an individual whose subjectivity is the product of its very gatherings.[70] Impressibility, a precursor to Deleuze's notion of affect and the fold, was nonetheless elaborated in a very different political climate than Deleuze's. Whereas for Deleuze the space of becoming opens up ontologies of assemblage that challenge the individuating principle of liberal humanism, the sentimental politics of life was itself constituted by the fantasy that regulating women's sexuality would control the fields and forces that penetrate and forge the civilized body. Nervous impressibility precludes any ontological distinction between affective movement, emotional or biological interiority, physical expression, and hereditary material, rendering internal sensations and external embodiment linked directionalities of nerve force that constitute the individual and species-body over time. The body is forged by its relations, horizontally within synchronic time as well as vertically through the time of generations. In this logic, vaginal folds enable the consolidation of the self, just as the framework of sexual difference creates the category of woman as a political identity. Impressibility rendered vaginal stimulation and racial development coextensive processes due to the enfolded nature of civilized sexual subjectivity in which surface and depth, interiority and exteriority, subject and object collapse into each other within the woman's body.

Yet the civilized could never imagine susceptibility to be completely contained by the bisexual pair, for the subjectivity and survival of the human depends on its organic nature, on the sticky, fluid acts of contact, copulation, birthing, nursing, eating, digesting, and excreting. "Folding or doubling is itself a Memory," Deleuze writes, "the 'absolute memory' or the memory of the outside, beyond the brief memory inscribed in strata or archives, beyond the relics remaining in the diagrams."[71] In the nineteenth century, the memory preserved in the vaginal folds, the memory of the origins of self outside the forces of one's own body, was the animal past from which civilization had risen and yet on which it remained dependent. The seemingly forward-moving evolutionary model of accumulation pivoted on regular recursive movements of the palimpsestic corpus, on children's recapitulation of prior evolutionary stages and on prior impressions that ever peek through. The responsibility for the reproductive labor of the fleshly body thus fell solely on women. Womanhood became identified with the enfolded genitalia in which the biological origins of the species, the remainder of the animal past, were simultaneously preserved and tucked away from civilized sight.[72] The vagina was where the flesh that exceeds the humanist ideal of an abstract, individuated body, the subject of rights—a body nonetheless dependent on flesh, on its sensory relations with objects that press on it for its own subjectivity—doubles back on itself, retreating inward. Containing the animal origin of the universe within the vaginal folds purifies white women's minds and white men's minds and bodies. Dominant frameworks of sexual differentiation did the work of quarantining the state of flesh, among the civilized, to white woman's reproductive anatomy.

We might think of Hortense Spillers' "hieroglyphics of the flesh" as the inverse of the fold, the constitutive outside to civilized subjectivation through the incorporation of impressions. For Spillers, the body, the vehicle that enables liberal individualist self-possession, comes into being as an abstract legal construct through its opposition to the flesh. Flesh is an embodied state that exists outside the recursively forward-moving temporal frame of civilization. For everyone but the civilized, Spillers writes, flesh characterizes the unchanging state of existence, "the concentration of ethnicity" mired in the "stillness" of "mythical time" to which they are consigned.[73] In this "eternal" state of raw captivity, of "that zero degree of social conceptualization that does not escape concealment under the brush of discourse," enslaved women and men are rendered raw biological material suitable for use as a "living laboratory" for slave economies and twentieth-century theory and policies alike.[74] A person rendered flesh, for Spillers, is stripped of the particularities of sex and temporality and therefore the allowance of rights. Flesh "bears in person the marks of a cultural text whose inside has been turned outside."[75] Hieroglyphics of the flesh are not traces left by others folded into the subject's interiority. Rather, they represent excavations mined from within. Flesh is the condition of "seared, divided, ripped-apartness," of "rupture," of having experienced the "tearing out" of "small portions" of the body, of having suffered the overseer's lash that "has popped [the] flesh open."[76] Flesh is "the calculated work of iron, whips, chains, knives, the canine patrol, the bullet," somatic material torn asunder and circulated as a source of profit.[77] This continual state of rupture—the exact opposite of enfolded tissue—for Spillers renders flesh a "cultural *vestibularity*," an access point where hegemonic culture can enter, extract, and deport raw materials, all the while minimizing the contaminations of base materiality themselves.[78] A conduit for the penetration of capital and culture, to be flesh was to be vestibularity, to be a permanent antechamber unable to gather any material into itself; to be vaginal, yet stripped of its impressibility.

Sexual differentiation works to tuck away the reproductive residue of flesh in the vagina of the white woman, thereby securing the rational disembodiment of civilized men, the subject of reason. The vagina was deemed to be the proper storehouse of civilization's animal remainder and the primitive past, the highly circumscribed passageway through which citizen bodies enter and exit in their fleshy impulses and squalling beginnings. By contrast, Elizabeth Blackwell and Mary Walker worked to develop an "anatamo-politics" of discipline, to use Foucault's term.[79] They understood the vagina of the civilized woman as the morphology of progress and the tactile site of her subjectivity, rather than a remnant of the civilization's racialized and animal origins. They did so, however, by consigning other people, and other orifices, to the debased realm of the flesh. Other orifices, not invested with the force of sexual differentiation and the specialized labors of reproduction, were therefore inappropriate junctures between individuals and between the body and the population.

Civilized sexuality was thus vaginal, rather than anal or oral. Dr. Walker stressed that while the excitement of the vaginal nerves was the foundation of civilized sexuality and women's mental development, the penetration of the anus was "barbarous" (UM, 108). Anal sex "lacerated" inelastic tissue unable to expand to such dimensions. The "filthy unnaturalness of such contact" results in fecal incontinence and the inflammation of women's "whole nerve system," ultimately resulting in "cancer of the bowels" (UM, 107–108). To fully understand the effects of this mode of primitive sexuality, one had only to ponder the "agonized death from inflammation" of Turkish harem boys, who were kept solely "for licentious acts in the rectum" (UM, 14). The anus was a primitive site of flesh, one often ripped apart and popped open. Anal tearing not only resulted in great pain for women, but would also contaminate the impressible tissue of the penis. Feces lodge in "the multitudinous folds" of the rectum, squirreled away from women's dutiful acts of bathing. "This filthiness is absorbed by men and produces a depravity that he cannot throw off" (UM, 108). Anal impressions contaminate the body with "worn-out, effete matter" (UM, 108). In effect, anal sex reverses the potential of impressibility to tenderize the brute material of the body with the vitalizing acts of civilization. It immerses impressible penises in decay, redirecting white men and women toward the path of barbarousness. To guard against this descent, Walker urged that the "proposition" of anal sex should be met with the dissolution of marriage. Its "compulsion" warranted "imprisonment for life"—an early expression of carceral feminism (UM, 108–109). Sexual restraint, rather than anal sex, was the moral method of preventing unwanted pregnancy (UM, 107). Walker revokes the racial attainment of nervous dimorphism most male scientists assigned to the civilized races, which freed men from the consequences of sex. Instead, she stresses that the penis and male body remain impressible neurological tissue that can communicate sympathetically with the rest of the male body and with the nervous systems of all sexual partners.

The mouth is likewise an unsuitable sexual orifice for Walker, its use a "degradation" of which both men and women are guilty. Sexual fluids are "thrown off" because they are "effete" waste materials no longer needed by the thriving body and thus inappropriate for consumption. Furthermore, the face lacks appropriate nervous elasticity. On the "eating of semen" or the "sipping of the exundations of women," she warned, "the whole expression of face is soon so hateful that one is repelled at a glance." Nerve force improperly applied results in odious expression, rather than stimulating impression. The brain deteriorates to the point of "insanity" (*UM*, 111). Walker's use of the language of dining for describing oral sex resonates with Kyla Wazana Tompkins's notion of "queer alimentarity," which denotes a form of nineteenth-century nonnormative eroticism centered on the mouth.[80] Eating, in Tompkins's argument, serves as a key site of sexual and racial formation, a process of self-constitution transpiring at the liminal oral space between the material world and the porous body. In other words, eating serves as a key domain for the sentimental regulation of the impressible body. For Walker, it is precisely the racial and sexual status of civilization that oral and anal sexual acts erode. Impressions involve the affective entering of objects into the body via the perceptual faculty, while excretions are the physical removal of objects of waste, and their strict separation is paramount. Oral and anal sexuality, however, hopelessly amalgamate the vital and the fetid.

Walker thereby illuminates the three-orifice hierarchy nested within the two-sex model of the civilized body. The vagina, under ideal conditions of inheritance, is properly elastic, lingual, potent, and sanguine. In contrast, the anus is unpliable, preverbal, weak, and feculent, conditions that abjure the attainment of civilized sexuality.[81] The mouth, designated as an organ of sensory impression, must be protected from the waste of sexual excretion. The contrast Walker draws between the elastic vagina and the rigid anus—an area altogether flesh, with no vitiating powers—replicates the hierarchy between the delicate civilized vagina, the location of white womanhood, and hardy primitive genitalia. Walker's formulation presages the AIDS discourse of the 1980s, in which the biology of anal intercourse foretold death. Scientists and journalists alike accounted for the virus's spread among gay men on the basis that the "vulnerable anus" and the "fragile urethra" were permeable barriers enabling the entry of pathogens; by contrast, they extolled how the "rugged vagina" withstood viral invasion, making heterosexual transmission unlikely.[82] Into the twentieth century, the vagina retained its role as the only vestibular space proper to civilized sexuality, as the condensation of sexual and racial health. These constructions crystallize the governmentality of the orifice, a biopolitical technology with considerable staying power.

For Walker, white men's sexual immorality could degenerate the civilized race's achievement of the sexually differentiated body. Drawing on patients from her own practice, Walker's illustrated chapter "Hermaphrodites" depicts

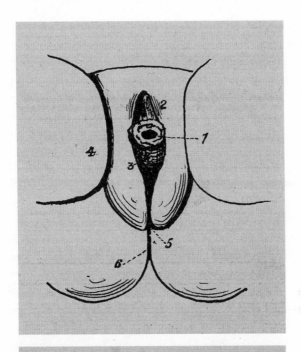

1. Internal labia and clitoris forming a defective penis.
2. External labia.
3. Lower part of the malformation.
4. Leg.
5. Where vagina should be.
6. Where the anus should be.

FIGS. 3.3 AND 3.4. "Hermaphrodite."
"1. Internal labia and clitoris forming a defective penis. 2. External labia.
3. Lower part of the malformation. 4. Leg. 5. Where vagina should be.
6. Where the anus should be." From Mary Walker, *Unmasked,
or, The Science of Immorality. To Gentlemen*
(New York: Wm. H. Boyd, 1878).

the physiological consequences of men's maltreatment of their wives. The chapter is the first known medical account of hermaphroditism published by a woman.[83] Walker explains that the fervent wishes of the abused wife to protect her future child can form mental impressions that transpire in her fetus in the form of "defects" (*UM*, 33). Children have been born to her patients who possess labia and a "clitoris forming a defective penis," yet are "utterly devoid of" the apertures of vagina or anus (*UM*, 36, 38). In Walker's account of racial atavism, white men's sexual vice undoes the two-sex model that characterizes the civilized races, resulting in atavistic offspring that are sexually indistinguishable and thoroughly impenetrable. For Walker, such debilities were "but legitimate results of abuse of either or both soul and body," evidence for all to see of the violation of natural law (*UM*, 32). "Nature," she opines, "has strange freaks in her efforts to enforce her law of the rights of woman to her own person" (*UM*, 81). In this stark image of the privatizing discipline inherent to the sentimental politics of life, the body's most private parts enact punishment in the absence of state action to protect what Louise Newman has aptly termed "white women's rights."[84] We might also think of Walker's account of intersex bodies as the product of women's sexual abuse as an early expression of cis women's rights, or the identification of genitalia as the location of not only female, but also feminist, subjectivity.

Womanhood emerges in the mid-nineteenth century as a political category of rights and a social subjectivity rooted in normative genitalia in contradistinction to the undifferentiated state of flesh, whether racialized and/ or intersex.[85] Genitalia are key among the body parts activated by biopower as dense sites of subjectivity. As the editors of a journal's special issue on viscerality have recently put it, biopower and colonialism engender "systems of meaning that have lodged in the gut."[86] Biopower activates the biological body down to the folds of the entrails, wrapping them within "logics of desire, consumption, disgust, health, disease, belonging, and displacement that are implicit in colonial and postcolonial relations."[87] Similarly, the identification of woman with the vaginal structure represents a site of biopolitical subjectivation, a form of biological materiality that nonetheless cannot exist before or outside power.[88] Biopolitics is waged within somatic materiality, and the capacities and appearance of the sexual organs ensure the vitality of some families, while others are relegated to illness, disability, impermeability, and death. In this context, woman emerges as a biopolitical subjectivity governed by the hierarchy of the orifice. The open, impressible vagina literalizes the status of sex and race difference as relational phenomena in the era before genetics—as a compendium of interactions, trapped in the folds.

Sexual differentiation marked not only a present physiological state but also the condensation of vital energies gathered over evolutionary time. In the dominant view, some species, races, and individuals lacked such energy, having drained it in profligate sexuality that failed to leave beneficial mental traces. Walker's account of the primitivity of her intersex patients anticipates the work of biologists Patrick Geddes and J. Arthur Thompson, who survey sexual differentiation in plants and animals in *The Evolution of Sex* (1889). They conclude that "hermaphroditism is the primitive condition, and the cases now existing either represent persistence or reversion," finding its "most abundant expression in sluggish and fixed animals," particularly parasites.[89] Parasites, living organisms that nonetheless lack the basic vitality to independently sustain their own life, typify the hermaphroditic condition of flesh. It is marked by stasis, by the inability to move forward through developmental stages reached by more advanced organisms.

By contrast, impressibility connotes plasticity and vitality, an active internal energetic force that enables the enfolded constitution of the self through its collisions with other bodies and objects over time. In this regard, nervous impressibility bears striking resemblances to current theories of affect. This scholarship portrays affect as an autonomic intensity of the body that exceeds the boundaries of the subject and a physicality alive to the world in which it is immersed that is itself constituted by the effects of its interactions. As the editors of *The Affect Theory Reader* put it, "Affect arises . . . in the capacities to act and be acted upon. . . . Affect is found in those intensities that pass body to body (human, nonhuman, part-body and otherwise), in those resonances that circulate about, between and sometimes stick to bodies and worlds, *and* in the very passages or variations between these intensities and resonances themselves."[90] Impressibility names a particular biopolitical affect regime, one that determines a body and race's viability on the basis of its receptivity to the circulation of influences out of which the individual and the species body accumulate layer by layer. Impressibility, in fact, is an unacknowledged kernel of contemporary theoretical interest in the vitality, plasticity, and affectivity of matter.

Impressibility signifies a body attuned to the vital forces circulating between and among bodies along the network of nerves that proceeds independently of the individual. Impressible nerves communicate directly with one another, establishing links both within the same human body and across corporeal boundaries even as, in the words of one nineteenth-century neurologist, "the mind is altogether unconscious."[91] In the nineteenth century, the brain was not the central seat of the nervous system that directed all its movements. Rather, ganglions of nerves throughout the body were thought to dispatch and process stimuli and form their own responses and attachments via a "sympathetic nervous link" with the body's organs.[92] The peripheral nervous system was characterized by a distributed consciousness that independently engaged in acts of movement, communication, and affiliation, such that "there were, in effect, many 'small brains' in the cerebrospinal nervous system."[93] In her feminist account of evolutionary nerve force, Antoinette Brown Blackwell surmised that women possess a highly specialized nervous system on account of their advanced reproductive functions, such that "there is more than one nervous plexus well developed in adult females. The brain is not, and cannot be, the sole or complete organ of thought and feeling."[94] Walker and Blackwell conceived of the vagina as the key additional nerve reticulation that enabled affective connections.

For Walker, that affectivity took the form of genital communication between the bifurcated sexes that surpassed the central nervous system's capacity of language. "The world is not large enough to get away from the great law of the language of the nerves," she cautioned men; the "nerves of the organs of sex, are wonderful knowing and have a wonderful power of *telling* before the brain does, and have power superior to the organs of speech in communicating" (UM, 46). Married couples learn of the "acts and motives" of their partner through affective genital-to-genital nervous transmission that circumvents the cerebrospinal axis (UM, 46). A direct sympathetic link between the uterus of a woman and the stomach of a man ensured that "morning sickness in men" was a widespread phenomenon resulting from men's immoral sex with their pregnant wives (UM, 48). Yet the vagina communicated most of all. "There cannot be a louder call than is made with the nerves of the vagina," Walker instructed, which is "intensified with menstrual flow that every month gives [them] new power" (UM, 73). Men must learn to comprehend and yield to its language at their own peril. The sentimental politics of life served as a mechanism to regulate the affective forces aggregating transgenerationally among the network of nerves, and for Walker, the vagina was its instrument.

Genitals are nervous conduits linked to the circulation of impressions throughout a milieu and throughout the epochal time of species-being that forges the population. Sex thereby immersed the impressible nervous system in intimate contact with not only the body of another, but with all the vital forces circulating within them. Walker insisted that white men, too, possess highly impressible genitalia that absorbs and transmits their sexual acts. Vital forces received from their lovers "become so much a part of him as are his feet or any other part," such that, regardless of provenance, "their children will inherit the traits and often the looks of their mistresses" (UM, 24, 25). Wives who can "*never* reach a perfection of orgasm" can be sure that the cause is due to their husbands' profligacy, which has sapped penile nerves of their magnetic power (UM, 21). Here, Walker intervened directly in an ongoing medical debate about women's capacity for orgasm, not only insisting on its possibility, but positing it as a condition of men's behavior. The opposite could also occur: men's dalliances contaminate wives "through his nerves in his sexual relation with her, impress[ing] her with the idea of indulging in variety also" (UM, 79). In extreme cases, white women will have sex with their male Chinese servants because their husbands have affectively stimulated primitive appetites (UM, 94). In gothic imagery that combined the circulation of nervous affect with blood, Walker warned of a philandering husband:

> The very elements of the unchaste, that the husband has gathered up in his former relationship with those unfortunate women, is circulating in the bones and muscles and nerves of his wife . . . and she can never eradicate it from her system. Not only will the children inherit more or less of all these traits, but in thousands of instances have the once pure wives had so much of the prostitute elements or drunken elements pervading their system from the husband inheritance, that they have eventually been overpowered by them. (UM, 26)

Impressible bodies are transformed in whole by the contact of just one part, rendering genital stimulations a risk to the body of the profligate spouse as well as that of all his lovers and any future children. Impressions are durable, transmissible to another person diachronically, as from parent to child, as well as synchronically, as between lovers through the "husband inheritance." For Walker, sperm was forged directly by nervous experience, having "received from the man the wonderful but as yet but partially understood impress upon the nerve centers, that time can never eradicate" (UM, 25). In the decades during the gradual consolidation of modern sexuality, hereditary material was understood to circulate broadly and diffusely throughout a milieu as precipitated feeling. Receptivity and porosity to affects, in this earlier epoch of biopower, served as the mechanisms of racial formation.

Heredity functioned along similar lines to how scholars write of affect today—not as a property of the body, but the materialization of contact within the fold. "Affect does not reside in an object or sign, but is an effect of the circulation between objects and signs," one that "sticks" to bodies, Sara Ahmed writes.[95] Yet biopower crafts its fatal hierarchies precisely by determining race and sex as a measure of relative stickiness. For many, the stickiest subject was the white woman. Educator and psychologist G. Stanley Hall stressed that woman's "whole soul, conscious and unconscious, is best conceived as a magnificent organ of heredity," rendering her the instrument of the racial future.[96] Impressibility may not distinguish between sensation, emotion, and thought—a condition Ahmed ascribes to affect as one of its theoretical assets—but it relies on a more fundamental logic of racial distinction that distinguishes the affectable body from the primitive body, which is benumbed in flesh. Impressibility regimes position vitality and affectivity as the exclusive guarded property of evolutionary whiteness, one that depends on sexual differentiation to maintain. In this light we can fully appreciate the tremendous importance of hygiene for self-identified Christian physiologists like Blackwell and nineteenth-century medicine more broadly: it is a discipline of the civilized body that could, in Blackwell's words, "counteract the evil influence of heredity" by policing its sensory contact.[97] By and large, new ontologies of affect, vitality, and materiality have neglected to engage with the genealogy of its central concepts within the biopolitical logic of racial and sexual differentiation, a methodological commitment that has shaped the overwhelming whiteness and, for some, apoliticization of the field. Yet we need to know how vitality and affectivity were themselves the stuff of heredity and racialization in order to dismantle, rather than unknowingly recapitulate, racial thought. This genealogy and ontology of affectivity is what impressibility paradigms offer contemporary affect theory.

HANDMAIDENS OF HEREDITY

Walker and Blackwell's vaginal vitalisms pose further connections to contemporary theoretical and political paradigms if we continue to plumb the implications of affective heredity. Hereditary transmission in this pregenetic epoch was not restricted to parental transmission before birth. Walker attested that sexual partners exchange hereditary material directly between one another. Heredity, she argued, is not only an inborn condition but also the precipitation of erotic contact throughout civilization. Impressibility required strict technologies of discipline in part because it granted fertile roles far outside the genetic lineage of direct descent. Its path of hereditary transmission encompassed the objects, animals, and peoples of the household, neighborhood, and community. Impressions are remains of momentary contact, preserved for posterity. Any external circumstances affecting an impressible nervous system contain an element of progeniture. The impressible body thus opened up space for a range of relationships outside of parentage to fall within the domain of the regenerative.

In impressibility theory, causation takes many forms. In the 1730s, David Hume expanded on Locke's theory of development via the impression, elaborating the notion of sensory impression into a theory of mental development. Sensory stimulation, resulting from a sensory organ coming into contact with an object or from "internal sensations," makes a second impression on the brain, which we refer to as an idea. Hume proposes that causation results not only when one idea "is the cause of the existence" of another, but also when the content of the idea "is the cause of any of the actions or motions of the other." The mind copies impressions of objects, transforming them into ideas, and it matters little whether the original source of the impressing sensation was a newly encountered object in the world or an idea already produced by a prior encounter. The key framework here is not the logic of temporality—which impression first created the idea—but that of contact, the act of one object making a trace on another. Furthermore, the power of motivating the action of another has the same result as the direct compulsion of that action. This causal logic of impressions is "the source of all the relations of interest and duty, by which men influence each other in society, and are placed in the ties of government and subordination." Social authority results from the power one class possesses over others to motivate their movement, through the mere "exertion of the will," often absent of applied force.[98] Power, for Hume, is the capacity to produce impressions through discourse, regardless of embodied action.

In the terms of relationality outlined by Hume, the practice of medicine could thereby maintain a causal relationship to racial health, for it directly produces "improved" generations, whether or not physicians reproduce themselves. Along these lines, Elizabeth Blackwell explained that the "medical profession" has a "special and weighty responsibility . . . to watch over the cradle of the race; to see that human beings are well born, well nourished, and well educated. The onward impulse to this great work would seem to be especially incumbent upon women physicians."[99] Women doctors who trained and cared for hundreds of families could more successfully impress the next generation than if their efforts were confined to their own domestic hearth. "These spiritual mothers of the race," she explained, "are often more truly incarnations of the grand maternal life, than those who are technically mothers in the lower physical sense."[100] Women physicians not only ensure that the traits of civilization will be transmitted to future generations, but have themselves escaped the material, embodied nature of reproductive motherhood. They are the mothers of the population, regulating the vital forces circulating among civilized biology as a whole.[101] To be sure, the hospital Blackwell and her sister Dr. Emily Blackwell established provided urgently needed medical attention to poor immigrant women, a group otherwise completely unserved in New York City. But Elizabeth, little interested in clinical work, soon devoted herself to writing the rhetoric of reform from her position of authority. Impressibility held either act to be generative.

Elizabeth and Emily argued that while the affective relations of women's "social intercourse" are "a very limited thing in a half civilized country," they "become in our centres of civilization a great power, establishing customs more binding than laws, imposing habits and stamping opinions, a tribunal from whose judgment there is hardly an appeal."[102] In their adaptation of Humean logic, the influence wielded by civilized women was capable of "stamping" vast urban populations through the medium of their "judgment" alone. They cleverly challenged the tenet of civilization theory that understood the chief proof of full sexual differentiation among a people to be women's complete exemption from labor.[103] Women were defined as the nonproductive, but early women doctors reworked the underlying logic of development to argue that white women's position at the helm of civilization ensured that their influence was in fact the work of racial production.

In outlining these eugenic goals, Elizabeth Blackwell was far more prolific than Mary Walker. For Blackwell, marriage must be formed of partners of equivalent age, race, virtue, "tastes and desires."[104] Disease disqualified an individual from matrimony; a couple in which both possess the risk of consumption or insanity "should be forbidden by law to intermarry, for the offspring are certain to be either idiots, cripples, or defective."[105] Just as the chronobiopolitics of civilization required the unfolding of sex after the youthful period of heightened impressibility has been passed, civilized adulthood was marked by an optimum period for reproduction. Blackwell deemed that men should not have intercourse before the age of twenty-five, but should father children by thirty. Blackwell and Walker's efforts to shore up the sexual health of the U.S. and British populations—in contrast to what they saw as the sexual barbarism of colonial India and the Middle East—worked to legitimate their unusual personal desires and professional ambitions. In Blackwell and Walker's rendering of the sentimental politics of life, the imperative of managing both the vertical and horizontal forms of hereditary transmission helped to justify new social roles for and between women.

Impressibility theory presents an intriguing perspective on queer history, opening up the possibility that nineteenth-century unmarried white women, including same-sex couples, could position themselves within the ranks of civilized sexuality. In the period ranging from Blackwell's graduation from Geneva Medical College in 1849 to 1930, nearly 70 percent of female physicians never married, and a significant portion had long-term relationships with female partners.[106] Blackwell elected to pursue medicine out of sheer ambition and as a way to stave off marriage, and eventually took in an orphaned girl, Kitty, as both servant and child to combat her loneliness.[107] Numerous other trailblazing early women physicians partnered among themselves, including Elizabeth's sister, Dr. Emily Blackwell, who lived with the gynecologist and surgeon Dr. Elizabeth Cushier for nearly thirty years, raising an adopted daughter together.[108] These relationships are key examples of the "Boston marriages" that united professional New England women in the late nineteenth century in domestic intimacy.[109] Walker, for her part, commandeered a visibly queer presence. Walker would brag of multiple arrests by New York City police for donning masculine attire; her dress outfit often included wing collar, bow tie, top hat, and tails.[110] Yet within the sensory regime of the sentimental politics of life, these queer desires, even if they seemingly challenged the logic of sexual differentiation, could contribute to civilized sexuality. Impressibility enabled Walker and the Blackwell sisters to explicitly argue that their professional work was productive of civilization. Implicitly, impressibility reconciles Walker's biopolitical moralizing with her exceedingly unconventional sexed presentation and perhaps romantic choices.[111] Having located feminine subjectivity securely in the vagina, Walker was free to modify her outward appearance in masculine fashion. Perhaps impressibility even legitimated Walker's masculine presentation as a choice enabled by a plastic and agential body, malleable to reformers' pursuit of progress and escape from what Walker denounced as "woman's ever changing, extravagant, licentious, debilitating, diseasing, immoral doll-baby dress" (UM, 106). Women physicians could leave their reformers' mark on the immoral habits imperiling civilized sexuality through the transitive properties of nerve power and heredity, without themselves embarking on the sticky relations of marriage and parenting. The impressibility of the civilized constitution and the perceived necessity of its careful protection thus enabled these doctors to frame themselves as generative and reproductive members of civilization, despite their unconventional domestic and professional lives.

The impressible body was deemed to have achieved an evolutionary stage of such plasticity that it was capable of generating more evolved forms of embodiment. "Humankind may be divided into three groups," quipped Sir William Osler, founder of Johns Hopkins Medical School: "men, women, and women physicians."[112] Osler's retort was clearly meant as an insult, though it could just as easily have been interpreted as evidence of female doctors' further specialization. As with the movement of time more generally in the era of recapitulation theory, progress often transpired recursively. For many, racial evolution promised that the continued development of Anglo-Saxons would eventually arrive at the beginning: the original forms of Adam and Eve.

FIG. 3.5. Dr. Mary Walker and unknown person, circa 1910. Legacy
Center Archives, Drexel University College of Medicine, Philadelphia.

The ultimate progression, the culmination of the circular chronobiopolitics of civilization, was to assume anew the harmonic perfection of the Garden of Eden, right on U.S. soil. To that end, Elizabeth looked backward, prior to the age of corrupting modernity, to Germanic legends of the prowess of the Teutonic peoples for models of the civilized womanhood of the future. She happily reports that their legendary foremothers "grew up in wild freedom," where they were prohibited from early marriage and demanded mature husbands as warlike as themselves. The robust wife of a duke "could crack nuts with her fingers, and drive a nail into a wall with her hand, as far as others with a hammer."[113] Another woman "bound her offending lover with her girdle, and slung him to a beam of the ceiling," a tale that occasions her to mourn women's loss of "stout virtue," as well as "the failure of our bodily powers."[114] Accounts of women who breakfasted on rounds of ale, quarts of wine, and enormous slabs of beef strike Blackwell's envy for their profound digestive muscle. Following Tompkins, we could surmise that what Blackwell envisions here are women whose bodily sovereignty entails the satisfaction of their appetites, both sexual and gustatory. Like other female figures in the sentimental politics of life, Blackwell envisions that working toward the racial health of the population by moderating its sexual activity would eventually reap gratifying physical pleasures for civilized women. For Blackwell, womanhood was an embodied and sexualized subjectivity, one born of generations of racial evolution.

Drs. Blackwell and Walker's efforts to elucidate the vitality of white women's sexuality and their own professional labors in contrast to the corruption, disease, and death of the primitive suggests the aptness of viewing their careers within the frame of presexology homonationalism, one in which the impressibility and expansiveness of civilized sexuality made room for generative desires between white women of means.[115] Sex differentiation could abet same-sex relationships—indeed, it underwrites the very concept—not only consign them to the primitive. Before the racial determinisms that scholar Siobhan Somerville argues were productive of the sciences of homosexuality at the turn of the century, the plasticity, vitality, and porosity of civilization opened up space for women's queer sexual agency—as both celibacy and partnership—within the frame of biopower.[116] As Morgensen emphasizes, the settler colonial biopolitics of modern sexuality conditions the emergence of queer social formations in the United States.[117] Blackwell and Walker's efforts to expand the strictures of civilized sexuality to include the pleasures and volition of white women by enlisting the logic of neurological impressibility played out within this context and the ramping up of the United States' overseas imperial projects, as well as the expansion of the British empire following the acquisition of the Suez Canal in 1869. Whereas they understood the savage to be unable to move through time—to be stuck in the wrong orifices, rather than pliable and sticky—civilization had progressed to the point that white woman's influence in Anglo America held the powers of regeneration. The racial history of sexuality was a pathway for white women's political agency and the cisnormative logic that women's subjectivity was intimately linked with genital morphology.

THE RACIAL HISTORY OF SEXUALITY

In Walker and Blackwell's writings on sexuality and the vagina, we can see the endpoint of the sentimental politics of life for many women reformers: impressibility could be used as a wholesale defense of white women's physiological, sexual, mental, and emotional capacities. Wielding the white woman's vagina as a biopolitical instrument, the doctors Blackwell and Walker argued that the neurobiology of progress culminated within its folds. Whereas contemporary physicians such as Edward Hammond Clarke infamously declared that the anatomy of the civilized woman rendered her advanced education inadvisable, for mental exertion redirected blood flow from the uterus and caused irreparable damage, Walker and Blackwell saw her body as the culmination of racial potential.[118] Stressing the impressibility of the vagina, Walker and Blackwell insisted that civilization depended on women's ability to regulate its use. For Blackwell, it was natural law that put women in the seat of civilized sexuality: "Through the guidance of sexual intercourse by the law of the female constitution, the increase of the race will be in accordance with reason, and our highest welfare."[119] For Walker, on the other hand, the health of civilization depended on women's rights, specifically "*woman always having supreme control of her person*, as regards an invasion by men" (*UM*, 145). Both physicians interpreted the belief that civilized women possessed heightened impressibility to underscore the biological imperatives of moral sexuality, but this entailed that sex be determined by women's organic rhythms rather than the desires of men.

But there is also a much larger point here. Civilization named the apex of hereditary malleability, dynamism, and porosity, conditions of susceptibility regulated over generations by women's advanced faculty of feeling. Biopower depends on the governmentality of the orifice: in particular, the portion of the population designated female must embrace their appointed role as preeminent vectors of the plasticity, absorptiveness, and vitality of whiteness, capacities located in the vaginal nerves.[120] Within this paradigm, the woman's body could be interpreted as so thoroughly endowed with vitality and race-building affective reception and transmission that space opened up for white women's social, sexual, and professional agency. Blackwell and Walker's gyno-neurology itself helped to establish sexual differentiation as a complex of mental, emotional, physiological, anatomical, and racial distinction and to elucidate a politics of women's rights rooted in genitalia-based interpretations of womanhood. Feminism, as the defense of women's political and social rights, works within the racial logics of sex differentiation. In other words, it's not only that "woman" is intersected by multiple other vectors of power that materialize as identity and experience, or that feminism as the politics of women's equality runs roughshod over trans* and other gender-variant folks who don't fall within the narrow confines of the category of woman. More fundamentally, racial power has delineated the notion of woman and its corresponding physical attributes and affective capacities. We are still within this social and intellectual legacy, which plays out in realms as varied as affect theory, white feminisms, the criminal justice system, mainstream gay rights movements, and trans exclusionary radical feminisms. The biopolitics of feeling lives on in the logics of binary sex, racialized gender ideals, and cisnormativity, which equates genital morphology with one's own sexed identity, casting all bodies that live otherwise into the debased realm of unaffectable and condemned flesh.

....

CHAPTER 4

Incremental Life

Biophilanthropy and the Child Migrants
of the Lower East Side

> I have so much trouble with girls I hire, I am almost persuaded if I have
> one to train up in my way from a child, I shall be able to keep them
> awhile.
>
> HARRIET WILSON, *Our Nig* (1859)

When writer and abolitionist Lydia Maria Child visited the infamous Five
Points tenement district in Manhattan's Lower East Side in September 1841,
she likened its ribald atmosphere to that of "an open tomb." The problem
with this tomb was its abundant fertility. She worried particularly about the
young children, the "little *girls*," who were raised in the midst of drunken-
ness, vagrancy, prostitution, and other illicit street trades, who would in turn
proliferate vice into the future.[1] Yet the only avenue she could envision for
interrupting the reproduction of depravity in the country's most notorious
neighborhood was to wish for the millennial return of Christ. Six weeks later,
however, Child briefly flirted with another possible solution. "The greatest
misfortune" of the "squalid little wretches . . . at Five Points," she reported to
her *National Anti-Slavery Standard* readers after a trip to the seaside Long-
Island Farm School for parentless children, "was that they were not orphans."
Consequently, they could not be removed from their pernicious neighborhood
to enjoy the "natural influences" of sea, shore, and matron that made the Farm
School so promising for civilizing indigent youth.[2] While Child remains to
this day one of the most famous proponents of sentimental ideology, when it
came to the tenement poor, parents' claims to their own children presented
obstacles in her vision of urban reform.

In contrast to Child's vision of the social benefits of orphanhood, consider
the pained brevity of recently rediscovered notes that parents pinned to the

swaddling clothes of infants they surrendered to the wicker cradle installed on the East Twelfth Street stoop of the New York Foundling, some three decades later. "This child name is Marie John Dunn—5 days old"; "Child of Mary E. Farmer"; and, devastatingly, a card that reads only, "O Cruel Poverty!"[3] More verbosely: "You can call my precious little darling Bella. She was baptized Nov. 7 in the Catholic Church, I hope she will be happy for it is breaking my heart to part with her but I am not able to see to her."[4] The lives of women and couples whose impoverishment in the aftermath of the city's industrial revolution forced them to relinquish their children to newly established city orphanages are largely untold. Thousands of poverty-stricken parents in the late nineteenth century turned to reform projects that removed children from their parents and neighborhoods, often out of desperation. Parents' stories, unrecoverable, register only as brief impressions on the page, traces of origin, attachment, and mourning that child welfare agencies often did their best to eradicate.[5]

How had Child's wish become reality? In the early 1850s, the young reformer, reverend, and author Charles Loring Brace (1826–1890) moved to New York City, fresh out of seminary, and embarked on a large-scale effort to undertake what Child had only indirectly considered: the orphaning of the children of the Lower East Side. Unlike Child, Brace proved to have no qualms about recruiting tens of thousands of poor immigrant children from their families and neighborhoods in an effort "calculated to redeem these children physically and morally."[6] He removed children from the tenements in order to reduce New York's skyrocketing crime rate, a result of rapid industrialization and its attendant immigration and poverty, and to make immigrant youth useful to the capitalist development of the nation. From the early 1850s until his death in 1890, Brace founded and built the Children's Aid Society (CAS) into the nation's most visible child welfare organization. By 1893, CAS maintained twelve industrial schools that had trained over 100,000 youth and managed over twenty New York lodging houses that had sheltered over 200,000. Nonetheless, the Society's favored project was its Emigration Plan, today best known as the "orphan trains." This landmark initiative migrated nearly 100,000 Irish, German, and Italian American children from Manhattan to serve as laborers in rural homes across the United States between 1854 and 1929 and inspired copycat programs that collectively migrated at least that many more during the same period. That nearly half of the migrated youth still had at least one living parent underscores the degree to which Brace fashioned orphaning as a biopolitical strategy of urban management. In his words, tenement parents' "affection for their children" was an obstacle standing in the way of national prosperity.[7] In this chapter, I take up Brace's child welfare reform work as one of the most dramatic instantiations of the sentimental politics of life, or the regulation of impressions circulating throughout a population via the instruments of disciplinary reform and population regulation.

I argue that the efforts of the Children's Aid Society and similar child migration organizations represent a key deployment of the instrument of *biophilanthropy*, or the elite and middle-class effort to impress a new heritable endowment on the bodies and minds of the children of the poor and otherwise allegedly uncivilized in order to render their labor profitable to the population as a whole.[8] This tactic of incremental life gradually extends the time of life of what Malthus referred to as a "redundant population," targeting bodies deemed undesirable, yet potentially redeemable, on account of their youthful impressibility.[9] Biophilanthropy works via the steady accumulation of impressions that will redirect a class or race from foreordained death and force it to persist, as a newly proletarianized group, for the economic and moral health of the settler colonial project. This could allegedly be achieved through the large-scale migration of children away from their families and out of the tenements, whereby "the change of circumstance, the improved food, the daily moral and mental influences, the effect of regular labor and discipline, and, above all, the power of Religion, awaken the[ir] hidden tendencies to do good . . . while they control and weaken and cause to be forgotten those diseased appetites or extreme passions which these unfortunate creatures inherit directly," effectively rewriting their hereditary material.[10] Reformers set about eradicating family connections. Yet despite these goals, youth and families drew on the services of CAS and similar organizations as part of a centuries-old strategy of labor in which indigent boys and girls contracted with rural families for several-year stints, earning room and board and relieving their poverty-stricken families of the same. Tenement dwellers availed themselves of biopolitical measures as an element of their own schemes to endure the ravages of industrialization. The deployment of the sentimental politics of life was a contested process, and its instruments were solicited for a variety of competing purposes. These include urban reformers' dreams of a city evacuated of, but nonetheless serviced by, the poor, and indigent parents' struggles to survive the vicissitudes of capitalism's uneven development.

The paucity of attention to Lamarckian evolutionary paradigms in Americanist scholarship has obscured the degree to which biopolitics, aimed at managing and optimizing the health of the species, flourished in the nineteenth century under the guise of sentimental and environmentalist approaches like Brace's that were rooted in ideas of the differential plasticity of the individual and the racial body. Biophilanthropy provides a useful corrective to scholarly tendencies that interpret sentimentalism as primarily a discursive event and understand models of biological plasticity as either new or inherently liberatory. Nineteenth-century biopolitics was not restricted to the rigid sciences of racial inequality and evolutionary models enshrining competition as the engine of species change. Rather, biopolitics was more frequently instituted as broad mechanisms of liberal reform premised on the possibility of physical, mental, and moral malleability. Brace summed up how the sentimental treatment of immigrant children would stimulate changes at the racial level of population: "The physical and moral care [of the] young," according to the guiding lights of "sympathy and unselfish benevolence," would provide "all the conditions which Evolution requires to form the perfect race or society."[11] Before the science of genetics positioned heredity as an immutable substrate impervious to influence, and even as racial science insisted that racial groups were constituted by distinct physiological and anatomical difference, heredity was nonetheless commonly understood to be pliable. Heredity had not yet taken shape as a static substance, but materialized first as an indexical one that precipitated out of milieus past and present. Biophilanthropy, a formula for reducing threats to the flourishing of the population by intervening directly in the formation of hereditary material during childhood, thus meets the criteria Francis Galton offered for eugenics: "the science which deals with all influences that improve the inborn qualities of a race."[12] Decades before 1907, when formal eugenics began with the passage of the nation's first sterilization law, reformers dedicated themselves to improving the hereditary material of immigrant groups and thereby inch them toward life through technologies of child welfare management. Outlining a path to racial progress through the transformation of the hereditary material of the poor, the sentimental politics of life thereby inaugurated the practice and culture of eugenic breeding in the United States.

THE INFLUENCES OF CHARLES LORING BRACE

Five months after Lydia Maria Child's trip to Five Points, the youthful Charles Loring Brace listened rapt to the family minister Horace Bushnell. That February evening, Brace confided to his journal the "strange" power of Bushnell's preaching, which had revealed the " 'secret and involuntary influences' " constantly shaping us unawares.[13] "The child looks and listens," Bushnell warned in this famous sermon, "and whatsoever tone of feeling or manner of conduct is displayed around him, sinks into his plastic, passive soul, and becomes a mould of his being ever after."[14] A decade later, freshly graduated from Yale, Brace moved to New York City and soon embarked on an ambitious project to shape the influences of the poor through the orphaning and subsequent emigration of the youth of the Lower East Side.[15] Several years before his death, Brace divulged to a young friend that Bushnell's sermon had "affected my whole life," a life now both celebrated and reviled for child welfare work that has earned Brace recognition as the putative father of foster care in the United States (*L*, 8). Brace sought to enact the theory his own life was proving: that managing the impressions of youth could shape the destiny of a population.

Charles Loring Brace sought to secure the health and safety of New York City by transforming the hereditary material of immigrants on the peripheries of the legal economy, a biopolitical goal that is at once far more chillingly calculating and wildly optimistic than current scholarship has recognized. Despite the long-term significance of Brace's work and his prolific publishing career in a variety of genres, which provides researchers with rich source material, scholars have overwhelmingly distilled the range of questions provoked by Brace's work into one hotly contested debate.[16] One side of this argument identifies Brace as a paradigmatic example of reformers' attempts to gain social control over the laboring classes by managing multiple aspects of their daily lives and relationships. The other praises his work initiating the orphan trains as an enlightened innovation in the care of needy, dependent children, on account of his forward-thinking recognition of street children as capable of humanitarian rehabilitation.[17] By contrast, I place Brace's child welfare efforts in the context of his own writings in the fields of ethnology, evolutionary theory, and domesticity, and within the larger framework of sentimental biopower. This perspective reveals that Brace's efforts to remove children from their urban, immigrant families were not designed merely for the benefit of the children themselves, any more than they were calculated primarily to serve present employers.[18] Rather, these two allegedly competing goals—to satisfy the capitalist class's demands for cheap labor and to provide the conditions for the sentimental transformation of the street vagrant into domestic laborer—are part and parcel of the sentimental politics of life paradigm.

Multiple trajectories of the sentimental politics of life converge in Brace's own biography. Brace moved within an elite network of family, friends, and acquaintances that enabled him to be at the forefront of Protestant theology (he was raised Calvinist and later worked for a Methodist mission in Five Points), evolutionary science, impressibility discourse, and social reform. Cousin to Harriet Beecher Stowe and Catharine and Henry Ward Beecher, Brace's relationships to the Beechers were strengthened by family connections on both his maternal and paternal sides. Another cousin was married to Asa Gray, the nation's most prominent botanist, which enabled Brace to become one of the first handful of people in the United States to read *On the Origin of Species*, just a month after its November 1859 publication.[19] At a meeting of the Transcendentalists in Concord a week after Brace read *Origin* during a Christmas visit with the Grays, it was Brace who first told Henry David Thoreau, Bronson Alcott, and the others gathered there of Darwin's theory of evolution, a theory that would profoundly shape their future work.[20] Through Gray's connections, Brace's study of evolution culminated with a visit to both Darwin and prominent geologist and naturalist Charles Lyell in England.[21] These family connections underwrote Brace's work at the fruitful intersections of sentimentalism and science.

When Brace moved to New York City in 1851, he arrived at an auspicious moment in the development of U.S. biopolitics. A range of government and nongovernment actors increasingly understood the residents of a region as forming a population, which denoted not only an administrative unit, but also a set of organic phenomena unto itself. For example, the 1850 census had tracked and tabulated, for the first time, the names of each member of a household, not only its head; rates of mortality, disability, and crime; measures of economic production such as wages, taxes, and real estate value; and social indices such as levels of schooling.[22] This biopolitics of population emerged in the midst of massive industrialization and urbanization, such that New York City seemed to be bursting at the seams as a result of a demographic explosion that increased the city's inhabitants from two hundred thousand to more than eight hundred thousand in just thirty years.[23] A variety of pictorial, literary, journalistic, and criminological accounts produced the crowded, multiethnic tenement districts of Five Points, Cherry Hill, the Bowery, and other neighborhoods of the Lower East Side as symbols of the perils of success. Middle-class culture widely portrayed the tenements as an active source of contagion that threatened not only the southeastern tip of Manhattan, but the health and vitality of the city as a whole.

Police Chief George Matsell had recently whipped up public concern over the danger thousands of children who lived their days and nights in the city's public thoroughfares posed to the emergent middle class, which was struggling to consolidate its power in a rapidly changing economic and political arena.[24] Matsell reported that district captains tabulated nearly three thousand street children engaged in a number of activities that jeopardized the legal economy, including theft at the docks where imported merchandise was unloaded; prostitution, often under the guise of the sale of small objects such as fruit or matchsticks; "Crossing Sweepers" who solicited change; and "Baggage Smashers" who offered to carry the parcels of arriving passengers at railroad stations and ferryboat landings. The actual numbers of children engaged in criminal trades, he advised, far exceeded those who had been officially enumerated. In his perspective, tenement economies violated liberalism's natural laws, troubling the city's claim to civilization. "The degrading and disgusting habits of these almost infants," Matsell continued, made it "humiliating to be compelled to recognize them as a part and portion of the human family."[25] Matsell's 1849 police report had a tremendous impact on Brace's decision to leave the pulpit in order to undertake direct service work with indigent youth (L, 178). Brace, too, saw the city as a population, an organic whole that was best managed by eliminating those elements that threatened its success.[26] Yet while Matsell condemned tenement parents for forsaking their own "blood" and for maintaining the habits of animals, Brace understood the circulation of bodily material to flow not only between parents, but also between all bodies within a milieu. For Brace, the solution to the rates of crime and poverty of immigrant children was therefore a biopolitical one: to work directly on the biology of the uncivilized themselves by altering their environment.

Brace deployed the tactics of sentimental biopower to formulate "the best method of disposing of our pauper and indigent children," thereby securing the health of the city's economy.[27] In the sentimental politics of life, disposal can look like tender care for the European-origin population. After the initial appearance of publicly and privately funded orphanages in the 1820s and 1830s, and the nation's first juvenile reformatory (founded in 1824), a flood of new institutions opened their doors in the 1850s.[28] For Brace, however, asylums "cultivated . . . [one] thousand bad and unnatural habits which grow poisonously" in the hothouse environment of the institutions ("BMD," 5). Instead, Brace implemented the "family system," replacing incarceration with domestic rehabilitation. The system divided youth into small units guided by a firm but caring guardian who would inspire their faith and spirit of individuality and, when necessary, squash their disobedience ("BMD," 10–11). The family is "God's reformatory," argued Brace, and was thus the institution most amenable to eradicating the inherited traits of poverty and viciousness ("BMD," 12). Teachers were instructed to "suppl[y] the link of sympathy" between the Christian classes and the "wolf-reared children" of the streets, an emotional bond that would indebt children to the institution and engender their receptiveness to learning the "habits of order, cleanliness, and punctuality" necessary for their entrance into the workforce.[29] Sympathy served as their chief inoculant, a securitizing force that would counteract existing hereditary traces through hereditary material itself, impressing new heritable traits into the flesh. CAS's work bore "natural fruit," and multiple metaphors of harvest underscore the endeavor's generative function (DC, 142). The Rivington Street Lodging House and industrial school was even decorated with the staples of high Victorian culture's romance with natural history: live and cut flowers, ferns and other plants, an aquarium, and an outdoor garden (see figure 4.1). As this undoubtedly idealized picture suggests, organic embellishments did their best to "tam[e] and refin[e], for the time, the rough

FIG. 4.1. "Poor Children among Flowers." From Charles Loring Brace,
The Dangerous Classes of New York, and Twenty Years' Work among Them
(New York: Wynkoop, 1880).

little subjects who frequented them" (DC, 332). Flowers and plants were
widely understood to provide pious models to children and young women
and functioned as their literary stand-ins. For Brace and many domestic
novelists, flowers represented civilized youth, whereas the children of the
poor were plants in need of careful tending. Their presence in a CAS facility
suggests that this analogy was understood as both figurative and literal.

Brace was able to gain financial support for his efforts to ameliorate "the
mental and physical constitutions" of the "dangerous classes" by manipulating two central tropes of middle-class culture: the threat of mass resistance to
capitalism and the promise of the malleable young orphan.[30] He worried that
the "great masses" of poor mistakenly believe that "capital . . . is the tyrant," a
position that would likely drive them to revolt, as had happened in Paris, Vi-
enna, Bern, and other metropoles in 1848, and threatened to "leave this city
in ashes and blood" (DC, 29). Furthermore, if left untreated, the infractions
of these boys "would not be like the stupid foreign criminal class," he warned,
for "their crimes, when they came to maturity, [will] show the recklessness,
daring, and intensity of the American character" (DC, 321). In Brace's America, even the crimes were exceptional. Brace both whipped up and defused the
danger that tenement children, emblems of increasing economic inequality,
posed to the bourgeoisie by offering a figure of individual transformation. The
exceedingly popular trope of orphanhood in domestic literature generally
framed the white child as malleable, her traits the offspring of environment

rather than parentage. Brace's innovation was to extend the middle-class orphan trope to the children, and especially the male youth, of poverty-stricken Irish and other Western European immigrants.

By the standards of dominant racial thought, the Irish were centuries behind the development of Anglo-Saxons, a primitivity that was both cause and effect of their fixed, rigid natures, which were capable of, if any change at all, only change for the worse. In contrast, Brace framed tenement children as primitive beings who were rapidly becoming plastic, flexible Americans by virtue of their birth and residence in the United States. The Children's Aid Society targeted the children of Irish, German, and to some degree Italian immigrants—and only children from these backgrounds—on account of Brace's belief that new behaviors could be stamped on these children. He virtually excluded African American children and the offspring of immigrants from all other nations, reasoning that such children lacked the requisite malleability for successful reform. Whereas Police Chief Matsell consigned all street children to the irredeemable limits of humanity, Brace identified Irish, German, and Italian children as animalistic subjects of evolutionary time who could be made redeemable through the repetitive movements of labor and the habits of civilization.

IMPRESSIBLE HEREDITY

Brace was one of many reformers in the second half of the nineteenth century who understood impressibility to grant the civilized agency in the process of human evolution. He wrote a particularly thorough account of the biological basis of biophilanthropy, at the heart of which lies Darwin's theory of pangenesis. Brace bragged of having read *On the Origin of Species* thirteen times, and this commitment to evolutionary thought came to supplement his Bushnellian framework of influences that circulate throughout the population with a Darwinian model of species change through environmental influence (*L*, 300). Yet the two models, as understood in the nineteenth century, had considerable overlap, and species change was broadly understood to be plastic in the activating presence of culture.

In *On the Origin of Species,* Darwin relied on the Lamarckian notion of the transmission of acquired characteristics to posit that variations that suddenly appeared in organisms might be found again among their offspring. Lamarck's theory proposes that repeated behavior and environmental influence accumulate impressions that enlarge or atrophy an organ, creating adaptations that descendants inherit. While Darwin merely enlisted Lamarck in *Origin,* a decade later he elaborated his own theory of heredity, pangenesis. For one of the first times in Western science, pangenesis proposed the existence of a discrete biological particle that is transmitted from one generation to the next.[31] Pangenesis offered an explanation of *how* organisms pass on their traits, including acquired characteristics, to offspring. Darwin proposed that each cell contains small units, which he termed "gemmules," that register its significant experiences.[32] In formulating this new substance of heredity he nonetheless continued to borrow from the language and metaphor of the impression, explaining that "it is probable that hardly a change of any kind affects either parent, without some mark being left on the germ . . . like those written on paper with invisible ink."[33] Cells continually produce gemmules, and any modifications wrought by experience are duly replicated in those gemmules produced after the stimulating event. Periodically, gemmules detach from the host and disperse throughout the body. All gemmules, whether in body cells or sex cells, could then be transmitted to offspring, ensuring that modifications in structure experienced anywhere in the organism would make their way to the next generation. Given favorable circumstances, gemmules will express themselves in the immediate offspring. In the absence of a nourishing environment, they will lay dormant for generations, potentially reappearing as an atavistic trait, the invisible ink suddenly apparent once more.[34]

In Brace's hands, gemmules provided the specific mechanism through which environmental influence impresses itself on the bodies of both present and future children, becoming hereditary material. Brace proposed that changing the individual's environment could radically alter an individual's gemmules, which he understood as encapsulating "latent tendencies, or forces" (DC, 43). While the "gemmules" inherited by a tenement prostitute from her similarly employed mother are "working in her blood, producing irresistible effects on her brain, nerves, and mental emotions," reformers could orchestrate other "moral, mental, and physical influences" that would prevent her latent desires from dictating her future (DC, 43, 43–44, 45). Sensation and influence constituted heredity; reformers could impose a new "inherited self-control" (DC, 23). Heredity, in the mid-nineteenth century, indexed a tendency of the environment rather than constituted a fixed lineage, and thus posed the solution to its own dilemma.

The popular notion of Darwinism in the nineteenth century United States— and indeed across the Americas—was notably Lamarckian. While Darwin emphasized that random variation produced most adaptations, which natural selection then put to the test, his nonspecialist contemporaries like Brace largely disregarded the prominent role of haphazard mutation and vigorous competition in species change.[35] They understood habitual tendencies to directly produce individual variation that determines long-term success. This is in contrast to the twentieth-century understanding that natural selection functions as a kind of tribunal that privileges, over time, traits that confer reproductive advantage. Brace summarized: "The races in which there is the highest development of sympathy, of benevolence, of sexual purity, of truth and justice, will tend to be the strongest in body . . . the most prosperous . . . and the most influential on inferior races" (GC, 471–472). Brace and his cousin's husband Asa Gray hotly debated the details of Darwinism, maintaining a sustained dialogue in which the esteemed botanist sought to curb Brace's flights of passion with the more tempered logic of empirical evidence.[36] "When you *unscientific people* take up a scientific principle you are apt to make too much of it," Gray chided after reviewing Brace's manuscript claiming that experiences such as water crossings had profoundly shaped the evolution of the Egyptian "race."[37] Like many others in the settler colonial West, Brace both championed Darwin's theories and interpreted them as much more compatible with the Lamarckian inheritance of acquired characteristics than the English naturalist or his U.S. colleague were willing to affirm.[38]

Lamarckism offered settler colonists the promise of crafting a race anew in their own image, and Brace in fact saw California as just such a place. California, he relishes, is "the land of handsome men. One sees great numbers of fine manly profiles, with full, ruddy cheeks, and tall, vigorous forms."[39] He speculated that in this beneficial climate "a new and powerful community is springing up, and possibly a new race forming."[40] Throughout his writings, he embraced the potential of the western frontier to evolve a new stage in racial supremacy, one that might altogether surpass the taxonomy of the Anglo-Saxon.

Darwin's nineteenth-century readers broadly understood natural selection in Lamarckian terms and set about amplifying conditions that would create beneficial modifications in the population and eliminating contagions in the form of environments and individuals. They understood evolution as a teleological, progressivist process of upward development, enacting what Cynthia Russett has aptly referred to as the era's popular "breeder's model of human evolution . . . whereby small individual differences in populations might be nudged and encouraged in certain directions to make change."[41] Following the 1930s modern evolutionary synthesis, however, which merged population genetics with natural selection, Darwinians came to stress the role of random variation and population pressure, which creates differential rates of reproduction and over time leads to modifications to species. Contemporary Darwinians now understand natural selection and population pressure to be the engine of evolution that renders some random variations useful adaptations that consequently persist in populations and consigns others to the dustbin of history. Natural selection, Elizabeth Grosz explains, functions as an intermediary factor that creates "a time lag, a delay, nick, or dislocation between variation and selection," that is, between the origins of an organic mutation and its relative chances of survival in the species over time.[42] By contrast, reformers like Brace saw themselves as immediately producing new variations in real time and taking selection directly into their own hands.

Brace's work as a scientific popularizer details his substantial interest in advancing the theory that civilization incurred the differential evolution of racial groups over time. In *The Races of the Old World: A Manual of Ethnology* (1863), the abolitionist Brace enlisted his Lamarckian interpretation of Darwinism, in the midst of the Civil War, to prove the monogenist thesis of the shared ancestry of all races on earth to a broad audience.[43] The book's early application of Darwinian evolution—published just three years after *On the Origin of Species*—to the fight against polygenist theories, which saw races as distinct species, largely pivots on environmental theories of species change. He stresses the radical dependence of the individual body on its environment for its form and function and the transmission of acquired characteristics to descendants.[44] Brace cites dramatic physiological amelioration when the colonized and enslaved come to the United States, adaptations acquired "merely by contact with whites and by a state of freedom" (*R*, 372). Like other students of race in the nineteenth century, Brace regarded the body as so unstable that he found the "most enduring token of race" to be language rather than physical difference, a position that retains the eighteenth-century account of racialization as a process of environmental effects rather than innate difference (*R*, 6). Brace nonetheless emphasized drastic divergence between racial groups, postulating that these differences in quality resulted from differential faculties of emotional self-regulation. Peoples not of Northern European descent generally lacked the capacities for self-control, he inveighed, and thus failed to moderate their sensations and acquire judicious modifications. Most likely, this is why CAS restricted participation to Irish, Italian, German, and Jewish youth, the only children whom Brace regarded as worthy biological investments. African Americans "might die out, as the Indian might die out, from the wear and tear and contact from a different and grasping race," Brace claimed, but an increasing capacity for self-control, especially among the Teutonic race, is leading "toward the progress and the final perfection of humanity" (*R*, 490). As Brace exemplifies, many Lamarckians had a sharply bifurcated image of evolutionary progress wherein civilized races ascend into evolutionary perfection and the primitive fade quietly into extinction.[45]

In nineteenth-century evolutionary models, inherited characteristics represent direct effects of a milieu, rather than innate and immutable traits put to the test in different environments. Lamarckians understood the eastern city as a dense, sensory-rich environment that would further mental development, but only among those races that had already developed the faculty of self-control.[46] Life in the city was a constant deluge of impressions, each of which presented the opportunity for further development or degeneration, depending on the individual's regulatory faculty of sentiment. Brace therefore sought to maintain the city for the civilized classes alone. Through his concurrent emigration of tenement children out of the urban center and advocacy of the construction of "suburbs" outside the city for working-class families, Brace promised a city reserved for the wealthy but serviced by the poor—a vision that neoliberal New York City, over a century later, currently undertakes with earnestness (DC, 51–63).

The horrors of twentieth-century racial determinisms have encouraged many scholars over the years to equate frameworks of physiological mutability and flexibility with antiracist agendas. Yet the very insidiousness of sentimental paradigms lies in the license it gives reformers and the state to directly manipulate the biological destiny of the population. Models of the cultural basis of racial difference and the resulting differential malleability of the body, rather than rigid biological determinisms, dominated the liberal imagination of the mid- to late nineteenth century. New administrative technologies of governance that sought to "improve" the hereditary material of the population were born of paradigms of plasticity, rather than determinism. The origins of eugenics, in other words, lie within the heart of the sentimental politics of life, and models of the cultural basis of racial difference are one of nineteenth-century biopower's most salient legacies.

EXILE AND EVOLUTION

The most cherished—and notorious—project CAS undertook was to remove from the city limits altogether any children who resisted the legal economy, in the simultaneous service of the perceived needs of the urban population and the settler colonial nation. Capitalizing on the rhetorical and biological potential of the West, Brace initiated the Emigration Plan in 1854. Until its closure in 1929, the project removed tenement youth from their parents and sent them to live with and work for rural families, where they would allegedly receive a new set of inherited instincts. Brace's chosen nomenclature of emigration, rather than migration, highlights the key mechanism of the project: exile. CAS dispatched trains to the West that made stops in small towns, often those in which they had previously advertised the availability of farmhands from New York. One rider later recalled that she was met at the station by a proxy "for the people who had ordered me. Like a package, I was addressed to my future parents."[47] Most of the children lined up, usually on stage in the town hall, while farmers passed through, often feeling their muscles and teeth to ascertain their suitability for labor. Those who were not absorbed into a family reboarded the train, which continued westward until bereft of child migrants. Migrated children were expected to work in exchange for their room and board between the ages of twelve and eighteen, at which point they were formally permitted to leave the home.

More than 100,000 children were shipped out on CAS's orphan trains over the seventy-five years of the program, and another 150,000 traveled with copycat schemes run by other organizations. Yet of the estimated 100,000 children CAS emigrated, the majority found themselves in upstate New York. The next most frequent destinations were southern states such as Virginia and Arkansas, and then finally the midwestern states, especially Indiana and Illinois. To some degree, then, Brace's mobilization of a romantic settler myth of an empty West that could serve as a "safety valve" for the labor shortages and workers' active organization against capitalist interests in the East did not reflect the migration patterns of many of the placed-out children.[48] Nonetheless, the rhetorical goal persisted. In the last decade of the programs, children were often told that theirs was the only such train car ever sent west, that they had been lucky recipients of a rare opportunity—a lie that is perhaps the culmination of sentimental biopower's technique of discipline through atomization.

Casting his Emigration Plan in settler colonial terms, Brace positioned the West as a space of rejuvenation that would transform his immigrant children into real Americans by bringing them into the service of civilization. Children's rural milieus were orchestrated to overwhelm earlier instincts and characteristics, forcing a new heredity on them. To ensure that migrated children's new milieu was totalizing, CAS forbade migrated children to contact their families or anyone else from their neighborhoods of origin. "The separation of children from parents, of brothers from sisters, and of all from their former localities, destroy[s] that continuity of influence which bad parents and grandparents exert," Brace explained (DC, 57). One rider even bemoaned that agents had pilfered the notecard recording his family's address from his jacket pocket as he slept on the westbound train.[49] Children were prohibited from bringing any items from home, even their own clothing. (Objects have agential value in impressibility schemes, casting off affects that are absorbed by other bodies, and must be regulated accordingly.) Many children nonetheless managed to smuggle small items onboard, remembrances they kept with them for decades after.[50] Biophilanthropy sought to move children incrementally toward useful life by thrusting new hereditary material on them and allowing traces of parental lineage to wither.

While the rhetorical subject of the Emigration Plan was almost uniformly masculine, 39 percent of the children CAS placed out to work were girls.[51] Among the hundreds of thousands of children who participated in the Society's day schools and lodging houses, males were privileged structurally and especially rhetorically. To Brace, girls' heightened vulnerability and penetrability impeded rather than enabled their progress. Bowery girls "inherit an unusual quantity of the human tendencies to evil," were too primitive, and lacked the self-control necessary to resist sexual temptation (DC, 302). Girls "develop body and mind earlier than the boy," therefore "the habits of vagabondism stamped on her in childhood are more difficult to wear off" (DC, 115). Female bodies betrayed the chronobiopolitical time lines of impressibility by reaching nervous fixity and sexual maturity too soon, rendering null reformers' efforts to impress a new layer on them. The results of their trade in the streets were "stamped" on them and left these girls beyond moral or physical redemption, guilty of the betrayal of what should have been their guiding instinct: "the desire of preserving a stock, or even the necessity of perpetuating our race" (DC, 116). Since girls were less capable of absorbing new tendencies after sexual maturity, it was their duty to protect any beneficial hereditary influences that passed through them; women were the conduits of reproductive monogamy. Yet street girls engaged in "crime and lust," and their "lower nature [was] awake long before [the] higher," triggering a degeneration that caused the girl child to "degrade its soul before the maturity of reason, and beyond all human possibility of cleansing!" (DC, 116). As a result, the Children's Aid Society refused to work with any female over the age of twelve on the assumption that she would already be engaged in the sex trade. A prostitute, we may surmise, would be too thoroughly saturated with the impressions of others.

What particularly worried Brace, however, was how difficult it was for even a learned ethnologist such as himself to distinguish those women who were spotlessly navigating the city streets from those plying the oldest profession. The source of endless grief at the Girl's Lodging House was the difficulty of enforcing its plan to prohibit the entry of sex workers, for these young women were masters at casting themselves as the heroines of Brace's own sentimental plot. Brace summarized the paradox earnestly: "Sweet young maidens, whom we guilelessly admitted, and who gave the most touching stories of early bereavement and present loneliness, and whose voices arose in moving hymns of penitence, and whose bright eyes filled with tears under the Sunday exhortation, turned out perhaps the most skillful and thorough-going deceivers, plying their bad trade by day, and filling the minds of their comrades with all sorts of wickedness in the evening" (DC, 306). For Brace, the subjects of his sentimental fiction had a disturbing tendency to come to life, robbing him of his self-appointed creative powers by turning the plot to their own advantage to obtain food and lodging.

By contrast, Brace presented newsboys as promising participants in a fertile homoerotic romance: the generative seeds of new hereditary material. Brace defended newsboys and other male vagrants as "at heart" not "much corrupted; his sins belong to his ignorance and his condition, and are often easily corrected by a radical change of circumstances" (DC, 114). He idealized the newsboys of the Bowery as masters of the entrepreneurial ethos who, when properly trained, captured the best of the American spirit. While street trade exacerbated women's tendencies to licentiousness, in young boys it developed their capacity for wit and cunning, the very roots of the free market system. The Children's Aid Society insisted on receiving payment from its male lodgers as a means of bolstering their entrepreneurial spirit, developing their sense of trust, and forging intimate relations between the children and the society's male agents. Furthermore, the agency set up a small system of savings for the boys to teach them "the desire for accumulation, which, economists tell us, is the base of all civilization."[52] Like many other proponents of capitalism during the Gilded Age, Brace held onto Adam Smith's formulation of trade as a "bond of union and friendship" between men that increases sympathy between individuals and nations.[53] Experiences of masculine camaraderie through market relations were primed to engineer tenement boys who could play a role in capitalist development, rather than threatening its demise.

This sentimental view of the business contract was one of the same qualities that so attracted ex-minister Horatio Alger to the Children's Aid Society in the decades following his dismissal from the pulpit on the grounds of pederasty. Alger wrote several dime novels about the work of the charity, kept both bed and desk at one of the boy's lodging houses, and occasionally took groups of boys home to live in his apartment. As these circumstances suggest, the eroticism and homosociality of street boys was not far below the surface of Alger's or Brace's narratives and behavior. Michael Moon argues that Alger's novels reformulate domestic fiction as a homoerotic male romance that celebrates intimacy between an older man and growing boy as the basic component of capitalist relations.[54] Brace's activities and rhetoric similarly present the market as a homosocial space that produces intimate relations between men, a necessary emotional condition for their upward evolution. Brace's sermons, Moon notes, emphasize boys' longings for an older and wiser male friend to love and support them.[55] This dynamic adds nuance to Brace's assertion that his organization supplies father and brother figures to the young charges. Frequently Brace was eager to cast himself in the fatherly and brotherly role in this masculine romance; he enthused to his sister, "I think there is nothing in the world so interesting as a healthy, manly boy and the attempt to help these fellows to help themselves is the most pleasant to me possible" (*L*, 161). Brace's rhetoric suggests a homoerotic restaging of the brother/father/lover trope germane to sentimental adoption fiction in which the roles of brother/mentor/lover superimpose one another.[56]

Brace's devotion to the young men engaging in the varied street trades, including sex work, of the first bustling gay neighborhood of the United States brings to mind some tantalizing details from his private correspondence.[57] A letter he wrote to a college friend in 1849, soon before departing for a months-long walking tour of the United Kingdom with John and Frederick Law Olmsted, is particularly suggestive of Brace's commitment to homoerotic domesticity: "Yet there is a love of friends, to men, which I have in some degree, and am having more and more, a confidence which cannot *think* of being shaken, earnest desire for their happiness, and a sympathy which possibly is the noblest that exists. . . . And I half believe that the love of two manly hearts to one another, who are struggling hard with evil, may be even a higher type of Love than man's to woman. What do you think? John and I, you know, are together,—a pleasant lodging-house" (*L*, 65).[58] That Brace elsewhere referred to relations between men as "revolting and abhorrent" (*GC*, 36) and claimed that a society that supports it is headed toward "disaster, ruin and death" is perhaps indicative of the "evil" which two men in "love" might be "struggling hard" to resist (*DC*, 116). Though Brace reported to John from Hungary that "the tall, strong, handsome men" there had taught him what "human beauty was," and he confessed that he had "become so used to kissing *men*, that [he] shall hardly know how to kiss a woman," Brace set himself to the act and married Letitia Neill in 1854 (*L*, 133).

At the Children's Aid Society, biophilanthropy constituted a homosocial reproduction in which older men transform the hereditary material of their young charges, thereby reproducing themselves. Impressibility theory rendered same-sex relations fertile, for in the period before modern sexual discourse, heredity was not yet confined to the union of sex cells at conception and materialized instead through habitual contact throughout life. As with the women physicians analyzed in the preceding chapter, same-sex intimacies among the civilized were sometimes understood as conforming to the emerging sexual norms of whiteness and thereby playing a positive role in evolutionary change. Brace interpreted children's malleability as rendering the bond between an older man and younger boy generative, reproductive, and central to the evolutionary advance of U.S. civilization. Heredity solidifies as the effect of intimacy between men. More broadly, biopolitical projects in the age of impressibility to "purify" the nation's heredity did not operate primarily by regulating poor women's fertility, as they did in the wake of genetics. Rather, they enacted a sentimental ethic of reproduction in which reformers brought the children of the poor under their own care. In fact, biophilanthropy often privileged men, over women, as the key motivators of racial evolution, as is similarly the case in the militarized off-reservation boarding schools for Native youth. Designed to improve the racial stock of the settler nation, biophilanthropy attempted to regulate the labors of the poor, a mode that prioritized intimacy between men in the composition of civilized inheritance.

THE CHILD VERSUS THE TROPE

While the Children's Aid Society organized the Emigration Plan to rupture youth's connections to immigrant networks and etch new heritable material into the soma, the indigent and working-class families who enlisted the assistance of placing-out services were motivated by a variety of desires and circumstances, only some of which were shared by CAS itself. In particular, families approached the Emigration Plan as a temporary labor placement service. This goal may have been entirely at odds with reformers' intentions to impress new characteristics into the body, but impoverished families had been sending children to other neighborhoods, towns, and states to work on a seasonal or annual basis for centuries. Such placing out supplied the child with room and board and made room for younger children back at home. The Emigration Plan was thus part of a centuries-long legacy of migratory child labor, yet its particular methodology of exile and evolution presented poor families with new opportunities and pitfalls.

Social historian Clay Gish argues that youth participation in the placing-out program was motivated by the needs of working-class families for temporary labor arrangements. Far from saving children from the brink of suicide, as CAS fundraising appeals invoked, Gish claims that the agency was used by working-class families "as an extension of strategies . . . long employed to ease family turmoil in times of crisis, to strengthen the family economy, and to smooth young people's transition from the home into the world."[59] Drawing on CAS intake and placement records from the beginning of the agency in 1853 until 1890, the year of Brace's death, Gish finds that the average age of participants in the program was far older than the rhetorical subject of CAS promotions, ranging from fourteen to seventeen years of age. Furthermore, his sample reveals that a full one-half of the youths came to the agency as a means to enter the labor force, sometimes with a parent, rather than being rescued from broken-down hovels by aid workers. The records reveal that "the vast majority of young people in the emigration program chose an employment arrangement rather than a familial relationship" with their hosts and frequently left for new situations within the first year.[60] Most surprisingly, given the entire absence of working-class family relations in Brace's writings or agency publications, more than one-half of youth who migrated were accompanied by their families. This picture of working-class self-determination differs strikingly from the sentimental, eroticized portraits of dependence and discipline painted by Brace.

A heart-wrenching record of the circumstances under which some children arrived under the auspices of Manhattan's children welfare organizations and placing-out programs currently resides in the New-York Historical Society Archives. Four leather-bound memo books, only recently rediscovered, collect notes and letters found affixed to the clothes of infants dropped off in the plain wicker cradle waiting on the front steps of the New York Foundling.[61] The Foundling placed out tens of thousands of children in its own emigration program, initially called "the baby train," in the wake of Brace's success. The notes provide a glimpse into the lives of women and men forced to, or who opted to, surrender their infants and toddlers to urban orphanages and western households. The Foundling's ledger books record 2,457 children left on the doorstep in their first two years of operation alone, a statistic evoking the dire need for child welfare services.[62]

The vast majority of the pinned notes—some of which still retain the perforations made 150 years ago—contain the child's name, and many give a birthdate. Among a good number, the child's name stands alone. Others record a baptism. Many parents list small means of support included for the child in the form of money and clothing; others issue promises to do so tomorrow, in a week, in the future. These vows linger in the century and a half separating their author and the reader. For all their detail, these specific pledges of support resonate not as commitments, but as fervent wishes for circumstances to be anything but what they are. Some notes stipulate that the child's residency at the Foundling will be only temporary, directives that may or may not have been respected by staff. Others hope the notes will serve as a form of identification when they come to reclaim their child as their circumstances improve. For example, one letter from November 9, 1869, the Foundling's first year, reads: "This little boy was born on Oct. 31; his father is a worthless man and his mother not being able to support herself and the child is obliged to give him to the kind care of Sister Irene until she is better able to support him. He will be called for again and the person that comes for him must have the piece of paper to harmonize with this. He was named Frankie. [Signed,] his mother." Simultaneously a contract for his future retrieval and a formal relinquishment of any claim over the infant's life—"he *was* named Frankie,"

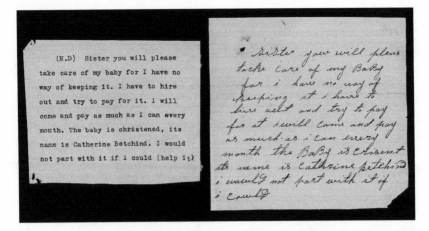

FIG. 4.2. "Sister you will please take care of my baby for I have no way of keeping it I have to hire out and try to pay for it I will come and pay as much as I can every month the baby is Christened its name is Catherine Betchind I would not part with it if I could[.]"
Note found pinned to infant left at the doorstep of the New York Foundling. From the Records of the New York Foundling Hospital, 1869–2009, MS 347, New-York Historical Society.

the use of the third person to describe herself—the words linger in the tension of mitigating circumstances. Some mothers plead forgiveness; other notes are authored by priests or police, relaying the circumstances under which the child came under their care, frequently in terms replete with bourgeois scolding. Some notes take pains to list the names of the child's mother, father, or both, while others wish to leave no familial trace. More than a few betray clear anxiety about the child's origins, insisting that the child is not "low," "degraded," or "illegitimate." Others testify to sheer fear of men's power over women's lives: "I am willing to give it up on account of my father. If I should keep it, he would kill me. This note is carried by my mother. Mary Fitzsoming."[63] Taken together, the notes are an evocative archive of feelings and histories largely left unrecorded, of origins and intimacies that biopolitical agencies took as their primary task to eradicate.

The children who left the city to take up washing, sewing, plowing, cooking, delivering, cleaning, tending livestock, raising younger children, and other tasks of the homestead obtained access to these situations. Families were instructed to send the children to basic schooling. Yet CAS provided very little oversight of the placements they arranged. Agents corresponded with the children or families once a year to inquire about their situation. More seldom, they conducted home visits. In effect, children were entirely at the

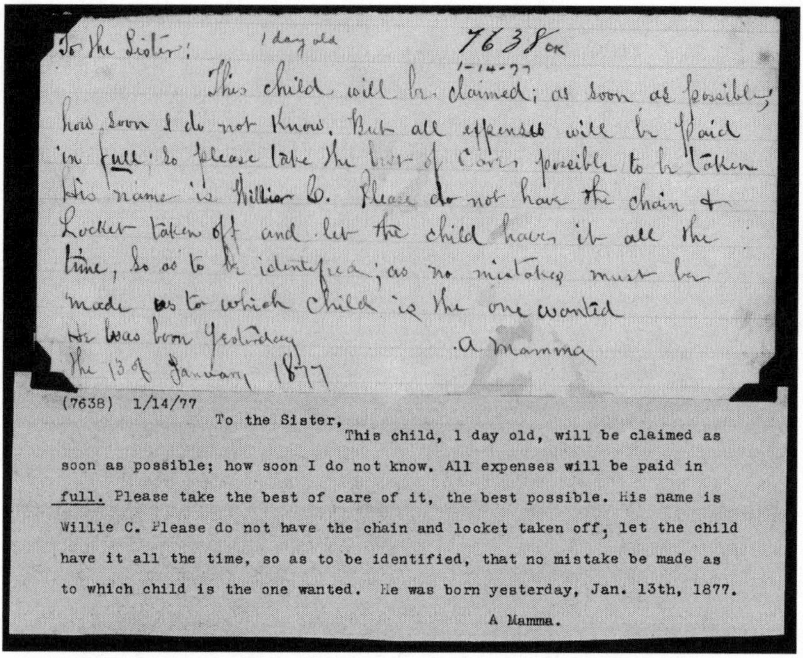

To the Sister: 1 day old 7638 ok
1-14-77
This child will be claimed; as soon as possible; how soon I do not know. But all expenses will be paid in full; so please take the best of care possible to be taken His name is Willie C. Please do not have the chain & Locket taken off and let the child have it all the time, so as to be identified; as no mistakes must be made as to which child is the one wanted
He was born Yesterday
The 13 of January 1877
A mamma

(7638) 1/14/77
To the Sister,
This child, 1 day old, will be claimed as soon as possible; how soon I do not know. All expenses will be paid in full. Please take the best of care of it, the best possible. His name is Willie C. Please do not have the chain and locket taken off, let the child have it all the time, so as to be identified, that no mistake be made as to which child is the one wanted. He was born yesterday, Jan. 13th, 1877.
A Mamma.

FIG. 4.3. "To the Sister: This child will be claimed; as soon as possible; how soon I do not know. But all expenses will be paid in *full*; so please take the best of care possible to be taken. His name is Willie C. Please do not have the chain & locket taken off and let the child have it all the time, so as to be identified; as no mistakes must be made as to which child is the one wanted. He was born yesterday, the 13 of January, 1877. A mamma." Note found pinned to infant left at the doorstep of the New York Foundling. From the Records of the New York Foundling Hospital, 1869–2009, MS 347, New-York Historical Society.

mercy of their new employers and families.[64] The oral histories of the last generation of orphan train riders, collected by family members and community activists when the programs came to broad attention in the late twentieth and early twenty-first century, are rife with accounts of malnourishment; overwork; and emotional, sexual, and physical abuse, as well as pointed silences that suggest some miseries are still too painful to articulate. Historians have estimated that as a consequence of the negligent management of the placing out of agency youth, more than half of the children were housed in homes where they were overworked, abused, and extremely unhappy.[65] Tales of running away and other resistance fill oral histories of orphan train riders, suggesting some of the ways that indigent youth negotiated a system that was

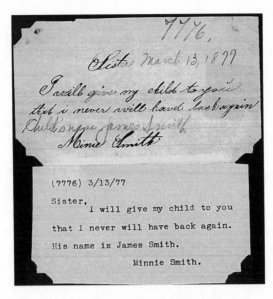

FIG. 4.4. "Sister, I will give my child to you
that I never will have back again, Minnie Smith."
Note found pinned to infant left at the doorstep of the New York
Foundling. From the Records of the New York Foundling Hospital,
1869–2009, MS 347, New-York Historical Society.

designed to rupture their connections and institute new behaviors according to their own terms.

Marguerite Thompson, a 1911 New York Foundling rider, recalls her youth spent among the Larsons, a wealthy Nebraska family whom she referred to as her own. Her duties included mopping floors, washing dishes, and cleaning bathrooms that she and her brother Teddy, another rider, were not allowed to use, all laborious tasks given the Larson's numerous boarders. Although she recalled that "between the ages of six and eleven I got many whippings. I can truthfully say I never got enough to eat," the agency never learned of these conditions. Thompson explained:

> Once a year, Mr. McPhealy would come from the New York Foundling Home to see how I was getting along. I had to tell him fine. I would have to speak a piece for him, or poetry as it is called now. The name of it was "Looking on the Bright Side." Then I had to dance the Irish jig for him, and when I was through, I was excused. I would go outside and cry and wish he would take me back with him. I wanted to tell him the truth about how I was treated, but I couldn't.[66]

Her sense of injustice sits uncomfortably alongside her references to the Larsons as "Mama" and "Papa," terms of endearment that highlight the tragedy of the domestic mimicry she was forced to perform: "Mama didn't like my New York accent at all. She wanted me to talk like they did, so I was slapped quite often in the mouth." Incremental life, for Thompson, took the form of impressions imposed brutally on her flesh.

While a number of different circumstances resulted in a youth or family placing out with CAS, the publications of the Society uniformly paint a portrait of an innocent young child rescued from the poisonous behavior of poor and working-class adults. Biophilanthropy projects to impress new characteristics on noncivilized children by removing them from their families attempted to actualize sentimental fiction's paradigmatic drama: the successful maturation of the orphaned child. Drawing on the popular literary modes of the gothic urban crime tale and the sentimental orphan plot, CAS crafted teleological narratives of base sensation evolving into reflective sentiment. In narrative retellings of children's uplift widely circulated for publicity and fundraising efforts, the children begin as enemies of the legal economy. They navigate urban mazes portrayed according to the conventions of urban sensational literature, where "murder has stained every floor of its gloomy stories, and Vice skulks or riots from one year's end to the other" (DC, 26). By the end of the tale, however, the child denizens of the gothic mysteries-of-the-city plot evolve into orphans deserving of pity and capable of progress, the sentimental heroes and heroines of domestic life. Such passages emphasize the brightness of the youth's eyes and the lightness of their hair; they also praise the hardy independence of young men and the maternal instincts of girls who devote themselves to the care of younger children. CAS promotion made extensive use of riders' own accounts. For literary critic Karen Sanchez-Eppler, children's letters and life stories brought the organization's sentimental frame to life, thereby "allowing middle-class readers to imagine and sympathize with the horrors of the street and to feel beneficent satisfaction over accounts of rescue and reform made possible by their contributions."[67] These familiar plots allowed a catharsis for donors, a variant of "the pleasure of being morally elevated by consumption" that Lauren Berlant finds central to the political work of the sentimental genre.[68] In this case, readers directly accessed the pleasures of acting the philanthropist.

In sharp contrast to children's mixed experiences of placing out, the iconography of the Children's Aid Society's Emigration Plan provided viewers with a visual map of the redemptive guarantees of orphanhood. An image often printed as the frontispiece of the organization's annual reports from the

1870s through 1890s demonstrates the evolution of the street boy from vagrant to adopted western son (figure 4.5). He begins, "homeless," huddled in the dark shadows of an urban corner familiar to nineteenth-century viewers as the habitat of rats and drunkards, his meager clothing providing glimpses of white skin and curly locks aimed to heighten the tragedy of the scene. After being removed from the neighborhood by a charity worker, he is shipped "off for the west" on a train as part of a group of uniformed youth. Now the only thing standing between the orphan boy and a new family is hard farm labor behind the plow. This tool highlights the boy's newly upright and triumphant gait he has acquired as an individual among the land of men, a realm in which the role of animals is clearly delineated from that of the civilized races; the horses' white flanks reflect the sun.[69] The light-drenched image contrasts sharply with the slouching carriage of his evolutionary beginnings among scurrying children taking shelter on dim sidewalks. Here, animals fall under his dominion, just as he belongs to a family off-scene.

A turn-of-the-century photograph of an orphan train on the Atchison, Topeka & Santa Fe line strikes a rather more ambivalent tone (figure 4.6). The photograph melds white youth and the classic symbol of settler modernity—the train—into one organic behemoth crossing the "empty" plains. Light-colored dresses on girls and dark-colored trousers and jackets on the boys display their acquisition of rigorous sex differentiation, a crucial stop on the tracks to civilization. The image illustrates one of Brace's greatest hopes: that the vast West will as easily absorb the youth as their own bodies will take to its ways. A composite of the visual markers of bourgeois progress, the youth appear at once within the legacy of triumphant images of civilization's conquest of the West and as a reminder of the profitability of orphan labor, bodies fully soldered to the mechanical horse. Despite the goals of placing out, however, reformers' intentions were often thwarted by migrated youth and their families themselves, who availed themselves of the service to survive the ravages of industrialization.

ORPHAN PLOTS

Biophilanthropic programs to migrate children often represented themselves as enacting sentimental literature's overwhelmingly popular trope of orphanhood, of bringing the domestic plot to life as a path of urban redemption. Yet cultural production, in the view of cultural materialists like Stuart Hall and Lisa Lowe, provides neither prescriptions for nor reflections of economic life.[70] Rather, cultural texts function to reconcile the contradictions between labor and capital, and capital and nation. Sentimental orphan literature, as

FIG. 4.5. "The Work of the Children's Aid Society." Frontispiece, *Annual Report of the Children's Aid Society* (1873). From the Records of the Children's Aid Society 1836–2006 (bulk 1853–1947); MS 111, series 3, volume 20, New-York Historical Society.

FIG. 4.6. "Orphan Train on the Atchison, Topeka, and Santa Fe Railroad." Kansas State Historical Society.

with orphan migration projects, works to harmonize capitalism's need for a wide labor force and expansive land acquisition with national ideas of cultural homogeneity by establishing the innate capacity for self-regulation among native-born white children, as against the need for enforced imitation among the poor.[71] In other words, these novels help consolidate the biopolitics of orphanhood, in which civilized children precipitate the vitality of life itself, while the primitive are relegated to positions of service that will enable their imitation of the sexed and sexual norms of civilization. Orphan heroines are widely portrayed as brimming with life, and eventually, despite their many hardships, they invariably find themselves in situations that foster their vitality. In these novels, heroines born of bourgeois parents learn how to regulate their own initially impulsive response to sensory impressions, either because of or, often, in spite of the will imposed by their new families—Susan Warner's *The Wide, Wide World* (1850) and Maria Cummins's *The Lamplighter* (1854) are paradigmatic in this regard. By contrast, the children of the immigrant poor were deemed to be just sufficiently impressible to transform into a useful labor force if they were trained in the arts of imitation by the needs of national capital. Their position is similar to the one that white abolitionist writers such as Stowe and Child assigned to black youth. Within the animacy hierarchy of the sentimental politics of life, imitation marks a body that is impressible but lacks the sentimental capacity of self-regulation. An imitative body can mimic the sensory repertoire of civilization so skillfully that its behaviors grind into the substrate; the mastery of movement partially compensates for the absence of agential and self-regulating qualities of self-command, self-direction, and elasticity.[72] Domestic labor, rather than independent adventures, marks the fate of sentimental literary orphans of color. These literary resolutions of national conflict help enact the biopolitical paradigm.

In turn, domestic fiction turned to child migrations to encourage biophilanthropic resolutions of the contradictions between heterogeneous immigrant neighborhoods and national racial ideals. Alice Wellington Rollins closely patterned *Uncle Tom's Tenement* (1888) after Stowe's popular protest novel in order to bring middle-class attention to the plight of Irish tenement children and the possibility of their rescue and redemption. The novel offers moral female figures who learn to choose the best path for their children that their station affords. For the tenement mother, this means releasing her claims to her child. A protective mother, "Eliza was bitterly conscious that in the year they had been there [in the tenements] Harry had caught ideas and habits and thoughts and language and tastes that perhaps all the years of his after life in comparative luxury and at least decency might never be able to eradicate."[73] To save Harry from the stimulations of immigrant life in the bustling metropolis, Eliza makes the leap of faith that had urged her literary foremother across the Ohio River. But instead of clutching him tightly and throwing herself onto a block of ice, Eliza realizes that she herself, a mother of the tenements, is the problem. "Will no one save him," she anguishes, "not from the slave-hunter or the blood-hounds, but from *me*, his *mother*, who can only give him too little food, too little air, indecency for shelter and vice for his companions?"[74] Eliza realizes that it is her duty to save Harry from herself, and she sends him off to the West with a child placement organization. To the middle class, true maternal affection among the urban poor dictates giving one's child up to reformers who redistribute tenement youth throughout the settling continent.

Despite the distinct racial destinies of fictional protagonists and migrated children, domestic novels helped solidify what we might think of as the sentimental ethic of reproduction, which prioritizes child raising alongside childbirth in cultivating the nation's racial stock. Given that the "ideas and habits and thoughts and language and tastes" of youth comprise hereditary material in the pregenetic epoch of the nineteenth century, biophilanthropy projects attempted to regulate the impressions of childhood to produce laborers that would optimize, rather than threaten, the racial health of the nation. Impressions accumulate palimpsestically in the orphaned body, moving it toward usefulness—and perhaps whiteness—generation by generation. Meanwhile, the migrated child herself, abstracted from community and family—the very means of her own production, such that orphanhood entails a kind of commodity fetish—facilitates the accumulation of wealth in the form of surplus value and broken-in land for the expanding middle class. The orphan becomes the quintessential symbol of the biological optimization at the heart of the Lamarckian nineteenth century and the accumulation strategies of industrializing racial colonialism. This convergence produced both child welfare strategies and popular domestic fiction as methods of harmonizing the racial norms of civilization with its need for the cheap labor by which it is sustained.

BIOPHILANTHROPY

The children and families impoverished by global industrialization who solicited CAS's child welfare services found themselves the newest participants in what was already a long history of the deployment of orphans as a significant political strategy in colonialism and settler colonialism the world over. The production and use of orphaned children provided labor, territory settlement, and, for some, the promise of gradually whitening an indigenous population through forced immersion with settler society.[75] Ann Laura Stoler notes that orphanages housing European and mixed-race origin children functioned as a "basic institution of imperial power" within French, British, and Dutch regimes in the nineteenth and twentieth centuries.[76] With goals similar to CAS's, the institutions aimed to control the spread of pauperism and prostitution by removing indigent children from the allegedly harmful influence of their milieus, particularly their mothers.[77] Within the United States, the most notorious use of children as an instrument of settler colonialism is the off-reservation boarding school movement, begun in Carlisle, Pennsylvania, in 1879, to upwardly evolve Native youth through military drills, Protestant education, and menial labor. Its founder, Richard Henry Pratt, took inspiration from what he understood as the beneficial effects of slavery on the enslaved and of imprisonment for conquered Native leaders. Both institutions brought the primitive into contact with civilization, where the "potency of environment" stimulated physical and mental adaptations.[78] Reconstruction-era campaigns to provide educational and religious training to black southern youth, from the Hampton Institute to the schools established by the Freedmen's Bureau, operated according to similar social evolutionary principles.

Over the next few decades, schools aiming to transform black and Indian youth into assets of the middle classes' capital accumulation, rather than threats to civilization, counted among their pupils children from a variety of groups that now fell under U.S. imperial governance, including Puerto Ricans, Filipinos, and other Pacific Islanders.[79] Throughout these endeavors, the child's body figures predominantly as a product of its milieu, rather than its parentage. Parents and ethnic communities become fatal environments poisoned by the stagnation of the past, while reformers pose as rescuers who drag innocent children into the bright light of modernity.

Biophilanthropy targets the organic body alongside the eternal soul, working within institutions of discipline such as charities, schools, churches, prisons, orphanages, and domestic homes, with the larger goal of creating useful cohorts of workers that would further the accumulation of labor power and wealth.[80] It largely proceeds, as much of nineteenth-century U.S. biopower did, through private institutions—particularly religious ones— rather than official arms of the state. Like nineteenth-century philanthropy more generally, biophilanthropy orients itself toward the future needs of capitalists.[81] It works through laborers' subjection to power at the level of the sensorium, of conscious responses and movements become automatic over the time of life and instinctual over the time of generations. It seeks to engrave the relentless rhythms of production and the contemplative chronology of Christian faith into the impulses of the flesh, tempering gratification with habitual deferral.

In an account of her first days at Carlisle, Yankton Dakota writer Zitkala-Sa provides one of the most captivating renditions of biophilanthropy's technique of overwhelming existing strategies of self-management through the sheer force of sensory immersion. "Strong glaring light . . . noisy hurrying of hard shoes upon a bare wooden floor . . . warm hands [that] grasped me firmly," "cold blades of the scissors against my neck" that "gnawed off" braids, and the "offensive" smell of turnips evoke the sensations that envelop her young body, engulfing hard-earned methods of bodily comportment cultivated by her mother and other tribal elders.[82] Within the sensory regime of the "civilizing machine," her powers of sight and hearing fail to provide opportunities for emotional immediacy and instead render her socially disabled, cut off from her teachers, "whose open eyes could not see my pain," such that she "trudged in the day's harness heavy-footed like a dumb sick brute."[83] The youths' favored activity of falling headlong into the snow "to see our own impressions"—a fitting metaphor for the ways sensory organization and emotional reflection facilitate subjectivity—incurs the faculty's anger and results in corporeal punishment.[84] Native youth's sensory self-direction and resultant self-knowledge threatens the heart of the biophilanthropic project. Affectively, the Indian child must be exiled beyond the human, to experience her own death as a self-knowing subject with intimate connections to others, before she can be remade in her makers' image.

According to its own logic, biophilanthropy reverses death, seizing members of a primitive population marked for expiration and forcing them to live by rending deleterious milieus out of the body layer by layer and violently imposing a new vitality on them. The first stage of this process is orchestrating the extermination of the past. Migrated youth must first undergo a kind of familial death, in which their parents perish literally or symbolically, and all the youths' prior influences expire as well. Parental contact, innate inheritance, domestic keepsakes—all are active contagions that must be ritually put to death to render the child capable of redemption. Children are then reborn to the nation as participants in its forward movements. The process aligns with theorist Achille Mbembe's account of the necropolitical assumption of subjectivity assigned to the racialized, in which the "confrontation with death" enables the individual to free itself from the animal and be "cast into the incessant movement of history"—a process that can take shape as the dispensation of mortal death or as a "benevolent" procedure involving "the destruction of a culture in order to 'save the people' from themselves."[85] For the racialized, death is the path to life.

Biophilanthropy's necropolitical mode shared key strategies in common with another monumental disciplinary strategy that solidified in the nineteenth century: incarceration. "To sentimental reformers," Caleb Smith writes of the architects of the penitentiary before the Civil War, "a virtual death was the first step toward the citizen-subject's glorious rebirth."[86] Within the walls of the prison, reformers rendered the body immobilized, isolated, and deprived of sensation, particularly through the technique of solitary confinement, in order to redeem the soul.[87] Biophilanthropic projects, in turn, work through the logic of sequential sensory management: first sensory deprivation to squelch the lingering past, and then sensory inundation within the productive flows of domesticated time to orchestrate rebirth to a new heritage.[88] Richard Henry Pratt infamously promised to "kill the Indian to save the man," a strategy he applied equally in the settings of Carlisle Industrial School and his first laboratory for social evolution, the prison.[89] He staged "before and after" photographs to demonstrate the success of the environmentally induced annihilation of indigeneity, likely going so far as to direct school officials to bring tribal clothing and adornments along with the children they recruited to create more dramatic photographs that highlighted the transition from savagery to civilization.[90] For Mbembe, "politics is therefore death that lives a human life."[91] Smith explains that while those reformers who created the prison system saw it as a humanizing institution that was inverse to the "dehumanizing violence" of the slave plantation, their commitment to performing "civil death" through captivity rendered the penitentiary "mutually constitutive" with Indian Removal and plantation slavery.[92] Biophilanthropy projects are counterparts of other forms of genocide, captivity, and unfree labor and were themselves constituted by the highly uneven distribution of life chances known as racialization.

Yet as Pratt's notion of redemption through genocide makes clear, not all subjects of biophilanthropy were granted equivalent terms of death and rebirth. Different groups of reformers adopted distinct stances toward which ethnic groups could be impressed and to what degree. The role of death as redemptive strategy plays a different role for different groups: figurative in the case of Irish families; literal for Native communities. Black residents were often declared already dead, as in Brace's organization, inert material that could not be made to evolve regardless of circumstance. Across the spectrum, biophilanthropic projects mete out death along racial lines of vital potential. Off-reservation boarding school children were forced into useful life, but within the larger apparatus of genocide. Indigenous death was the precondition that enabled the birth of the settler colonial nation.[93] Indeed, the United States was often figured as an orphan of Europe, a parentless and youthful empty continent.[94] Yet when targeting the allegedly more malleable bodies of Irish- and German-origin children through the tactics of urban charity, biophilanthropists worked not through the foundational genocide of settler colonialism, nor by enacting the exhaustive "social death" of enslavement that cut off all ties to the past as well as recognition of personhood in the present, but by rebirthing immigrant children into the family of whiteness.[95] In this light, the Emigration Plan forms an important, largely untold episode in the story of how the Irish became white, as against the Native and Latino populations in the West they helped to displace.[96] An element of racial capitalism that targets groups for simultaneous whitening and/or proletarianization, biophilanthropy illuminates how the racial category of whiteness emerges in conjunction with capitalist development of the "conquered" western plains, figuratively cleansed of original inhabitants.

Biophilanthropy is an instrument of biopower particularly suited to settler colonialism. A population made to live, but only incrementally, serves the settler colonial logic of "erasure and replacement," wherein the white settler gradually incorporates perceived aspects of indigenous life as sources of rejuvenation.[97] Whereas Comte de Buffon and other European naturalists had condemned residents of the Americas as unfailingly degenerate on account of a humid and otherwise unfavorable climate, Lamarckian schemes in the New World could vindicate the racial potential of colonists by promising self-directed evolution through their access to extraordinary natural resources. These resources included the sometimes-useful "wildness" of Native peoples themselves, as in the recapitulationist logic of Frederick Jackson Turner's famous "frontier thesis," which posits that contact with Natives is an invigorating engagement with primitivity that compels further evolutionary growth. Biophilanthropy followed a similar course: the redemption of the children of European immigrants by removing them from the city and planting them as autochthonous products of western climes, bodies whose natural ownership of the land was patently reflected in their very composition. Along these lines, Horatio Alger celebrated the physical transformation of the eponymous hero of *Julius; or, The Street Boy Out West* (1874). Julius "had grown three inches in height; his form had expanded; the pale, unhealthy hue of his cheek had given place to a healthy bloom, and his strength had considerably increased."[98] Impressible bodies sanction the milieu that produced them, for better or worse.

Lauren Berlant clarifies that biopower's maxim to foster life or to permit death involves "the power to *make* something to live or to let it die . . . the authority to *force* living not just to happen but to endure and appear in particular ways."[99] Biophilanthropy is a particular deployment of making live, taking place at the level of sensory experience, that recruits children from surplus populations who threaten the health of the wage economy. Its mode of incremental life builds up children originally marked for death in order to suspend them in exploitable life, enabling the nation to extract their vital energies for agrarian, domestic, and reproductive labor.[100] Biophilanthropy is thus the precursor to "slow death," Berlant's widely adopted term for "a condition of being worn out by the activity of reproducing life" that takes place during the unremarkable time of ordinariness, as opposed to the exceptional event.[101] Within unrelenting conditions of precarity marked by ongoing and gradual deterioration, slow death becomes a kind of agency located in the nonactivity, rather than the strident resistance, of the sensory faculty. It is the refusal to overinvest in "habit" and action as biopolitical dictates of self making, taking shelter instead in "coasting . . . the shifting, diffuse, sensual space between pleasure and numbness."[102] Eating, sleeping, and zoning out emerge as sensorial modes of self-sovereignty simultaneously produced by, and in resistance to, late capitalist biopower.[103] The sensory inculcation of biophilanthropy—and sentimental biopower more generally—helps explain how this came to be, how the reprieve of "releasing the subject into self-suspension" can be simultaneously an effect of the wearing out of labor and a mode of survival within it, of escaping the relentless project of sensorial discipline.[104]

But within the logics of biopower, sensation itself is a key criteria of disaggregating the population into those who deserve sensory autonomy and those who must be animated, in whom the rhythms of productive life must be incubated. Slow death relies on the perceived or felt vitality, in the first place, of the population that can self-suspend in the quotidian space of the everyday. As resistance, slow death is predicated on whiteness. In the course of the development of U.S. capital, racialized groups were first targeted for life to reduce their threat to the nation, and then dispatched to accumulate the traits of the civilized so that their labor could then be gradually extracted. Making live happens in different racial registers in different regimes of empire, with different effects of prolonging, accumulating, extracting, and escaping life.

FROM THE SENTIMENTAL POLITICS OF LIFE TO STERILIZATION

While the Emigration Plan enjoyed broad public support in its first two and a half decades, by the late 1870s it began to unravel. The growing power of the Catholic Church enabled it to register complaints that CAS and other agencies were trying to breed out their religion by placing Irish youth in Protestant homes. Catholic activists began to organize their own child welfare agencies in New York and other eastern cities that would guarantee that Irish and other children would be housed in institutions and placed in families of like faith, measures that expanded the reach of biophilanthropic projects. Yet the impact of Catholic opposition was minor compared to the wide-ranging effects of shifts in the practices of the biological and social sciences. As the next chapter explores, a growing trend in a range of scientific practice posited heredity to be fixed material, not precipitated habit. This theoretical shift became apparent in the wide reception of Richard Dugdale's *The Jukes* (1877), a sociological study of the inmates of an upstate New York prison system that claimed to have traced more than 76 convicted criminals, 18 brothel-keepers, 120 prostitutes, over 200 relief recipients, and 2 cases of feeble-mindedness to a single eighteenth-century ancestor.[105] While Dugdale argued the Lamarckian position that "environment tends to produce habits which may become hereditary," his work was nonetheless widely received as proof that some poor families carry immutable hereditary taints.[106] The study was instrumental in gathering public support for sterilizing indigent women in the early twentieth century; W. E. B. Du Bois lamented that opponents of racial uplift ubiquitously cited the study well into the 1940s.[107] When Gregor Mendel's work on genetics was rediscovered in 1900, it signaled the solidification of a new era of fixed inheritance, in which genes impervious to environmental influence were thought to determine one's physical appearance and behavior.

The new regime of innate and immutable heredity threw the project of biophilanthropy into doubt. Brace's own project fell victim to the shifting tide. Influenced by the growing suspicion of the inefficacy of changing character through experience, members of the new profession of criminology in the Midwest during the late 1870s began to accuse Brace of dumping the eastern poor in their environs and polluting their regional stock. CAS was sending "criminal juveniles . . . vagabonds, and gutter snipes" to midwestern states, one official charged, where they would proceed to indulge in the criminal behaviors their natures dictated.[108] Faced with the accusation that correctional facilities were swelling with emigrant inmates, Brace began a series of in-house studies that would prove the efficacy of CAS reform efforts. Their results validated their own program. These defensive efforts didn't quell unrest in the industrializing Midwest, however, which was in the midst of its own crisis of family and child poverty. As a consequence, CAS began sending large shipments of children to Virginia, Iowa, Missouri, Kansas, and Nebraska instead, mostly during agricultural peaks in fall and spring.[109]

The rhetoric of child welfare shifted starkly at the turn of the century, away from the malleable heredity and social atomization of biophilanthropy and toward the notion that reproductive sexuality created innate family units that ought to be preserved. Beginning in the 1880s, social work professionals in the Midwest argued that scientifically managed institutions were far superior mechanisms of rehabilitation than Brace's domestic model and accused CAS and other faith-based child welfare organizations of "sentimental ineptitude."[110] So numerous and widespread were the concerns about the agency's fictionalized records, its cavalier approach to selecting host families, its sloppy follow-through, and its agenda to break up families that the Emigration Plan is credited as indirectly launching the social welfare movement.[111] As we have seen, on this last point the agency was rather better at helping working-class families stay together than its promotion allowed. Furthermore, awareness grew that a majority of the children Brace placed out were not in fact orphans, a fact that jarred with the increasing value placed on children's affective and emotional, rather than physical, labor.[112] As a result of several high-profile scandals in which tenement parents accused the agency of stealing their children and instances where children used the service as a means to run away without their parents' knowledge, CAS implemented parental surrender forms in 1895.[113] CAS stopped recruiting from the tenement districts, and instead sourced children from city orphanages, whose needs better fit the agency's goals of permanent placement.

Yet humanitarian concerns were not the ultimate cause of the end of the placing-out system. Rather, new forms of so-called "better breeding" replaced their predecessor. Unconvinced that habitual impressions would redeem tenement children, midwestern leaders put the Society on the defensive and began passing legislation in the 1890s that prohibited the transport of indigent children across state lines. These laws ought to be considered local versions of the anti-immigration legislation debated continuously in Washington from the early 1880s until the passage of the Johnson Reed Act in 1924, which were most prominently supported by leading eugenicists. In 1899, Indiana, Illinois, and Minnesota passed statutes forbidding the placement of children with mental deficiencies and certain diseases within their state lines and implemented standards for selecting foster homes. More states followed soon thereafter, while others, like Kansas, required children to have attestations of good character backed up by bonds in amounts of five thousand dollars in order to be permitted entrance.[114] The new evolutionary paradigm that understood heredity to be destiny guided this legislation, and as a consequence, the children of the immigrant poor were increasingly considered contagions to be prevented from migrating to the inner core of the continent. Alice Bullis Ayler, one of the last three orphan train riders sent to Kansas in 1929, recalls that her midwestern home spurned her as "bad blood. I was always looking at my veins and wondering what could be bad about it."[115] "The bad blood is supposed to carry the bad things down from your parents. And you don't have a chance to do better."[116] In 1929, Texas, the last state to legally permit child migrants, closed its doors to the placing-out system, and the orphan trains ground to a halt.[117] By the turn of the century, reformers were largely dedicated to regulating who gave birth in the first place, rather than controlling the environments of children already born. Brace's method of sentimental eugenics was losing its credibility in competition with the immutable gene. Meanwhile, anti-immigrant legislation remade internal migrations as well as international labor flows according to the new paradigm of innate racial stock.

Today, attitudes toward orphan trains are polarized nearly to the degree that sentimentalism is pitted as an opponent of the so-called Darwinian

FIG. 4.7. "Young girl with stroller." From the Records of the Children's Aid Society, 1836–2006 (bulk 1853–1947); MS 111, box 988, folder 3, New-York Historical Society.

mandates of the robber barons of the Gilded Age. For example, the play *The Orphan Train* (Aauran Harris, 1998) promises audiences "inspirational adventures" in a "moving and amusing heart-warmer."[118] By contrast, a recent *New York Times* article on binge drinking in Wyoming blamed the problem in part on the "psychic print" left by orphan train migrations, even though by 1893 the Children's Aid Society had emigrated fewer than ten children to the state.[119] These schisms obscure the ways that sentimental biopower stitched together free market capitalism, urban reform, western settlement, domestic literature, and child welfare as complementary endeavors that could remake the hereditary material of indigent youth and, by extension, the racial health of the settler nation. Above all, the broad convergence of sentimental discourse and Lamarckian evolution produced the figure of the malleable child as the embodiment of progress. This trope prepared the way for eugenics to emerge as a primary agenda of racial governmentality.[120]

The broad appeal of biophilanthropy in the latter half of the nineteenth century suggests that to trace the course of biopolitics, we must be attentive to the multiplicity of ways that the politics of heredity, reproduction, and evolution take shape. Child migration projects reveal that eugenics campaigns were initially implemented in liberal child welfare schemes that regulated child-rearing, decades before they took the form of restricting women's child-bearing capacities. Lamarckian-Darwinian evolution offered a blueprint for hereditary optimization by impressing the nervous systems of children, a eugenic reproduction scheme that targeted bodily material conceived of as plastic. With the arrival of harder heredity and genetics at the turn of the century, these models of inoculation-based reform, in which implanting new tendencies in youth would combat "unfit" inherited influences, gave way to state sterilization mandates that surgically prevented "unfit" women from conceiving. Furthermore, new ideas of immutable hereditary material fell within the solidifying model of sexuality that coordinated all impressions, interactions, and erotic stimulations into an identity-based paradigm. Genetics and modern sexuality emerged together at the turn of the century. Increasingly, they positioned hereditary transmission as the exclusive provenance of heterosexuality, a regime in which genetic relations were distinct and inviolable. Biophilanthropy projects, which positioned masculine intimacy as an instrument of racial progress, accordingly lost credibility. Yet to exclude these efforts from the trajectory of eugenic race-cleansing is to embrace reformers' child-saving rhetoric and dismiss their own accounts of directing human evolution by manipulating heredity. This position obfuscates the structural place of racial optimization, hinged on the promise of plasticity, within liberal social reform. The notion of plastic heredity on which biophilanthropy rests does not disqualify the tactic from eugenic aims. Rather, the calculation of relative corporeal mutability and fixity and the development of programs designed to differentially optimize hereditary material are themselves constitutive of biopolitics regimes across the centuries.

CHAPTER 5

From Impressibility to Interactionism

W. E. B. Du Bois, Black Eugenics,

and the Struggle against Genetic Determinisms

> The mass of ignorant Negroes still breed carelessly and disastrously, so
> that the increase among Negroes, even more than the increase among
> whites, is from that part of the population least intelligent and fit, and
> least able to rear their children properly. . . . They must learn that among
> human races and groups, as among vegetables, quality and not mere
> quantity really counts.
>
>   CLARENCE GAMBLE, "Birth Control and the Negro" (1939)

Clarence Gamble, heir to the Proctor and Gamble family fortune, devoted
a considerable amount of his time and wealth to the international fight for
birth control in the first half of the twentieth century. For Gamble as for many
others, increasing the use of birth control among the poor and/or racialized promised eugenic outcomes. Physician, founder of multiple contraception clinics, and prominent advocate of sterilization in the United States and
Puerto Rico, Gamble had a multifaceted career that reflects the strong—yet
still insufficiently understood—links between birth control and eugenics in
the early years of the reproductive rights movement. Gamble's appeal, quoted
in the epigraph, for financial support for the "Negro Project" circulates today
as one of the most frequently cited examples of the nefarious dimensions
of the campaign for contraception access.[1] The Negro Project began in 1939
under the auspices of Margaret Sanger's Birth Control Federation of America (BCFA) and was soon steered by the newly formed Planned Parenthood.
Its stated goals were to demonstrate that a birth control program among the
southern black working class would improve black well-being and reduce
state health and welfare expenditures.[2] Gamble's lament provides scholars
with a key piece of evidence for their argument that racist and eugenic goals,

rather than a desire for black women's reproductive self-determination, drove the initiative. Today, the continuing political stakes of the eugenic rhetoric Sanger and her associates championed in the Negro Project are suggested by the popularity of the pro-life strategy to recruit African American activists into the movement by casting Margaret Sanger's various birth control campaigns—the most notorious of which is the Negro Project—as racist and genocidal in intent. The Negro Project has thus again become a topic of conversation; in 2017, it dominates the earliest returns in Google searches for the keyword *Margaret Sanger*.

Yet Clarence Gamble did not originally pen the bald-faced eugenic appeal cited above. Rather, it is the work of the famed African American intellectual and uplift leader W. E. B. Du Bois, who himself served as one of the Negro Project's National Negro Advisory Council members.[3] Gamble quoted verbatim from Du Bois's article "Black Folks and Birth Control" (1932), which was printed twice in the *Birth Control Review*, a publication founded and initially edited by Margaret Sanger.[4] The Negro Project later printed Du Bois's article advocating that black families reproduce according to "quality" over "mere quantity" as a promotional leaflet to recruit poor black women to its two experimental birth control clinics. The project distributed nearly twenty thousand copies to county health departments, African American nurses' associations, the black press, African American women's groups, and prominent individuals in rural South Carolina and Nashville, Tennessee.[5]

Why would Du Bois, or Margaret Sanger and Clarence Gamble for that matter, turn to the eugenic strategy of promoting the reproduction of the "fit" in their advocacy of women's access to birth control? In this concluding chapter, I offer a new vantage on the oft-murky collusion between reproductive rights and eugenics in the early twentieth century by analyzing how both birth control and eugenic campaigns emerged out of long-standing biopolitical frameworks. New movements for women's and African American rights were embedded within a larger structure of disciplinary cultivation and populational optimization that had been flourishing for decades, even as new determinist theories of fixed heredity were increasingly accompanied by shifts in biopolitical tactics. As we saw in the last chapter, the consolidating genetic paradigm positioned heredity as destiny and dismissed sentimental models of biological transformation through sensory regulation as illegitimate and unscientific. Projects to transform hereditary material through experience, such as orphan migration, accordingly came to a close. In response to the brutal hierarchies of the new determinisms that identified racial inequality as a basic fact of nature, multiethnic scientists such as Du Bois brought impressibility into the twentieth century and adapted the sentimental politics of life for the unfolding genetic age. They accommodated growing skepticism of the feasibility of the inheritance of acquired characteristics, while simultaneously insisting on the possibility of biosocial transformation. They did so in part by turning away from child-rearing and toward birth control and eugenic regulation of contraception as key tactics of racial progress.

The disposition of nineteenth-century U.S. biopower and its reliance on the layered axes of the civilizationist racial hierarchy contextualizes the later politics of Du Bois's turn toward eugenics and Sanger's birth control campaigns. Du Bois's vast and varied output makes an important case study of the ongoing relevance of the sentimental politics of life into the twentieth century, even as disciplinary biopower was increasingly accompanied by security biopolitical tactics that focused on population-level regulation rather than individual transformation. For one, his relationship to eugenics has been a point of scholarly controversy, such that Du Bois's work represents a litmus test for the parameters of eugenics and, by extension, antiracist leaders' implication in the course of biopower. Some scholars reassure readers that Du Bois's interest in reproductive politics was feminist and, while perhaps elitist, was certainly not eugenic.[6] A recent edited volume devoted to the politics of gender and sexuality in Du Bois's life and work neglects the topics of birth control and eugenics altogether, a silence that registers the acute discomfort Du Bois's relationship to family planning continues to provoke.[7] By contrast, scholars Daylanne English, Marouf Hasian Jr., Gregory Dorr, and Angela Logan have illuminated and contextualized Du Bois's long-standing investment in eugenics.[8] Some of this work, however, threatens to minimize the oppressive nature of black uses of birth control for racial betterment by framing eugenics to be primarily about race, and thus potentially an antiracist strategy in the hands of black leaders.[9] For example, reversing an earlier stance that excused Du Bois from eugenic leanings, Dorothy Roberts has recently asserted that "white eugenicists promoted birth control as a way of preserving an oppressive racial structure. Blacks promoted birth control as a way of toppling it."[10] This characterization discounts the hierarchies of class position, normative sexuality, sex differentiation, and mental and physical ability central to eugenic strategies of racial purification and indeed the notion of race itself. As we have seen throughout this book, race consolidated in the nineteenth century as a compound structure of civilizationist ideals in which culture, faith, and political economy were understood to etch themselves into the body palimpsestically over the time of generations, rather than a discrete designation of distinct and eternal biological type. The accomplished social theory and visible reproductive activism of Du Bois, in particular, reveals that civilizationist hierarchies of cultural, physical, and mental fitness persisted well into the twentieth century as a method to resist mainline Mendelian-based U.S. eugenics.[11]

In this final chapter, I show how Du Bois's eugenic investments illuminate larger shifts in biopolitical governance as sensory-based reform lost power in the wake of the immutable gene. The first section below explores how mainline eugenic scientists and leaders positioned their work in genetics as a modern, experimental, and rigorous science of heredity that revealed the inherent and fixed inequality of the races. Their determinist work challenged what they framed as premodern, speculative, and sentimental theories about the Lamarckian transmission of acquired traits to descendants and hence the possibility of gradually ameliorating a race over time. I reveal that eugenicists identified "sentimentalists" as their principal enemy, demonstrating their dependence on earlier biopolitical paradigms, however oppositional, for their own emergence.[12] I next show how impressibility continued to serve as a resource for reformers into the genetic era by analyzing how Du Bois challenged determinist race science through a reassertion of the premise that race materializes as an index of cultural development over time, rather than as a fixed and innate biological difference. Du Bois, along with his sometime associate Franz Boas, adapted the sentimental politics of life in order to develop the oppositional theory that race is contingent on culture, rather than a genetic condition. Yet Du Bois shared the commitment common to both sentimental reformers and eugenic scientists: to improve the racial stock. I demonstrate here that in the first four decades of the twentieth century, Du Bois developed a eugenic plan for uplift that incorporated family planning measures such as birth control and adoption as tools for the biocultural transformation of the black working class. Drawing on the Planned Parenthood archives, I explore the details of Du Bois's involvement with the Negro Project in the final section. Overall, I argue that some of the most celebrated and criticized aspects of Du Bois's work today—his innovative understanding of race as largely a cultural phenomenon and his investment in eugenic "better breeding"—are part and parcel of his adaptation of a fading biopolitical paradigm as a method of resisting a new one whose antiblackness was increasingly virulent.

Accordingly, eugenics is germane, not incidental, to Du Boisian political thought. Yet my goal is neither to condemn nor to exonerate Du Bois, nor to argue for the existence of a kinder, gentler eugenics. Instead, I focus on Du Bois to show how the sentimental politics of life transitioned into newer biopolitical strategies of race improvement as well as theories that race is the product of the interaction of biology and culture. Du Bois and his debate with genetic determinists provide a compelling example of how the biocultural model of embodiment bifurcated in the twentieth century into the allegedly distinct domains of culture and biology and how racialized subjects resisted this move. Mainstream eugenicists won the day, however, and sentimentalism retracted from its broad function as a method of biopolitical governance and scientific epistemology to the discredited feminine world of emotion and consumer culture. Yet Du Bois refused to capitulate to this new determinist binary and turned to both science and literature to modernize impressibility discourse's account of the heritability of culture. He turned away from increasingly discredited biocultural models that sought to manage the growth of the individual and race through physical impressions, and instead embraced new birth control and eugenics technologies as the means of biological change. Du Bois's work reveals how the vital politics of sentimentalism could transform into modern eugenic practice. The sentimental politics of life thus functions as a shared origin of interactionist theories of difference and the eugenic period of the modern birth control movement.

THE RISE OF GENETIC DETERMINISM

Biophilanthropy was premised on the possibility of changing immigrant groups' hereditary makeup, an idea that increasingly lost favor in scientific circles by the turn of the century. Yet the orphan trains and similar projects conditioned the emergence of eugenic campaigns to regulate women's fertility, even as these new campaigns replaced sentimental models of transformation through sensory regulation. In this section, I trace the emergence of dominant eugenic science, uncovering how eugenicists explicitly positioned themselves against the "sentimentalists" they were supplanting, whom they derided as unscientific and irresponsible. Genetic determinists, I suggest, played a significant role in stripping sentimentalism of its prior function as scientific epistemology and disciplinary governance. Biopolitical tactics shifted accordingly, away from conceiving of bodily material on an impressible/unimpressible binary best managed through discipline and toward a populational notion of racial capacity best managed by the state.

New scientific and political methodologies developed beginning in the 1870s enabled the rise of determinism. The psychometrist Francis Galton's new term *eugenics*, meaning "well-born," emerged out of his studies in heredity and his development of the field of statistics to track multiple variables within intervals of time. His analysis of family traits throughout generations—infamously begun by exploring the illustriousness of his own family, including his half-cousin Charles Darwin—suggested that family characteristics remained remarkably static over generations. His graphs showed that prominent features such as individual weight and height formed bell curve patterns when plotted over the life span of multiple individuals, normative groupings that reflected hereditary continuity from one generation to the next. Bell curves illustrate relative consistency around a mean, in this case across time, a phenomenon Galton named regression. Sharp spikes and valleys, in contrast, would have implied dramatic changes in bodily form from one generation to the next, such as a Lamarckian paradigm would anticipate. Galton's theory of heredity suggested a substance that was as immutable as it was innate, a fixed, discrete material inured to human actions.

Galton's idea soon had experimental evidence. In the 1880s biologist August Weismann proposed that multicellular organisms have two types of cells— somatic cells and germ plasm, the latter of which comprises eggs and sperm— and that the germ plasm is unaffected by anything somatic cells experience over the organism's lifetime. His experiments investigating this hypothesis, in which he chopped the tails off five generations of white mice and bore witness to the continued sprouting of these appendages in their progeny, strongly suggested to many that the cells that transmitted hereditary material were not in fact transformed by repeated impressions on the nervous system. Weismann's work significantly advanced newly deterministic models of development in which hereditary material is impervious to individual experience, the precise opposite of what Lamarckians proposed and impressibility discourse reflected. His experiments also helped set a new methodological agenda for biology: empirical experimentation rather than theoretical speculation.[13] Through Galton and Weismann, heredity took shape in the form of an innate, immutable particle impervious to contact with the bodily cells of its host, or the bodies of others, that remained remarkably stable over time. Modern heredity was born.[14]

Many biologists embraced Weismann's research and the correlated growing prestige of their own field. Other life scientists and social scientists, however, protested that his demonstrations made a crude mockery of Lamarckism, which stressed the impact of repeated and habitual impressions—a far cry from one bad encounter with a knife. To many, Weismann's experiments were far from convincing, and Lamarckism continued to have significant presence in the Americas. U.S. social science, psychology, and medicine in particular held onto the paradigm until the First World War, and biologists, public health officials, and others in Latin America until the 1950s.[15] Popular belief in the inheritance of acquired characteristics continued to flourish in North America long after it faded from professional discourse. One plastic surgeon writing to a general audience in 1934, for example, reflected that physicians of his emergent specialty were so "frequently called upon to remove a deformity that has marked a family for generations" that he was compelled to caution, "Unfortunately, eradication of the defect in the parent does not prevent its transmission to the child!"[16] Yet among biologists, the tide had shifted toward conceiving of the body as a discrete space fortified from the world at large, a body determined by immutable genes and defended from germs by an army of immunity.[17]

The rediscovery of Gregor Mendel's principles of heredity by three different European scientists in 1900 bolstered Weismann's research, contributing to biologists' gradual rejection of the Lamarckian concept that repeated impressions on the senses alter hereditary material.[18] Mendel's hybridization of multiple generations of pea plants had demonstrated that individuals inherit two sets of "factors" (termed *genes* in 1908) for each trait, one from each parent. While scientists had previously widely believed that the traits of two individuals blend in their progeny, Mendel's work showed that traits are inherited on an all-or-none basis and are tied to a single gene. To many biologists, the existence of discrete unit characters confirmed that hereditary material did not blend with the cells of reproductive partners and passed unaltered from one generation to the next.

In the Lamarckian era, reformers like Charles Loring Brace had turned to the technique of discipline to manipulate heredity. Foucault characterizes discipline as a technology of power that "analyzes and breaks down; it breaks down individuals, places, times, movements, actions, and operations" in an attempt to move individuals toward a predetermined "optimal model."[19] Disciplinary biopower divides those who can be impressed toward this norm, through the self-regulation of feeling, from those who cannot. Brace sought to improve the heredity of the nation through the atomizing effects of rural domesticity, a disciplinary eugenics project that sought to move Irish immigrant children into the service of a settler agrarian national ideal. Galton, in turn, helped instantiate what Foucault names the "instrument of security," the biopolitical tool of population management through the calculation of chance, probabilities, and risk in order to establish homeostasis at the abstract level of the biological species. While targeted at the temporal level of population, rather than the spatial frame of discipline, Foucault emphasizes that the two methods are neither sequential nor distinct: rather, security brings specific techniques of population management to assist in the functioning of discipline.[20] Eugenics after Galton continued to take heredity as its target, but increasingly turned to the calculation of risk as its instrument. Security, as with Galton's bell curves, entails "the plotting of the normal and the abnormal, of different curves of normality, and the operation of normalization consists in establishing an interplay between these different distributions of normality and [in] acting to bring the most unfavorable in line with the more favorable."[21] Security works through probability calculations of variables inherent to the biological field itself and governing through managing these "material givens": the birth rate was thus one of its first objects.[22]

Biophilanthropy had helped lead the way toward security tactics, shaping the population according to the inherent potential of the body itself through the manipulation of heredity at the level of individual discipline. The rise of determinisms entailed a shift in the practice of security away from institutional reforms targeting youthful impressibility and toward biological interventions that targeted the subindividual level of women's reproductive capacity through broad-reaching state and federal policies. In the case of eugenics, security tactics sought to regulate a rapidly changing national demographic through techniques of imminence, rather than external control. Indigent, queer, and otherwise "unfit" women were sterilized for the sake of racial purification, while civilized women were encouraged to reproduce for the health of the nation.

Genetics informed the security agenda to optimize the biopotential of the population at the level of national policy, scientific research, and reform projects. Across these divergent arenas, the focus was increasingly on genes, not the conditions surrounding the development of a child. Eugenics quickly flourished as both the science of identifying desirable and undesirable traits in the racial stock and the practice of implementing corresponding policy. Leading eugenics researcher Charles B. Davenport, founder of the Eugenics Record Office at Cold Spring Harbor, which functioned as the de facto headquarters of eugenic science, explained that Mendel's experiments had shown unit characters to be "absolutely constant, unalterable, indivisible things."[23] Genes were a wholly distinct substance from the malleable and porous hereditary material figured by sentimental reformers. Eugenics helped occasion shifts in the meanings of the body in which the wax-like impressibility of hereditary tissue gave way to "fixed and rigid" unit characters, impervious to touch.[24] Whereas in the nineteenth century heredity was understood to be a diffuse quality of the body, the precipitate of movement and contact, eugenic science conceived of discrete, static, microscopic units squirreled away deep within the body and apparent only to the technologically enhanced vision of the scientist.

Like others of his cohort, Davenport's interpretation of Mendelian unit characters was so strict that he proclaimed that racial mixing violated the laws of heredity and was thus doomed to produce degenerate offspring. "The idea of a 'melting pot' belongs to a pre-Mendelian age," Davenport wrote. "Now we recognize that characters are inherited as units and do not readily break up."[25] Political priorities shifted in tandem. In the words of a prominent historian of eugenics, whereas neo-Lamarckians blended biological and social reform, "the new genetics caused eugenists to turn from social reforms to biological ones, on the understanding that social reforms were limited in their effect to a single generation."[26] Following the passage of the first sterilization law in Indiana in 1907, twenty-nine other states legalized involuntary sterilization with the intent of eliminating the indigent, disabled, queer, and the otherwise "unfit" from the national future, policies upheld in the 1927 Supreme Court case *Buck v. Bell*. Widely popular Fitter Family and Better Baby contests at state fairs across the country attempted to encourage increased reproduction among the fit, so that they would transmit their traits into the future.

The stark determinism of this new generation of eugenicists is well known. Less understood, however, is how the dominance of their biopolitical security tactics depended on discrediting sentimentalism as a scientific discourse and social reform strategy. Across scientific, legislative, and popular arenas, eugenicists and their supporters frequently identified "sentimentalists" and "sentimentalism" as the principal opponents of their efforts to improve the national population through the application of genetic science. Madison Grant's popular 1916 diatribe *The Passing of the Great Race*, for example, asserts that the belief that the effects of culture and environment could ameliorate the unfit is a position of hopeless sentimentality. For Grant, each of the "moral perverts, mental defectives, and hereditary cripples" plaguing the nation is perhaps deserving of being "nourished, educated and protected by the community during his lifetime, but the state through sterilization must see to it that his line stops with him, or else future generations will be cursed with an ever increasing load of misguided sentimentalism."[27] Eugenicists claimed that no amount of public charity, assistance, or sympathy could alter the unit characters that controlled for feeblemindedness, sexual perversion, alcoholism, racial status, and other conditions they understood to be hereditary.[28] Increasingly, sentimentalism came to signify outmoded views of evolutionary change and public charity that threatened public health.

The new scientists of heredity positioned sentimentalism as an emotional and dangerous attachment to pseudoscience, effectively stripping it of its prior iteration as a theory of empirical knowledge. Sentimentalism now represented a kind of premodern bogey that, when excised, rendered science objective and rational through its very absence. As we saw in the first chapter, Louis Agassiz in the 1840s drew on sentimental reflection as a scientific method to explain why he embraced polygenesis after contact with black waiters at a hotel. Several decades later, Edward Drinker Cope drew on the sentimental account of empiricism to develop an evolutionary theory in which the regulation of the senses drives species change. Eugenicists, in contrast, challenged not only the belief in acquired characteristics, but also sentimentalism's claim to scientific knowledge production more generally. They characterized sentimental methods as facile, puerile, and driven by emotion, rather than reason. Looking back on the development of eugenic science from the standpoint of the mid-1930s, the key architect of the modern Darwinian synthesis, Julian Huxley, remarked that eugenicists had been "rightly shocked at the intellectual excesses of the perfectionists and sentimental environmentalists, who adhered to the crudest form of Lamarckism and believed that improvements in education and social conditions would be incorporated in an easy automatic way into human nature itself and so lead to continuous and unlimited evolutionary progress."[29] For Huxley, eugenic scientists such as Davenport and his colleagues had actually gone too far in ruling out any role of environmental influence in shaping human development, but this exuberance had been understandable given the outlandishly premodern Lamarckism within the biological sciences that they had to displace.

In the work of eugenic scientists and their promoters one can thus trace not only an epistemological shift in the nature of scientific knowledge, but also a shift in the meanings attached to sentimentalism as an epistemology. Increasingly, sentimentalism—a discourse about the truth claims of feeling—was thought to address only emotional feeling. The physical dimensions of feeling receded from its purview. In other words, as impressibility lost its cultural purchase, sentimentalism, its regulatory instrument, lost authority as a physiological discourse and scientific method. Sentimentalism has become, now, so interchangeable with emotionality that its previous ontological and empirical dimensions have been largely forgotten, both in the term's common usage and in scholarly work. This transformation of sentimentalism is in part the genetic determinists' triumph.

The shift in the meaning of heredity away from malleable impressibility and toward biological determinism was accompanied by a corresponding shift away from associating femininity with progress and toward investing it with a sense of weakness, contamination, and premodernity. Advocates for women's moral and political influence—whether feminist or conservative— in the late eighteenth and nineteenth centuries had embraced the impressible body, as we saw in the case of gynecological feminism and the work of black feminists. Femininity's long-standing associations with susceptibility and penetrability became an advantage in this context, in which the sensitivity, elasticity, and openness of the body was linked to its capacity for progress. As heredity was increasingly seen as impervious to the environment, however, both feminine impressibility and the domestic home and its analogues in orphanages, hospitals, and asylums gradually lost status. Pliancy was becoming a liability: eugenicists built on the neurasthenic panic that the drawing rooms and desk jobs of the professionalizing classes dangerously softened the "overcivilized" white body, creating a nervous weakness that left men and women woefully unsuited to the responsibilities of administering a growing empire.[30] After genetics, they repositioned the white woman's utility from lying within her beneficial susceptibility to the outside world and her transmission of affect to wholly contained within her role as a carrier of seed, the "mother of tomorrow" who would proliferate beneficial hereditary material and carry the nation into the future.[31] Reproduction now transpired through sex chromosomes, restricted to the new notion of heterosexuality that also appeared at the turn of the century.

No less savvy a strategist than Margaret Sanger quickly registered this shift in the material importance of white feminine corporeality from the capacities of its elastic tissue to its function as an empty vessel. By the early 1920s, merely a handful of years since she had illegally opened the nation's first birth control clinic in an immigrant Brooklyn neighborhood, Sanger increasingly distanced herself from the frameworks of women's self-determination and the right to sexual pleasure she had previously articulated in her struggle for the legalization of contraception.[32] In its place, she embraced eugenics rhetoric.[33] She argued that "society at large is breeding an ever-increasing army of under-sized, stunted, and dehumanized slaves; [and] that the vicious circle of mental and physical defect, delinquency and beggary is encouraged, by the unseeing and unthinking sentimentality of our age, to populate asylum, hospital and prison."[34] Birth control would get to the root of the problem and limit the production of unfit generations altogether. Earlier generations of feminists interpreted sentimentalism to inoculate their efforts to care for the underprivileged, rendering their actions fertile across generations. Sanger, by contrast, explicitly positioned birth control as a modern antidote to the feminine weakness for public charity that proliferated disability, vice, and exploitation. Her position reflects a wider shift under way that moved from the disciplinary measures of enclosing individual bodies and to directly regulating the capacity to generate life on the broad scale of population through national policy.

Sanger also specifically challenges sentimentalism's claim to empirical knowledge, associating sentiment with "unseeing and unthinking" emotionality and thereby facilitating the reproduction of the sensory and cognitively impaired. In so doing, she associated birth control with the prestige of modern masculinist science and its new technologies of vision, divorcing it from the feminized and tactile rhetoric of sentimentalism and large-scale public welfare projects.[35] As sight emerged as the preeminent sensory capacity in the twentieth century, and one mastered by contemporary scientific practice, sentimentalism's deployment of impressibility and contact as a theory of knowledge and as the engine of

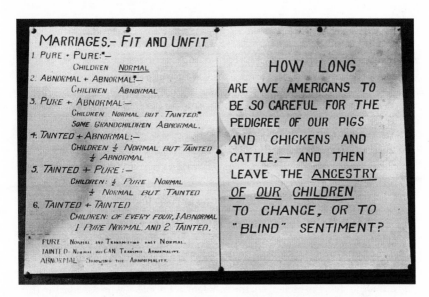

FIG. 5.1. "How long are we Americans to be so careful for the pedigree
of our pigs and chickens and cattle,—and then leave the *ancestry of
our children* to chance, or to 'blind sentiment?'" Chart used at Kansas
Free Fair showing "marriages fit and unfit" with outcomes of "pure" and
"abnormal" unions, circa 1929. American Philosophical Society.

social change became one of its many liabilities. Scientific sight, it would seem,
was only in part a sensory phenomenon, having achieved a mythic status of an
impartial, disembodied "view from nowhere."[36] To consider touch and physical
feeling a reliable epistemology was to be "blind" to the facts of science. Sight, not
touch, now reigned supreme, and eugenicists positioned sentimental sympathy
as a disabling condition that jeopardized the future health and bodily integrity
of the nation. The new security regime muted the flesh altogether and relied
on the calculations of science to avert crisis.

To be clear, this change in the meanings attributed to sentimentalism does
not represent the triumph of cold, unfeeling eugenic science over the sympathetic, charitable intentions of sentimentalists. Rather, it represents one
biopolitical instrument building on and overshadowing another. The career
of Edward Drinker Cope's protégé, the geologist Henry Fairfield Osborn
(1857–1935), makes this particularly clear. Following in his mentor's footsteps,
Osborn was an adherent of neo-Lamarckism at the start of his career. After
Weismann's attacks, however, he gradually moved away from endorsing the
belief that hereditary material was modifiable. While Cope and the American School of Evolution, a generation earlier, had drawn on sentimentalism

as a scientific epistemology to develop an agenda for racial purity, Osborn positioned modern eugenic science as a leader in rejecting "sentimentalism, which is fostered by ignorance."[37] For Osborn, genetics had "proved" that for humans, the impact of "environment" and "education have an immediate, apparent, and temporary influence, while heredity has a deep, subtle, and permanent influence on the actions of men."[38] Yet rhetorically, Osborn echoes the dimensional and temporal language of absorptive impressibility and the circulation of influence even as he insists that environmental stimuli make no changes in future generations. Characterizing environmental effects as fleeting and shallow in contrast to the spatial and temporal depth of heredity, Osborn rejects impressibility while nonetheless revealing his own indebtedness to its conceptual framework.

Finally, the epistemological shift in the status of sentimental knowledge was accompanied by a shift in the ontological status of the targets of sentimental sympathy. The human cast of sentimental characters—the disabled, the poor, the sick, the racialized, the indigent yet noble—whose suffering provided an occasion for the civilized to refine their own higher faculties of sympathy were increasingly cast as contagions, rather than catalysts, of national vitality. For mainline eugenicists, progress now depended on moderating the gene pool instead of upwardly evolving the primitive—or, in the case of Malthus, watching them suffer. Under this new regime of heredity, the "lowly," as Harriet Beecher Stowe termed the black subjects of *Uncle Tom's Cabin*, rapidly lost their utility to the civilized. At the same time, *sentimentalism* as a term increasingly came to signify an affected proclivity toward seeing emotional worth in something or someone that others rationally recognize as worthless—animals, the disabled, children of color, aged household effects, women's popular culture, women. It is in this context that James Baldwin penned his famous excoriation of *Uncle Tom's Cabin* in 1949, deftly characterizing sentimental literature as violent objectification: "Sentimentality, the ostentatious parading of excessive and spurious emotion, is the mark of dishonesty.... The wet eyes of the sentimentalist betray his aversion to experience, his fear of life, his arid heart; and it is always, therefore, the signal of secret and violent inhumanity, the mark of cruelty."[39] Sentimentalism was becoming the sign of disabling affectation that marked a full retreat from life itself. Sympathy, and its affective objects, no longer explicitly represented an epistemology of emotion or scientific truth, even as governmentality increasingly depended on privatized structures of attachment and identification over the course of the twentieth century.[40] In the place of sentimental science, a sanctified genetic science of heredity had emerged, seemingly cleansed of its nonrational origins.

Broadly popular eugenic applications of classical genetics interpreted social reform measures and human sympathy to be actively harmful to the future of the nation, for assistance merely prolonged and proliferated the lives of the unfit. The work of W. E. B. Du Bois represents a particularly interesting case study for understanding how the sentimental politics of life gradually dissolved into newer models of biopolitical security in which heredity dwelled within innate material and was best governed through reproduction management, rather than materialized through lifelong contact. For one, he was among the earliest and most vocal of critics of the way race science and hereditarian science in particular were popularly understood and he drew the wide attention of black audiences. For example, in 1929 Du Bois met fellow Harvard PhD and leading white supremacist Lothrop Stoddard in a highly publicized Chicago debate responding to the prompt, "Should the Negro Be Encouraged to Cultural Equality?" The sold-out crowd of four thousand, three-quarters of whom were black, often erupted into cheers as Du Bois scored points against one of the demagogues of U.S. racialism.[41]

Decades earlier, Du Bois had quickly comprehended that fixed heredity presented a profound challenge to the liberal theory of progress itself, which enshrines the actions of the individual as the heart of freedom. "Advocates of peace, the workers of social uplift and the believers in human brotherhood," he lamented, "have often made their voices falter and tinged their arguments with apology. Why is this? It is because the splendid scientific work of Darwin, Weismann, Galton and others has been widely and popularly interpreted as meaning that there is such essential and inevitable inequality among men and the races of men as no philanthropy can or ought to eliminate; that civilization is a struggle for existence whereby the weaker nations and individuals will gradually succumb and the strong will inherit the earth."[42] Du Bois keenly registered how the dominant interpretation of new hereditarian theories radically undermined a belief in the potential for the universal brotherhood of man and the possibility of social transformation. The mid-nineteenth-century belief "in the religion of equality and sympathy," for Du Bois exemplified by figures like John Brown and William Lloyd Garrison, was now discarded. Garrison, for example, now seemed to be "an anachronism in the age of Darwin," for he had devoted his life "to lift not the unlifted but the unliftable."[43] The biophilanthropic tactic of accumulating hereditary modifications was now seen as folly, and the new sciences of heredity were interpreted as enshrining racial subordination.

To resist encroaching genetic determinisms and offer divergent interpretations of the work of Darwin and Weismann, Du Bois enlisted a familiar framework: he modernized many elements of the sentimental politics of life. Du Bois was among a growing group of African American men and women who had the academic background necessary to take on biological determinists on their own terms.[44] He was thus part of a century-long tradition of black uses of the natural sciences for projects of freedom and liberation.[45] He was also part of a small, multiethnic cohort offering nondeterminist interpretations of the new biological sciences. Fellow sociologist Lester Frank Ward, for example, remained unconvinced that the "current speculations" of Weismann and other scientists about the impermeability of sex cells to experience had successfully disproved the "comforting popular belief" in the inheritance of acquired characteristics, proposing instead that "it may perhaps be as well to continue for a time to hug the delusion" that acquired characteristics are inherited.[46] Ward's image of embracing misbelief fittingly captures the function of sentimental epistemology as a particular relationship to evidence, one in which emotional and physical feelings have the status of truth, and in which physical contact is the means by which such truth is known. Unlike Ward, however, Du Bois wasn't about to close his eyes to new scientific developments and "hug" any "delusions." Rather, he challenged racial determinist theories by rethinking the dynamic relationship between science and sympathy and the body and its environment. During these decades before his turn to Marxism led him to develop a political economic account of racial exploitation, Du Bois largely adhered to an emotional and biohistorical account of race relations. If "the belief in racial or national superiority," he posed to readers of his Crisis editorial in 1911, "is largely due . . . to unenlightened psychological repulsion and underestimation of the dynamic or environmental factors," then a commitment to sympathy and the malleability of the body, mind, and spirit and to the vitality of life itself served the most effective weapons against racial discrimination.[47] His strategy to counter Davenport and his ilk was to carve out a social science that could draw on emotion as a methodology in order to identify the influence of environment on social well-being and to chart how African American families were advancing, however unevenly, toward civilization.

While geneticists were increasingly distinguishing their work as a discipline in which sentiment had no place as either a method or an object of analysis, social scientists devoted themselves to the study of emotions and affective states. Several critics have noted that Du Bois was deeply interested in the shifting epistemological status of sympathy and sentiment at the turn of the century.[48] Molly Hiro insightfully observes that The Souls of Black Folk represents "a kind of sociology of cross-racial sympathy" that proposes that "emotions . . . ought to be conceived as among the data sociology should interrogate," a perspective stemming from his pre-Marxist conviction that race relations were rooted in emotional and affective antipathies.[49] Yet for Du Bois, the stakes of sympathy were larger even than the meanings of intimacy and fellow feeling. More generally, the epistemological and ontological status of sympathy and sentiment shaped what the body was thought to be capable of, what science could do, and what kinds of political and biological change were conceived to be possible. Thus for Du Bois sympathy functioned not only as a fitting object of social scientific analysis but also as a method. "Facts, in social science, I realized, were elusive things," Du Bois reflected, "emotions, loves, hates, were facts; and they were facts in the souls and minds of the scientific student, as well as in the persons studied. Their measurement, then, was doubly difficult and intricate."[50] Eager to acknowledge his own implication in his data, Du Bois insisted on the possibility of a twentieth-century scientific subject affectively attached to his own study. Du Bois proposed that social science could offer a corrective to the popularity of studies like Frederick Hoffman's *The Race Traits and Tendencies of the American Negro* (1896), which gleefully predicted the oncoming extinction of African Americans. In-depth study of the vitality of African American communities, such as he undertook for over fifteen years at Atlanta University, offered empirical accounts of the viability of the races.

Yet for Du Bois, empiricism was not dispassionate objectivity, but a strategy of racial advocacy. In this, his approach to science held much more in common with an earlier generation of sentimental empiricists than it did with the rising tide of biological determinists who understood scientific neutrality to be as resolute as the seemingly impervious genetic unit itself. Committed to an emotional, rather than structural, account of racial relations, Du Bois accordingly understood that the manner in which the scientist approached his material—for example, one might contrast Hoffman's necropolitical delight with Du Bois's sentimental account of rural southern black lives in *The Souls of Black Folk*—as integral to the cause of justice. Furthermore, Du Bois saw the social scientist as implicated in his own research in part because he was committed to a sentimental model of individual and social growth as dynamic and progressive, rather than predetermined. In the sentimental framework, merely coming into contact with knowledge can spur social transformation.

This commitment to sentimental models of knowledge subtended Du Bois's remarkable productivity across multiple genres. For example, Du Bois immediately followed up a detailed, social scientific study totaling more than two thousand pages of an African American intentional community in Lowndes County, Georgia, written for the Census Bureau—which the Bureau did not publish and instead destroyed—with his 1911 sentimental novel, *The Quest of the Silver Fleece*. In both texts, he stresses the mastery of self-discipline and domestic virtue that propelled black communities up the social evolutionary ladder toward civilization. Literary critic Maria Farland uncovers the publication history of these two sequential projects in order to expose the "forgotten links between Du Bois's literary and scientific writing," pointing out that Du Bois turned to the popular genre of sentiment on account of his lack of access to the scientific mainstream. Yet her insistence that his turn toward the romantic plot after the Bureau's callous destruction of his research represents a "surprising choice of genre, [in that] DuBois chose to affiliate himself with a domain of writing that was popular, socially engaged, and primarily female," overlooks the historical continuities between science and sentiment and treats sentiment as primarily a genre rather than an epistemology.[51] Farland works backward from the contemporary premise that science and sentiment must be at odds.

Yet Du Bois's turn to sentiment was viable not only because his scientific work wasn't gaining the purchase it deserved but also because sentiment had long been a constitutive framework of scientific study, one that subtended evolutionary models of racial formation. Sentimentalism, for Du Bois, was an epistemological, ontological, and political stance that remained useful into the twentieth century. As Mia Bay has argued, the scholarly tendency to position Du Bois as a progenitor of multiple modern social science disciplines has occluded a thorough understanding of Du Bois's significant interventions into late nineteenth-century sciences, the immediate context for his own research.[52] Du Bois's career is situated at the crossroads of two centuries, a useful marker for tracing how both the sentimental politics of life gradually unraveled and security biopower gradually came to overshadow methods of individual optimization through nervous impressibility.

FROM IMPRESSIBILITY TO SOCIAL HEREDITY

Du Bois emphasizes sympathy, contact, time, movement, and the vitality of life itself as engines of racial development. This commitment to the vitality of culture and the responsiveness of the mind shaped Du Bois's evolutionary understanding of race as a set of shifting and reproducible cultural commonalities that gradually become materialized, rather than an immutable genetic condition. Given his emphasis on the role of culture in shaping racial belonging, scholars have celebrated Du Bois's racial philosophy as a key precursor to social construction theory.[53] For example, Joel Olson claims that after around 1906, "culture and geography replace biology and destiny as [Du Bois's] explanations for race."[54] This scholarship rejects Kwame Anthony Appiah's influential critique that Du Bois remained tied to a biological notion of race that compromised his progressive political aims and instead emphasizes Du Bois's landmark efforts to develop a cultural account of race that divorced group identity from physiology.[55] Yet Du Bois's notion of culture is itself a legacy of impressibility, a framework in which culture becomes somatic over time. While he emphasized the impact of culture on racial formation, he also understood race in the biopolitical terms of species: a dynamic, mutable, shifting phenomenon that exists only over the span of generation upon generation. We can thus think of Du Bois as a progenitor of assemblage theories in which the body materializes as the ongoing interplay between biology and culture.

More specifically, Du Bois can be seen as helping to inaugurate a post-Lamarckian interactionist notion of development, one in which biological and social factors have distinct processes over the course of individual lifetimes, but intertwine over the course of phylogenetic development. Evolutionary and hereditary theories positing that culture is transmitted from one generation to the next subtend Du Bois's groundbreaking understanding of race as a set of collective cultural traits shared across generations. A social scientist, Du Bois refused to equate biological investigation with necessarily determinist interpretations and saw the black body as deserving of study and, consequently, improvement. The debate about Du Bois as either a determinist or a social constructionist misses the trajectory of his work and consequently its utility for our current postgenomic era, in which scholars and activists are once again conceptualizing models of biocultural development and in particular the hereditary impact of trauma.

Du Bois was explicit and astute about the political stakes of the new heredity. In a 1904 lecture, "Heredity and the Public Schools," he addressed the Principals' Association of the Colored Schools in Washington, DC, informing black educators of the consequences of Weismann's research for their enterprise.

> Weismann's conception is that no acquired characteristics of the individual after birth are ever transmitted to his descendants . . . [and] upon this distinction is based nearly all the modern doctrine of higher and lower races, of superior and inferior nations: for it is said how impossible it is to make an Anglo-Saxon out of a Zulu, since no matter how educated the individual Zulu may become his acquired education can never be transmitted to his children. . . . He can never be raised or lowered; he is fated to be what by inexplicable creation he was made. If any of you have noted, in the last decade or so, a weakening of interest in the public school, a lessening of faith in what human training may accomplish, and a general tendency to sit back and watch the lower classes and the lower races waver and wander on, unhelped and with little sympathy from above, you may be sure that the source of this new attitude is the conception of heredity.[56]

In response to this crisis of feeling, Du Bois sought to change the interpretation of Weismann's work. He insisted that 90 percent of a person's makeup comes by way of social rather than physical inheritance.[57] This left Du Bois free to retain a Lamarckian view of cultural transmission, even as he explicitly accommodated Weismann's critique that acquired characteristics were not heritable. Du Bois made an important intervention in response to Lamarckism's declining status, asserting that the body evolves at a different rate than mental traits. As he explained, while physical changes transpire "through long ages of environmental pressure . . . marked changes in mass education, in public sentiment, and in environment . . . may . . . materially transform mental characteristics in a generation or two."[58] The body thus evolved out of pace with social inheritance, which made dramatic and rapid transformations, including quickly improving the qualities of the mind. In this mind/body split, he made a sharp departure from sentimentalists, whose twinning of physiological and psychological states determinists brought to its logical conclusion.

Du Bois's qualified Lamarckian approach grants different temporalities to the body and culture and enlists contact, impressibility, and inheritance as interfaces between the two. For Du Bois, there are two ways to acquire characteristics: through social heredity and physical heredity. He borrowed James Mark Baldwin's concept of "social heredity," which outlines the process by which the cultural attainments of one generation become their legacy to the next through "maternal instruction, imitation, gregarious life," and other processes of training.[59] Baldwin emphasized direct and indirect teaching and opposed the concept of physical transmission. While the body was thus not open to manipulation, Du Bois enlisted social heredity to explain the development of mental traits "acquired by the individual after he is grown by the thoughts, souls, and deeds which influence and mould his life."[60] As he explained, "the tendency to permanence in acquired character is what is known as heredity," making a subtle but crucial shift in the Lamarckian framework from "characteristics" to "character," and thus from the physiological to the cultural and psychological.[61] Providing an example of social heredity for his audience of black schoolteachers, Du Bois took a page straight out of the biophilanthropist's playbook: "Take for instance a boy; he is born and reared in the slums of New York; conceive now of a boy of exactly similar endowment, born on a farm in Ohio. . . . In the one place the social influences of the slums of New York are going to form a street Arab, quick, keen, depraved, perhaps criminal, while the surroundings of the other boy are going to give to the world a slower, more honest, and more open nature."[62] Cultural influence had dramatic psychological effects.

Du Bois disentangled what was now understood to be a Lamarckian conflation of social influence and physical inheritance, but his approach to race nonetheless retained the tactic of disciplining the impressible body to enable its rise in the ranks of civilization. To formulate how culture could be transmitted from one generation to the next, Du Bois drew on the conceptual riches of the sentimental politics of life. "Culture-contact," he proposed, represented one of the major elements of a race's journey toward civilization (the others were subsistence, accumulation, and education) and is continuously molding the next generation, for better or worse. It was reformers' duty to ensure that such contact would enable "growth" rather than give way to "debauchery"; yet this was a tall order, given the wide circle of influence on the young, who absorb their lessons "at the feet of teachers and preachers, by contact with surrounding society, by reverence for the dead Hand—for that mighty accumulation of customs and traditions handed down generation after generation."[63] While Du Bois doesn't use the specific vocabulary of the impression often, he nonetheless employs its metaphors, casting both God and past generations as crafters of the delicate touch that shapes young minds. Explaining how the southern black poor were slowly advancing toward civilization "by infinite gradation," Du Bois emphasized how much their development depended on their social context, such that "hard pressed they may sink into crime; encouraged they may rise to comfort, but never to wealth." Riches, he explained, were out of the question because of the training "they and their fathers" had received, for what did "a slave know of saving? What can he know of forethought?"[64] The black poor must be impressed with the concepts of futurity and its material analogue, accumulation, to mobilize the race's development out of present-oriented sensation, accreted each generation, layer by layer.

A familiar set of tools led all the way to a new notion of race as predominantly, though not entirely, cultural inheritance. The models of the racial palimpsest and social heredity enabled Du Bois to formulate race as largely a cultural accumulation. Increasingly unmoored from the physiological, race became "a complex of habits and manners," and those "persons sharing this experience formed a race no matter what their blood may be."[65] Yet it is important to remember that Du Bois was not rejecting scientific explanations of race in favor of cultural constructionist notions per se but drawing on a different tradition of heredity and embodiment than the eugenic determinism of Davenport, Galton, and others. As the historian of anthropology George Stocking Jr. has lucidly explained, "In a milieu of ascendant biological evolutionism, Lamarckianism helped to explain the evolution of the races and the mental evolution of man in terms which gave what we would now call 'culture' a crucially determining role."[66] Race took shape as the interaction between individual experience and the inherited racial body, itself the product of culture.

While Franz Boas has received the lion's share of the credit for this shift toward cultural relativism and away from biological and hierarchical accounts of race, recently scholars have stressed the significance of Du Bois's own work in this direction, happening simultaneously and sometimes in partnership with Boas's efforts.[67] Adolph Reed Jr., for example, has claimed that Du Bois's work before 1915 bears the stamp of a discursive field dominated by Lamarckian thinking, a context that enabled Du Bois to reject the racial determinisms sweeping biology and other life sciences. The liberal tradition of impression theory proved similarly important in the emergent notion of race as predominantly a cultural phenomenon, or, in the vitalist terms Du Bois articulated toward the end of his life, as a "group of contradictory forces, facts and tendencies."[68] As Boas explained, a broad-based understanding "of the achievements of the Negro" would necessitate a study of how "he has developed in his own natural surroundings. The conditions for gaining a clear insight into this question are particularly unfavorable in North America, where loss of continuity of development and an inferior social position have made a deep impress on the race that will be slow to disappear."[69] Boas and Du Bois described cultural acquisition in terms of sensory impressions, hereditary tendencies, and evolutionary adaptations that were reproduced generation after generation. The racial palimpsest model continued to have influence, registering the trace of culture on the mind and body of past, present, and future generations.

While Du Bois worried about the way determinists interpreted Darwinian thought to authorize the survival of the fittest, he also approached evolutionary thought as a resource. As he saw it, there is a "fundamental fallacy involved in taking a static instead of a dynamic, a momentary instead of a historic, a fixed instead of a comparative, point of view of peoples," for racial groups are dynamic systems rather than stationary points on a hierarchy.[70] Determinists saw physiological, intellectual, and psychological characteristics as coconstitutive of one another, such that each aspect of a person's profile was an index not only of their overall quality as an individual, but also of their racial group's level of civilization. By contrast, Du Bois underscored the dynamism of the social group. Those who would declare that "the backward races of today are of proven inefficiency and not worth the saving" were giving voice to "the arrogance of peoples irreverent toward Time and ignorant of the deeds of men."[71] Du Bois embedded African Americans in time, overturning one of the key registers of antiblackness that suspends bodies in eternal and unchanging flesh. Both individuals and racial groups functioned as moving variables for Du Bois, whose multidirectional shifts it was the task of the social scientist to plot. As Vilashini Cooppan has argued, Du Bois aimed to differentiate among African Americans, to show that the race did not form a singular mass fixed in the prehistorical spatiotemporal plane of the primitive.[72] Du Bois thus challenged the entire premise of determinism, posing the provocative question "How shall we compare the present with the past, nation with nation, and group with group"?[73] What measure could possibly capture a dynamic, vibrant, variant mass of people and freeze them unilaterally in a moment of time? He contested racial determinisms by drawing on the evolutionary—and biopolitical—notion of population, a fluctuating, malleable entity conceivable only through the measures of temporality and change.

Du Bois thereby enlisted evolutionary narratives to fashion new models of biopolitical subjectivity. Lamarck and Darwin had extended the secular framework of human time from the biological limits of the individual body to the epochal timeframe of the species. For Du Bois, evolution therefore dramatically rent the liberal individual subject asunder. The person now belonged to a generation, itself merely one stage of a larger process, rather than represented a discrete unit entirely contained within itself. "What the age of Darwin has done," Du Bois explained, "is to add to the eighteenth century idea of individual worth the complementary idea of physical immortality of the human race. And this, far from annulling or contracting the idea of human freedom, rather emphasizes its necessity and eternal possibility—the boundlessness and endlessness of possible human achievement. Freedom has come to mean not individual caprice or aberration but social self-realization in an endless chain of selves."[74] Darwin had inaugurated a new kind of collective political subject, one that came to being through the inevitable movements of time and bound individuals together "in an endless chain of selves." Freedom for Du Bois becomes access to time itself, and equality a condition of group potential, "of opportunity for unbounded future attainment," rather than an individuated capacity of self-possession. The vitality of the subject exceeds the human life span and the measure of time. We have seen how nineteenth-century discourses of temporality denied African Americans access to the possibility of not just progress, but the movements of time more generally. Du Bois instead calls on evolutionary theory to shatter the finite mortality of the individual subject, bound by the human body, granting humans access to an eternal plane of development. Heredity thus becomes social in two senses for Du Bois: not only because it results from influences from the cultural environment but also because the subject of development and of "self-realization" is now a collective group with an infinite temporal frame. Freedom, in other words, exists in the form of population.

Du Bois's biopolitical notion of freedom included the effects of social experience on the physical body. Throughout endeavors ranging from quantitative social science and anthropological study to curating photographic displays, Du Bois sought to investigate and validate the strength of the black body alongside demonstrating the achievements of black culture. Importantly, Du Bois's civilizing efforts were not only about the politics of respectability— seen especially in his photographic documentation of black families' acquisition of the traditional civilizationist markers of sex-differentiated decorum, fine domestic interiors, and an appreciation of classical Western culture[75]—but also about optimizing the black body and documenting morbidity and fatality caused by impoverishment. The decade-long series of conferences and proceedings he organized at Atlanta University investigating the condition of urban African Americans involved "a consideration of human physique and the conditions of physical life" alongside the study of social organization.[76] A resultant volume, *Health and Physique of the Negro American* (1906), features tables of comparative physical measurements such as brain weight, chest dimension, and hair texture, as well as comparative charts of "feeblemindedness," "venereal diseases," and mortality rates. On the basis of such biomedical data, the conference committee—two-thirds of whom were Du Bois and Boas—resolved that there was not "adequate scientific warrant for the assumption that the Negro race is inferior to other races in physical build or vitality."[77] Instead, Du Bois and Boas identified poor health care as the cause of high mortality rates and instances of disease.

Du Bois surveyed, documented, and calculated the physical health of urban and rural black communities, with the long-term goal of reducing risk and stabilizing health outcomes. For Du Bois, biopolitical approaches of regulating populations over time could be enlisted as uplift resources, given that a changing political and scientific climate now dismissed the racial consequences of individual change and transformation. Lamarckism enabled him to conceive of cultural transmission across generations as a type of inheritance—a seeming social constructionist paradigm—but it also enabled a species approach to racial justice, one in which biological and social factors interact over the span of generations. Security biopolitics proved a resource to Du Bois to contest genetic determinisms, a position that both harked back to the nineteenth-century sentimental politics of life and reached toward the epigenetic present.

REPRODUCTION AS LIBERATION

If equality and freedom materialize in an endless chain of selves that stretches across generations, then reproduction becomes a central strategy of liberation. Like others during the dawn of genetics, Du Bois transformed social evolutionary models into reproductive protocols. This effort had particular urgency for Du Bois, for traditional social evolutionary models froze blacks in prehistory, rendering progress impossible. Both time and the political potential of race itself manifest through the fertility of women.[78] In this section, I look in detail at Du Bois's endorsement of eugenic reproduction, an example of how the sentimental politics of life model could be refashioned as support of both birth control and eugenics in the genetic era.

Explicit neo-Lamarckism begins to fade out of Du Bois's social scientific framework by 1915, in keeping with trends in the discipline.[79] During this same period, however, Du Bois became an ardent advocate of birth control.[80] The rejection of Lamarckism meant that effects of reform movements were limited to the present generation. Accordingly, reformers turned to birth control in order to shape the evolution of future generations. In other words, while reformers could no longer understand their work as molding hereditary material, they could influence which women would transmit their genes. Du Bois embraced birth control as a means to catalyze the progressive development of the African American population, manifesting the slippage between eugenics and contraception endemic to the early to mid-twentieth-century U.S. birth control movement as a whole.[81] Du Bois overwhelmingly positioned birth control as a method of guiding racial progress through "science and sense" rather than a means by which heterosexual couples could make independent reproductive choices.[82] Du Bois's work illuminates how nineteenth-century strategies to improve human evolution helped precipitate twentieth-century eugenic agendas.

The sentimental politics of life not only subtended Du Bois's innovative approach to race as a social phenomenon, but also conditioned his understanding of "better breeding" as a political strategy. His writings advocating birth control as a tactic of racial advance show the depth of his interest in strategic reproduction as a broad social remedy and illuminate the fluidity between the eugenics of the sentimental politics of life and that of the subsequent genetic era. "The Negro," Du Bois proclaimed, ought to be "breeding for an object," so that he may hold his own "surrounded in the modern world by men who have been bred for brains, for efficiency, for beauty."[83] Targeted reproduction included coupling across class and race lines, for physical attractiveness and intellectual capacity were not correlated to racial stock. Fictional narratives like the speculative story "The Comet" and his romance novel *Dark Princess: A Romance* (1928) were particularly hospitable genres for fantasizing about productive unions. In both of these stories, mixed-race reproduction is chief among the protagonists' "great constructive deeds" that challenge racial economies.[84] In the words of Alys Weinbaum, "Even as *Dark Princess* succeeds in severing maternity from the logic of racial nationalism, it reinserts the black mother into a logic of internationalism, casting reproduction as the motor of black belonging in the world."[85] Aesthetic principles broadly guided Du Bois's vision of a stronger race and influenced the agendas of the organizations he shaped. Daylanne English has argued that as editor of the NAACP's magazine *The Crisis*, Du Bois assembled "a kind of eugenic 'family album,' a visual and literary blueprint—for the ideal, modern black individual" throughout the 1920s.[86] Recurring features such as "Men of the Month," photographs of the winners of NAACP "prize baby contests," and an annual children's number that once featured images of "Five Exceptional Negro Children" as well as their IQ scores exemplify the eugenic visual culture of the magazine under his editorship.[87] Echoing the eugenic rallying cry popularized by President Theodore Roosevelt, he even praised the "sturdy family of a teacher" who was preventing "race suicide."[88] When Margaret Sanger requested that Du Bois supply a statement endorsing the birth control agenda to be read at a major birth control conference, Du Bois prepared a brief public address that claimed "the regulation of birth by reason and common sense instead of by chance and ignorance" was second in importance for the cause of "human advance" only "to the abolition of war."[89] Rather than abandoning the possibility of control over evolution that Lamarckian theories promised, Du Bois and other activists dedicated to improving the nation's racial stock transferred their allegiance from a belief in the ability to directly manipulate species change to the imperative of regulating women's fertility. Evolutionary thought provided Du Bois with a framework for conceiving of race as cultural affiliation, rather than fixed physiological heritage, as well as a model for eugenic uplift.

In keeping with the impressibility framework, Du Bois approached racial uplift as multiple kinds of contact between growing individuals and grown adults, which took place in marriages, public schools, adoption programs, urban neighborhoods, and rural hollows. Adoption played an important role, as it had for the sentimental reformers of the prior century. Du Bois's work in the annual *Crisis* children's issues not only promoted adoption as a means to expand the ranks of the civilized, but also directly facilitated adoptions by matching prospective parents with birth mothers.[90] He explained: "There are to be sure not enough children of the better class; and this is a matter for earnest thought among us. . . . If children are not born to the family, why not adopt them?" Du Bois argues that these children of the "better classes"— implicitly adopted or birthed—will uplift the children of the less civilized by virtue of their very proximity: "The masses of this world have always been unpleasant companions and only by contact with the better can they be made more pleasant and more useful."[91] He proposed that "perfection" could thus be a possibility for "the modern American family," through "long training and carefully fostered ideals and persistent purging of the socially unfit."[92] "The Worst carry contamination and death and pose the threat of corrupting the quality of the Best," he similarly proposed in the "Talented Tenth," an essay in which he defines slavery in part as "the legalized survival of the unfit."[93] By way of solution, he infamously proposed that the elite men of the race would lift the fit yet less evolved into civilization through both contact and example.

Du Bois, however, was hardly the only uplift leader touting strategic birth control as racial improvement. Classrooms at black colleges such as Tuskegee and Howard, a special issue of Sanger's *Birth Control Review* devoted to African American reproduction, and psychologists cited in the *Crisis* alike agreed that "eugenics will improve the Negro of the future."[94] Scholars Gregory Dorr and Angela Logan have shown that prize baby contests functioned as an important component of NAACP fundraising from the mid-1920s until Du Bois's resignation from the organization in 1934. Du Bois and the NAACP field secretary launched eugenic baby competitions whose proceeds funded the organization's efforts to combat lynching. Within three years, over half of the three hundred local branches had held contests; within six, the pageants had raised over eighty thousand dollars.[95] That the NAACP organized eugenic pageants to fight the epidemic of lynching reflects the interdependence of biological and social approaches to racial equality Du Bois and others adopted in the era. As biopower situates the race as the central axis of political life, so too does biopower necessarily animate landmark antiracist strategies, especially among the middle class. The twinning of antilynching and better babies campaigns suggests that scholars still have much to learn about how biopower shapes multiethnic resistance strategies to biopower itself.

To be clear, Du Bois maintained important differences in his approach to better breeding from that of mainline eugenicists. He took pains to object to the three central political goals of Anglo-American eugenics: coercing sterilization, illegalizing immigration, and preventing cross-racial relationships. Along with other African American intellectuals, he tracked rapidly proliferating sterilization legislation—twenty-four U.S. states had laws by the end of the 1920s legalizing the sterilization of "unfit" individuals without consent—and was vigilant about its potential use as a method of black genocide. Du Bois called for blacks to serve as sterilization watchdogs.[96] He cautioned: "The burden of this crime will, of course, fall upon colored people, and it behooves us to watch the law and the courts and stop the spread of the habit."[97] Furthermore, he criticized the anti-immigrant hysteria sweeping North America in these decades. "COME NORTH! . . . The demand for Negro labor is endless," he exhorted southern blacks in a 1920 *Crisis* editorial. "Immigration is still cut off, and a despicable and indefensible drive against all foreigners is shutting the gates of opportunity

to the outcasts and victims of Europe."[98] Transnational class solidarity motivates Du Bois to see European immigrants as sharing the same economic interests as the majority of African Americans. Rather than simply reading the 1917
immigration restriction as an advantageous opportunity for black workers to
migrate northward, he positions black laborers as acting in the class interests
of both sets of "outcasts and victims." It is this opposition to eugenics policies
and the racial logic of strict hereditarianism more generally that has led some
scholars to cast Du Bois in the role of fierce eugenics critic. As we have seen,
however, these criticisms of Mendelian-based eugenic projects that emphasized racial purity rather than uplift do not foreclose Du Bois's support of
eugenics altogether. While Du Bois did voice many important concerns about
the brutal hereditarian logic of eugenic policies, such criticism registers his
resistance to mainline eugenics specifically rather than demonstrating his
opposition to the attempt to optimize life itself through strategic breeding.

DU BOIS AND THE NEGRO PROJECT

The lens of the sentimental politics of life illuminates the biopolitical under-
pinning of Du Bois's approach to birth control specifically, and marriage more
generally, as uplift strategies. This is not contradictory: the movement for
women's reproductive rights emerged out of the dominant political frame, not
in opposition to it.[99] Du Bois advocated that "future marriages" be guided by
"survival of the fittest by peaceful personal and social selection," which incorporated "not the methods of the jungle, not even the careless choices of the
drawing room, but the thoughtful selection of the schools and laboratory."[100]
Ever the reformer, Du Bois would seemingly submit life's most private desires to careful study and planning. Forced sterilization and other repressive
means for eugenic breeding were anathema to Du Bois. Instead, he advocated
"peaceful" individual and collective mate selection. But what could a collective
decision about reproductive fitness look like, aside from the campaigns promoted by Stoddard and his ilk—which had sterilized at least twenty thousand
people by the mid-1930s?[101]

A little-explored element of Du Bois's engagement with the birth control
movement provides insight. His service as a member of the National Negro
Advisory Council of the now-notorious Negro Project offers a key example
of the rhetorical muscle Du Bois lent to family planning movements on the
ground. The Negro Project represented the Birth Control Federation of
America's first national effort to reach African American populations. The
Negro Project—soon renamed Planned Parenthood's Division of Negro
Services—opened three demonstration birth control sites in Nashville and
two rural South Carolina counties, Berkeley and Lee, to illustrate the viability

of such services among poor African Americans. The strategy to create short-term demonstration clinics, rather than long-term facilities supported by the field work of an appointed doctor and minister, represented Clarence Gamble and the funders' victory over Margaret Sanger's original vision.[102] In historian Johanna Schoen's summation, this "halfhearted approach to providing contraceptive services for the black community was the rule rather than the exception" in the birth control movement more generally.[103] The project also attempted a nationwide educational program among black communities.[104] According to an internal organizational chart, the project's objectives were to "1. Reduce Negro material and infant mortality and morbidity 2. Reduce health expenditures for cummunity [sic] 3. Reduce relief and welfare expenditures."[105] Project goals were broadly biopolitical, targeted at stabilizing the dynamics of population. Regulation of both the life and death of southern blacks for the benefit of regional economic health trumped concern for individual families' reproductive self-determination.

Du Bois initially joined the project in late 1939, its first year of existence. He served as a member of the Georgia State Committee, one of several advisory boards formed through invitations to individuals listed in the *Colored Who's Who* directory. When the project eliminated state-level committees in 1941, Du Bois accepted Sanger's written invitation to join the National Negro Advisory Council, which comprised around forty-five public figures, including Mary Church Terrell, Walter White, and E. Franklin Frazier.[106] He is not listed as present in any of the extant minutes of Advisory Council Meetings. His "Black Folk and Birth Control" article quoted in this chapter's epigraph, which was used as promotional material, and his name on the project's letterhead form the bulk of his service. For Planned Parenthood staff, the National Negro Advisory Council functioned performatively: its purpose was largely achieved by the existence of the body itself. In the privately expressed words of Clarence Gamble, the project should "appear to be of, by and especially for the colored race," as "there is a great danger [it] will fail because the Negroes think it a plan for extermination. Hence lets appear to let the colored run it as we appeared to let south do the conference at Atlanta."[107] The Advisory Council was designed to provide cultural legitimacy and contacts among African Americans—as if southern sharecropper families would feel that Du Bois and his cohort had interests closely aligned with their own—rather than to offer significant guidance or organizational muscle to division staff.

Du Bois's involvement, however limited, with the Division of Negro Services offers a particularly compelling episode to reflect on the larger shift from evolutionary models of uplift to security tactics of maintaining population equilibrium in the aftermath of the Darwinian synthesis and World War II.

World War II provided occasion for birth control advocates to cast contraception as a "means for reducing evils" far outside the scope of individual family planning. Planned Parenthood promoted birth control as necessary for a nation at war in order to match the "physical fitness" recently achieved by Germany in "one generation" in part through "birth control centers."[108] Advocates trumpeted birth control as a remedy for unfavorable rates of poverty, criminality, urban density, and other populational ills. Advisory Council members shared Planned Parenthood's belief that birth control was an important strategy for redressing severe health and economic inequality among black southerners, stimulating racial uplift, and enabling African Americans to play their part in a nation in the midst of global war. As U.S. troops joined the front lines in Europe and the Pacific, the division's promotional literature featured council members boosting birth control's role in bringing "into the world the healthy and the fit to be prepared for the responsibilities of citizenship."[109] More broadly, birth control for African Americans, Planned Parenthood avowed, could prevent "the ultimate price of impaired health, delinquency, dependency and death,"[110] or, in other words, could "conserv[e] for race-building, the waste of Negro life which now takes place."[111]

It is unclear what makes up this waste: too many unfit births, or too many tragic deaths. These goals convey a broad security strategy of modulating the vitality of the race itself through the as-yet-undefined elimination of waste, rather than an older strategy of uplifting individuals into the ranks of civilization. The work of the Division of Negro Services reflects shifts under way in reproductive politics. Reformers were moving increasingly away from the disciplinary measures of molding individuals through institutions of "enclosure" and toward tactics of broad-scale population "modulation" that target the dynamics of life itself, tactics Foucault terms "security measures" and Deleuze calls "societies of control."[112]

Compared to the populational rhetoric of other Advisory Council members and to Planned Parenthood promotional material, Du Bois more consistently framed the importance of reproduction as simultaneously a strategy for producing optimal individuals and as a broad race vitality measure. Over the decades, he remained committed to blending a disciplinary emphasis on training the poor in the behavior and habits of civilization with a security tactic of steering broad demographics by modulating fertility itself, an approach informed by nineteenth-century biopower techniques. As late as 1948 Du Bois issued a mandate to the talented tenth to civilize the rest of the race. In an address to Wilberforce College students memorializing his "Talented Tenth" lecture, Du Bois proposed that their role as race leaders included molding the

FIG. 5.2. Planned Parenthood Federation of America pamphlet. "Better Health for 13,000,000," 1943. Creator: Planned Parenthood Federation of America, Inc. From the Florence Rose Papers, Sophia Smith Collection, Smith College (Northampton, Massachusetts).

reproductive habits of the poor: "We would want to impress on the emerging generations of Negroes in America, the ideal of plain living and high thinking, in defiance of American noise, waste and display; the rehabilitation of the indispensable family group, by deliberate planning of marriages, with mates selected for heredity, physique, health and brains, with less insistence on color, comeliness or romantic sex lure, mis-called [sic] love; youth should marry young and have a limited number of healthy children; the home must be a place of education, rather than cleaning and cooking, with books, discussion and entertainment."[113] More than several years after the Nazi's atrocities were widely known and public opinion began to shift away from explicit breeding strategies, Du Bois continued to endorse a quasi-biophilanthropic reformism premised on the ability of elites to "impress on the emerging generations" the ideals of restraint, eugenic marriage, cultural attainment, biological vigor, and domestic space isolated from the pressures of labor.

The sentimental-Lamarckian notion of cultural inheritance provided Du Bois with important intellectual resources that enabled him to dislocate the notion of race from its purported location in immutable hereditary material. His notion of the role of social context in shaping cultural inheritance led him both to conceive of race as a socially contingent, rather than a fixed and innate quality, and to turn toward eugenic applications of birth control, a contradictory set of legacies in contemporary terms. Yet appreciating the contours of nineteenth-century biopower reveals a broad commitment across both disciplinary and security regimes to the impact of cultural habit and social policy on racial vitality. Du Bois adapted and modified this tradition to challenge new deterministic regimes in which biology was destiny while simultaneously meeting the new strictures of twentieth-century heredity. The result was an early example of twentieth-century interactionist theory that attempts to reconcile the dynamic role of culture with genetic heredity.

Du Bois held on to disciplinary biopower even as it was being eclipsed by security measures. While emphasis on individual sensorial discipline gave way to networks of control over women's fertility, managed by professionals both male and increasingly female, it did not disappear entirely. Rather, new measures superimposed, even accentuated, the goals of individual behavioral reform both in the implementation of hegemonic biopower and in styles of resistance. For Du Bois, the population was a sphere of social self-realization where individual ambitions could come to full fruition over evolutionary time. With respect to reproduction and racial health, his strategy of racial justice worked within the framework of biopower, even as he challenged its hegemonic forms. Managed reproduction that selected for positive traits, for Du Bois, was a way to direct the physical and mental development of the race in the midst of a new biological regime that discounted attempts to uplift African Americans as dangerously misguided sentimentalism.

RACIAL VITALITY

Du Bois adaptated the theory of uplift through impressibility and the transmission of culture over generations into the forms of new social science and practices of reproductive politics. His work suggests the transformations in the sentimental politics of life over the course of the early twentieth century. Multiple factions split off from the sentimental epistemology that had tied together groups as politically disparate as black feminists, race scientists, and urban child welfare reformers. Despite their differences, a common belief that the civilized could direct their own evolution had stemmed from their shared conceptual framework in which civilization was inherited and then improved on by the impressible body's continual absorption of new influences. However, sentimentalism underwent dramatic shifts as the Lamarckian paradigm gradually lost scientific credibility beginning in the 1880s. Yet it did not disappear entirely. Du Bois's work illuminates how the legacy of the sentimental politics of life transpired in at least three different ways in the early twentieth century: eugenic scientists' efforts to discredit sentimentalism and promote biological determinism; the work of figures like Du Bois and Boas who interpreted the dynamic inheritability of culture as the basis of racial affiliation; and in the work of birth control advocates who turned to regulating conception, rather than managing the impressions of the children of the less fit, in order to shape the growth of the population.

The contemporary critical commitment to understanding race as an exclusively cultural phenomenon renders Du Bois's investment in racial vitality illegible and his eugenic efforts incomprehensible. The social constructionist paradigm most frequently interprets biological thinking as necessarily determinist; antiracism, by extension, becomes the rejection of the biological. (The corollary of this paradigm, as we have seen in earlier chapters, insists that ideas of bodily malleability are necessarily antiracist, an equally specious proposition.) Yet Du Bois's interest in racial vitality makes sense if examined from the perspective of racial thinking in the decades prior to and concurrent with his work rather than through a false opposition between antiracism and ontological approaches. In his era, many black intellectuals were on board with the agenda to imbue the race and nation with life. In the words of Du Bois collaborator Dr. Thomas Wyatt Turner, a charter member of the NAACP and a professor at Howard, Tuskegee, and Hampton Universities, social reform would be most beneficial if it were to "aim not only at ameliorating the conditions of life but also at bettering life itself."[114] Cultural theorist Donna Jones elaborates the extensive use of Bergsonian vitalism in Negritude movements across the Caribbean in the mid-twentieth century, highlighting how vitalist discourse functions simultaneously as a framework for racial difference and colonial emancipation.[115] Dominant racial discourses such as Hoffman's condemned African descendants as evolutionary holdovers, sapped of life, who would perish in the face of the onslaught of progress. In contrast, black leaders turned to a range of scientific and theoretical investigations of the vitality of the black body to insist on blacks' rightful place in the forward movements of time, as liberal individuals and as a collective race.

Recognizing Du Bois's engagement with biopower to fight for racial justice makes particularly apparent that racial formation is best understood as neither a deterministic nor a socially constructed phenomenon. Rather, the political work done by race is that of relationality, of condensing a compound of interactions between physiology and the environment over time. Race functions as a consistent target of biopower on account of its presumed porosity and malleability, at the level of the individual and/or the population. Race takes shape as a dynamic that coheres through processes of optimization, management, and modulation, targeting individuals over time and their layering, generation by generation, in palimpsestic formation. Accordingly, our analyses of race need to move beyond binaries of determinism and social construction, to see how biocultural accounts of race are rooted in the practices of capitalism, colonialism, and neocolonialism as well as in modes of belonging to resist their effects. Just as importantly, new models of analyses in the humanities that celebrate the vitality of matter and the porosity of bodies as a radical shift in Western theories of matter need to come to terms with sentimental biopwer, which promoted sensitivity and malleability as the criteria of racial hierarchy. The ongoing and shifting calculation of the relative role of biology and culture in shaping the matter of the body is one of biopower's primary conceptual legacies.

EPILOGUE

....

The Afterlives of Impressibility

> In the future attention undoubtedly will be centered on the genome,
> and with greater appreciation of its significance as a highly sensitive
> organ of the cell, monitoring genomic activities and correcting com-
> mon errors, sensing the unusual and unexpected events, and respond-
> ing to them, often by restructuring the genome.
>
> BARBARA MCCLINTOCK, "Nobel Lecture" (1983)

As the twenty-first century matures, the limitations of the cultural theory
of race have become increasingly apparent. The framework in which "race"
marks solely the accretion of social structures with little relation to physiological phenomena, sometimes credited to social scientists including W. E. B. Du
Bois and Franz Boas to counter eugenic determinisms as explored in the last
chapter, has ceased to serve as a viable resource for progressive politics. The
strategic celebration of cultural difference that both masks and justifies stark
economic inequalities; the mostly successful dismantling of affirmative action
programs on the grounds that such programs discriminate on the basis of race,
itself a category declared to exist only within the left-leaning institutions that
perpetuate its harmful fiction; and shrill accusations from the Right that white
candidates who talk about race and show their intimate relationships with nonwhite individuals are committing acts of racism, among many other examples,
make clear that the conception of racial belonging as a primarily social construct can easily be recruited to naturalize neoliberal racial capitalism.[1]

From the perspective elaborated in *The Biopolitics of Feeling*, what is problematic about the social construction theory of race is not only the inert role
it assigns to the material body, a formulation that often renders the body a

passive receptor of social scripts. More fundamentally, the general practice of developing intellectual and political frameworks by calculating the relative influence of heredity versus the environment on both ontogenetic and phylogenetic development—in this case, models that divorce culture from biological existence—has provided biopower with some of its most fertile soil. Problems inherent in binary models of biology and culture are equally clear with regard to the notion of gender. In the 1950s, gender was first conceived as the social role of sexed identity by sexologist John Money. He drew on a familiar conceptual vocabulary to articulate this new concept: the impression. Money built on ethologist Konrad Lorenz's studies of attachment among baby geese for their caregiver, a process Lorenz called *imprinting*, to conceive of gender as a stage-specific consolidation of social experience that "imprinted" by the age of two.[2] Money thereby updated impressibility for the Cold War era to outline normative codes of behavior. The concept of gender was later developed by decades of feminist critics within the context of a sex/gender distinction in which the former represents a given physiological state, and the latter an unfolding social process. (This same division has been challenged for most of its existence, yet nonetheless remains a core feminist pedagogical concept.) Money's work has become infamous as the grounds for a debate about the relative influence of biology and culture on gender development and is particularly notorious for his handling of the John/Joan case, which regendered a young male who had lost his penis during a botched circumcision. Money's chief critic, the sexologist Milton Diamond, brought "Joan's" eventual failure at female gender socialization into the public eye in the 1990s as evidence of the grotesque inaccuracy of the socialization theory of gender identity.[3] Yet Money and Diamond's professional turf war reaffirmed the larger postwar structure of biology and culture as distinct and separable spheres whose relative influence at the level of the individual could be delineated, calculated, and ranked. In the words of Jemima Repo, their "debate over biology and culture itself confirms the dichotomy as the only imaginable or legitimate parameters according to which the truth of sex can be conceived from the latter half of the twentieth century onward."[4] Understood in this way, social construction theories recapitulate, rather than interrogate, the grounds of difference claims initially elaborated within the gradual deployment of biopower over the course of the nineteenth century.

In its emphasis on the body as primarily the work of discursive production, social construction theory largely remains within the terms of the biology and culture split induced by modern sexuality and heredity a century prior. It thereby echoes the dominant biopolitical frame of the twentieth century.[5] At the close of the nineteenth century, notions of embodiment gradually shifted from marking the condensation of relations within the milieu to issuing forth from an internal genetic script, a shift in which models of race, sexuality, and heredity all moved inward to nominalize individualized properties of the self. In the late twentieth century, social construction theory moved the process of subjectivity and self-constitution outward, identifying it as a process of externally imposed social scripts.[6] Yet both the modern notions of race and sex and social constructionist theories are rooted in the demarcation, calculation, and modulation of the mind and body's relative affectability by the world in which it is immersed that characterized nineteenth-century biopower.

In this book, I have endeavored to show how calibrations of an organism's degree of receptivity to its surroundings are key to the consolidation and operation of biopower and its materializations of racial and sexual difference over the course of the nineteenth century. Exploring the decades in which the modern notions of race and sex were formed, I reveal how biopower coalesced within a conceptual field that understood the individual and species body, in its ideal form, to be a mutable entity, one that readily receives its shape and significance from the sensory impressions made on it. Indeed, sensory and emotional receptivity to the environment rapidly rose to the fore of biopower's ontologizing structures. I argue that the relative capacity of impressibility served to delineate sex, race, and species, as well as to provide a method of individual and population regulation—regulation that took the form of sentimental technologies of sensory discipline and emotional reflection. Sentimental biopower was deployed to govern the expanding population of the United States by regulating its differential capacity of impressibility in the form of private technologies that would manage the body's impulses and appetites, such as the home, church, factory, plantation, prison, and reform meeting. Biopower modulated the flow of impressions circulating throughout the population, itself a newly conceived biological-political entity of governance understood to emanate from the capacity to issue and/or receive sensory impressions within a milieu. The population was administered through an evolutionary animacy hierarchy that measured a body's vitality, and assigned it a status of species, race, and/or sex accordingly, on the basis of its relative impressibility. This hierarchy clearly distinguished those refined bodies that could be affected and move through time—and had absorbed the habits of civilization over the course of generations—from those animalized, unimpressible bodies mired in primitivity that could only affect, and therefore contaminate, the settler colonial nation.

The modern notions of race and sex could thus be said to operate at the spatiotemporal level of species-being, rather than at the individual level of static biological difference (a lingering characterization of nineteenth-century thought) or the interior psychic space of identity and subjectivity (in the modern sexuality and social construction models). I suggest that ideas of embodiment in the nineteenth century took shape in the form of a palimpsestic model of development in which race and sex are composed of archives of relationality. In the context of civilization that gradually softens and inscribes the body's material substrate, the body accretes generation by generation through layers of impressions. Heredity, in this pregenetic age, was understood to precipitate from sensory experience throughout the lifetime of the civilized; contact, touch, and proximity were fertile relations. The racial palimpsest is a particular type of assemblage, one that differentiates between somatic material on the grounds of its ability to accrete, however recursively, over the span of generations. Civilization enabled the only corporeality capable of further adaptations, yet the nature of that development depended on the circumstances of environment. Racial difference thus figured within an evolutionary model of accumulation that rendered whiteness the crystallization of simultaneous capacity and precarity. Biopolitics developed in this context—not to manage fixed and resolute incarnations of difference, but to moderate the corporeal vulnerability at the level of population on which racial progress hinged. Its tactics are the identification, transformation, domestication, and/or removal of life-forms determined to lack accumulative potential.

The greatest attainment of the racial palimpsest was allegedly the specialized quality of binary sex. Sex difference stabilized the vulnerability of the impressible body by dividing the civilized body into two and consigning the susceptibility and penetrability of the receptive body onto its female half. As a consequence, the notion of sex difference is central to the function of racialization and biopolitics more generally, despite its much smaller role in most scholarly analyses of biopower. Conversely, both antifeminist and feminist claims to rights and representation on the grounds of sex difference issue from within biopolitical formulations, a legacy with which feminist critics are just beginning to grapple and trans activists have been struggling for decades. Similarly, defenses of queer sociality that rest on same-sex love and domesticity as engines of civilization also emerged from within racializing biopower; indeed, they began making their appearance as early as the 1870s.

How might understanding race and sex to denote relational rather than static phenomena inform contemporary justice struggles? What does recognizing the prominent role of biopolitics in shaping sex-positive black and white feminisms, child welfare innovations, and the cultural notion of racial and gender formation illuminate for the politics of the present? How do we proceed with the knowledge that feminism, as well as queer rights, have issued from racializing structures in which sex difference is located in the pelvis and figures as a function of whiteness? For one, the much-bemoaned contemporary fracturing of the Left can be understood as one of biopower's most salient outcomes, for biopower not only materializes identity categories through techniques of individual discipline but also involves the far more nefarious act of populational modulation, which materializes at the site of relational capacity. One of biopower's most insidious effects is that it produces the scene of the social as a zero-sum game that disposes of some bodies to safeguard others. Biopower poisons the well of social life, drawing people together through a common contagion, rather than shared need. Biopower turns us against each other, asking us to see, like T. R. Malthus, the suffering and death of others as the grounds of our own virtue. Biopower has consolidated at the site of the body's capacity to perceive, feel, emote, and express and thereby modulates our very sense of collectivity, of communion, and of companionship. Race, sex, and sexuality coalesce as the products of our sensory stimulations, emotional entanglements, and affective interactions. In other words, "identity politics" is not necessarily to blame for the divisiveness of Left politics. Rather, to restructure the political, we need to reconceive the very grounds of the organic and the social.

Are the effects of impressibility on the body politic indelible? We currently lack a viable ontoepistemological frame that can understand experience as a process that forges the organic and psychic development of the individual and the bonds of the collective, rather than places individuals in direct or indirect competition with one another on account of their accumulated difference. And while impressibility frameworks were deployed as biopower's force of differentiation, they might also contain the seeds of a way to imagine the social otherwise—as befits both Marxian and Foucauldian models of resistance in which hegemony cultivates its own undoing. As the twenty-first century unfolds, the status of the relations between ontogenetic and phylogenetic development and an organism's environment is once again in flux. More than the relative importance of the interplay between biology and culture is currently up for negotiation: the feasibility of delineating between the two phenomena itself has been reopened as a properly scientific and theoretical site of investigation.[7] New models of heredity emerge in conjunction with shifting political contexts. This suggests the possibility of a coming epistemic break that departs from the specific forms of calculation and administration of immutable genetic potential characteristic of the twentieth century, forms of governance rooted in biological determinism that shaped the course of twentieth-century biopower.

Epigenetics has reintroduced the possibility that the expression of heredity material is shaped by life events, proposing that descendants can inherit effects of paternal—but especially maternal—experience.[8] The vocabulary of epigenetic science explicitly echoes the age of impressibility, further indicating the aptness of framing current research within a political time line that reaches back to the era prior to the gene. "Genomic imprinting" refers to the capacity of a limited number of genes to be "imprinted" by the parent who contributed it, which prevents its expression in progeny. Such imprinting can happen over the course of the parent's lifetime, implying "that developmental modifications can be transmitted across generations in the absence of the original, precipitating conditions."[9] Epigenetics may seem to evoke the Lamarckian principle of the inheritance of acquired characteristics down to its reliance on the language of the transmitted impression, but there is an important difference: it locates the mechanism of inherited adaptations in the act of gene expression through methylation pathways, rather than in modifications to genetic material itself. Given this book's suggestion that overarching frameworks of the interplay between heredity and the environment structure biopolitical epochs, this shift to epigenetics—which harks back to the pregenetic era—perhaps implies that new opportunities to reimagine the political can take shape, forms of belonging that can ideally avoid recapitulating the pitfalls of the past. Nonetheless, new social justice models will need to work against, rather than through, dominant epigenetic accounts in the life sciences. Epigenetics as an emergent paradigm generally identifies sex difference as hardwired in the brain, saddles the female body alone with the burden of reproductivity, and positions cultural conditions—in a moment in which culture has absorbed the meanings earlier generations assigned to race—as the causative factors of economic inequality.[10]

Yet two recent accounts of corporeal development point to how conceiving of the body as an assemblage of corporeal and environmental processes may nonetheless prove to refine, rather than undermine, feminist social justice paradigms. These models reopen the question of the physiological component of racialization and sexual differentiation so popular in the nineteenth century, yet do so within a frame that understands biological processes as imbricated effects, rather than causative agents, of power relations. Anne Fausto-Sterling offers one framework for conceiving of biology as a plastic and adaptive force in continuous interplay with the routines of psychic self-development, behavior, and culture, such that anatomical structure, physiological function, and gender role take shape through the molds of behavior. In *Sex/Gender: Biology in a Social World* (2012), she proposes that gendering shapes the highly malleable brains of toddlers through dopamine reward cycles triggered by behavior comforting to the child and/or desirable by their caretakers as well as "aversive conditioning" resulting from behavior that brings no such reward.[11] Fausto-Sterling applies the principle of neuroplasticity, in which the brain's synaptic connections refine or erode within an organism's lifetime according to the emotional intensity and frequency of their stimulation, to propose that social gender role shapes both physiological function and anatomical structure.[12] For Fausto-Sterling, "[to] understand sex and gender we have to study how sensory, emotional, and motor experience becomes embodied."[13] In this interaction model, gender functions as a feedback loop between cultural and biological processes, to the extent to which these can even be separated in the first place.

Philosopher Sylvia Wynter offers another interpretation of the dopamine reward cycle, in this case to call for an expanded mode of neuroscience investigation. Wynter considers consciousness to be the outcome of an extended interplay between neural development and social context, rather than the organic outcome of the specialized human brain. She builds on Frantz Fanon's notion of "sociogenesis," or the development of the self among humans through social experience, which accompanies the ontogenetic and phylogenetic development of the organism and species. Wynter proposes that scientific accounts of human development must take into account individual subjective experience, such as the experience of racialization, as fundamental to the fact of consciousness. She calls for a form of hybrid science that can recognize "the sociogenic principle as a culturally programmed rather than genetically articulated *sense of self* with the 'property' of the mind or human consciousness being located only in the dynamic processes of symbiotic interaction between the opioid reward and punishment system of the brain and the culture-specific governing code or sociogenic principle (as the semantic activating agent) specific to each of our hybrid nature-culture modes of being."[14] In other words, Wynter hinges the human capacity of self-awareness, and the development of self over the time of individual life, on the interplay of organic and cultural development that neuroplasticity entails. She thereby overturns decades of reductionist scientific models that place the capacity of consciousness at the mercy of the internal genetic code. Together, Wynter and Fausto-Sterling offer the potential for understanding the effects of racialization, gendering, and the uneven distribution of economic and political resources in terms that exceed traditional mind/body boundaries and capture the psychological *and* physiological aspects of emotion, trauma, impoverishment, environmental racisms, climate precarity, and collective belonging. If we understand this experience to potentially impact the genetic expression of progeny in the case of trauma, then we have a new appreciation of the insidious effects of biopower over the time of generations.

Reopening the notion of the plasticity of biological material thus can have a distinctly different political valence than the vitalist revival in new materialism, which generally articulates the liveliness of matter as both a novel and liberatory idea, one that can escape the effects of Western rationality. Biological plasticity can also potentially offer new perspectives on how race and gender write themselves into the body, effecting drastically disparate health outcomes, life expectancy, and quotidian modes of anxiety, fear, and/or hopefulness, processes that interpretive models that hew only to the social aspects of identity precipitation preclude from view. The risks of a biocultural approach to social justice paradigms are clear, and indeed we have the very course of the nineteenth century, and the eugenic policies of the twentieth, as models for understanding the dangers in approaching models of plasticity and policies of biological manipulation as a means of social remediation and vice versa. For W. E. B. Du Bois, models of the interplay between biology and culture abetted eugenic approaches to birth control. In sum, plasticity frameworks can naturalize inequality in cultural behavior.

Nonetheless, how can we fully understand the nearly thirty-year discrepancies in life expectancy in neighboring zip codes in metropolitan regions such as Oakland and Chicago without reconsidering the biosocial effects of structural racism?[15] The interplay of biology and culture can enable an understanding of race, sex, and gender as accumulations of the experiences of slavery, empire, capitalism, colonization, techniques of labor, sexuality, and domesticity, accounts that would better enable us to grapple with their corrosive work on the mind *and* body. Furthermore, if race is inherited trauma, it is also affective belonging. What if one of the reasons there is so little scholarship on affect and racialization is because we have such scanty language to account for the ways violence registers in the body, the ways resilience, hope, and love take material form? To account for how many activist, intellectual, and artistic groups race, sex, and sexuality serve also as generative resources, as life-giving structures of attachment, enabling constraints born from the ashes of trauma? Analyzing the imbrication of the cultural and material worlds does not necessarily entail the horrors of race science, eugenics, or sociobiology, though it certainly poses that risk. A wide embrace of models of plasticity or determinism, full stop, recapitulates the biopolitical cycles we've been repeating for the last two hundred years. Yet a careful assemblage theory could also be a tool to more fully understand the hybrid nature of life itself and to build political models that sustain our collective bonds, rather than subjugating to economic imperatives our very capacities of feeling.

NOTES

....

INTRODUCTION

1. DiAngelo, "White Fragility."
2. I riff here on Michele Landis Dauber's notion of the "sympathetic state." Dauber, *The Sympathetic State.*
3. See in particular Berlant, *The Female Complaint*; Barnes, *States of Sympathy*; and Wexler, *Tender Violence.*
4. Two scholars who explicitly and importantly theorize sentimentalism in relation to biopower include Strick, *American Dolorologies*; and Romero, *Home Fronts.* See also Luciano, *Arranging Grief.*
5. The topic of sentimentalism has generated a large secondary literature. The first twenty years of scholarship were dominated by a debate about the political relevance of sentimental ideology. Ann Douglas infamously accuses sentimentalism of functioning as an enervating force that sapped the strength from an "authentic," thoughtful, and masculine public culture by helping to bring about "the exaltation of the average which is the trademark of mass culture." Douglas, *The Feminization of American Culture*, 4. Jane Tompkins, in contrast, commends sentimental mass literature for serving as an enlivening tradition whose very "familiarity and typicality . . . are the basis of their effectiveness," particularly in formulating a feminine politics that understands submission as power. Tompkins, *Sensational Designs*, xvi. A second wave of scholarship by key figures including Lora Romero, Glenn Hendler, and Laura Wexler examines how sentimentalism is itself productive of political, social, and economic relations, a move that has significantly expanded our understanding of the terrain of the sentimental into visual culture, artistic practice, political theory, racial thought, business culture, and legal practice, among other arenas. For particularly rich collections, see Chapman and Hendler, *Sentimental Men*; and Shirley Samuels, *The Culture of Sentiment.* More recently, studies of affect have turned to sentimentalism as a prime mode that cultivates structures of political attachment. See Berlant, *The Female Complaint.*
6. Rose, *The Politics of Life Itself.*
7. Douglas, *The Feminization of American Culture.* For this critic, "by such self-baptism, feminine authors become characters in their own sentimental effusions: hothouse products, they are self-announced refugees from history" (186).

8. Douglas, *The Feminization of American Culture*, 195; Young, *Darwin's Metaphor*.

9. Hendler, *Public Sentiments*, 36.

10. Shelley Streeby argues that the sensational and sentimental modes of popular and political culture are always intertwined. Here I expand her framework to analyze the interdependence of physiological and emotional discourses and practices of feeling more broadly. See Streeby, *American Sensations* and *Radical Sensations*.

11. In the eighteenth century, Denis Diderot explained that sensibility is the capacity "to perceive impressions of external objects," and sentiment, in turn, is "an emotional 'movement' in response to a physical sensation." Quoted in Jessica Riskin, *Science in the Age of Sensibility*, 1.

12. I build here on Dana Luciano's crucial analysis of the chronobiopolitics of sentimentalism, in which sentiment entails the capacity of reflection over time—as opposed to the primitive immediacy of sensation—that enables racial progress. Luciano, *Arranging Grief*.

13. Thanks to Ed Cohen for help with this point.

14. Keller, *The Mirage of a Space between Nature and Nurture*, 5.

15. I emphasize the influence of sentiment beyond the domestic novel, prioritizing less well-analyzed aesthetic and political traditions.

16. This methodological pairing perhaps demands justification. Science and sentiment have been familiar groupings almost exclusively as superlative polarities. Currently, however, the seeming naturalness of this opposition is falling apart in the wake of the ontological turn. See, for example, Murison, *The Politics of Anxiety*, 17–46.

17. Brennan, *The Transmission of Affect*, 6.

18. S.v. "impression, n.," Oxford English Dictionary Online, accessed June 3, 2015, http://www.oed.com.proxy.libraries.rutgers.edu/view/Entry/92725.

19. S.v. "impression, n.," Oxford English Dictionary Online, accessed June 3, 2015, http://www.oed.com.proxy.libraries.rutgers.edu/view/Entry/92725.

20. S.v. "impression, n.," Oxford English Dictionary Online, accessed June 3, 2015, http://www.oed.com.proxy.libraries.rutgers.edu/view/Entry/92725; emphasis added.

21. There is a limited discussion of the notion of impressibility in Victorian studies that approaches the concept as a quality of the mind important in the development of psychology. See, for example, Vrettos, "Defining Habits."

22. Buchanan, *Outlines of Lectures on the Neurological System of Anthropology*, 39. Buchanan identified impressibility in phrenological terms: a region of the brain that only a few possess. I use the term more broadly.

23. Dr. Elizabeth Blackwell, for example, explained that in contrast to the "savage," the member of the civilized races "approaches more nearly to the true type of man, and has acquired the capacity of transmitting increased capacities to his children." Blackwell, *Essays in Medical Sociology*, 181.

24. Buchanan, *Buchanan's Journal of Man*, 322.

25. On racialization as the eternal state of flesh, see Spillers, "Mama's Baby, Papa's Maybe," 66–67.

26. On Lamarck's notion of the milieu, see Canguilhem and Savage, "The Living and Its Milieu," 11.

27. Foucault, *Security, Territory, Population*, 20–21.

28. Nikolas Rose contrasts the molar scale of earlier biopower from the molecular emphasis of the contemporary moment. Rose, *The Politics of Life Itself*, 11–12.

29. Malthus, *An Essay on the Principle of Population*. I further explore Malthus's text in chapter 2.

30. James Chandler defines sentiment as "distributed feeling. It is emotion that results from social circulation, passion that has been mediated by a sympathetic passage through a virtual point of view." Chandler, *An Archeology of Sympathy*, 11–12.

31. Bushnell, *Unconscious Influence*, 16 (hereafter cited parenthetically as *UI*).

32. For example, Adam Smith, *The Theory of Moral Sentiments*. For insightful analysis, see Barker-Benfield, *The Culture of Sensibility*.

33. Chiles, *Transformable Race*; Wheeler, *The Complexion of Race*.

34. As Diane Paul clarifies: "In the nineteenth century, however, 'innate' did not imply 'determined,' for it was generally believed that the environment shaped heredity. Thus an inherited trait could be suppressed or redirected by changes in the condition of life." Paul, *Controlling Human Heredity*, 32.

35. Hunt, *Glances and Glimpses*, 102.

36. Chiles, *Transformable Race*.

37. Elizabeth A. Wilson argues that Darwin and Freud's notion of the body incorporates, via Lamarckism, "a permeable, heterogeneously constituted biology" that includes, in the case of Darwin, "psychological, cultural, geological, oceanic, and meteorological" factors all bound in reciprocal relation. Wilson, *Psychosomatic*, 70, 69. Other work in this vein includes Murison, *The Politics of Anxiety*; and Castiglia, *Interior States*.

38. Gossett, *Race*; Horsman, *Race and Manifest Destiny*.

39. Nyong'o, *The Amalgamation Waltz*, 83.

40. For example, Ellen Samuels, *Fantasies of Identification*, 18. The book works from the premise that race in the nineteenth century was figured as a fixed and immutable effect of heredity that was "biological and therefore inescapable" (27).

41. Mel Chen illuminates animacy, or a sentience hierarchy rooted in linguistic principles, as a broad biopolitical tactic to order life according to its relative vitality. Chen, *Animacies*.

42. Anna Julia Cooper, *A Voice from the South*, 9, 52.

43. For another account of the tension between nineteenth-century accounts of racial fixity and the transformational work of civilization, see Blencowe, "Biology, Contingency and the Problem of Racism in Feminist Discourse."

44. These criteria were codified by the ethnologists Lewis Henry Morgan and E. B. Tylor.

45. Freud, "A Note upon the 'Mystic Writing Pad,'" 208. Dana Seitler aptly observes that Freud's Wolf Man case reveals that in psychoanalysis, as with modernity more generally, "the nonhuman is not always the abject result of the more civilized human" but is, rather, contained in the human itself. Seitler, *Atavistic Tendencies*, 53.

46. Puar here builds on Rey Chow's notion of the "ascendancy of whiteness." Puar, *Terrorist Assemblages*, 200.

47. Clough, introduction to *The Affective Turn*, 2.

48. Puar, "Prognosis Time."

49. Drawing on the philosophy of reason and the history of science, Denise F. da Silva names the condition of racialization as "affectability," or the idea that some humans are composed solely of exteriority, are wholly "subjected to outer determination," and lack the self-constituting capacity of autopoesis possessed by Europeans. Da Silva, *Toward a Global Idea of Race*, 47. In my reading of nineteenth-century racial thought, the capacity to absorb the effects of impressions over time distinguishes the civilized state of impressibility from the racialized quality of being easily moved and yet unable to retain the effects of those movements.

50. Cope, *Origin of the Fittest*, 381, 285.

51. On primitive sensation versus sentimental reflection, see Luciano, *Arranging Grief*, 25–68.

52. Spillers, "Mama's Baby, Papa's Maybe," 67.

53. Quoted in Hayot, "Chinese Bodies, Chinese Futures," 103. See also Lye, *America's Asia*.

54. The racialized body as machine was celebrated by national capital, which replaced enslaved labor with indentured Chinese labor in the 1860s, and railed against by California's threatened white working class. On the simultaneous ending of legal slavery and beginning of the importation of coolie labor, see Jung, *Coolies and Cane*.

55. Cope, *Origin of the Fittest*, 235.

56. Ngai, *Ugly Feelings*, 89–125.

57. Ngai, *Ugly Feelings*, 91.

58. Repo, *The Biopolitics of Gender*, 13. On *biopower* as an umbrella term, see Cohen, *A Body Worth Defending*, 20.

59. The sentimental politics of life was a key epoch of transition in which disciplinary and security power overlapped. Disciplinary techniques of isolation, atomization, control, supervision, and the goal of perfection attempted to manage phenomena increasingly conceived of as "physical processes," or elements of the real, of measurable and predictable crisis, risk, and danger that affected the population within a certain milieu. Foucault, *Security, Territory, Population*, 57.

60. Foucault, *Security, Territory, Population*, 45–48.

61. Ahuja, *Bioinsecurities*, xii; Puar, *Terrorist Assemblages*, 32–36; Mbembe, "Necropolitics," 39. For an opposing view that delineates biopower from necropower, see Boggs, *Animalia Americana*, 10–21.

62. Mbembe, "Necropolitics," 23.

63. Da Silva, *Toward a Global Idea of Race*, xl.

64. Mason, introduction to *The Poems of Philip Henry Savage*, xvii.

65. Russett, *Sexual Science*; Laqueur, *Making Sex*. Lynn Wardley argues that Mary Wollstonecraft "sees woman's bodies and minds *as* matter, which means that they are shaped by the vicissitudes of other material systems, including culture." Wardley, "Lamarck's Daughters."

66. Sears, *Arresting Dress*; Kogan, "Sex-Separation in Public Restrooms."

67. Thanks to Arev Pivazyan for help with this point.

68. Looby, "The Man Who Thought Himself a Woman," 242.

69. Looby, "The Man Who Thought Himself a Woman," 252–253.

70. Looby, "The Man Who Thought Himself a Woman," 241.

71. I depart here from Nancy Leys Stepan's pivotal essay "Race and Gender: The Role of Analogy in Science." I see race and sex in the period as operating in interlocking, rather than analogical, relation, in which sex establishes the materialization of racial difference itself.

72. I avoid the term *gender* throughout this project on account of its inapplicability to the pre–World War II period. Gender, a term introduced in its present sense as the social role of biological sex by sexologist John Money, emerges out of a later epoch of biopolitics than the period I examine. The nineteenth century made no distinction between biological and social roles of sex—sexual difference was itself seen as an achievement of civilization. For accounts of the emergence of "gender" and associated biopolitical technologies see Preciado, *Testo Junkie*; and Repo, *The Biopolitics of Gender*. For a different take on the applicability of gender prior to the twentieth century, see LaFleur, "Sex and 'Unsex.'"

73. Ferguson builds here on Chandan Reddy. Ferguson, *Aberrations in Black*, 3.

74. Foucault, *"Society Must Be Defended"* and *Security, Territory, Population*.

75. Welter, "The Cult of True Womanhood."

76. On bodily disaggregation, see Allewaert, *Ariel's Ecology*.

77. Luciano, *Arranging Grief*.

78. Blackwell, *Counsel to Parents*, 7.

79. Mason, introduction to *The Poems of Philip Henry Savage*, xxx. See Mao, *Fateful Beauty*; Gaskill, "Vibrant Environments"; Noble, *The Masochistic Pleasures of Sentimental Literature*; Kyla Wazana Tompkins, *Racial Indigestion*; Lauren Klein, "Matters of Taste"; Pascoe, *Relations of Rescue*.

80. Shah, *Contagious Divides*, 12, 84.

81. Shah, *Contagious Divides*, 77.

82. Keeling, *The Witch's Flight*, 20.

83. I build here on José Muñoz's performative idea of race as something a body does, not something a body is. Muñoz, "Feeling Brown, Feeling Down." For key primary sources, see Adam Smith, *The Theory of Moral Sentiments*, 234–268; Morgan, *Ancient Society*.

84. Foucault, *The History of Sexuality*, 106.

85. Berlant, *The Female Complaint*, 41.

86. Mbembe, "Necropolitics."

87. Foucault, *Lectures on the Will to Know*.

88. On the many dimensions of nineteenth-century domesticity and their relationship to U.S. empire, see Amy Kaplan's seminal essay "Manifest Domesticity."

89. In her important early work on sentiment and biopower, Lora Romero illuminates how Harriet Beecher Stowe performs a "hygienist critique of patriarchal power" in which norms of physical health provide the shape and structure of Stowe's analysis of slavery. For Romero, little Eva is a casualty of the rigid mind/ body split that slavery imposes on the white and black populations, respectively; Eva's body is quickly "used up" on account of her sympathetic relations with her family's slaves. Romero, *Home Fronts*, 81, 79.

90. Stoler, *Carnal Knowledge and Imperial Power*.

91. Stoler, *Carnal Knowledge and Imperial Power*, 120.

92. Foucault characterizes governmentality as the institutions and practices that enable a form of "power that has the population as its target, political economy as its major form of knowledge, and apparatuses of security as its essential technical instrument." Foucault, *Security, Territory, Population*, 108.

93. Cope, *Origin of the Fittest*, 29.

94. I use the term *eugenic sciences*, rather than dismissing them as pseudoscience, because they were leading fields of biological thought in their day. Referring to disciplines such as phrenology, Lamarckism, and eugenics as pseudoscience positions science as a transcendent form of knowledge that is independent from its shifting means of knowledge production.

95. Subramaniam, *Ghost Stories for Darwin*, 45–69.

96. Quoted by Paul, *Controlling Human Heredity*, 3. Similarly, the influential Henry Fairfield Osborn defined eugenics as the practice of reproducing the "best spiritual, moral, intellectual, and physical forces of heredity" in the national population. Osborn, preface to *The Passing of the Great Race*, ix.

97. Scholars in Latin American, African American, and disability studies, in particular, have demonstrated that eugenics is a flexible program that can be adapted to a number of scientific, political, racial, and national frameworks. See English, *Unnatural Selections*; Ordover, *American Eugenics*; Stepan, *The Hour of Eugenics*; and Kline, *Building a Better Race*.

98. Deleuze, "Postscript on the Societies of Control"; Rose, *The Politics of Life Itself*; Preciado, *Testo Junkie*.

99. Rose, *The Politics of Life Itself*, 3.

100. Rose, *The Politics of Life Itself*, 1–7.

101. Rose, *The Politics of Life Itself*, 18, 19.

102. Rose, *The Politics of Life Itself*, 16.

103. Rose, *The Politics of Life Itself*, 61, 62.

104. Melinda Cooper, *Life as Surplus*.

105. Preciado, *Testo Junkie*, 105–106. Pharmacopornopower signals Preciado's notion that the convergence of the chemical and sexual revolutions and expanding media empires in the mid-twentieth century ushered in a new era of biopolitics.

106. Accounts of the new symbolic importance of affective labor tend to overlook the continued semiotic and material significance of industrial production. For a critique of this work, see Martín-Cabrera, "The Potentiality of the Commons."

107. Vora, *Life Support*, 3.

108. Mitchell and Snyder, *The Biopolitics of Disability*, 7.

109. Willey, "A World of Materialisms," 1000.

110. Willey, "A World of Materialisms."

111. Pitts-Taylor, *The Brain's Body*, 40.

112. Pitts-Taylor, *The Brain's Body*, 123.

113. Stacy Alaimo celebrates nineteenth-century Darwinian feminisms as anticipating new materialisms, a move which neglects the civilizationist hierarchies subtending their views of the dynamism of (white) bodily matter. Alaimo, "Sexual Matters."

114. Ahmed, "Orientations Matter," 247.

115. Ahmed, "Orientations Matter," 247.

116. Gaskill, "Vibrant Environments," 69–115; Gilman, *The Dress of Women.*

117. Coole, "The Inertia of Matter and the Generativity of Flesh," 92.

118. On the latter, see da Silva, *Toward a Global Theory of Race.*

119. Jordy Rosenberg proposes that new materialists and others problematically position the object world as existing in a distinct and prior temporality from the social world of the present, thereby echoing the racial structures of colonialism. Rosenberg, "The Molecularization of Sexuality," n.p.

120. Da Silva, *Toward a Global Theory of Race.*

121. Willey, "A World of Materialisms," 1000.

122. Da Silva, *Toward a Global Theory of Race,* 47.

123. Subramaniam, *Ghost Stories for Darwin,* 52.

124. Agamben, *Homo Sacer.*

125. Haines, "Martin Delany."

126. Müller-Wille and Rheinberger, "Heredity," 20.

127. López-Beltrán, "The Medical Origins of Heredity," 125.

128. Müller-Wille and Rheinberger, "Heredity," 3–34.

129. Müller-Wille and Rheinberger, "Heredity," 16–24.

130. Stoler, *Race and the Colonial Education of Desire*; Luibhéid, *Entry Denied.*

131. Coviello, *Tomorrow's Parties*; LaFleur, *The Natural History of Sexuality.*

132. Coviello, *Tomorrow's Parties,* 22.

133. Puar, *Terrorist Assemblages,* 35.

134. Puar, *Terrorist Assemblages,* 211.

135. Somerville, *Queering the Color Line.*

136. Stocking, *Race, Culture, and Evolution,* 251.

137. Puar, *Terrorist Assemblages,* 9–10.

138. Keller, *The Mirage of a Space between Nature and Nurture,* 21, 22. Keller argues that Darwin and Galton are the two figures most responsible for this development.

139. Keller, *The Mirage of a Space between Nature and Nurture,* 11.

140. Heredity discourse thus parallels the biopolitical work of immune discourse, which delineates a body from the milieu in which it is immersed, that Ed Cohen theorizes in *A Body Worth Defending.*

141. Eliza Slavet argues that Freud drew extensively on neo-Lamarckism in conceptualizing Jewish identity as the inheritance of ancestral memories. Slavet, *Racial Fever.*

142. On the emergence of the X chromosome as the genetic site of sex difference in the 1920s, see Richardson, *Sex Itself.*

143. Keller, *The Mirage of a Space between Nature and Nurture.*

144. Coviello, *Tomorrow's Parties.*

145. Julian Huxley coined the term to note the rise of an evolutionary theory that accounted for both the mechanism of Mendelian heredity and the dynamics of population pressure. On Mexico, see Stern, "Eugenics beyond Borders."

146. Foucault, *Security, Territory, Population,* 78. Foucault dates this shift to Darwin himself, rather than the way Darwin was received.

147. Deleuze, "Postscript on the Societies of Control," 3.

148. Deleuze, "Postscript on the Societies of Control," 4.

149. Repo, *The Biopolitics of Gender*; Melamed, "The Spirit of Neoliberalism."
150. Puar, *Terrorist Assemblages*; Weheliye, *Habeas Viscus*; Ahuja, *Bioinsecurities.*

1. TAXONOMIES OF FEELING

1. The name riffs on the earlier American School of Ethnology, now infamous for its racist theory of polygenesis.
2. The broad enthusiasm in the United States for Lamarckian evolutionary paradigms, rather than the competition of natural selection, has received remarkably little scholarly attention outside the history of science, even in the midst of the current emphasis on the role of the life sciences in everyday life. Among those projects that do attend to Lamarckian cultural politics, Lamarckian evolutionary theories have often appeared as progressive alternatives to so-called social Darwinism, an evaluation influenced by claims such as that made by American School affiliate Joseph Le Conte in the epigraph to this chapter.
3. My own research for this chapter was greatly enabled by the libraries of UC Berkeley, which hold Le Conte's personal collection of published and manuscript neo-Lamarckian science, some of which is shelved in the open stacks of the Bioscience and Natural Resources Library.
4. Cope, "Two Perils," 2052–2054, 2070–2071.
5. Cope, "The Oppression of Women," 4104.
6. Cope, "The Present Problems of Organic Evolution," 572–573; Cope, "Ethical Evolution," 1525.
7. Cope, "Energy of Life Evolution," 790.
8. Jessica Riskin points to Denis Diderot's definition of sentiment as "an emotional 'movement' in response to a physical sensation." Riskin, *Science in the Age of Sensibility*, 1.
9. Cope, "Ethical Evolution," 1523.
10. Bowler, "Edward Drinker Cope and the Changing Structure of Evolutionary Theory," 252.
11. Barber, *The Heyday of Natural History*, 28.
12. Dana D. Nelson, " 'No Cold or Empty Heart' "; Walls, "Textbooks and Texts from the Brooks"; Hallock, "Male Pleasures and the Genders of Eighteenth-Century Botanic Exchange."
13. Thanks to Ann Fabian for help with this point.
14. Quoted in Menand, *The Metaphysical Club*, 105; emphasis added.
15. Gould, *The Mismeasure of Man*, 44.
16. On late nineteenth-century scientists who investigated sympathy and emotion, see Levander, "The Science of Sentiment."
17. Riskin, *Science in the Age of Sensibility*, 21, 6, 2, 7.
18. Van Sant, *Eighteenth-Century Sensibility*, 1.
19. Figlio, "Theories of Perception and the Physiology of Mind in the Late Eighteenth Century," 191.
20. Van Sant, *Eighteenth-Century Sensibility*, 1–4.
21. Stocking, *Race, Culture, and Evolution*, 265, 263.

22. Cope, *Origin of the Fittest*, 385.

23. Draaisma, *Metaphors of Memory*, 24.

24. Burnyeat, *The Theaetetus of Plato*, 325.

25. Burnyeat, *The Theaetetus of Plato*, 329.

26. Burnyeat, *The Theaetetus of Plato*, 329.

27. Barnes, *The Complete Works of Aristotle*, vol. 1, 674.

28. Barnes, *The Complete Works of Aristotle*, vol. 1, 674.

29. Barnes, *The Complete Works of Aristotle*, vol. 1, 619.

30. Barnes, *The Complete Works of Aristotle*, vol. 1, 619.

31. Barnes, *The Complete Works of Aristotle*, vol. 1, 619.

32. "Let us then suppose the Mind to be, as we say, white Paper, void of all characters, without any *Ideas*," Locke proposed. Locke, *Essay concerning Human Understanding*, 104. Contrary to common assertion, the phrase *tabula rasa* (blank slate) does not appear anywhere in the final draft of Locke's *Essay*. See Walker, *Locke, Literary Criticism, and Philosophy*, 31–32. Walker explains that the image of the "mind as an imprinted substance" was common among the seventeenth-century innatists Locke was seeking to overturn, and he asserts the "epistemological neutrality of the imprinted substance metaphor," for it was enlisted to support both innatist and experiential positions (34). For my purposes, I wish to underscore the ubiquity of the impression metaphor of the mind, such that it was common language rather than grounds of the debate.

33. Locke, *Essay concerning Human Understanding*, 117.

34. Locke, *Essay concerning Human Understanding*, 123.

35. Locke, *Essay concerning Human Understanding*, 123.

36. Allewaert, *Ariel's Ecology*, 3.

37. Allewaert, *Ariel's Ecology*, 2.

38. Locke, *Essay concerning Human Understanding*, 118, 64.

39. Cultural theorist Lisa Lowe stresses that attending to Locke's own participation in settler colonial ventures, such as his involvement in the settlement of the Carolina colony and his work as treasurer for the English Council for Trade and Foreign Plantations, suggests that the juncture of "liberalism and colonialism is not one of biographical complicity. . . . It is precisely by liberal principles that political philosophy provided for colonial settlement, slavery, and indenture." Lowe, *Intimacies of Four Continents*, 9.

40. Quoted in Lowe, *Intimacies of Four Continents*, 10.

41. Locke, *Essay concerning Human Understanding*, 118.

42. Lord, "The Natural and the Spiritual," n.p.

43. Quoted in Wardley, "American Fiction and Civilizing House," v.

44. The description of Darwin's theory as capturing the "struggle for existence" was coined by Herbert Spencer.

45. Hyatt self-consciously built on Lamarck's work, of which he learned from Agassiz. Cope became aware of Lamarck after he had begun developing his own theories about the effects of the use and disuse of body parts on an organism.

46. Darwin, preface to the Third Edition of *On the Origin of Species*, n.p.

47. Figlio, "Theories of Perception," 195.

48. Lamarck, *Philosophie Zoologique*, 221, 219.

49. Lamarck, *Philosophie Zoologique*, 219.

50. In a recent semester of my "Gender and Science" course, a precocious student remarked that Lamarck's theory of the inheritance of acquired characteristics had always seemed patently false to him, for despite their continued and vigorous use, penises did not grow larger each generation. I was delighted to tell the class that Lamarck in fact had precisely penises in mind—perhaps in hopes of the very evolutionary outcome my student so clearly articulated.

51. Lamarck, *Philosophie Zoologique*, 106.

52. Lamarck, *Philosophie Zoologique*, 321.

53. Lamarck, *Philosophie Zoologique*, 222, 322.

54. Lamarck, *Philosophie Zoologique*, 333, 336.

55. According to Foucault's chronology. Foucault, *"Society Must Be Defended."*

56. Foucault, *"Society Must Be Defended,"* 243.

57. Foucault, *"Society Must Be Defended,"* 62.

58. Foucault, *"Society Must Be Defended,"* 255.

59. Foucault, *"Society Must Be Defended,"* 254.

60. Quoted in Gould, *The Mismeasure of Man*, 50.

61. Cope, *Origin of the Fittest*, 210.

62. See, for example, Margulis and Sagan, *Acquiring Genomes*.

63. Cope, *The Primary Factors of Organic Evolution*, v.

64. Cope, *Origin of the Fittest*, 229.

65. Cope, "Energy of Life Evolution," 790, 790–791.

66. Cope, "Descent of Man," 167–168.

67. Powell, "The Growth of Sentiency," 167.

68. Cope, *Origin of the Fittest*, 40.

69. Cope, "Energy of Life Evolution," 789–800.

70. Lamarck, *Philosophie Zoologique*, 324, 326.

71. Cope, *Origin of the Fittest*, 281, 386.

72. Cope, *Origin of the Fittest*, 381.

73. Cope, "Two Perils," 2054.

74. Herzig, *Suffering for Science*, 24, 22, 24.

75. Cope, "Two Perils," 2053.

76. Cope, "Two Perils," 2054.

77. TallBear, *Native American DNA*, 45–48, 136–138.

78. TallBear, *Native American DNA*, 137.

79. Cope, "Descent of Man," 169.

80. Le Conte, "The Theory of Evolution and Social Progress," 493. Cope, by contrast, argued that some amount of struggle characterizes evolution even at the highest levels of racial development.

81. Cope, "Ethical Evolution," 1525.

82. Quoted in Lanzoni, "Sympathy in *Mind* (1876–1900)," 270.

83. Lanzoni, "Sympathy in *Mind* (1876–1900)," 285.

84. Packard and Cope, "Editors' Table" 16, no. 6, 491.

85. Hendler, *Public Sentiments*; Barnes, *States of Sympathy*, ix.

86. Hartman, *Scenes of Subjection*.

87. Luciano, *Arranging Grief*, 18.

88. Luciano, *Arranging Grief*, 20, 153.

89. For an influential reading of the sentimental ideal of female bodilessness, see Noble, *The Masochistic Pleasures of Sentimental Literature*.

90. Pernick, *A Calculus of Suffering*, 157.

91. Cope, "On the Hypothesis of Evolution," 177.

92. Cope, "On the Hypothesis of Evolution," 175–177.

93. Foucault, *"Society Must Be Defended,"* 60–61.

94. Foucault, *"Society Must Be Defended,"* 61.

95. Van Sant, *Eighteenth-Century Sensibility*, 4.

96. Bederman, *Manliness and Civilization*; Lutz, *American Nervousness*.

97. See, for example, Morgan, *Ancient Society*.

98. Cope, "The Relation of the Sexes to Government," 722.

99. Cope, "What Is the Object of Life?," 51.

100. Cope, "The Relation of the Sexes to Government," 723, 721.

101. Todd, *Sensibility*, 8.

102. Cope, "The Future of Thought in America," 23.

103. Packard and Cope, "Editors' Table" 16, no. 1, 34.

104. Cope, "Oppression of Women," 4104.

105. Cope, *Origin of the Fittest*, 238.

106. Cope, "What Is the Object of Life?," 49.

107. Cope, "Psychology," 399.

108. Cope, "Oppression of Women," 4104.

109. E. D. Cope to Julia Cope, March 27, 1888, Edward Drinker Cope, Letters (MSS.C67), American Museum of Natural History Archives, New York.

110. Cope, "Oppression of Women," 4104.

111. Le Conte, "The Relation of Biology and Sociology to the Woman Question."

112. Cope, "Two Perils," 2070.

113. Cope, "The Marriage Problem," 1324.

114. Cope, "The Applied Metaphysics of Sex," 399, 400.

115. Hyatt, "The Influence of Woman," 91.

116. Cope, "Two Perils," 2070.

117. Hyatt, "The Influence of Woman," 90, 91.

118. Over three decades, Marsh similarly dedicated himself to thwarting Cope's fossil discoveries through methods both scientific and scandalous.

119. See Jaffe, *The Gilded Dinosaur*.

120. Haller, *Outcasts from Evolution*, 201.

121. Bowler, *The Non-Darwinian Revolution*.

122. Peirce, "Evolutionary Love," 180.

123. See Bowler, *The Eclipse of Darwinism*.

124. Packard and Cope, "Editors' Table" 19, no. 7, 691.

125. Cope, "Letter to the Editor: The African in America," 2399.

126. Cope and Kingsley, "Editorials," 451.

127. See Daston and Galison, *Objectivity*.

128. Quoted in Snyder and Mitchell, *Cultural Locations of Disability*, frontispiece.

129. Cope, "What Is Republicanism?," 4897; emphasis in the original.

130. See, for example, Mason, *Civilized Creatures*.

2. BODY AS TEXT, RACE AS PALIMPSEST

1. Redding, *To Make a Poet Black*; Peterson, "'Further Liftings of the Veil.'"

2. Claudia Tate argues that the very conventionality of the sentimental genre successfully conceals the radical political desires of Harper and other late nineteenth-century black feminist novelists. Tate, *Domestic Allegories*. More recently, P. Gabrielle Foreman similarly contends that "sentimental modes of expression often camouflage what is hidden in plain sight," namely, the complex social and political movements Harper and other writers advanced through their fictional texts. Foreman, *Activist Sentiments*, 7.

3. Harper's speech was delivered at the World's Congress of Representative Women, the only forum permitting women speakers at the World's Columbian Exhibition.

4. Harper, "Woman's Political Future."

5. Kazanjian, *The Colonizing Trick*, 119.

6. This approach is inspired by Jasbir Puar's methodological provocation to analyze biopolitics from the position of the occupied. Puar, "Inhumanist Occupation."

7. Foreman, *Activist Sentiments*, 7.

8. Foster, *A Brighter Coming Day*, 278.

9. "Politics of respectability" demarcates the belief that "freed of crippling, invidious, racial discriminations, blacks are capable of meeting the established moral standards of white middle-class Americans." Higginbotham, *Righteous Discontent*, 17.

10. David Kazanjian argues that processes of "racial governmentality" within colonization position race as the means through which populations are quantified and managed in order to secure freedom. In the process, freedom and colonization become intertwined. Kazanjian, *The Colonizing Trick*.

11. See, for example, Roediger, *The Wages of Whiteness*.

12. Anna Julia Cooper is another contender for this title. On the robust intellectual tradition of black women, one that makes a convincing case for Anna Julia Cooper's position at its helm, see Brittney Cooper, *Beyond Respectability*.

13. Foster, introduction to *A Brighter Coming Day*, 13.

14. Melba Joyce Boyd, *Discarded Legacy*, 15.

15. The increased legal reach of the institution of slavery in the 1850s galvanized Harper into political work. Maryland's 1853 decree that any African American who entered the state from its northern border could be taken into slavery, regardless of their legal status, was the immediate impetus of her lecturing career. See Melba Joyce Boyd, *Discarded Legacy*, 36–40.

16. Quoted in Melba Joyce Boyd, *Discarded Legacy*, 6.

17. An exception includes Stancliff, *Frances Ellen Watkins Harper*, which analyzes Harper's work as part of the black rhetorical tradition.

18. Harper, *Iola Leroy*, 244. See also Field, "Frances E. W. Harper and the Politics of Intellectual Maturity"; Gillman, *Blood Talk*.

19. Harper, *Iola Leroy*, 244.

20. Anna Julia Cooper, *A Voice from the South*, 11, 144.

21. Foster, *A Brighter Coming Day*, 221.

22. Foster, *A Brighter Coming Day*, 228.

23. Lynn Wardley has argued that the "representation of the uncanny power of Victorian material culture to elicit emotion, provoke somatic response, bewitch, heal, or avenge wrong," not only resonates with the Catholic practice of the relic and the role of the commodity in capitalism as a fetish of its conditions of production, but also emerges from a Lamarckian belief in the power of transmission and "the Pan-African religions of the antebellum South." Wardley, "Relic, Fetish, Femmage," 205. On relations between humans and commodities in sentimental culture more broadly, see Merish, *Sentimental Materialism*. Performance studies scholar Robin Bernstein's theory of "scriptive things" captures how material culture in the era invites a specific repertoire of behavior in its use, such that objects incur experiences that press into the flesh. Bernstein, *Racial Innocence*, 92–145.

24. Foster, *A Brighter Coming Day*, 81.

25. Foster, *A Brighter Coming Day*, 59.

26. Foster, *A Brighter Coming Day*, 61.

27. See, for example, Schwartz, *Birthing a Slave*; Briggs, *Reproducing Empire*; Strick, *American Dolorologies*.

28. Quoted in Strick, *American Dolorologies*, 103.

29. Simon Strick argues that pain "functions as a relay between the sentimental and biopolitical circumscriptions of politics," a thesis that posits their "intersection" and "collaboration": a framework just shy of figuring their fundamental interdependence. Strick, *American Dolorologies*, 4.

30. Fretwell, "Senses of Belonging," 14.

31. Harper, *Iola Leroy*, 254.

32. Watkins, "Address Delivered before the Moral Reform Society in Philadelphia," 165, 157; emphasis in the original.

33. Foster, *A Brighter Coming Day*, 286.

34. Harper, "Trial and Triumph," 195.

35. Foster, *A Brighter Coming Day*, 104.

36. Manning, *Politics of Touch*, 62.

37. Van Sant, *Eighteenth-Century Sensibility*, 90.

38. Van Sant, *Eighteenth-Century Sensibility*, 97.

39. Van Sant, *Eighteenth-Century Sensibility*, 91.

40. Figlio, "Theories of Perception and the Physiology of Mind in the Late Eighteenth Century."

41. Van Sant, *Eighteenth-Century Sensibility*, 95.

42. This framework is opposed to neoliberal models in which biological potential is disaggregated, dispersed, and maximized at the level of the cell. See Vora, *Life Support*; and Lee, *The Exquisite Corpse of Asian America*.

43. Howes, *Sensual Relations*, 5.

44. Mark Smith, *Sensing the Past*, 109–110.

45. Quoted in Mark Smith, *Sensing the Past*, 108. On embroidery, see Classen, "Feminine Tactics." Classen argues that "ladies'" work was understood as a more refined version of working-class domestic labor, but that it "never rose above its shared sensory basis with housework" (228).

46. Mark Smith, *Sensing the Past*, 100.

47. Classen, "Feminine Tactics," 228.

48. Mark Smith, *Sensing the Past*, 108. The passage quotes Alain Corbin.

49. Bauer, " 'In the Blood,'" 62.

50. Noble, *The Masochistic Pleasures of Sentimental Literature*, 114, 34.

51. Still, *Underground Railroad*, 779–780, quoted in Melba Joyce Boyd, *Discarded Legacy*, 43.

52. Harper, "Trial and Triumph," 259.

53. Harper, "Trial and Triumph," 261.

54. Harper, "Trial and Triumph," 264.

55. The passage suggests the multiple functions of white women's gloves in bourgeois culture—in addition to protecting skin from the sun's darkening rays, they also sheathed porous hands from contaminating grasps. Thanks to Sarah Blackwood for pointing this out.

56. The belief that shame required a degree of self-awareness and self-government unattainable by African Americans was widespread and most famously articulated by Thomas Jefferson.

57. Nyong'o, *The Amalgamation Waltz*, 76.

58. Hartman, *Scenes of Subjection*.

59. Harper, *Iola Leroy*, 219.

60. Carby, *Reconstructing Womanhood*, 80. Critics such as Deborah McDowell, Houston A. Baker, and Ann duCille similarly emphasize what they see as Harper's "passionless" characters that result from her efforts to defend the black capacity of civilization. DuCille, *The Coupling Convention*, 43–47.

61. Tavia Nyong'o approaches sexuality as a prominent site of the class struggle inherent to respectability politics. Nyong'o, *The Amalgamation Waltz*, 85. Antebellum black sexuality, in his reading, is not only a site of trauma but also a space of creative invention and expression.

62. Sanborn, "Mother's Milk," 707.

63. Sanborn, "Mother's Milk," 703, 698.

64. Ahmed, *Cultural Politics of Emotion*; Sedgwick, *Touching Feeling*.

65. Harper, "Sowing and Reaping," 137.

66. Harper, "Sowing and Reaping," 266–267; emphasis added.

67. Harper, "Sowing and Reaping," 267; emphasis added.

68. Harper, "Trial and Triumph," 267.

69. Hawthorne, "The Birth-Mark" (hereafter cited parenthetically).

70. Darwin, *The Expression of Emotions in Man and Animals*, 322.

71. Carby, *Reconstructing Womanhood*, 109. On the "sexual economy" informing the lynching of black men and women, see Wiegman, *American Anatomies*, 81–113.

72. Tate, *Domestic Allegories*, 4.

73. Coviello, *Tomorrow's Parties*.

74. Harper, "Trial and Triumph," 185.

75. Noble, *The Masochistic Pleasures of Sentimental Literature*, 25.

76. Noble, *The Masochistic Pleasures of Sentimental Literature*, 5; emphasis in the original.

77. Foucault, *"Society Must Be Defended,"* 239–264.

78. Foster, *A Brighter Coming Day*, 289.

79. Logan, "Prenatal and Hereditary Influences," 211–212.

80. Carby, *Reconstructing Womanhood*; Spillers, "Mama's Baby, Papa's Maybe."

81. Mitchell, *Righteous Propagation*, 7.

82. Anna Julia Cooper, *A Voice from the South*, 28.

83. Harper, "Sowing and Reaping," 155.

84. Foster, *A Brighter Coming Day*, 289–290.

85. See Luciano, *Arranging Grief*.

86. Foster, introduction to *Three Rediscovered Novels*, xxiii–xxv.

87. For example, Harper and Cooper both explicitly reference the key study of the Juke family, which purported to demonstrate the proliferating effects over time of the inheritance of the qualities of pauperism, sexual licentiousness, and criminality. Harper also draws on the 1880s laboratory work of August Weismann, which challenged the Lamarckian theory of the inheritance of acquired characteristics.

88. Mitchell, *Righteous Propagation*, 97.

89. Rusert, *Fugitive Science*, 18. Here I extend Rusert's frame for an antebellum movement into the postbellum period.

90. Foster, *A Brighter Coming Day*, 275.

91. Foster, *A Brighter Coming Day*, 227.

92. Harper, *Iola Leroy*, 78.

93. See English, *Unnatural Selections*; Dorr and Logan, " 'Quality, Not Mere Quantity, Counts' "; Hasian, *The Rhetoric of Eugenics in Anglo-American Thought*; and Mitchell, *Righteous Propagation*. On "aspiring class," see Mitchell, *Righteous Propagation*.

94. Dorr and Logan, " 'Quality, Not Mere Quantity, Counts,' " 69.

95. Sánchez-Eppler, *Touching Liberty*, 135; Hendler, *Public Sentiments*, 10.

96. McHenry, *Forgotten Readers*, 188.

97. See, for example, Brinton, *Library of Aboriginal American Literature*.

98. Cope, "Editors' Table."

99. Harper, "Trial and Triumph," 203; emphasis added.

100. Foster, *A Brighter Coming Day*, 96–99.

101. McGill, "Frances Ellen Watkins Harper and the Circuits of Abolitionist Poetry," 62.

102. Ivy Wilson, *Specters of Democracy*, 63.

103. Ivy Wilson, *Specters of Democracy*, 9.

104. Gruesz, *Ambassadors of Culture*, 26.

105. Warner, *The Letters of the Republic*, xiii. See also Anderson, *Imagined Communities*.

106. Anderson, *Imagined Communities*; Warner, *Publics and Counterpublics*, 90.

107. Foucault, *"Society Must Be Defended,"* 246.

108. Slavet, *Racial Fever*.

109. Hunt, *Glances and Glimpses*, 146.

110. Godwin, *The Enquirer*.

111. Foucault calls this "the power of regularization." Foucault, *"Society Must Be Defended,"* 247.

112. Malthus, *An Essay on the Principle of Population*, 143.

113. Malthus, *An Essay on the Principle of Population*, 144.

114. Malthus, *An Essay on the Principle of Population*, 145.

115. Malthus explained: "The impressions and excitements of this world are the instruments with which the Supreme Being forms matter into mind, and that the necessity of constant exertion to avoid evil and to pursue good is the principal spring of these impressions and excitements . . . give[s] a satisfactory reason for the existence of natural and moral evil . . . which arises from the principle of population." *An Essay on the Principle of Population*, 157–158.

116. Malthus, *An Essay on the Principle of Population*, 150.

117. Malthus, *An Essay on the Principle of Population*, 57.

118. De Quincey, "The Palimpsest of the Human Brain."

119. Thanks to El Glasberg for keen insights into the significance of the palimpsest metaphor.

120. Dillon, *The Palimpsest*, 2.

121. Anna Julia Cooper, *A Voice from the South*, 234–235.

122. Hume, *The Essential Philosophical Works*, 220.

123. Sacks, *The Man Who Mistook His Wife for a Hat*, 29–30, 39.

124. Foster, *A Brighter Coming Day*, 132.

3. VAGINAL IMPRESSIONS

1. Blackwell, *Essays in Medical Sociology*, 55.

2. Blackwell, *Essays in Medical Sociology*, 81.

3. Blackwell, *Essays in Medical Sociology*, 63.

4. Walker, *Unmasked* (hereafter cited parenthetically as *UM*).

5. Blackwell's *Counsel to Parents on the Moral Education of Their Children* was rejected by fourteen London publishing houses. Blackwell, "A Medical Address on the Benevolence of Malthus," 5. Only a handful of copies of Walker's sex advice book, *Unmasked*, are extant today.

6. An exception: Krug, "Women Ovulate, Men Spermate."

7. O'Connell, Sanjeevan, and Hutson, "Anatomy of the Clitoris."

8. Harris, *Dr. Mary Walker*, 58; Jonathan Katz, *Gay American History*, 246.

9. The secondary literature consistently positions Blackwell as an unscientific, morally driven reformer who rejected the momentous discoveries in medicine of her time, such as vaccination, germ theory, and vivisection. This portrait is often drawn through contrast to the superior experimental and clinical abilities of her contemporary, Dr. Mary Jacobi. See, for example, Morantz-Sanchez, *Conduct Unbecoming a Woman*.

10. Faderman, *To Believe in Women*, 36.

11. Quoted in Faderman, *To Believe in Women*, 259.

12. Historian Cynthia Eagle Russett explains that by the dawn of the twentieth century "a genuine scientific consensus emerged" in which women differed from men with respect to "anatomy, physiology, temperament, and intellect." Russett, *Sexual Science*, 11.

13. Schaefer, *Religious Affects*, 23.

14. For Mel Chen, animacy signifies "an ontology of affect." Chen, *Animacies*, 212.

15. Murison, *The Politics of Anxiety*, 2–3.

16. After several literary biographies of Elizabeth Blackwell penned by women in the late 1940s, the second wave of attention came in the form of the recovery work of the 1970s and 1980s. As with other recuperative feminist projects of the era, the tone of this work is largely celebratory, emphasizing what they frame as women's democratic efforts to resist an overwhelmingly repressive male medical establishment. By the 1990s, portrayals of women's valiant attempts to gain scientific legitimacy gave way to analyses of how gender, race, and power shaped the medical profession more generally. More recently, scholars in fields such as medical humanities have joined historians of women and gender in emphasizing women as actors in the construction of scientific authority.

17. While historians beginning with Regina Morantz-Sanchez have not failed to mention Elizabeth Blackwell's eugenic commitments, little work makes her racial framework central to the analysis. Critical work that does take up Walker's and especially Blackwell's desire to protect the civilized race tends to portray these aspects of their thought as evidence that they could not entirely escape the strictures of their environment, rather than constitutive elements of their trailblazing medical practice. See, for example, the otherwise superb biographies Julia Boyd, *The Excellent Doctor Blackwell*, and Harris, *Dr. Mary Walker*.

18. Quoted in Julia Boyd, *The Excellent Doctor Blackwell*, 252.

19. For example, writing of Charlotte Perkins Gilman's novel *The Crux*, Dana Seitler suggests that Gilman's narrative represents a key example of "eugenic feminism" on account of its "producing and stabilizing a distinct set of cultural meanings about sexuality, race, and gender that root identity in biology" and "inhabit[ing] scientific discourse as a mode of female agency." Here Gilman's work is problematic not specifically because of her eugenic and civilizationist agenda but because positions emphasizing the corporeal body and the life sciences per se are threats to feminist political goals. Rather, we might understand Gilman within a lens that illuminates the historical importance of biopolitics (in both white supremacist and black uplift modes) as an organizing schematic of feminism. Seitler, *Atavistic Tendencies*, 197.

20. Cody, "Review: *Engendering Science*," 215.

21. Hamlin, *From Eve to Evolution*, 19, 20.

22. Markowitz, "Pelvic Politics"; McWhorter, *Racism and Sexual Oppression in Anglo-America*.

23. Murphy, *Seizing the Means of Reproduction*, 10.

24. Harris, *Dr. Mary Walker*, 54.

25. She continued wearing the medal even after a U.S. military board revoked her honor, along with that of nearly 1,000 others, in 1916. Harris, *Dr. Mary Walker*, 73–74, 251.

26. Julia Boyd, *The Excellent Doctor Blackwell*, 215; Blackwell, *Essays in Medical Sociology*, 94–95. Blackwell and many other feminists were vehemently opposed to state sponsorship of prostitution. Subsequent additions to the British Contagious Diseases Act included new stipulations, such as submitting sex workers to "internal examination" to assess their health. Quoted in Julia Boyd, *The Excellent Doctor Blackwell*, 216.

27. Murison, *The Politics of Anxiety*, 3.

28. Krug, "Women Ovulate, Men Spermate," 63.

29. Antoinette Brown Blackwell, *The Sexes throughout Nature*, 118.

30. Antoinette Brown Blackwell, *The Sexes throughout Nature*, 20.

31. Antoinette Brown Blackwell, *The Sexes throughout Nature*, 221.

32. Morgensen, "Settler Homonationalism."

33. Blackwell, *Essays in Medical Sociology*, 23; Blackwell, "A Medical Address on the Benevolence of Malthus," 21.

34. Blackwell, *The Laws of Life*, 171.

35. Blackwell, *Essays in Medical Sociology*, 54.

36. Jagose, *Orgasmology*, 20–21.

37. On the debate about women's orgasmic capacity, see Laqueur, *Making Sex*.

38. Walker, *Unmasked*, 10. See also Blackwell, *Essays in Medical Sociology*, 53.

39. Krug, "Women Ovulate, Men Spermate," 63.

40. Blackwell, *Essays in Medical Sociology*, 181. For Elizabeth and other millennialists, Adam and Eve represented the true type of humanity.

41. Blackwell, "A Medical Address on the Benevolence of Malthus," 26.

42. Blackwell, *Essays in Medical Sociology*, 67, 69.

43. Blackwell, *Essays in Medical Sociology*, 67–69.

44. Blackwell, "A Medical Address on the Benevolence of Malthus," 23.

45. Luciano illuminates the crucial role of temporality in the deployment of sexuality in the United States, highlighting how notions of embodied time gave structure to racial and sexual formation. Luciano, *Arranging Grief*.

46. Blackwell, *Essays in Medical Sociology*, 35, 60.

47. Blackwell, *How to Keep a Household in Health*, 140; Blackwell, *Essays in Medical Sociology*, 218.

48. Blackwell, *Essays in Medical Sociology*, 65.

49. Blackwell, *Essays in Medical Sociology*, 60–61.

50. Blackwell, *Essays in Medical Sociology*, 67.

51. Schiebinger, *Nature's Body*, 156–158; Briggs, "The Race of Hysteria."

52. Briggs, "The Race of Hysteria."

53. Quoted in Briggs, "The Race of Hysteria," 260.

54. Kapsalis, *Public Privates*, 11–30.

55. Briggs, "The Race of Hysteria," 263.

56. Blackwell praises Sims in her autobiography *Pioneer Work in Opening the Medical Profession to Women*, 229. See also Morantz-Sanchez, *Conduct Unbecoming a Woman*, 71–72. The Blackwells operated the New York Infirmary with Dr. Marie Zakrzewska, the subject of the fictional account *Dr. Zay* quoted in this chapter's epigraph.

57. Blackwell, *Essays in Medical Sociology*, 125.

58. Blackwell, *The Religion of Health*, 7.

59. Blackwell, *How to Keep a Household in Health*, 8.

60. Blackwell, *How to Keep a Household in Health*, 22.

61. Blackwell, *Essays in Medical Sociology*, 61.

62. Blackwell, *Essays in Medical Sociology*, 66.

63. Blackwell, *Essays in Medical Sociology*, 92.

64. Blackwell, "A Medical Address on the Benevolence of Malthus," 30.

65. Blackwell, *The Religion of Health*, 24.

66. Blackwell, "A Medical Address on the Benevolence of Malthus," 28.

67. Blackwell, "A Medical Address on the Benevolence of Malthus," 20–21.

68. Blackwell, *Essays in Medical Sociology*, 52–53.

69. Deleuze, *Foucault*; Deleuze, *The Fold*.

70. Deleuze, *Spinoza*, 125.

71. Deleuze, *Foucault*, 88.

72. On the fold as the remainder of what is excised from the liberal construct of the human, see Nyong'o, *The Amalgamation Waltz*, 18–20.

73. Spillers, "Mama's Baby, Papa's Maybe," 66.

74. Spillers, "Mama's Baby, Papa's Maybe," 68.

75. Spillers, "Mama's Baby, Papa's Maybe," 67.

76. Spillers, "Mama's Baby, Papa's Maybe," 67, 68.

77. Spillers, "Mama's Baby, Papa's Maybe," 67.

78. Spillers, "Mama's Baby, Papa's Maybe," 67; emphasis in the original.

79. Foucault, *The History of Sexuality*, 139.

80. Kyla Wazana Tompkins, *Racial Indigestion*, 68.

81. For the contemporary legacy of this association, see Nash, "Black Anality."

82. Quoted in Treichler, "AIDS, Homophobia, and Biomedical Discourse," 267.

83. Harris, *Dr. Mary Walker*, 158.

84. Newman, *White Women's Rights*.

85. By contrast, Eric Plemons argues that in the early twenty-first century, facial features have come to be identified as a location of female sexual difference. Plemons, *The Look of a Woman*.

86. Holland, Ochoa, and Tompkins, "On the Visceral," 395.

87. Holland, Ochoa, and Tompkins, "On the Visceral," 395.

88. I build here on Weheliye's critique of Agamben's "bare life." Weheliye, *Habeas Viscus*.

89. Geddes and Thompson, "The Evolution of Sex," 79, 77.

90. Gregg and Seigworth, *Affect Theory Reader*, 1.

91. Quoted in Salisbury and Shail, *Neurology and Modernity*, 15.

92. Salisbury and Shail, *Neurology and Modernity*, 16. This idea is partially returning, with the gut figuring as the second brain in the field of neuroenterology. See Elizabeth A. Wilson, *Psychosomatic*, 31–47; Elizabeth A. Wilson, *Gut Feminisms*.

93. Clarke and Jacyna, *Nineteenth-Century Origins of Neuroscientific Concepts*, 31; see also 29–57.

94. Antoinette Brown Blackwell, *The Sexes throughout Nature*, 124.

95. Ahmed, *Cultural Politics of Emotion*, 45.

96. Quoted in Russett, *Sexual Science*, 61.

97. Quoted in Julia Boyd, *The Excellent Doctor Blackwell*, 269. On Christian physiology, see Whorton, *Crusaders for Fitness*.

98. All above quotes are from Hume, *The Essential Philosophical Works*, 18.

99. Blackwell, *Pioneer Work in Opening the Medical Profession to Women*, 274–275.

100. Blackwell, *The Influence of Women in the Profession of Medicine*, 8.

101. This queer maternal position is reminiscent of the paternal, yet sexualized, relations with patients that Peter Coviello argues Walt Whitman cultivated in Civil War hospitals. Coviello, *Tomorrow's Parties*, 53–54.

102. Blackwell and Blackwell, *Medicine as a Profession for Women*, 5.

103. Russett, *Sexual Science*, 83.

104. Blackwell, *Counsel to Parents*, 94–95, 232.

105. Blackwell, *How to Keep a Household in Health*, 8.

106. Faderman, *To Believe in Women*, 270.

107. Elizabeth wrote to Emily that she adopted Kitty out of her wish to "train [her] up into a valuable domestic. . . . I gave a receipt for her, and the poor thing trotted after me like a dog." Quoted in Julia Boyd, *The Excellent Doctor Blackwell*, 150.

108. Cushier attended the Blackwells' Women's Medical College as a student; she later joined the faculty, after which she and Blackwell initiated a relationship.

109. Faderman, *Surpassing the Love of Men*. On the structural overlap between celibacy and Boston marriages as modes of queer life in the period, see Kahan, *Celibacies*, 33–55.

110. Harris, *Dr. Mary Walker*, 81–83.

111. Harris notes that Walker's romantic relationships were a topic of speculation among the popular press during her lifetime. Harris, *Dr. Mary Walker*, 94, 107.

112. Morantz-Sanchez, *Sympathy and Science*, 142.

113. Blackwell, *The Laws of Life*, 20–21.

114. Blackwell, *The Laws of Life*, 21.

115. I build here on Greta LaFleur's apt phrase "pre-sexology sexuality." LaFleur, "Precipitous Sensations," 116. "Homonationalism" marks the biopolitical process in which race, religion, and nation mark some queer bodies as deserving of protection and incorporation into the nation while others, especially within terrorist discourse, are marked as primitive and monstrous threats to the social order. See Puar, *Terrorist Assemblages*.

116. Somerville, *Queering the Color Line*, 15–38.

117. Morgensen, "Settler Homonationalism," 105–131.

118. Clarke, *Sex in Education*.

119. Blackwell, "A Medical Address on the Benevolence of Malthus," 34.

120. See Kyla Wazana Tompkins on the oral orifice as a key locus of the disciplinary regime. Tompkins, *Racial Indigestion*.

1. Child, *Letters from New-York*, 17.
2. Child, *Letters from New-York*, 43.
3. Quotes are verbatim. Collins, "Glimpses of Heartache."
4. Notes Left with Children, Records of the New York Foundling Hospital, New-York Historical Society, New York, NY.
5. The New York Foundling maintained four notebooks filled with such notes, which suggests that the institution viewed these remembrances as their property, rather than the children's.
6. Brace, *The Children's Aid Society of New York*, 28.
7. Quoted in Holt, *The Orphan Trains*, 128.
8. My heartfelt thanks to Allison Miller for proposing this wonderfully apt neologism.
9. Malthus, *An Essay on the Principle of Population*, 137.
10. Brace, *The Dangerous Classes of New York*, 45–46 (hereafter cited parenthetically as DC).
11. Brace, *Gesta Christi*, 475 (hereafter cited parenthetically as GC).
12. Galton, *Essays in Eugenics*, 35.
13. Emma Brace, ed., *The Life of Charles Loring Brace*, 7 (hereafter cited parenthetically as L).
14. Bushnell, *Unconscious Influence*, 19.
15. Brace, *The Children's Aid Society of New York*, 28.
16. Furthermore, this debate is situated almost exclusively within social history.
17. Scholars who argue that Brace reinforced the class hierarchy by breaking apart immigrant families include Michael B. Katz, *In the Shadow of the Poorhouse*, and, to some degree, Boyer, *Urban Masses and Moral Order in America*, and Bullard, "Saving the Children." The far more common argument about Brace consists of a somewhat measured celebration of his programs as humanitarian efforts that provided much-needed care for dependent children and successfully overcame many of the period's prejudices toward the poor. For prominent examples, see Holt, *The Orphan Trains*; Bender, *Toward an Urban Vision*; and O'Connor, *Orphan Trains*. Several historians have escaped (and similarly identified) this paradigm. See Gish, "Rescuing the 'Waifs and Strays' of the City."
18. Some authors have noted Brace's scientific commitments but view them as distinct from his other influences. Claudia Nelson, for example, argues that Brace's thinking was shaped more by religious principles than by scientific thinking. See Nelson, *Little Strangers*, 27.
19. Darwin sent two copies stateside: one to Louis Agassiz and the other to Gray. Ratner, "Evolution and the Rise of the Scientific Spirit in America," 105.
20. Dupree, *Asa Gray*, 267; Helkie, "An Interview with C. Loring Brace," 852. C. Loring Brace, the reformer's great-grandson, is a noted physical anthropologist who played a significant role in the discipline's move away from understanding race as a biological category in the mid-twentieth century.
21. Brace, "Darwinism in Germany," 287 (hereafter cited parenthetically as D).

22. U.S. Census, 1850.

23. Boyer, *Urban Masses and Moral Order in America*, 67.

24. Matsell, *Semi-Annual Report*.

25. Quoted in Stansell, *City of Women*, 195.

26. Matsell, *Semi-Annual Report*.

27. Brace, *The Best Method of Disposing of Our Pauper and Vagrant Children*, 9 (hereafter cited parenthetically as BMD).

28. Carp, *Family Matters*, 7–8.

29. Brace, *Address on Industrial Schools*, 4, 3; Brace, "Wolf-Reared Children," 543.

30. CAS was supported by a mixture of public and private funds. The first large sum of private money was redirected from an original earmark for the American Colonization Society (DC, 283–284). Miriam Langsam estimates that one-third of the CAS budget came from government sources, one-third from private individuals, and one-third from miscellaneous sources such as churches and the fees boys paid to the lodging houses. While Brace extolled the virtues of the middle classes as the heart of civilization and the backbone of the CAS, significant funds came from New York's elite. In some years, more than half of the private money came from a few very wealthy people, including the Astors and the Vanderbilts. See Langsam, "Children West," 41.

31. Darwin, *The Variation of Animals and Plants under Domestication*, 349.

32. Darwin, *The Variation of Animals and Plants under Domestication*, 370.

33. Darwin, *The Variation of Animals and Plants under Domestication*, 26.

34. Darwin, *The Variation of Animals and Plants under Domestication*, 374.

35. Bowler, *Evolution*. See also Bannister, *Social Darwinism*.

36. Brace reflected that "he owed a great deal intellectually" to his relationship with Asa Gray and boasted of their "incessant talks and disputations on Darwinism" (*L*, 443, 303).

37. A. Gray and J. L. Gray, *Letters of Asa Gray*, 457; emphasis in the original. The text in question was Brace's "Egyptian Monotheism."

38. Gray chided Darwin himself for "read[ing] quite Lamarckian" in his reliance on the inheritance of acquired characteristics and referred to these passages as the "weakest point of the book." A. Gray and J. L. Gray, *Letters of Asa Gray*, 457.

39. Brace, *The New West*, 369.

40. Brace, *The New West*, iv.

41. Russett, *Sexual Science*, 87.

42. Grosz, *The Nick of Time*, 50.

43. Brace, *The Races of the Old World* (hereafter cited parenthetically as R).

44. Whereas some polygenists relied on Lamarckian theories to argue that different racial groups had descended from different ancestral species, John Haller Jr. emphasizes that other scientific thinkers, like Brace, enlisted Lamarckism in the defense of monogenesis. Haller, *Outcasts from Evolution*, 74–79. Frederick Douglass's "The Claims of the Negro Ethnologically Considered" is a key example of work in the latter vein.

45. In the apt words of George Fredrickson, "Brace's pioneering effort to develop a Darwinist ethnology in opposition to the American School, although animated to

some degree by antislavery humanitarianism, had demonstrated that most of the hierarchical assumptions of the polygenists could be justified just as well, if not better, in Darwinian terms." Fredrickson, *The Black Image in the White Mind*, 235.

46. E. D. Cope, *Origin of the Fittest*, 389. See also Brace, *The Dangerous Classes of New York*, 47–50.

47. New York Foundling, *1993 Orphan Train Rider Reunion*.

48. On the gender and racial politics of the "safety valve" theory, see Streeby, *American Sensations*.

49. Graham, *American Experience: The Orphan Trains*.

50. Kleinman, "Interview with Christina Baker Kline."

51. Brace, *The Children's Aid Society of New York*, 40.

52. Brace, *The Children's Aid Society of New York*, 16.

53. Adam Smith, quoted in Brace, *Free Trade*, 9.

54. Moon, "'The Gentle Boy from the Dangerous Classes.'"

55. Moon, "'The Gentle Boy from the Dangerous Classes.'"

56. On the brother/father/lover trope in sentimental adoption fiction, see my essay "The Biology of Intimacy."

57. Chauncey, *Gay New York*, 33–46.

58. I have suppressed a paragraph break and the ellipsis mark where the editor, Brace's daughter, excised the remainder of this intriguing train of thought.

59. Gish, "Rescuing the 'Waifs and Strays' of the City," 125.

60. Gish, "Rescuing the 'Waifs and Strays' of the City," 132.

61. I first visited the New York Foundling archives in the basement of its West Village building in order to see the notebooks in 2007, but they had been misplaced for years. Richard Reilly, the volunteer archivist, was unaware of their existence. Reilly later found them and had them transferred, along with other Foundling records, to the New-York Historical Society.

62. Collins, "Glimpses of Heartache."

63. Notes Left with Children, Records of the New York Foundling Hospital, New-York Historical Society, New York, NY.

64. Children's domestic vulnerability partly resulted from their status in legal limbo, outside both the emergent framework of adoption and the lingering practice of indenture.

65. See, for example, Holt, *The Orphan Trains*.

66. Thompson, "Marguerite Thompson."

67. Sánchez-Eppler, *Dependent States*, 183.

68. Berlant, *The Female Complaint*, 54.

69. Colleen Glenney Boggs argues that animals in the nineteenth century were enlisted as barometers of biopolitical subjectivity, functioning as "the 'other' *and* as the ground from which liberal subject formation becomes possible" through their humane treatment. Boggs, *Animalia Americana*, 35.

70. Lowe, *Immigrant Acts*, ix–xii.

71. Capital's need for a labor force in excess of the quantity of available jobs in order to keep wages low and surplus value high encourages large-scale shifts in social relations, including migration and immigration, that threaten the

homogeneous racial ideals of the nation-state. In Roderick Ferguson's terms, "as capital disrupts social hierarchies in the production of surplus labor, it disrupts gender ideals and sexual norms that are indices of racial difference," creating population shifts that violate the norms of race, culture, and nation. Ferguson, *Aberrations in Black*, 17.

72. For the contrasting positions of imitation and elasticity in representations of racialized and white youth in sentimental literature, see my essay "The Biology of Intimacy."

73. Rollins, *Uncle Tom's Tenement*, 73.

74. Rollins, *Uncle Tom's Tenement*, 170.

75. Orphan settlement projects took place across the Americas and came to a close only in the 1960s. London orphanages sent around one hundred thousand "Home Children" to Canada, Australia, New Zealand, and South Africa between 1869 and the late 1930s.

76. Stoler, *Carnal Knowledge and Imperial Power*, 69–70.

77. Stoler, *Carnal Knowledge and Imperial Power*, 69–70.

78. Pratt, "How to Deal with the Indians," n.p.

79. See, for example, Stehney, "The Carlisle 62."

80. Thanks to Allison Miller for help with this point.

81. Flew, "Unveiling the Anonymous Philanthropist."

82. Zitkala-Sa, *American Indian Stories*, 49, 50, 56, 60.

83. Zitkala-Sa, *American Indian Stories*, 66.

84. Zitkala-Sa, *American Indian Stories*, 57.

85. Mbembe, "Necropolitics," 14, 22n38. In the latter passage, Mbembe cites David Theo Goldberg.

86. Caleb Smith, *The Prison and the American Imagination*, 29.

87. Caleb Smith, *The Prison and the American Imagination*.

88. On domestic time, see Freeman, *Time Binds*, 39–41.

89. For Pratt's views on the similarity of prisons and off-reservation boarding schools, see Pratt, *Battlefield and Classroom*.

90. This was a technique Pratt learned at Hampton. Samuel Armstrong to Richard Henry Pratt, 27 August [1878], Box 1, Pratt Papers, Beinecke Library, Yale Collection of Western Americana, Yale University, New Haven, CT.

91. Mbembe, "Necropolitics," 14–15.

92. Caleb Smith, *The Prison and the American Imagination*, 12, 41, 18.

93. See Byrd, *The Transit of Empire*.

94. Melville, "Hawthorne and His Mosses."

95. Patterson, *Slavery and Social Death*.

96. Yet this transformation could take place only if migrated children were sent to work for white settler colonists. In 1904, the U.S. Supreme Court ruled that the best interest of migrated orphans was the opportunity to achieve and maintain whiteness, rather than continuity of religious faith. See Gordon, *The Great Arizona Orphan Abduction*.

97. Morgensen, "The Biopolitics of Settler Colonialism," 56.

98. Alger, *Julius*, 78.

99. Berlant, *Cruel Optimism*, 97; emphasis in the original.

100. On vital energy, see Vora, *Life Support*, 3.

101. Berlant, *Cruel Optimism*, 100.

102. Berlant, *Cruel Optimism*, 99.

103. Berlant, *Cruel Optimism*, 117.

104. Berlant, *Cruel Optimism*, 116.

105. Dugdale, *The Jukes*. Brace, by contrast, included Dugdale's study in later editions of *The Dangerous Classes of New York* as evidence of the efficacy of his own methods of environmental influence.

106. Dugdale, *The Jukes*, 66. Platt argues that Dugdale's research "was distorted almost beyond recognition by anti-intellectual supporters of hereditary theories of crime." See Platt, *The Child Savers*, 25.

107. Du Bois, *Dusk of Dawn*.

108. Quoted in Holt, *The Orphan Trains*, 121.

109. Langsam, "Children West," 25–26.

110. Quoted in Holt, *The Orphan Trains*, 171.

111. Holt, *The Orphan Trains*, 118–155.

112. For an excellent history of the sentimentalization of children at the turn of the century, which produced the child as "economically worthless and emotionally priceless," see Zelizer, *Pricing the Priceless Child*.

113. O'Connor, *Orphan Trains*, 304.

114. Holt, *The Orphan Trains*, 148–150.

115. Ayler, "Alice Bullis Ayler."

116. Graham, *American Experience: The Orphan Trains*.

117. Interestingly, 1929 was also the year that the last state without an adoption law legalized the practice. Claudia Nelson suggests that this clarifies the extent to which children were now seen as important for their emotional qualities, rather than their labor output. See Nelson, *Little Strangers*, 2.

118. Virginia Wadsworth Wirtz Center for the Performing Arts, *2006–2007 Mainstage Season*. Thanks to Jinah Kim for sending me this announcement.

119. Egan, "Boredom in the West Fuels Binge Drinking." On the number of Wyoming placements, see Brace, *The Children's Aid Society of New York*, 40.

120. On racial governmentality, see Kazanjian, *The Colonizing Trick*.

5. FROM IMPRESSIBILITY TO INTERACTIONISM

1. Most scholars who attribute the passage solely to Gamble and the Birth Control Federation of America (BCFA) follow Linda Gordon's precedent in *Woman's Body, Woman's Right: Birth Control in America*. Gordon, *Woman's Body*, 328. Gordon's revised edition continues to attribute the phrase to the BCFA. See Gordon, *The Moral Property of Women*, 235. Texts that cite this passage include Davis, *Women, Race, and Class*, 215; Ordover, *American Eugenics*, 152; and Schoen, *Choice and Coercion*, 47–48.

2. "Special Negro Project, under the direction of the Birth Control Federation of America, Inc.," Florence Rose Papers, 1832–1970, Sophia Smith Collection, Smith College, Northampton, MA.

3. Correcting her earlier citation of Gordon, Roberts also alerts readers to Du Bois's responsibility for this quote in "Margaret Sanger and the Racial Origins of the Birth Control Movement," 203.

4. Du Bois, "Black Folk and Birth Control." After the first printing, the article was renamed "Negroes and Birth Control."

5. On the number of pamphlets distributed, see Florence Rose to W. E. B. Du Bois, Margaret Sanger Papers, 1761–1995, Sophia Smith Collection, Smith College, Northampton, MA.

6. Scholars who argue that Du Bois's interest in birth control and/or evolutionary improvement was not eugenic include Shawn Michelle Smith, *Photography on the Color Line*; Gordon, *Woman's Body*; Roberts, *Killing the Black Body*; and Rodrique, "The Black Community." Alys Weinbaum praises Du Bois's intervention into what she terms the "race/reproduction bind" as "gender-conscious, even feminist in its persistent attention to issues of maternity, reproduction, and genealogy." Weinbaum, *Wayward Reproductions*, 190.

7. Gillman and Weinbaum, *Next to the Color Line*.

8. See in particular Dorr and Logan, " 'Quality, Not Mere Quantity, Counts' "; Mitchell, *Righteous Propagation*; English, *Unnatural Selections*; and Hasian, *The Rhetoric of Eugenics in Anglo-American Thought*.

9. Scholars who have come to acknowledge Du Bois's investment in eugenics often do so in a reluctant manner that attempts to defend his eugenics as antihierarchical and merely reflective of the era. Roberts, for example, positions Du Bois's involvement as significant insofar as it illuminates the influence of eugenics at large, rather than suggesting anything intrinsic to his politics or thought itself. I have similar concerns about Dorr and Logan's term "oppositional eugenics" to describe black eugenics projects. Attempts to improve the racial stock and challenge white supremacy by limiting the birth rate of the poor and celebrating the rising fitness of the race were oppositional in a very limited sense.

10. Roberts, "Margaret Sanger and the Racial Origins of the Birth Control Movement," 203.

11. The language of "mainline" eugenics comes from Kevles, *In the Name of Eugenics*.

12. Grant, *The Passing of the Great Race*, 16.

13. See Kevles, *In the Name of Eugenics*, 43.

14. I use Evelyn Fox Keller's useful characterization of modern heredity, though I suggest it emerges from the work of Weismann and Galton, rather than Darwin and Galton, as she argues. Keller, *The Mirage of a Space between Nature and Nurture*, 21–26.

15. See Stern, "Eugenics beyond Borders"; Stepan, *The Hour of Eugenics*; and Stocking, *Race, Culture, and Evolution*.

16. Maliniak, *Sculpture in the Living*, 62.

17. On the role of militaristic immune discourse in conceiving of the body as a discrete milieu unto itself, see Cohen, *A Body Worth Defending*.

18. Elazar Barkan characterizes the first two decades of twentieth-century biology as embroiled in "unparalleled theoretical turmoil" as Mendelian, Lamarckian,

biometric, and other approaches all found favor among biologists. Barkan, *The Retreat of Scientific Racism*, 138.

19. Foucault, *Security, Territory, Population*, 56, 57.

20. Foucault, *Security, Territory, Population*, 10.

21. Foucault, *Security, Territory, Population*, 63.

22. Foucault, *Security, Territory, Population*, 22.

23. Davenport, *The Trait Book*, 1.

24. Grant, *The Passing of the Great Race*, 18.

25. Quoted in Kevles, *In the Name of Eugenics*, 47.

26. Stepan, *The Hour of Eugenics*, 65.

27. Grant, *The Passing of the Great Race*, 45, 46.

28. Grant continued: "There exists to-day a widespread and fatuous belief in the power of environment . . . to alter heredity. Thus the view that the Negro slave was an unfortunate cousin of the white man, deeply tanned by the tropic sun and denied the blessings of Christianity and civilization, played no small part with the sentimentalists of the Civil War period and it has taken us fifty years to learn that speaking English, wearing good clothes, and going to school and church does not transform a Negro into a white man." Grant, *The Passing of the Great Race*, 16.

29. The Darwinian synthesis reconciled natural selection with population genetics, resulting in the dominant evolutionary paradigm still endorsed today. Huxley, "Eugenics and Society," 13.

30. Bederman, *Manliness and Civilization*; Briggs, "The Race of Hysteria."

31. Kline, *Building a Better Race*, 16.

32. For an example of Sanger's belief in women's right to sexual pleasure free from worries of unwanted pregnancy, see Sanger, *Woman and the New Race*.

33. See Gordon, *The Moral Property of Women*; and Roberts, "Margaret Sanger and the Racial Origins of the Birth Control Movement."

34. Sanger, *The Pivot of Civilization*, 175.

35. Sanger maintained important tactical differences with leading eugenic scientists and theorists, however. While she agreed with the general approach to purify the race and to "bring reason and intelligence to bear upon *heredity*," she argued that birth control represented a practical program for effecting these changes, one that enabled wealthier women to have fewer children. Sanger, *The Pivot of Civilization*, 172. Eugenic scientists were generally loath to limit the fertility of the "fit" and thus often opposed efforts to promote birth control among well-off whites.

36. Haraway, "Situated Knowledges," 584.

37. Osborn, preface to *The Passing of the Great Race*, ix.

38. Osborn, preface to *The Passing of the Great Race*, viii, vii.

39. James Baldwin, *Notes of a Native Son*, 14.

40. Berlant, *The Queen of America*; Berlant, *The Female Complaint*.

41. Lewis, *W. E. B. Du Bois*, vol. 2, 235. See also Taylor, "W. E. B. Du Bois' Challenge to Scientific Racism," 449.

42. Du Bois, "Evolution of the Race Problem," 149.

43. Du Bois, "Evolution of the Race Problem," 150.

44. Du Bois was the first African American to earn a PhD from Harvard. On Jewish and black resistance to biological determinisms, see Stepan and Gilman, "Appropriating the Idioms of Science."

45. Rusert, *Fugitive Science*.

46. Ward, "The Transmission of Culture," 314, 319.

47. Du Bois, "Races," 157.

48. Mizruchi, "Neighbors, Strangers, Corpses"; Hiro, "How It Feels to Be without a Face."

49. Hiro, "How It Feels to Be without a Face," 194n14.

50. Du Bois, "My Evolving Program for Negro Freedom," 57.

51. Farland, "W. E. B. Du Bois, Anthropometric Science, and the Limits of Racial Uplift," 1019.

52. Bay, " 'The World Was Thinking Wrong about Race.' " For a recent influential account of Du Bois as a progenitor of social science, see Morris, *Scholar Denied*.

53. For example, see Gilroy, *The Black Atlantic*; Baker, *From Savage to Negro*.

54. Olson, "W. E. B. Du Bois and the Race Concept," 218.

55. Appiah, "The Uncompleted Argument."

56. Du Bois, "Heredity and the Public Schools," 116–117.

57. This is the same ratio of social to innate factors in development currently asserted by epigeneticists. However, as Keller argues, such a ratio can only be conceived at the populational level, not at the level of an individual.

58. Du Bois, "Races," 157.

59. James Mark Baldwin, "Physical and Social Heredity," 423. In a lengthy debate with Edward Drinker Cope on the evolution of the mind, Baldwin denied Lamarckian transmission as a factor in intelligence, claiming that conscious imitation was more than enough to account for the acquisition of education and skills.

60. Du Bois, "Heredity and the Public Schools," 119.

61. Du Bois, "Heredity and the Public Schools," 117.

62. Du Bois, "Heredity and the Public Schools," 117.

63. Du Bois, "Development of a People," 296–297.

64. Du Bois, "Development of a People," 306.

65. Du Bois, "Talented Tenth Memorial Address," 164.

66. Stocking, *Race, Culture, and Evolution*, 256.

67. On Du Bois's and Boas's collaborations, such as the anthropologist's contributions to *Crisis* and the inaugural meeting of the NAACP and joint work on the Atlanta conferences, see Baker, *From Savage to Negro*, 119.

68. Du Bois, *Dusk of Dawn*, 133.

69. Quoted in Baker, *From Savage to Negro*, 124.

70. Du Bois, "Races," 157.

71. Du Bois, *The Souls of Black Folk*, 162.

72. Cooppan, "Move On down the Line," 48–49.

73. Du Bois, "Development of a People," 293.

74. Du Bois, "Evolution of the Race Problem," 152.

75. Shawn Michelle Smith, *Photography on the Color Line*.

76. Du Bois, *Health and Physique*, 5.

77. Du Bois, *Health and Physique*, 110.

78. Cooppan, "Move On down the Line," 65n16.

79. Reed, *W. E. B. Du Bois*, 93–126.

80. Many Du Bois scholars have noted that Du Bois was an early and prominent supporter of birth control movements in the United States. See, for example, Lewis, *W. E. B. Du Bois*, 273.

81. Gordon, *The Moral Property of Women*; McCann, *Birth Control Politics*. For a good global overview, see Klausen and Bashford, "Fertility Control."

82. Quoted in English, "W. E. B. Du Bois's Family *Crisis*," 294.

83. Du Bois, "Opinion of W. E. B. Du Bois," *Crisis* 24, no. 4, 152–153.

84. Du Bois, *Dark Princess*, 42.

85. Weinbaum, *Wayward Reproductions*, 215.

86. English, *Unnatural Selections*, 48.

87. English, *Unnatural Selections*, 49–51.

88. English, *Unnatural Selections*, 49–51.

89. Aptheker, *Correspondence of W. E. B. Du Bois*, 301. Furthermore, Du Bois did not take this opportunity to critique the increasing cooptation of birth control by white supremacist eugenicists—some of whom, such as Lothrop Stoddard and Henry Fairfield Osborn, served on Sanger's various committees.

90. English, *Unnatural Selections*, 48.

91. Du Bois, "Opinion of W. E. B. Du Bois," *Crisis* 32, no. 6, 283.

92. Du Bois, "Development of a People," 305.

93. Du Bois, "The Talented Tenth," 134.

94. Dorr and Logan, " 'Quality, Not Mere Quantity, Counts,' " 77; *Birth Control Review* 16, no. 6 (1932), quoted in Dorr and Logan, " 'Quality, Not Mere Quantity, Counts,' " 75.

95. Dorr and Logan, " 'Quality, Not Mere Quantity, Counts,' " 86, 88.

96. Some scholarship suggests that U.S. eugenicists rarely targeted nonwhites because their assumptions of the degeneracy of racialized stock made such control unnecessary and segregation barred people of color from the institutions possessing sterilization technology. Larson, *Sex, Race, and Science*. Recent work has brought new regions and archives into the history of eugenics that complicates this frame. See, for example, Natalia Molina's archival work in the Mexican consulate in Los Angeles, which reveals scores of letters from Mexican citizens living in the United States writing to the consulate for protection from local eugenic and hygienic measures. Molina, *Fit to Be Citizens?*, 116–157.

97. Quoted in Ordover, *American Eugenics*, 153.

98. Du Bois, "Opinion of W. E. B. Du Bois," *Crisis* 19, no. 3, 105.

99. On the common ground of birth control advocates and opponents in the biopolitical language of liberalism, see Weingarten, *Abortion in the American Imagination*.

100. Du Bois, "Evolution of the Race Problem," 156.

101. Kevles, *In the Name of Eugenics*, 112.

102. Margaret Sanger to Mrs. Cele Damon, November 24, 1939, Florence Rose Papers, 1832–1970, Sophia Smith Collection, Smith College, Northampton, MA. On Sanger's disagreements with colleagues about the goals of the project, see McCann, *Birth Control Politics*, 160–168.

103. Schoen, *Choice and Coercion*, 50.

104. Margaret Sanger to W. E. B. Du Bois, November 11, 1930; W. E. B. Du Bois to Margaret Sanger, November 17, 1930, Reel 32, Margaret Sanger Papers, 1761–1995, Sophia Smith Collection, Smith College, Northampton, MA.

105. "Special Negro Project."

106. Florence Rose to W. E. B. Du Bois, July 22, 1941, Reel 32, Margaret Sanger Papers, 1761–1995, Sophia Smith Collection, Smith College, Northampton, MA.

107. Clarence Gamble to Mrs. Rinehart, November 1, 1939, Margaret Sanger Papers, 1761–1995, Sophia Smith Collection, Smith College, Northampton, MA. The latter quote is also cited in Gordon, *The Moral Property of Women*, 235.

108. "Why Planned Parenthood Is Important *Now*," Margaret Sanger Papers, 1761–1995, Sophia Smith Collection, Smith College, Northampton, MA.

109. "Why Planned Parenthood Is Important *Now*."

110. "Better Health for 13,000,000," 3, Florence Rose Papers, 1832–1970, Sophia Smith Collection, Smith College, Northampton, MA.

111. "Why Planned Parenthood Is Important *Now*."

112. Deleuze, "Postscript on the Societies of Control," 6.

113. Du Bois, "Talented Tenth Memorial Address," 351.

114. Dorr and Logan, " 'Quality, Not Mere Quantity, Counts,' " 79.

115. Jones, *The Racial Discourses of Life Philosophy*.

EPILOGUE

1. Consider, for example, California's Proposition 209, which banned consideration of race and ethnicity by public institutions, and then-outgoing New York City mayor Michael Bloomberg's accusation that Bill de Blasio ran a "racist" campaign on the grounds that his mixed-race family appeared in advertisements and other materials. Jodi Melamed writes that neoliberalism increasingly "deploys a normative cultural model of race (which now sometimes displaces conventional racial reference altogether) as a discourse to justify inequality for some as fair or natural." Melamed, "The Spirit of Neoliberalism," 14.

2. Money, Hampson, and Hampson, "Imprinting and the Establishment of Gender Role."

3. Over the course of his long career, John Money also became one of the first scientists to develop the notion of sexual differentiation in the brain. See Jordan-Young, *Brain Storm*, 31.

4. Repo, *The Biopolitics of Gender*, 36.

5. Key theorists such as Donna Haraway nonetheless developed complex biosocial models throughout the heyday of social construction theory that drew on the theory's insight into the productive role of language.

6. For an early influential example, see Gagnon and Simon, *Sexual Conduct*.

7. In critical theory, see Frost, *Biocultural Creatures*.

8. On the emphasis on maternal effects in epigenetics, see Richardson, "Maternal Bodies in the Postgenomic Order."

9. Lawrence V. Harper, "Epigenetic Inheritance," 341.

10. Richardson, "Plasticity and Programming"; Pitts-Taylor, *The Brain's Body*. On the postwar logic of race, see Melamed, *Represent and Destroy*.

11. Fausto-Sterling, *Sex/Gender*, 117.

12. Neuroplasticity is another nineteenth-century notion of malleable and regenerative neural substance once more in play after nearly a century of determinist brain localization theory that understood the brain's structure and the lifetime of neurons to be finite and irreversible. For an accessible introduction to neuroplasticity and brain localization theory, see Doidge, *The Brain That Changes Itself*.

13. Fausto-Sterling, *Sex/Gender*, 123.

14. Wynter, "Towards the Sociogenic Principle," 59.

15. Virginia Commonwealth University, "Mapping Life Expectancy."

BIBLIOGRAPHY

....

ARCHIVAL COLLECTIONS

The Bancroft Library, University of California, Berkeley
The New-York Historical Society, New York, NY
    The Records of the Children's Aid Society, 1836–2006
    The Records of the New York Foundling Hospital, 1869–2009
Research Library, American Museum of Natural History, New York, NY
    Edward Drinker Cope Letters
Sophia Smith Collection, Smith College, Northampton, MA
    Florence Rose Papers, 1832–1970
    Margaret Sanger Papers, 1761–1995 (Bulk: 1900–1966)
    Planned Parenthood Federation of America Records, 1918–1974 (PPFA I)
Yale Collection of Western Americana, Beinecke Rare Book and Manuscript Library,
    Yale University Library, New Haven, CT
    Richard Henry Pratt Papers

PRIMARY SOURCES

Alger, Horatio. *Julius; or, The Street Boy Out West.* 1874. Reprint, New York: Holt,
    Rinehart and Winston, 1967.
Aptheker, Herbert, ed. *Correspondence of W. E. B. Du Bois,* vol. 1: *Selections, 1877–1934.*
    Amherst: University of Massachusetts Press, 1997.
Ayler, Alice Bullis. "Alice Bullis Ayler." National Orphan Train Complex. Accessed May 5,
    2015. http://orphantraindepot.org/orphan-train-rider-stories/alice-bullis-ayler/.
Baldwin, James. *Notes of a Native Son.* Boston: Beacon, 2012.
Baldwin, James Mark. "Physical and Social Heredity." *American Naturalist* 30, no. 353
    (1896): 422–430.
Barnes, Jonathan, ed. *The Complete Works of Aristotle: The Revised Oxford Translation.*
    Princeton, NJ: Princeton University Press, 1984.
Blackwell, Antoinette Brown. *The Sexes throughout Nature.* New York: G. P. Putnam's
    Sons, 1875.
Blackwell, Elizabeth. *Counsel to Parents on the Moral Education of Their Children, in
    Relation to Sex.* New York: Brentano's Literary Emporium, 1880.

Blackwell, Elizabeth. *Essays in Medical Sociology.* Vols. 1–2. 1902. Reprint, New York: Arno, 1972.

Blackwell, Elizabeth. *How to Keep a Household in Health: An Address Delivered before the Working Woman's College Household.* London: W. W. Head, 1870.

Blackwell, Elizabeth. *The Influence of Women in the Profession of Medicine.* London: George Bell and Sons, 1889.

Blackwell, Elizabeth. *The Laws of Life, with Special Reference to the Physical Education of Girls.* Reprint, New York: Garland, 1986.

Blackwell, Elizabeth. "A Medical Address on the Benevolence of Malthus, Contrasted with the Corruptions of Neo-Malthusianism." London: T. W. Danks & Co., 1888.

Blackwell, Elizabeth. *Pioneer Work in Opening the Medical Profession to Women.* Amherst, NY: Humanity Books, 2005.

Blackwell, Elizabeth. *The Religion of Health: A Lecture.* 2nd ed. London: S. W. Partridge and Co., 1869.

Blackwell, Elizabeth, and Emily Blackwell. *Medicine as a Profession for Women.* New York: W. H. Tinson, 1860.

Brace, Charles Loring. *Address on Industrial Schools, Delivered to the Teachers of the Schools, November 13, 1868.* New York: Wynkoop & Hallenbeck, 1868.

Brace, Charles Loring. *The Best Method of Disposing of Our Pauper and Vagrant Children.* New York: Wynkoop, Hallenbeck, & Thomas Printers, 1850.

Brace, Charles Loring. *The Children's Aid Society of New York: Its History, Plan and Results.* New York: Children's Aid Society, 1893.

Brace, Charles Loring. *The Dangerous Classes of New York, and Twenty Years' Work among Them.* 3rd ed. New York: Wynkoop, 1880.

Brace, Charles L. "Darwinism in Germany." *North American Review* 110, no. 227 (1870): 284–299.

Brace, Charles Loring. "Egyptian Monotheism." *New Princeton Review* 1 (1888): 346–361.

Brace, Charles L. *Free Trade, as Promoting Peace and Goodwill among Men.* New York: New York Free Trade Club, 1879.

Brace, Charles L. "The Fruits of Free Labor in the Smaller Islands of the British West Indies." *Atlantic Monthly* 9, no. 53 (1862): 273–282.

Brace, Charles Loring. *Gesta Christi: or, A History of Humane Progress under Christianity.* New York: A. C. Armstrong & Sons, 1883.

Brace, Charles Loring. *The New West: or, California in 1867–1868.* New York: G. P. Putnam & Son, 1869.

Brace, Charles L. *The Races of the Old World: A Manual of Ethnology.* London: John Murray, 1863.

Brace, Charles Loring. "Wolf-Reared Children." *St. Nicholas: An Illustrated Magazine for Young Folks* 9, no. 7 (1882): 542–554.

Brace, Emma, ed. *The Life of Charles Loring Brace: Chiefly Told in His Own Letters.* New York: Scribner's Sons, 1894.

Brinton, Daniel. *Library of Aboriginal American Literature.* Philadelphia: Brinton, 1882.

Buchanan, Joseph R. *Buchanan's Journal of Man.* Vol. 1. Cincinnati: J. R. Buchanan, 1888.

Buchanan, Joseph R. *Outlines of Lectures on the Neurological System of Anthropology.* Cincinnati: J. R. Buchanan, 1854.

Burnyeat, Myles. *The Theaetetus of Plato*. Translated by M. J. Levett Hackett. Indianapolis: Hackett, 1990.

Bushnell, Horace. *Unconscious Influence, a Sermon*. London: Partridge & Oakey, 1852.

Caton, John Dean. "Unnatural Attachments among Animals." *American Naturalist* 17, no. 4 (1883): 359–363.

Child, Lydia Maria. *Letters from New-York*. Edited by Bruce Mills. Athens: University of Georgia Press, 1998.

Child, Lydia Maria. *A Romance of the Republic*. Lexington: University Press of Kentucky, 1997.

Clarke, Edward Hammond. *Sex in Education; or, A Fair Chance for Girls*. Boston: James R. Osgood and Company, 1875.

Collins, Glenn. "Glimpses of Heartache, and Stories of Survival." *New York Times*, September 3, 2009. http://www.nytimes.com/2007/09/03/nyregion/03foundling.html.

Cooper, Anna Julia. *A Voice from the South*. New York: Oxford University Press, 1988.

Cope, E. D. "The Applied Metaphysics of Sex." *American Naturalist* 19, no. 8 (1885): 820–824.

Cope, E. D. "Descent of Man." *Modern Science Essayist* 1, no. 7 (1889): 161–175.

Cope, E. D. "Editors' Table." *American Naturalist* 24, no. 284 (1890): 747–748.

Cope, E. D. "The Energy of Life Evolution, and How It Has Acted." *Popular Science Monthly* 27 (October 1885): 789–800.

Cope, E. D. "Ethical Evolution." *Open Court* 3, no. 82 (1889): 1523–1525.

Cope, E. D. "The Future of Thought in America." *Monist* 3, no. 1 (1892): 23–29.

Cope, E. D. "Letter to the Editor." *New York Times*, February 4, 1887. ProQuest Historical Newspapers: *New York Times* (94566826).

Cope, E. D. "Letter to the Editor: The African in America." *Open Court* 4, no. 151 (1890): 2399–2400.

Cope, E. D. "The Marriage Problem." *Open Court* 2, no. 65 (1888): 1320–1324.

Cope, E. D. "On the Hypothesis of Evolution: Physical and Metaphysical." In *Half Hours with Modern Scientists*, edited by Noah Porter, 180–187. New Haven, CT: Chatfield, 1872.

Cope, E. D. "The Oppression of Women." *Open Court* 8, no. 354 (1894): 4103–4105.

Cope, E. D. *Origin of the Fittest: Essays on Evolution*. New York: D. Appleton and Co., 1886.

Cope, E. D. "The Present Problems of Organic Evolution." *The Monist* 5, no. 4 (1895): 563–573.

Cope, E. D. *The Primary Factors of Organic Evolution*. Chicago: Open Court, 1896.

Cope, E. D. "Psychology: Sex in Government." *American Naturalist* 21, no. 4 (1887): 399–400.

Cope, E. D. "The Relation of the Sexes to Government." *Popular Science Monthly* 33 (October 1888): 722–730.

Cope, E. D. "Sex in Government." *American Naturalist* 21, no. 4 (1887): 399–401.

Cope, E. D. "Two Perils of the Indo-European" (part 1 of 2). *Open Court* 3, no. 126 (1889): 2052–2054.

Cope, E. D. "Two Perils of the Indo-European" (part 2 of 2). *Open Court* 3, no. 127 (1889): 2070–2071.

Cope, E. D. "What Is Republicanism?" *Open Court* 10, no. 453 (1896): 4897–4899.

Cope, E. D. "What Is the Object of Life?" *Forum* 4, no. 1 (1887): 49–57.

Cope, E. D., and J. S. Kingsley. "Editorials." *American Naturalist* 27, no. 317 (1893): 450–451.

Darwin, Charles. *The Expression of Emotions in Man and Animals.* New York: D. Appleton and Company, 1899.

Darwin, Charles. Preface to the Third Edition of *On the Origin of Species* (1861). Talk Origins Archive. Accessed June 6, 2015. http://www.talkorigins.org/faqs/origin /preface.html.

Darwin, Charles. *The Variation of Animals and Plants under Domestication.* London: John Murray, 1868.

Davenport, Charles Benedict. *The Trait Book.* Cold Spring Harbor, NY: Cold Spring Harbor, 1912.

De Quincey, Thomas. "The Palimpsest of the Human Brain" (1845). *Quotidiana,* edited by Patrick Malden. Accessed February 5, 2015. http://essays.quotidiana.org /dequincey/palimpsest_of_the_human_brain.

Douglass, Frederick. "The Claims of the Negro Ethnologically Considered." In *Life and Writings of Frederick Douglass,* vol. 2, edited by Philip S. Foner, 289–309. New York: International Publishers, 1950.

Du Bois, W. E. B. "Black Folk and Birth Control." *Birth Control Review* 16, no. 6 (1932): 166–167.

Du Bois, W. E. B. *Dark Princess.* Jackson, MS: Banner Books, 1995.

Du Bois, W. E. B. "Development of a People." *International Journal of Ethics* 14, no. 3 (1904): 292–311.

Du Bois, W. E. B. *Dusk of Dawn: An Essay toward an Autobiography of a Race Concept.* New Brunswick, NJ: Transaction, 1997.

Du Bois, W. E. B. "Evolution of the Race Problem." *Proceedings of the National Negro Conference* (1909): 142–158.

Du Bois, W. E. B. *The Health and Physique of the Negro American.* Reprint, New York: Arno and the *New York Times,* 1968.

Du Bois, W. E. B. "Heredity and the Public Schools." In *Du Bois on Education,* edited by Eugene F. Provenzo Jr., 111–122. Lanham, MD: Rowman and Littlefield, 2002.

Du Bois, W. E. B. "My Evolving Program for Negro Freedom." In *What the Negro Really Wants,* edited by Rayford W. Logan, 31–70. Chapel Hill: University of North Carolina Press, 1944.

Du Bois, W. E. B. "Opinion of W. E. B. Du Bois." *Crisis* 19, no. 3 (1920): 105–110.

Du Bois, W. E. B. "Opinion of W. E. B. Du Bois." *Crisis* 24, no. 4 (1922): 151–155.

Du Bois, W. E. B. "Opinion of W. E. B. Du Bois." *Crisis* 32, no. 6 (1926): 283.

Du Bois, W. E. B. "Races." *Crisis* 2, no. 4 (1911): 157–158.

Du Bois, W. E. B. *The Souls of Black Folk: Authoritative Text, Contexts, Criticism.* Edited by Henry Louis Gates Jr. and Terri Hume Oliver. New York: Norton, 1999.

Du Bois, W. E. B. "The Talented Tenth." In *The Future of the Race,* edited by Henry Louis Gates Jr. and Cornell West, 133–158. New York: Alfred A. Knopf, 1996.

Du Bois, W. E. B. "Talented Tenth Memorial Address." In *W. E. B. Du Bois: A Reader*, edited by David Levering Lewis, 347–353. New York: Holt, 1995.

Dugdale, R. L. *The Jukes: A Study in Crime, Pauperism, Disease, and Heredity.* New York: G. P. Putnam's Sons, 1877.

Edwards, Charles L. "An Expression of Animal Sympathy." *American Naturalist* 21, no. 12 (1887): 1127–1129.

Foster, Frances Smith, ed. *A Brighter Coming Day: A Frances Ellen Watkins Harper Reader.* New York: Feminist Press at CUNY, 1993.

Freud, Sigmund. "A Note upon the 'Mystic Writing Pad.' " In *General Psychological Theory*, 207–212. New York: Touchstone, 1997.

Galton, Francis. *Essays in Eugenics.* London: Eugenics Education Society, 1909.

Galton, Francis. *The Life History Album.* London: Macmillan, 1884.

Geddes, Patrick, and J. Arthur Thomson. *The Evolution of Sex.* London: Walter Scott, 1889.

Gilman, Charlotte Perkins. *The Dress of Women: A Critical Introduction to the Symbolism and Sociology of Clothing.* Westport, CT: Greenwood, 2001.

Gilman, Charlotte Perkins. *Women and Economics: A Study of the Economic Relation between Men and Women as a Factor in Social Evolution.* Boston: Small, Maynard, & Co., 1898.

Godwin, William. *The Enquirer: Reflections on Education, Manners, and Literature, in a Series of Essays.* London: G. G. and J. Robinson, 1797.

Grant, Madison. *The Passing of the Great Race; or, The Racial Basis of European History.* New York: Charles Scribner's Sons, 1922.

Gray, Asa, and Jane Loring Gray. *Letters of Asa Gray.* Vol. 2. Boston: Houghton, Mifflin and Co., 1894.

Harper, Frances E. W. *Iola Leroy.* Boston: Beacon, 1897.

Harper, Frances E. W. "Sowing and Reaping." In *Minnie's Sacrifice, Sowing and Reaping, and Trial and Triumph: Three Rediscovered Novels*, edited by Frances Smith Foster, 93–176. Boston: Beacon, 1994.

Harper, Frances E. W. "Trial and Triumph." In *Minnie's Sacrifice, Sowing and Reaping, and Trial and Triumph: Three Rediscovered Novels*, edited by Frances Smith Foster, 177–287. Boston: Beacon, 1994.

Harper, Frances E. W. "Woman's Political Future" (May 20, 1892). Accessed June 6, 2015. http://archive.vod.umd.edu/civil/harper1893int.htm.

Harper, Lawrence V. "Epigenetic Inheritance and the Intergenerational Transfer of Experience." *Psychological Bulletin* 131, no. 3 (2005): 340–360.

Hawthorne, Nathaniel. "The Birth-mark." In *Mosses from an Old Manse*, vol. 10 of *The Centenary Edition of the Works of Nathaniel Hawthorne*, edited by William Charvat, Roy Harvey Pearce, and Claude M. Simpson, 36–56. Columbus: Ohio State University Press, 1964.

Hume, David. *The Essential Philosophical Works.* Ware, Hertfordshire: Bibliophile Books, 2011.

Hunt, Harriet K. *Glances and Glimpses; or Fifty Years Social, including Twenty Years Professional Life.* Boston: John P. Jewett and Co., 1856.

Huxley, Julian. "Eugenics and Society." *Eugenics Review* 28, no. 1 (1936): 11–31. Eugenics Archive. Accessed January 30, 2012. http://www.eugenicsarchive.org/eugenics /view_image.pl?id=1825.

Hyatt, Alpheus. "The Influence of Woman in the Evolution of the Human Race." *Natural Science* 11, no. 65 (1897): 89–93.

Kleinman, Loren. "Interview with Christina Baker Kline: #1 *New York Times* Bestselling Author of Orphan Train." *Huffington Post*, April 18, 2014. http://www .huffingtonpost.com/loren-kleinman/interview-with-christina-_b_5175099.html.

Lamarck, Jean-Baptiste Pierre. *Philosophie Zoologique* [Zoological Philosophy]. Translated by Hugh Elliot. London: Macmillan, 1914.

Le Conte, Joseph. "The Effect of Mixture of Races on Human Progress." *Berkeley Quarterly* 1, no. 2 (1880): 81–104.

Le Conte, Joseph. "The Factors of Evolution." *The Monist* 1 no. 3 (1891): 321–335.

Le Conte, Joseph. "The Relation of Biology and Sociology to the Woman Question." Unpublished manuscript, 189?, University of California Archives, Bancroft Library, University of California, Berkeley.

Le Conte, Joseph. "The Theory of Evolution and Social Progress." *Monist* 5, no. 4 (1895): 481–500.

Locke, John. *Essay concerning Human Understanding*. Edited and with a foreword by Peter H. Nidditch. New York: Oxford University Press, 1975.

Logan, Adella Hunt. "Prenatal and Hereditary Influences." In *"We Are Coming": The Persuasive Discourse of Nineteenth-Century Black Women*, edited by Shirley Wilson Logan, 211–214. Carbondale: Southern Illinois University Press, 1999.

Looby, Christopher, ed. "The Man Who Thought Himself a Woman." In *"The Man Who Thought Himself a Woman" and Other Queer Nineteenth-Century Short Stories*, edited by Christopher Looby, 94–108. Philadelphia: University of Pennsylvania Press, 2016.

Lord, Dr. "The Natural and the Spiritual." *The North Star*, March 31, 1848. Accessible Archives. http://www.accessible.com.proxy.libraries.rutgers.edu/accessible/print.

Maliniak, Jacques M. *Sculpture in the Living: Rebuilding the Face and Form by Plastic Surgery*. New York: Romaine Pierson, 1934.

Malthus, T. R. *An Essay on the Principle of Population*. Edited by Geoffrey Gilbert. New York: Oxford University Press, 2008.

Mason, Daniel Gregory. Introduction to *The Poems of Philip Henry Savage*, edited by Daniel Gregory Mason. Boston: Small, Maynard & Company, 1900.

Matsell, George W. *Semi-Annual Report of the Chief of Police from May 1, to October 31, 1849* (1850): 58–66. History Matters. Accessed June 6, 2015. http://historymatters .gmu.edu/d/6526/.

McClintock, Barbara. "The Significance of Responses of the Genome to Challenge." In *Nobel Lectures, Physiology or Medicine 1981–1990*, edited by Tore Frängsmyr, 180–199. Singapore: World Scientific, 1993.

Melville, Herman. "Hawthorne and His Mosses." In *The Norton Anthology of American Literature*, 2nd ed., edited by Nina Baym et al., 1:2163–2174. New York: Norton, 1985.

Money, John, Joan G. Hampson, and John L. Hampson. "Imprinting and the Establishment of Gender Role." *American Medical Association: Archives of Neurology & Psychiatry* 77, no. 3 (1957): 333–336.

Morgan, Lewis Henry. *Ancient Society*. Tucson: University of Arizona Press, 1985.

New York Foundling. *1993 Orphan Train Rider Reunion*. VHS. Author's collection.

Osborn, Henry Fairchild. Preface to *The Passing of the Great Race; or, The Racial Basis of European History*, by Madison Grant, vii–xiv. New York: Charles Scribner's Sons, 1922.

Packard, A. S., Jr., and E. D. Cope. "Editors' Table." *American Naturalist* 16, no. 1 (1882): 33–35.

Packard, A. S., Jr., and E. D. Cope. "Editors' Table." *American Naturalist* 16, no. 6 (1882): 487–492.

Packard, A. S., Jr.. and E. D. Cope. "Editors' Table." *American Naturalist* 19, no. 7 (1885): 691–693.

Peirce, Charles. "Evolutionary Love." *Monist* 3, no. 1 (1892): 176–200.

Phelps, Elizabeth Stuart. *Doctor Zay*. Boston: Houghton, Mifflin and Company, 1882.

Powell, John W. "The Growth of Sentiency." *Forum* 11 (1891): 167.

Pratt, Richard Henry. *Battlefield and Classroom: Four Decades with the American Indian, 1867–1904*. New Haven, CT: Yale University Press, 1964.

Pratt, Richard Henry. "How to Deal with the Indians: The Potency of Environment." Washington, DC: Library of Congress Photoduplication Service, 2006.

Ratner, Sidney. "Evolution and the Rise of the Scientific Spirit in America." *Philosophy of Science* 3, no. 1 (1936): 104–122.

Rollins, Alice Wellington. *Uncle Tom's Tenement*. Boston: William E. Smythe Co., 1888.

Sanger, Margaret. *The Pivot of Civilization*. New York: Brentano's, 1922.

Sanger, Margaret. *Woman and the New Race*. New York: Brentano's, 1920.

Sedgwick, Catharine Maria. *A New-England Tale; or, Sketches of New-England Character and Manners*. New York: Oxford University Press, 1995.

Sigourney, Lydia Howard. *Letters to Mothers*. Hartford, CT: Hudson & Skinner, 1838.

Smith, Adam. *The Theory of Moral Sentiments*. New York: Gutenberg, 2011.

Standing Bear, Luther. *The Land of the Spotted Eagle*. Lincoln, NE: Bison Books, 1933.

Still, William. *Underground Railroad: A Record of Facts, Authentic Narrative, Letters, etc.* Philadelphia: Porter & Coates, 1872.

Stowe, Harriet Beecher. *Uncle Tom's Cabin*. Edited by Elizabeth Ammons. New York: W. W. Norton, 1993.

Thompson, Marguerite. "Marguerite Thompson." National Orphan Train Complex. Accessed April 4, 2015. http://orphantraindepot.org/orphan-train-rider-stories/marguerite-thompson.

Virginia Commonwealth University. Center on Society and Health. "Mapping Life Expectancy." Accessed October 5, 2016. http://www.societyhealth.vcu.edu/work/the-projects/mapping-life-expectancy.html.

Virginia Wadsworth Wirtz Center for the Performing Arts. *2006–2007 Mainstage Season*. Evanston, IL: Northwestern University, 2006.

Walker, Mary. *Unmasked, or, The Science of Immorality. To Gentlemen*. New York: Wm. H. Boyd, 1878.

Ward, Lester Frank. "The Transmission of Culture." *The Forum* 11 (1891): 312–319.

Watkins, William. "Address Delivered before the Moral Reform Society in Philadelphia." In *Early Negro Writing 1760–1837*, edited by Dorothy Porter, 155–166. Baltimore: Black Classic Press, 1995.

Wilson, Harriet E. *Our Nig: or, Sketches from the Life of a Free Black.* New York: Vintage Books, 2011.

Zitkala-Sa. *American Indian Stories.* Lincoln, NE: Bison Books, 1985.

SECONDARY SOURCES

Agamben, Giorgio. *Homo Sacer: Sovereign Power and Bare Life.* Stanford, CA: Stanford University Press, 1998.

Ahmed, Sara. *The Cultural Politics of Emotion.* New York: Routledge, 2004.

Ahmed, Sara. "Orientations Matter." In *New Materialism: Ontology, Agency, and Politics,* edited by Diana Coole and Samantha Frost, 234–257. Durham, NC: Duke University Press, 2010.

Ahuja, Neel. *Bioinsecurities: Disease Interventions, Empire, and the Government of Species.* Durham, NC: Duke University Press, 2016.

Alaimo, Stacy. "Sexual Matters: Darwinian Feminisms and the Nonhuman Turn." *J19: Journal of Nineteenth Century Americanists* 1, no. 2 (2013): 390–396.

Allewaert, Monique. *Ariel's Ecology: Plantations, Personhood, and Colonialism in the American Tropics.* Minneapolis: University of Minnesota Press, 2013.

Anderson, Benedict. *Imagined Communities: Reflections on the Origin and Spread of Nationalism.* New York: Verso, 2006.

Appiah, Anthony. "The Uncompleted Argument: Du Bois and the Illusion of Race." *Critical Inquiry* 12, no. 1 (1985): 21–37.

Baker, Lee D. *From Savage to Negro: Anthropology and the Construction of Race, 1896–1954.* Berkeley: University of California Press, 1998.

Bannister, Robert C. *Social Darwinism: Science and Myth in Anglo-American Thought.* Philadelphia: Temple University Press, 1979.

Barber, Lynn. *The Heyday of Natural History, 1820–1870.* New York: Doubleday, 1980.

Barkan, Elazar. *The Retreat of Scientific Racism: Changing Concepts of Race in Britain and the United States between the World Wars.* Cambridge: Cambridge University Press, 1992.

Barker-Benfield, G. J. *The Culture of Sensibility: Sex and Society in Eighteenth-Century Britain.* Chicago: University of Chicago Press, 1992.

Barnes, Elizabeth. *States of Sympathy: Seduction and Democracy in the American Novel.* New York: Columbia University Press, 1997.

Bauer, Dale. "'In the Blood': Sentiment, Sex, and the Ugly Girl." *differences: A Journal of Feminist Cultural Studies* 11, no. 3 (1999): 57–75.

Bay, Mia. "'The World Was Thinking Wrong about Race': The Philadelphia Negro and Nineteenth-Century Science." In *W. E. B. Du Bois, Race, and the City,* edited by Michael B. Katz and Thomas J. Sugrue, 40–59. Philadelphia: University of Pennsylvania Press, 1998.

Baym, Nina. *American Women of Letters and the Nineteenth-Century Sciences: Styles of Affiliation.* Baltimore: Johns Hopkins University Press, 2002.

Baym, Nina. *Woman's Fiction: A Guide to Novels by and about Women in America, 1820–1870.* 2nd ed. Chicago: University of Illinois Press, 1993.

Bederman, Gail. *Manliness and Civilization: A Cultural History of Gender and Race in the United States, 1880–1917.* Chicago: University of Chicago Press, 1996.

Bender, Thomas. *Toward an Urban Vision: Ideas and Institutions in Nineteenth Century America*. Baltimore: Johns Hopkins University Press, 1982.

Berlant, Lauren. *Cruel Optimism*. Durham, NC: Duke University Press, 2011.

Berlant, Lauren. *The Female Complaint: The Unfinished Business of Sentimentality in American Culture*. Durham, NC: Duke University Press, 2008.

Berlant, Lauren. *The Queen of America Goes to Washington City: Essays on Sex and Citizenship*. Durham, NC: Duke University Press, 1997.

Bernstein, Elizabeth. "Militarized Humanism Meets Carceral Feminism." *Signs: A Journal of Women in Culture and Society* 36, no. 1 (2010): 45–72.

Bernstein, Robin. *Racial Innocence: Performing American Childhood from Slavery to Civil Rights*. New York: New York University Press, 2011.

Blencowe, Claire. "Biology, Contingency and the Problem of Racism in Feminist Discourse." *Theory, Culture, and Society* 28, no. 3 (2011): 3–27.

Boggs, Colleen Glenney. *Animalia Americana: Animal Representations and Biopolitical Subjectivity*. New York: Columbia University Press, 2013.

Bowler, Peter J. *The Eclipse of Darwinism: Anti-Darwinian Evolution Theories in the Decades around 1900*. Baltimore: Johns Hopkins University Press, 1992.

Bowler, Peter J. "Edward Drinker Cope and the Changing Structure of Evolutionary Theory." *Isis* 68, no. 2 (1977): 249–265.

Bowler, Peter J. *Evolution: The History of an Idea*. Berkeley: University of California Press, 2003.

Bowler, Peter J. *The Non-Darwinian Revolution: Reinterpreting a Historical Myth*. Baltimore: Johns Hopkins University Press, 1988.

Boyd, Julia. *The Excellent Doctor Blackwell: The Life of the First Female Physician*. Charleston, SC: History Press, 2006.

Boyd, Melba Joyce. *Discarded Legacy: Politics and Poetics in the Life of Frances E. W. Harper, 1825–1911*. Detroit: Wayne State University Press, 1994.

Boyer, Paul. *Urban Masses and Moral Order in America, 1820–1920*. Cambridge, MA: Boston University Press, 1992.

Brennan, Teresa. *The Transmission of Affect*. Ithaca, NY: Cornell University Press, 2004.

Briggs, Laura. "The Race of Hysteria: 'Overcivilization' and the 'Savage' in Late Nineteenth-Century Obstetrics and Gynecology." *American Quarterly* 52, no. 2 (2000): 246–273.

Briggs, Laura. *Reproducing Empire: Race, Sex, Science, and U.S. Imperialism in Puerto Rico*. Berkeley: University of California Press, 2002.

Brodhead, Richard H. "Sparing the Rod: Discipline and Fiction in Antebellum America." *Representations* 21 (1988): 67–96.

Browne, Simone. *Dark Matters: On the Surveillance of Blackness*. Durham, NC: Duke University Press, 2015.

Bullard, Katharine Sara. "Saving the Children: Discourses of Race, Nation and Citizenship in America." PhD diss., University of Illinois at Urbana-Champaign, 2004.

Burgett, Bruce. *Sentimental Bodies: Sex, Gender, and Citizenship in the Early Republic*. Princeton, NJ: Princeton University Press, 1998.

Byrd, Jodi. *The Transit of Empire: Indigenous Critiques of Colonialism*. Minneapolis: University of Minnesota Press, 2011.

Canguilhem, Georges, and John Savage. "The Living and Its Milieu." *Grey Room* 3, no. 2 (2001): 7–31.

Carby, Hazel. *Reconstructing Womanhood: The Emergence of the Afro-American Woman Novelist.* New York: Oxford University Press, 1989.

Carp, E. Wayne. *Family Matters: Secrecy and Disclosure in the History of Adoption.* Cambridge, MA: Harvard University Press, 1998.

Carpenter, Cari M. *Seeing Red: Anger, Sentimentality, and American Indians.* Columbus: Ohio State University Press, 2008.

Castañeda, Claudia. *Figurations: Child, Bodies, Worlds.* Durham, NC: Duke University Press, 2002.

Castiglia, Christopher. *Interior States: Institutional Consciousness and the Inner Life of Democracy in the Antebellum United States.* Durham, NC: Duke University Press, 2008.

Chandler, James. *An Archeology of Sympathy: The Sentimental Mode in Literature and Cinema.* Chicago: University of Chicago Press, 2013.

Chapman, Mary, and Glenn Hendler, eds. *Sentimental Men: Masculinity and the Politics of Affect in American Culture.* Berkeley: University of California Press, 1999.

Chauncey, George. *Gay New York: Gender, Urban Culture, and the Making of the Gay Male World 1890–1940.* New York: Basic Books, 1994.

Chen, Mel. *Animacies: Biopolitics, Racial Mattering, and Queer Affect.* Durham, NC: Duke University Press, 2012.

Child, Brenda J. *Boarding School Seasons: American Indian Families, 1900–1940.* Lincoln: University of Nebraska Press, 1998.

Chiles, Katy. *Transformable Race: Surprising Metamorphoses in the Literature of Early America.* New York: Oxford University Press, 2014.

Clarke, Edwin, and L. S. Jacyna. *Nineteenth-Century Origins of Neuroscientific Concepts.* Berkeley: University of California Press, 1987.

Classen, Constance. "Feminine Tactics: Crafting an Alternative Aesthetics in the Eighteenth and Nineteenth Centuries." In *The Book of Touch*, edited by Constance Classen, 228–239. Oxford: Berg, 2005.

Clough, Patricia. Introduction to *The Affective Turn: Theorizing the Social*, edited by Patricia Clough and Jean Halley, 1–33. Durham, NC: Duke University Press, 2007.

Cody, Lisa Forman. "Review: *Engendering Science*." *Journal of Women's History* 22, no. 3 (2010): 214–223.

Cohen, Ed. *A Body Worth Defending: Immunity, Biopolitics, and the Apotheosis of the Modern Body.* Durham, NC: Duke University Press, 2009.

Coole, Diana. "The Inertia of Matter and the Generativity of Flesh." In *New Materialism: Ontology, Agency, and Politics*, edited by Diana Coole and Samantha Frost, 92–115. Durham, NC: Duke University Press, 2010.

Cooper, Brittney. *Beyond Respectability: The Intellectual Thought of Race Women.* Champaign: University of Illinois Press, 2017.

Cooper, Melinda. *Life as Surplus: Biotechnology and Capitalism in the Neoliberal Era.* Seattle: University of Washington Press, 2008.

Cooppan, Vilashini. "Move On down the Line: Domestic Science, Transnational Politics, and Gendered Allegory in Du Bois." In *Next to the Color Line: Gender,*

Sexuality, and W. E. B. Du Bois, edited by Susan Gillman and Alys Weinbaum, 35–68. Minneapolis: University of Minnesota Press, 2007.

Coviello, Peter. *Tomorrow's Parties: Sex and the Untimely in Nineteenth-Century America*. New York: New York University Press, 2013.

da Silva, Denise Ferreira. *Toward a Global Idea of Race*. Minneapolis: University of Minnesota Press, 2007.

Daston, Lorraine J., and Peter Galison. *Objectivity*. Cambridge, MA: MIT Press, 2010.

Dauber, Michele Landis. *The Sympathetic State: Disaster Relief and the Origins of the American Welfare State*. Chicago: University of Chicago Press, 2012.

Davis, Angela Y. *Women, Race, and Class*. New York: Random House, 1981.

Deleuze, Gilles. *The Fold: Leibniz and the Baroque*. Translated by Tom Conley. Minneapolis: University of Minnesota Press, 1992.

Deleuze, Gilles. *Foucault*. Translated by Sean Hand. Minneapolis: University of Minnesota Press, 1988.

Deleuze, Gilles. "Postscript on the Societies of Control." *October* 59, no. 1 (1992): 3–7.

Deleuze, Gilles. *Spinoza: Practical Philosophy*. Translated by Robert Hurley. San Francisco: City Lights Books, 1988.

DiAngelo, Robin. "White Fragility." *International Journal of Critical Pedagogy* 3, no. 3 (2011): 54–70.

Dikötter, Frank. "Race Culture: Recent Perspectives on the History of Eugenics (Review Essay)." *American Historical Review* 103, no. 2 (1998): 467–478.

Dillon, Elizabeth Maddock. *The Gender of Freedom: Fictions of Liberalism and the Literary Public Sphere*. Stanford, CA: Stanford University Press, 2007.

Dillon, Sarah. *The Palimpsest: Literature, Criticism, Theory*. New York: Bloomsbury Academic, 2013.

Doidge, Norman. *The Brain That Changes Itself: Stories of Personal Triumph from the Frontiers of Brain Science*. New York: Viking, 2007.

Dorr, Gregory Michael, and Angela Logan. " 'Quality, Not Mere Quantity, Counts': Black Eugenics and the NAACP Baby Contests." In *A Century of Eugenics in America: From the Indiana Experiment to the Human Genome Project*, edited by Paul A. Lombardo, 68–94. Bloomington: Indiana University Press, 2011.

Douglas, Ann. *The Feminization of American Culture*. New York: Farrar, Straus and Giroux, 1998.

Draaisma, Douwe. *Metaphors of Memory: A History of Ideas about the Mind*. Cambridge: Cambridge University Press, 2000.

duCille, Ann. *The Coupling Convention: Sex, Text, and Tradition in Black Women's Fiction*. New York: Oxford University Press, 1993.

Dupree, A. Hunter. *Asa Gray, 1810–1888*. Cambridge, MA: Harvard University Press, 1959.

Egan, Timothy. "Boredom in the West Fuels Binge Drinking." *New York Times*, September 2, 2006. http://www.nytimes.com/2006/09/02/us/02binge.html.

Elliott, Michael A. *The Culture Concept: Writing and Difference in the Age of Realism*. Minneapolis: University of Minnesota Press, 2002.

Ellison, Julie. *Cato's Tears and the Making of Anglo-American Sentiment*. Chicago: University of Chicago Press, 1999.

English, Daylanne K. *Unnatural Selections: Eugenics in American Modernism and the Harlem Renaissance*. Chapel Hill: University of North Carolina Press, 2004.

English, Daylanne. "W. E. B. Du Bois's Family *Crisis*." *American Literature* 72, no. 2 (2000): 291–319.

Faderman, Lillian. *Surpassing the Love of Men: Romantic Friendship and Love between Women from the Renaissance to the Present*. New York: HarperCollins, 1998.

Faderman, Lillian. *To Believe in Women: What Lesbians Have Done for America—A History*. New York: Houghton Mifflin, 1999.

Farland, Maria. "W. E. B. Du Bois, Anthropometric Science, and the Limits of Racial Uplift." *American Quarterly* 58, no. 4 (2006): 1017–1044.

Fausto-Sterling, Anne. *Sex/Gender: Biology in a Social World*. New York: Routledge, 2012.

Ferguson, Roderick A. *Aberrations in Black: Toward a Queer of Color Critique*. Minneapolis: University of Minnesota Press, 2004.

Field, Corrine T. "Frances E. W. Harper and the Politics of Intellectual Maturity." In *Toward an Intellectual History of Black Women*, edited by Mia Bay, Farah J. Griffin, and Barbara Dianne Savage, 110–128. Chapel Hill: University of North Carolina Press, 2015.

Figlio, Karl M. "Theories of Perception and the Physiology of Mind in the Late Eighteenth Century." *History of Science* 12 (1975): 177–212.

Fisher, Philip. *Hard Facts: Setting and Form in the American Novel*. New York: Oxford University Press, 1985.

Flew, Sarah. "Unveiling the Anonymous Philanthropist: Charity in the Nineteenth Century." *Journal of Victorian Culture* 20, no. 1 (2015): 20–33.

Foreman, P. Gabrielle. *Activist Sentiments: Reading Black Women in the Nineteenth Century*. Urbana: University of Illinois Press, 2009.

Foster, Frances Smith. Introduction to *A Brighter Coming Day: A Frances Ellen Watkins Harper Reader*, edited by Frances Smith Foster, 3–42. New York: Feminist Press at CUNY, 1993.

Foster, Frances Smith. Introduction to *Minnie's Sacrifice, Sowing and Reaping, and Trial and Triumph: Three Rediscovered Novels*, edited by Frances Smith Foster, xi–xxxviii. Boston: Beacon, 1994.

Foucault, Michel. *Discipline and Punish: The Birth of the Prison*. Translated by Alan Sheridan. New York: Vintage Books, 1995.

Foucault, Michel. *The History of Sexuality*, vol. 1: *An Introduction*. Translated by Robert Hurley. New York: Vintage, 1990.

Foucault, Michel. *Lectures on the Will to Know: Lectures at the Collège de France, 1970–1971*. Translated by Graham Burchell. New York: Picador, 2013.

Foucault, Michel. *Security, Territory, Population: Lectures at the Collège de France, 1977–1978*. Translated by Graham Burchell. New York: Picador, 2004.

Foucault, Michel. *"Society Must Be Defended": Lectures at the Collège de France, 1975–1976*. Translated by David Macey. New York: Picador, 2003.

Fredrickson, George M. *The Black Image in the White Mind: The Debate on Afro-American Character and Destiny, 1817–1914*. New York: Harper & Row, 1971.

Freeman, Elizabeth. *Time Binds: Queer Temporalities, Queer Histories*. Durham, NC: Duke University Press, 2010.

Fretwell, Erica. "Senses of Belonging: The Synaesthetics of Citizenship in American Literature, 1862–1903." PhD diss., Duke University, 2011.

Frost, Samantha. *Biocultural Creatures: Toward a New Theory of the Human*. Durham, NC: Duke University Press, 2016.

Gagnon, John H., and William Simon. *Sexual Conduct: The Social Source of Human Sexuality*. Chicago: Aldine, 1973.

Gaines, Kevin K. *Uplifting the Race: Black Leadership, Politics, and Culture in the Twentieth Century*. Chapel Hill: University of North Carolina Press, 1996.

Gaskill, Nicholas. "Vibrant Environments: The Feel of Color from the White Whale to the Red Wheelbarrow." PhD diss., University of North Carolina, 2010.

Gianquitto, Tina. *"Good Observers of Nature": American Women and the Scientific Study of the Natural World, 1820–1885*. Athens: University of Georgia Press.

Gillman, Susan. *Blood Talk: American Race, Melodrama, and the Culture of the Occult*. Chicago: University of Chicago Press, 2003.

Gillman, Susan, and Alys Eve Weinbaum, eds. *Next to the Color Line: Gender, Sexuality, and W. E. B. Du Bois*. Minneapolis: University of Minnesota Press, 2007.

Gilroy, Paul. *The Black Atlantic: Modernity and Double Consciousness*. Cambridge, MA: Harvard University Press, 1993.

Gish, Clay. "Rescuing the 'Waifs and Strays' of the City." *Journal of Social History* 33, no. 1 (1999): 121–141.

Gonzalez, John M. "The Warp of Whiteness: Domesticity and Empire in Helen Hunt Jackson's *Ramona*." *American Literary History* 16, no. 3 (2004): 437–465.

Gordon, Linda. *The Great Arizona Orphan Abduction*. Cambridge, MA: Harvard University Press, 1999.

Gordon, Linda. *The Moral Property of Women: A History of Birth Control Politics in America*. Urbana: University of Illinois Press, 2007.

Gordon, Linda. *Woman's Body, Woman's Right: Birth Control in America*. New York: Penguin, 1990.

Goshgarian, G. M. *To Kiss the Chastening Rod: Domestic Fiction and Sexual Ideology in the American Renaissance*. Ithaca, NY: Cornell University Press, 1992.

Gossett, Thomas F. *Race: The History of an Idea in America*. New York: Oxford University Press, 1997.

Gould, Stephen Jay. *The Mismeasure of Man*. New York: Norton, 1981.

Gould, Stephen Jay. *Ontogeny and Phylogeny*. Cambridge, MA: Harvard University Press, 1977.

Graham, Janet, dir. *American Experience: The Orphan Trains*. DVD. PBS Home Video, 1995.

Gregg, Melissa, and Gregory J. Seigworth, eds. *The Affect Theory Reader*. Durham, NC: Duke University Press, 2010.

Grosz, Elizabeth. *The Nick of Time: Politics, Evolution, and the Untimely*. Durham, NC: Duke University Press, 2004.

Gruesz, Kirsten Silva. *Ambassadors of Culture: The Transamerican Origins of Latino Writing*. Princeton, NJ: Princeton University Press, 2002.

Haines, Christian. "Martin Delany, or, Para-Ontologies of Blackness." Paper presented at the biennial meeting of C19: The Society of Nineteenth-Century Americanists, State College, PA, March 17–20, 2016.

Haller, John S., Jr. *Outcasts from Evolution: Scientific Attitudes of Racial Inferiority, 1859–1900*. Urbana: University of Illinois Press, 1971.

Hallock, Thomas. "Male Pleasures and the Genders of Eighteenth-Century Botanic Exchange: A Garden Tour." *William and Mary Quarterly* 62 (October 2005): 697–718.

Hamlin, Kimberly A. *From Eve to Evolution: Darwin, Science, and Women's Rights in Gilded Age America*. Chicago: University of Chicago Press, 2014.

Haraway, Donna. "Situated Knowledges: The Science Question in Feminism and the Privilege of Partial Perspective." *Feminist Studies* 14, no. 3 (1988): 575–599.

Harding, Sandra, ed. *The "Racial" Economy of Science: Toward a Democratic Future*. Bloomington: Indiana University Press, 1993.

Harris, Sharon M. *Dr. Mary Walker: An American Radical, 1832–1919*. New Brunswick, NJ: Rutgers University Press, 2009.

Hart, Jamie. "Who Should Have the Children? Discussions of Birth Control among African-American Intellectuals, 1920–1939." *Journal of Negro History* 79, no. 1 (1994): 71–84.

Hartman, Saidiya V. *Scenes of Subjection: Terror, Slavery, and Self-Making in Nineteenth-Century America*. New York: Oxford University Press, 1997.

Hasian, Marouf, Jr. *The Rhetoric of Eugenics in Anglo-American Thought*. Athens: University of Georgia Press, 1996.

Hayot, Eric. "Chinese Bodies, Chinese Futures." *Representations* 99, no. 1 (2007): 99–129.

Helkie, Ferrie. "An Interview with C. Loring Brace." *Current Anthropology* 38, no. 5 (1997): 851–869.

Hendler, Glenn. *Public Sentiments: Structures of Feeling in Nineteenth-Century American Literature*. Chapel Hill: University of North Carolina Press, 2001.

Herzig, Rebecca. *Suffering for Science: Reason and Sacrifice in Modern America*. New Brunswick, NJ: Rutgers University Press, 2006.

Higginbotham, Evelyn Brooks. *Righteous Discontent: The Women's Movement in the Black Baptist Church 1880–1920*. Cambridge, MA: Harvard University Press, 1994.

Hiro, Molly. "How It Feels to Be without a Face: Race and the Reorientation of Sympathy in the 1890s." *Novel: A Forum on Fiction* 39, no. 2 (2006): 179–203.

Hofstadter, Richard. *Social Darwinism in American Thought*. New York: G. Braziller, 1956.

Holland, Sharon P., Marcia Ochoa, and Kyla Wazana Tompkins. "On the Visceral." *GLQ: A Journal of Lesbian and Gay Studies* 20, no. 4 (2014): 391–406.

Holt, Marilyn Irvin. *The Orphan Trains: Placing Out in America*. Lincoln, NE: Bison Books, 1994.

Horsman, Reginald. *Race and Manifest Destiny: The Origins of American Racial Anglo-Saxonism*. Cambridge, MA: Harvard University Press, 1986.

Howard, June. "What Is Sentimentality?" *American Literary History* 11, no. 1 (1999): 63–81.

Howes, David. *Sensual Relations: Engaging the Senses in Culture and Social Theory*. Ann Arbor: University of Michigan Press, 2004.

Jacobson, Matthew Fry. *Whiteness of a Different Color: European Immigrants and the Alchemy of Race*. Cambridge, MA: Harvard University Press, 1998.

Jaffe, Mark. *The Gilded Dinosaur: The Fossil War between E. D. Cope and O. C. Marsh and the Rise of American Science*. New York: Crown, 2000.

Jagose, Annamarie. *Orgasmology*. Durham, NC: Duke University Press, 2012.

Jones, Donna. *The Racial Discourses of Life Philosophy: Negritude, Vitalism, and Modernity*. New York: Columbia University Press, 2010.

Jordan-Young, Rebecca. *Brain Storm: The Flaws in the Science of Sex Difference*. Cambridge, MA: Harvard University Press, 2011.

Jung, Moon-Ho. *Coolies and Cane: Race, Labor, and Sugar in the Age of Emancipation*. Baltimore: Johns Hopkins University Press, 2009.

Kahan, Benjamin. *Celibacies: American Modernism and Sexual Life*. Durham, NC: Duke University Press, 2013.

Kaplan, Amy. "Manifest Domesticity." *American Literature* 70, no. 3 (1998): 581–606.

Kapsalis, Terri. *Public Privates: Performing Gynecology from Both Ends of the Speculum*. Durham, NC: Duke University Press, 1997.

Katz, Jonathan. *Gay American History: Lesbians and Gay Men in the U.S.A., a Documentary History*. New York: Thomas Crowell, 1976.

Katz, Michael B. *In the Shadow of the Poorhouse: A Social History of Welfare in America*. New York: Basic Books, 1996.

Kazanjian, David. *The Colonizing Trick: National Culture and Imperial Citizenship in Early America*. Minneapolis: University of Minnesota Press, 2003.

Keeling, Kara. *The Witch's Flight: The Cinematic, the Black Femme, and the Image of Common Sense*. Durham, NC: Duke University Press, 2007.

Keller, Evelyn Fox. *The Mirage of a Space between Nature and Nurture*. Durham, NC: Duke University Press, 2010.

Kelley, Mary. *Private Woman, Public Stage: Literary Domesticity in Nineteenth-Century America*. 2nd ed. Chapel Hill: University of North Carolina Press, 2002.

Kevles, Daniel. *In the Name of Eugenics: Genetics and the Uses of Human Heredity*. Cambridge, MA: Harvard University Press, 1995.

Klausen, Susanne, and Alison Bashford. "Fertility Control: Eugenics, Neo-Malthusianism, and Feminism." In *The Oxford Handbook of the History of Eugenics*, edited by Alison Bashford and Philippa Levine, 98–115. New York: Oxford University Press, 2010.

Klein, Lauren. "Matters of Taste: Eating, Aesthetics, and American Identity, 1720–1865." PhD diss., City University of New York, 2011.

Klein, Rachel N. "Harriet Beecher Stowe and the Domestication of Free Labor Ideology." *Legacy* 18, no. 2 (2001): 135–152.

Kline, Wendy. *Building a Better Race: Gender, Sexuality, and Eugenics from the Turn of the Century to the Baby Boom*. Berkeley: University of California Press, 2001.

Kogan, Terry Stuart. "Sex-Separation in Public Restrooms: Law, Architecture, and Gender." *Michigan Journal of Gender and Law* 14, no. 1 (2007): 3–58.

Krug, Kate. "Women Ovulate, Men Spermate: Elizabeth Blackwell as a Feminist Physiologist." *Journal of the History of Sexuality* 7, no. 1 (1996): 51–72.

Ladd-Taylor, Molly. *Mother-Work: Women, Child Welfare, and the State, 1890–1930*. Urbana: University of Illinois Press, 1994.

LaFleur, Greta. *The Natural History of Sexuality: Race, Environmentalism, and the Human Sciences in British Colonial North America*. Forthcoming.

LaFleur, Greta. "Precipitous Sensations: Herman Mann's *The Female Review* (1797), Botanical Sexuality, and the Challenge of Queer Historiography." *Early American Literature* 48, no. 1 (2013): 93–123.

LaFleur, Greta. "Sex and 'Unsex': Histories of Gender Trouble in Eighteenth-Century North America." *Early American Studies: An Interdisciplinary Journal* 12, no. 3 (January 2014): 469–499.

Langsam, Miriam Z. "Children West: A History of the Placing-Out System of the New York Children's Aid Society." MS thesis, University of Wisconsin–Madison, 1961.

Lanzoni, Susan. "Sympathy in *Mind* (1876–1900)." *Journal of the History of Ideas* 70, no. 2 (2009): 265–287.

Laqueur, Thomas. *Making Sex: Body and Gender from the Greeks to Freud*. Cambridge, MA: Harvard University Press, 1992.

Larson, Edward J. *Sex, Race, and Science: Eugenics in the Deep South*. Baltimore: Johns Hopkins University Press, 1996.

Lee, Rachel. *The Exquisite Corpse of Asian America: Biopolitics, Biosociality, and Posthuman Ecologies*. New York: New York University Press, 2014.

Levander, Caroline. *Cradle of Liberty: Race, the Child, and National Belonging from Thomas Jefferson to W. E. B. Du Bois*. Durham, NC: Duke University Press, 2006.

Levander, Caroline F. "The Science of Sentiment: The Evolution of the Bourgeois Child in Nineteenth-Century American Narrative." *Modern Language Studies* 30, no. 1. (2000): 27–44.

Lewis, David Levering. *W. E. B. Du Bois*, vol. 1: *Biography of a Race*. New York: Holt, 1993.

Lewis, David Levering. *W. E. B. Du Bois*, vol. 2: *The Fight for Equality and the American Century*. New York: Holt, 2000.

López-Beltrán, Carlos. "The Medical Origins of Heredity." In *Heredity Produced: At the Crossroads of Biology, Politics, and Culture, 1500–1870*, edited by Staffan Müller-Wille and Hans-Jörg Rheinberger, 105–132. Cambridge, MA: MIT Press, 2007.

Lowe, Lisa. *Immigrant Acts: On Asian American Cultural Politics*. Durham, NC: Duke University Press, 1996.

Lowe, Lisa. *Intimacies of Four Continents*. Durham, NC: Duke University Press, 2015.

Luciano, Dana. *Arranging Grief: Sacred Time and the Body in Nineteenth-Century America*. New York: New York University Press, 2007.

Luibhéid, Eithne. *Entry Denied: Controlling Sexuality at the Border*. Minneapolis: University of Minnesota Press, 2002.

Lutz, Tom. *American Nervousness, 1903: An Anecdotal History*. Ithaca, NY: Cornell University Press, 1991.

Lye, Colleen. *America's Asia: Racial Form and American Literature, 1893–1945*. Princeton, NJ: Princeton University Press, 2004.

Manning, Erin. *Politics of Touch: Sense, Movement, Sovereignty*. Minneapolis: University of Minnesota Press, 2007.

Mao, Douglas. *Fateful Beauty: Aesthetic Environments, Juvenile Development, and Literature, 1860–1960*. Princeton, NJ: Princeton University Press, 2010.

Margulis, Lynn, and Dorian Sagan. *Acquiring Genomes: A Theory of the Origin of the Species*. New York: Basic Books, 2003.

Markowitz, Sally. "Pelvic Politics: Sexual Dimorphism and Racial Difference." *Signs* 26, no. 2 (2001): 389–414.

Martín-Cabrera, Luis. "The Potentiality of the Commons: A Materialist Critique of Cognitive Capitalism from the Cyberbracer@s to the Ley Sinde." *Hispanic Review* 80, no. 4 (2012): 583–605.

Mason, Jennifer. *Civilized Creatures: Urban Animals, Sentimental Culture, and American Literature, 1850–1900.* Baltimore: Johns Hopkins University Press, 2005.

Mbembe, Achille. "Necropolitics." *Public Culture* 15, no. 1 (2003): 11–40.

McCann, Carole R. *Birth Control Politics in the United States, 1916–1945.* Ithaca, NY: Cornell University Press, 1994.

McGill, Meredith. "Frances Ellen Watkins Harper and the Circuits of Abolitionist Poetry." In *Early African American Print Culture,* edited by Lara Langer Cohen and Jordan Stein, 53–74. Philadelphia: University of Pennsylvania Press, 2012.

McHenry, Elizabeth. *Forgotten Readers: Recovering the Lost History of African American Literary Societies.* Durham, NC: Duke University Press, 2002.

McWhorter, Ladelle. *Racism and Sexual Oppression in Anglo-America: A Genealogy.* Bloomington: Indiana University Press, 2009.

Melamed, Jodi. *Represent and Destroy: Rationalizing Violence in the New Racial Capitalism.* Minneapolis: University of Minnesota Press, 2011.

Melamed, Jodi. "The Spirit of Neoliberalism: From Racial Liberalism to Neoliberal Multiculturalism." *Social Text* 24, no. 4 (2006): 1–24.

Menand, Louis. *The Metaphysical Club: A Story of Ideas in America.* New York: Farrar, Straus and Giroux, 2001.

Merish, Lori. *Sentimental Materialism: Gender, Commodity Culture, and Nineteenth-Century American Literature.* Durham, NC: Duke University Press, 2000.

Mitchell, David T., and Sharon L. Snyder. *The Biopolitics of Disability: Neoliberalism, Alienation, and Peripheral Embodiment.* Ann Arbor: University of Michigan Press, 2015.

Mitchell, Michele. *Righteous Propagation: African Americans and the Politics of Racial Destiny after Reconstruction.* Chapel Hill: University of North Carolina Press, 2004.

Mizruchi, Susan. "Neighbors, Strangers, Corpses: Death and Sympathy in the Early Writings of W. E. B. Du Bois." In *The Souls of Black Folk: Authoritative Text, Contexts, Criticism,* edited by W. E. B. Du Bois, Henry Louis Gates Jr. and Terry Hume Oliver, 273–295. New York: Norton, 1999.

Molina, Natalia. *Fit to Be Citizens? Public Health and Race in Los Angeles, 1879–1939.* Berkeley: University of California Press, 2006.

Moon, Michael. " 'The Gentle Boy from the Dangerous Classes': Pederasty, Domesticity, and Capitalism in Horatio Alger." *Representations* 19, no. 1 (1987): 87–110.

Morantz-Sanchez, Regina. *Conduct Unbecoming a Woman: Medicine on Trial in Turn-of-the-Century Brooklyn.* New York: Oxford University Press, 1999.

Morantz-Sanchez, Regina. *Sympathy and Science: Women Physicians in American Medicine.* New York: Oxford University Press, 1985.

Morgensen, Scott L. "The Biopolitics of Settler Colonialism: Right Here, Right Now." *Settler Colonial Studies* 1 (2011): 52–76.

Morgensen, Scott L. "Settler Homonationalism: Theorizing Settler Colonialism with Queer Modernities." *GLQ* 16, nos. 1–2 (2010): 105–131.

Morris, Aldon. *The Scholar Denied: W. E. B. Du Bois and the Birth of Modern Sociology*. Berkeley: University of California Press, 2015.

Müller-Wille, Staffan, and Hans-Jörg Rheinberger. "Heredity—The Formation of an Epistemic Space." In *Heredity Produced: At the Crossroads of Biology, Politics, and Culture, 1500–1870*, edited by Staffan Müller-Wille and Hans-Jörg Rheinberger, 3–34. Cambridge, MA: MIT Press, 2007.

Muñoz, José Esteban. "Feeling Brown, Feeling Down: Latina Affect, the Performativity of Race, and the Depressive Position." *Signs* 31, no. 3 (2006): 675–688.

Murison, Justine. *The Politics of Anxiety in Nineteenth-Century American Literature*. New York: Cambridge University Press, 2011.

Murphy, Michelle. *Seizing the Means of Reproduction: Entanglements of Feminism, Health, and Technoscience*. Durham, NC: Duke University Press, 2012.

Nash, Jennifer C. "Black Anality." *GLQ: A Journal of Lesbian and Gay Studies* 20, no. 4 (2014): 439–460.

Nelson, Claudia. *Little Strangers: Portrayals of Adoption and Foster Care in America, 1850–1929*. Bloomington: Indiana University Press, 2003.

Nelson, Dana D. Introduction to *A Romance of the Republic*, by Lydia Maria Child. Lexington: University Press of Kentucky, 1997.

Nelson, Dana D. " 'No Cold or Empty Heart': Polygenesis, Scientific Professionalization, and the Unfinished Business of Male Sentimentalism." *differences* 11, no. 5 (1999–2000): 29–56.

Newman, Louise Michele. *White Women's Rights: The Racial Origins of Feminism in the United States*. New York: Oxford University Press, 1999.

Ngai, Sianne. *Ugly Feelings*. Cambridge, MA: Harvard University Press, 2007.

Noble, Marianne. *The Masochistic Pleasures of Sentimental Literature*. Princeton, NJ: Princeton University Press, 2000.

Nyong'o, Tavia. *The Amalgamation Waltz: Race, Performance, and the Ruses of Memory*. Minneapolis: University of Minnesota Press, 2009.

O'Connell, Helen E., Kalavampara V. Sanjeevan, and John M. Hutson. "Anatomy of the Clitoris." *Journal of Urology* 174, no. 4 (2005): 1189–1195.

O'Connor, Stephen. *Orphan Trains: The Story of Charles Loring Brace and the Children He Saved and Failed*. Chicago: University of Chicago Press, 2004.

Olson, Joel. "W. E. B. Du Bois and the Race Concept." In *Racially Writing the Republic: Racists, Race Rebels, and Transformations of American Identity*, edited by Bruce Baum and Duchess Harris, 214–230. Durham, NC: Duke University Press, 2009.

Ordover, Nancy. *American Eugenics: Race, Queer Anatomy, and the Science of Nationalism*. Minneapolis: University of Minnesota Press, 2003.

Pascoe, Peggy. *Relations of Rescue: The Search for Female Moral Authority in the American West, 1874–1939*. New York: Oxford University Press, 1993.

Patterson, Orlando. *Slavery and Social Death: A Comparative Study*. Cambridge, MA: Harvard University Press, 1985.

Paul, Diane B. *Controlling Human Heredity, 1865 to the Present*. Amherst, NY: Humanity Books, 1995.

Pearson, Susan J. *The Rights of the Defenseless: Protecting Animals and Children in Gilded Age America*. Chicago: University of Chicago Press, 2011.

Pernick, Martin S. *A Calculus of Suffering: Pain, Professionalism, and Anesthesia in Nineteenth-Century America*. New York: Columbia University Press, 1985.

Peterson, Carla L. " 'Further Liftings of the Veil': Gender, Class, and Labor in Frances E. W. Harper's *Iola Leroy*." In *Listening to Silences: New Essays in Feminist Criticism*, edited by Elaine Hedges and Shelley Fisher Fishkin, 97–112. New York: Oxford University Press, 1994.

Pittenger, Mark. *American Socialists and Evolutionary Thought, 1870–1920*. Madison: University of Wisconsin Press, 1993.

Pitts-Taylor, Victoria. *The Brain's Body: Neuroscience and Corporeal Politics*. Durham, NC: Duke University Press, 2016.

Platt, Anthony M. *The Child Savers: The Invention of Delinquency*. Chicago: University of Chicago Press, 1977.

Plemons, Eric. *The Look of a Woman: Facial Feminization Surgery and the Aims of Trans- Medicine*. Durham, NC: Duke University Press, 2017.

Preciado, Paul B. *Testo Junkie: Sex, Drugs, and Biopolitics in the Pharmacopornographic Era*. Translated by Bruce Benderson. New York: Feminist Press at CUNY, 2013.

Puar, Jasbir K. "Inhumanist Occupation: Palestine and the 'Right to Maim.' " *GLQ: A Journal of Lesbian and Gay Studies* 21, nos. 2–3 (2015): 218–221.

Puar, Jasbir K. "Prognosis Time: Towards a Geopolitics of Affect, Debility, and Capacity." *Women and Performance: A Journal of Feminist Theory* 19, no. 2 (2009): 161–172.

Puar, Jasbir K. *Terrorist Assemblages: Homonationalism in Queer Times*. Durham, NC: Duke University Press, 2007.

Redding, Saunders. *To Make a Poet Black*. Ithaca, NY: Cornell University Press, 1988.

Reed, Adolph L., Jr. *W. E. B. Du Bois and American Political Thought: Fabianism and the Color Line*. New York: Oxford University Press, 1997.

Repo, Jemima. *The Biopolitics of Gender*. New York: Oxford University Press, 2016.

Richardson, Sarah S. "Maternal Bodies in the Postgenomic Order: Gender and the Explanatory Landscape of Epigenetics." In *Postgenomics: Perspectives on Biology after the Genome*, edited by Sarah S. Richardson and Hallam Stevens, 210–231. Durham, NC: Duke University Press, 2015.

Richardson, Sarah S. "Plasticity and Programming: Feminism and the Epigenetic Imaginary." *Signs: Journal of Women in Culture and Society* 43, no. 1 (2017): 29–52.

Richardson, Sarah S. *Sex Itself: The Search for Male and Female in the Human Genome*. Chicago: University of Chicago Press, 2013.

Riskin, Jessica. *Science in the Age of Sensibility: The Sentimental Empiricists of the French Enlightenment*. Chicago: University of Chicago Press, 2002.

Ritvo, Harriet. *The Platypus and the Mermaid and Other Figments of the Classifying Imagination*. Cambridge, MA: Harvard University Press, 1997.

Roberts, Dorothy. *Killing the Black Body: Race, Reproduction, and the Meaning of Liberty*. New York: Vintage, 1997.

Roberts, Dorothy. "Margaret Sanger and the Racial Origins of the Birth Control Movement." In *Racially Writing the Republic: Racists, Race Rebels, and Transformations of American Identity*, edited by Bruce Baum and Duchess Harris, 196–213. Durham, NC: Duke University Press, 2009.

Rodrique, Jessie M. "The Black Community and the Birth Control Movement." NWSA *Journal* 1, no. 4 (1989): 755–756.

Roediger, David R. *The Wages of Whiteness: Race and the Making of the American Working Class*. New York: Verso, 2007.

Romero, Lora. *Home Fronts: Domesticity and Its Critics in the Antebellum United States*. Durham, NC: Duke University Press, 1997.

Rose, Nikolas. *The Politics of Life Itself: Biomedicine, Biopower, and Subjectivity in the Twenty-First Century*. Princeton, NJ: Princeton University Press, 2006.

Rosenberg, J. "The Molecularization of Sexuality: On Some Primitivisms of the Present." *Theory and Event* 17, no. 2 (2014). muse.jhu.edu/article/546470.

Rusert, Britt. *Fugitive Science: Empiricism and Freedom in Early African American Culture*. New York: New York University Press, 2017.

Russett, Cynthia. *Sexual Science: The Victorian Construction of Womanhood*. Cambridge, MA: Harvard University Press, 1991.

Sacks, Oliver. *The Man Who Mistook His Wife for a Hat*. New York: Touchstone, 1998.

Salisbury, Laura, and Andrew Shail, eds. *Neurology and Modernity: A Cultural History of Nervous Systems, 1800–1950*. New York: Palgrave Macmillan, 2010.

Samuels, Ellen. *Fantasies of Identification: Disability, Gender, Race*. New York: New York University Press, 2014.

Samuels, Shirley, ed. *The Culture of Sentiment: Race, Gender, and Sentimentality in Nineteenth-Century America*. New York: Oxford University Press, 1992.

Sanborn, Geoffrey. "Mother's Milk: Frances Harper and the Circulation of Blood." ELH 73, no. 3 (2005): 691–715.

Sánchez-Eppler, Karen. *Dependent States: The Child's Part in Nineteenth-Century American Culture*. Chicago: University of Chicago Press, 2005.

Sánchez-Eppler, Karen. *Touching Liberty: Abolition, Feminism, and the Politics of the Body*. Berkeley: University of California Press, 1993.

Schaefer, Donovan O. *Religious Affects: Animality, Evolution, and Power*. Durham, NC: Duke University Press, 2015.

Schiebinger, Londa. *Nature's Body: Gender in the Making of Modern Science*. Boston: Beacon, 1993.

Schoen, Johanna. *Choice and Coercion: Birth Control, Sterilization, and Abortion in Public Health and Welfare*. Chapel Hill: University of North Carolina Press, 2005.

Schuller, Kyla. "The Biology of Intimacy: Biopower and the Orphan Novel in the Age of Lamarck." *Arizona Quarterly*. Forthcoming.

Schwartz, Marie Jenkins. *Birthing a Slave: Motherhood and Medicine in the Antebellum South*. Cambridge, MA: Harvard University Press, 2010.

Sears, Clare. *Arresting Dress: Cross-Dressing, Law, and Fascination in Nineteenth-Century San Francisco*. Durham, NC: Duke University Press, 2014.

Sedgwick, Eve Kosofsky. *Touching Feeling: Affect, Pedagogy, Performance*. Durham, NC: Duke University Press, 2003.

Seitler, Dana. *Atavistic Tendencies: The Culture of Science in American Modernity*. Minneapolis: University of Minnesota Press, 2008.

Shah, Nayan. *Contagious Divides: Epidemics and Race in San Francisco's Chinatown*. Berkeley: University of California Press, 2001.

Slavet, Eliza. *Racial Fever: Freud and the Jewish Question*. New York: Fordham University Press, 2009.

Smith, Caleb. *The Prison and the American Imagination*. New Haven, CT: Yale University Press, 2009.

Smith, Mark. *Sensing the Past: Seeing, Hearing, Smelling, Tasting, and Touching in History*. Berkeley: University of California Press, 2008.

Smith, Shawn Michelle. *American Archives: Gender, Race, and Class in Visual Culture*. Princeton, NJ: Princeton University Press, 1999.

Smith, Shawn Michelle. *Photography on the Color Line: W. E. B. Du Bois, Race, and Visual Culture*. Durham, NC: Duke University Press, 2004.

Snyder, Sharon L., and David T. Mitchell. *Cultural Locations of Disability*. Chicago: University of Chicago Press, 2006.

Somerville, Siobhan. *Queering the Color Line: Race and the Invention of Homosexuality in American Culture*. Durham, NC: Duke University Press, 2000.

Spillers, Hortense. "Mama's Baby, Papa's Maybe: An American Grammar Book." *Diacritics* 17, no. 2 (1987): 64–81.

Stancliff, Michael. *Frances Ellen Watkins Harper: African American Reform Rhetoric and the Rise of a Modern Nation State*. New York: Routledge, 2011.

Stansell, Christine. *City of Women: Sex and Class in New York: 1789–1860*. Chicago: University of Illinois Press, 1987.

Stanton, William. *The Leopard's Spots: Scientific Attitudes toward Race in America, 1815–59*. Chicago: University of Chicago Press, 1960.

Stehney, Valerie Nanaturey Vargas. "The Carlisle 62." *Issues in Caribbean Amerindian Studies* 2, no. 1 (1999–2000): 1–4.

Stepan, Nancy Leys. *The Hour of Eugenics: Race, Gender, and Nation in Latin America*. Ithaca, NY: Cornell University Press, 1991.

Stepan, Nancy Leys. "Race and Gender: The Role of Analogy in Science." *Isis* 77, no. 2 (1986): 261–277.

Stepan, Nancy Leys, and Sander Gilman. "Appropriating the Idioms of Science: The Rejection of Scientific Racism." In *The "Racial" Economy of Science: Toward a Democratic Future*, edited by Sandra Harding, 170–200. Bloomington: Indiana University Press, 1993.

Stern, Alexandra. *Eugenic Nation: Faults and Frontiers of Better Breeding in Modern America*. Berkeley: University of California Press, 2005.

Stern, Alexandra Minna. "Eugenics beyond Borders: Science and Medicalization in Mexico and the U.S. West, 1900–1950." PhD diss., University of Chicago, 1999.

Stocking, George W., Jr. *Race, Culture, and Evolution: Essays in the History of Anthropology*. Chicago: University of Chicago Press, 1982.

Stoler, Ann Laura. *Carnal Knowledge and Imperial Power: Race and the Intimate in Colonial Rule*. Berkeley: University of California Press, 2002.

Stoler, Ann Laura. *Race and the Colonial Education of Desire: Foucault's History of Sexuality and the Colonial Order of Things*. Durham, NC: Duke University Press, 1995.

Streeby, Shelley. *American Sensations: Class, Empire, and the Production of Popular Culture*. Berkeley: University of California Press, 2002.

Streeby, Shelley. *Radical Sensations: World Movements, Violence, and Visual Culture*. Durham, NC: Duke University Press, 2013.

Strick, Simon. *American Dolorologies: Pain, Sentimentalism, Biopolitics*. Albany: SUNY Press, 2015.

Subramaniam, Banu. *Ghost Stories for Darwin: The Science of Variation and the Politics of Diversity*. Champaign: University of Illinois Press, 2014.

TallBear, Kim. *Native American DNA: Tribal Belonging and the False Promise of Genetic Science*. Minneapolis: University of Minnesota Press, 2013.

Tate, Claudia. *Domestic Allegories of Political Desire: The Black Heroine's Text at the Turn of the Century*. New York: Oxford University Press, 1992.

Taylor, Carol M. "W. E. B. Du Bois' Challenge to Scientific Racism." *Journal of Black Studies* 11, no. 4 (1981): 449–460.

Terry, Jennifer. *An American Obsession: Science, Medicine and Homosexuality in Modern Society*. Chicago: Chicago University Press, 1999.

Todd, Janet. *Sensibility: An Introduction*. London: Methuen, 1986.

Tompkins, Jane. *Sensational Designs: The Cultural Work of American Fiction, 1790–1860*. New York: Oxford University Press, 1986.

Tompkins, Kyla Wazana. *Racial Indigestion: Eating Bodies in the 19th Century*. New York: New York University Press, 2012.

Trachtenberg, Alan. *The Incorporation of America: Culture and Society in the Gilded Age*. New York: Hill and Wang, 1982.

Treichler, Paula A. "AIDS, Homophobia, and Biomedical Discourse." *Cultural Studies* 1, no. 3 (1987): 263–305.

Van Sant, Ann Jessie. *Eighteenth-Century Sensibility and the Novel: The Senses in Social Context*. New York: Cambridge University Press, 1993.

Vora, Kalindi. *Life Support: Biocapital and the New History of Outsourced Labor*. Minneapolis: University of Minnesota Press, 2015.

Vrettos, Athena. "Defining Habits: Dickens and the Psychology of Repetition." *Victorian Studies* 42, no. 3 (1999/2000): 399–426.

Walker, William. *Locke, Literary Criticism, and Philosophy*. Cambridge: Cambridge University Press, 2006.

Walls, Laura Dassow. "Textbooks and Texts from the Brooks: Inventing Scientific Authority in America." *American Quarterly* 49, no. 1 (1997): 1–25.

Wardley, Lynn. "American Fiction and Civilizing House: 1850–1925." PhD diss., University of California, Berkeley, 1988.

Wardley, Lynn. "Lamarck's Daughters: Evolution, Feminism, and American Fiction, 1790–1925." Unpublished manuscript.

Wardley, Lynn. "Relic, Fetish, Femmage: The Aesthetics of Sentiment in the Work of Stowe." In *The Culture of Sentiment: Race, Gender, and Sentimentality in Nineteenth-Century America*, edited by Shirley Samuels, 203–220. New York: Oxford University Press, 1992.

Warner, Michael. *The Letters of the Republic*. Cambridge, MA: Harvard University Press, 1992.

Warner, Michael. *Publics and Counterpublics*. New York: Zone Books, 2005.

Weheliye, Alexander. *Habeas Viscus: Racializing Assemblages, Biopolitics, and Black Feminist Theories of the Human*. Durham, NC: Duke University Press, 2014.

Weinbaum, Alys Eve. *Wayward Reproductions: Genealogies of Race and Nation in Transatlantic Modern Thought*. Durham, NC: Duke University Press, 2004.

Weingarten, Karen. *Abortion in the American Imagination: Before Life and Choice, 1880–1940*. New Brunswick, NJ: Rutgers University Press, 2014.

Welter, Barbara. "The Cult of True Womanhood: 1820–1860." *American Quarterly* 18, no. 2, pt. 1 (1966): 151–174.

Wexler, Laura. *Tender Violence: Domestic Visions in an Age of U.S. Imperialism*. Chapel Hill: University of North Carolina Press, 2000.

Wheeler, Roxann. *The Complexion of Race: Categories of Difference in Eighteenth-Century British Culture*. Philadelphia: University of Pennsylvania Press, 2000.

Whorton, James C. *Crusaders for Fitness: The History of American Health Reformers*. Princeton, NJ: Princeton University Press, 1982.

Wiegman, Robyn. *American Anatomies: Theorizing Race and Gender*. Durham, NC: Duke University Press, 1995.

Willey, Angela. "A World of Materialisms: Postcolonial Feminist Science Studies and the New Natural." *Science, Technology, and Human Values* 41, no. 6 (2016): 991–1014.

Wilson, Elizabeth A. *Gut Feminisms*. Durham, NC: Duke University Press, 2015.

Wilson, Elizabeth A. *Psychosomatic: Feminism and the Neurological Body*. Durham, NC: Duke University Press, 2004.

Wilson, Ivy. *Specters of Democracy: Blackness and the Aesthetics of Nationalism in the Antebellum U.S.* New York: Oxford University Press, 2011.

Wynter, Sylvia. "Towards the Sociogenic Principle: Fanon, Identity, the Puzzle of Conscious Experience, and What It Is Like to Be 'Black.'" In *National Identities and Sociopolitical Changes in Latin America*, edited by Mercedes F. Durán-Cogan and Antonio Gómez-Moriana, 30–66. New York: Routledge, 2001.

Young, Robert M. *Darwin's Metaphor: Nature's Place in Victorian Culture*. New York: Cambridge University Press, 1985.

Zelizer, Viviana A. *Pricing the Priceless Child: The Changing Social Value of Children*. Princeton, NJ: Princeton University Press, 1994.

INDEX

....

Note: Page numbers in *italics* indicate illustrations.

affect, 6; animacy hierarchy of, 102; biopower and, 20; debility and, 13; impressibility and, 10, 13, 117, 123; privatization
and, 20; racialization and, 212, 218n49
affect theory, 15, 123; impression in,
6, 126
affirmative action, 205, 244n1
African Americans: birth control and,
197–200; black death, 1; eugenics and,
174, 197; futurity, 88, 191; middle class,
70–71; plasticity of, 72; police killings of,
1; as primitive, 69; primitivism and, 62,
84; pro-life recruitment of, 173; sexual
differentiation and, 88; shame and, 81,
228n56; social science and, 187; time and,
192–195; unimpressibility of, 142, 164;
youth, 161–162. *See also* black feminism;
Du Bois, W. E. B.
Agamben, Giorgio, 28
Agassiz, Louis, 39–41, 222n45; on polygenesis, 58, 180
Ahmed, Sara, 26, 125–126
Ahuja, Neel, 15
Alcott, Bronson, 138
Alger, Horatio, 149, 165
Allewaert, Monique, 44, 45
American School of Ethnology, 5; polygenesis
and, 58, 222n1
American School of Evolution, 32, 35–38,
41; eugenics and, 65; feeling, rhetoric of,
38–39; history of science and, 62; im-
pressibility in, 50, 53; impression theory
of, 53; legacy of, 65; as neo-Lamarckians,

50; origins of, 46–49; race and, 51, 55;
racial hierarchy of, 55; reproduction
and, 37; sentiment, emphasis on, 57;
sentimentalism of, 183–184; sex difference
and, 59, 64–65. *See also* Cope, Edward
Drinker; neo-Lamarckians
animal consciousness, 51, 53
Anthony, Susan B., 102
anthropology, colonial, 12
antiblackness, ontology of, 13
Aristotle: on impressibility, 43; on sensory
impressions, 41, 42–43; on touch, 77
Ayler, Alice Bullis, 168

Baker, Houston A., 228n60
Baldwin, James (novelist), 184
Baldwin, James Mark (philosopher), 190,
242n59
Barnes, Elizabeth, 56
Bay, Mia, 188
Beecher, Catharine, 46, 138
Beecher, Henry Ward, 138
Bennett, Jane, 25
Berlant, Lauren, 20; on biopower, 165; on
consumption, 156
biophilanthropy, 21, 136–137, 185; capitalism
and, 162; child labor and, 165, 168; decline
of, 166–167, 170; impressions, regulation
of, 161; liberal reform and, 137; pangenesis
and, 142; poor labor and, 151; racialization and, 164; security and, 179; sensory
management and, 163; sentimental fiction
and, 156; settler colonialism and, 136,

biophilanthropy (cont.)
164–165; slow death and, 165–166; youthful bodies and, 162–163

biopolitics, 13–15, 49, 226n6; v. biopower,
14–15; of birth control, 173; black feminists and, 68, 70, 98, 102; chronobiopolitics, 24, 88; eugenics and, 173; of feeling,
11, 143; feminism and, 17–18, 103, 105–106;
necropolitics and, 163–164; orphanhood
and, 159; of population, 15, 86, 139; race
and, 33–34; of racial uplift, 71, 175–176;
sentiment and, 96; sentimentalism and,
227n29; sex and, 33–34; sex difference
and, 17, 69, 110; subjectivity and, 237n69;
of touch, 77, 85; vaginal, 104–105, 115–116;
whiteness and, 13, 22, 102, 116. See also
sentimental biopower; sentimental
politics of life

biopower: affect and, 20; biological determinism and, 36; v. biopolitics, 14–15;
biotechnology and, 25; bodies, disciplining of, 14–15, 49, 147; defined, 2, 14–15;
disciplinary, 178; domesticity and, 20;
Du Bois and, 202, 203–204; the family
and, 20; feeling, regulation of, 79, 178;
feminism and, 103–106; governmentality
and, 132; impressibility and, 4, 8, 36, 54,
209; liberal democracy and, 2; population regulation of, 6, 174; race and, 13,
66, 204; racial difference and, 60; racial
hierarchies of, 125–126; racialization and,
164; as regulatory mechanism, 79; respectability and, 71; security power and,
49; sensation and, 166; sentiment and,
36, 49, 219n80; sentimentalism and, 2, 75;
sex and, 13; sex hierarchies of, 125–126;
subjectivity and, 122. See also sentimental
biopower

biotechnology, 24; imperial biopower and, 25

birth control: African Americans and, 200;
biopolitics of, 173; Du Bois and, 174,
195–196, 198, 212, 240n6; eugenics and,
172–173, 176, 195, 202, 241n35; racial progress and, 174, 195; racial uplift and, 200;
Sanger and, 182, 196; of the unfit, 182;
World War II and, 200

Birth Control Federation of America
(BCFA), 172, 239n1

"Birth-Mark, The" (Hawthorne), 83–84

black feminism, 63, 69; biopolitics of, 68,
70, 98, 102; eugenics and, 88–90; heredity
in, 86, 89, 181; impressible body in, 181;
pleasure in, 81–82; womanhood and, 88.
See also Cooper, Anna Julia; feminism;
Harper, Frances; Hopkins, Pauline

Black Lives Matter, 1–2, 3

blackness: pain and, 78; primitivism and, 62,
84; as static, 54

Blackwell, Antoinette Brown, 105, 108; on
nervous system, 124

Blackwell, Elizabeth, 5, 18, 33, 216n23, 231n16;
anatamo-politics of, 118–119; on civilized
sexuality, 112, 131–133; eugenics and,
127–128; on heredity, 128; on impressibility, 109–110, 114–115, 128; on masturbation, 111–113; moralism of, 104, 105, 111,
126; on prostitution, 111, 232n26; race and,
231n17; reception of, 101, 230n5; same-sex
relationships of, 129–130, 234n107; as
unscientific, 230n9; on the vagina,
100–101, 108–111, 116, 124; vaginal biopolitics of, 104–105, 116; on women's
suffrage, 104

Blackwell, Emily, 102, 104, 127–128; same-sex
relationships of, 129

Boas, Franz, 175, 192, 203, 205

bodies, 217n37; Asian, 13; as biocultural
formations, 41; biopower and, 14–15, 49,
70, 147; black, 13–14, 54, 75, 113–114, 181,
203; of children, 162; civilized, 12, 16, 44,
59, 96, 108–111, 117–119, 182; disciplining
of, 14–15, 49, 147, 162–163; discourse of,
3; enslaved, 118; environment and, 5–6;
epistemology and, 6; impressibility of, 21,
181; impressions on, 9, 41–42, 100; intersex, 120–123; marketizing of, 2; Native, 21,
55, 72, 162–165; as palimpsestic, 117, 161;
primitive, 56, 165; racialized, 13–14, 55;
sentimentalism and, 3, 4–5, 20; sex and,
108, 110; sex difference and, 16, 59, 117–119;
sexuality and, 108, 111–116; species difference and, 6; unimpressible, 72; vitality
of, 102, 203; women's, 102, 113–114, 182; of
youth, 162–163

Boggs, Colleen Glenney, 237n69

Bonnot, Étienne (Abbé de Condillac), 78

137, 176; genetics and, 185; Gilman and, 231n19; as heredity science, 175; impressibility and, 21, 88–89; as pseudoscience, 220n94; racial governmentality and, 170; racial progress and, 174; racial uplift and, 90, 175; racism and, 172, 243n96; risk and, 178–179; Sanger and, 172, 183, 241n35; security and, 178–180; v. sentimentalism, 168, 176, 180–181; in twentieth century, 65, 137; "unfit" persons and, 183; whiteness and, 241n28, 243n96. *See also* Du Bois, W. E. B.; heredity

evolution, Darwinian, 5, 35, 138–139, 144; agency in, 51; competition in, 46, 50, 222n44; Darwinian synthesis, 181, 241n29; gemmules, 143; impressibility and, 142–143; impression metaphor in, 143; natural selection in, 31, 46, 63, 95, 143; population in, 31; racial hierarchies of, 105; species change in, 46, 142; time in, 57. *See also* Darwin, Charles

evolution, Lamarckian, 5, 35, 50–51, 136, 165, 217n37; acquired characteristics, inheritance of, 29, 47, 50, 73, 142–145, 174–175, 177; on animal orgasms, 47; the civilized and, 145; environment and, 166–167; impressibility discourse of, 47–48; milieu in, 48; pleasure/pain in, 46–47, 52–53; race and, 191; species change in, 46; in U.S., 222n2. *See also* American School of Evolution; heredity; Lamarck, Jean-Baptiste; neo-Lamarckians

evolutionary theory: colonial hierarchy and, 71; human agency and, 63–64; literature and, 91; modern, 144; population and, 31; progress and, 63–64; racism and, 50. *See also* American School of Evolution

Fanon, Frantz, 211
Farland, Maria, 188
Fausto-Sterling, Anne, 210–212
feminism: biological, 105; biopolitics and, 17–18, 103, 105–106; biopower and, 103–106; civilization and, 102; Darwinian, 105, 220n113; eugenics and, 231n19; evolutionary, 105; gynecological, 181; impressibility in, 25, 181; whiteness and, 103. *See also* black feminism

Ferguson, Roderick, 17, 238n71
Foucault, Michel: on biopolitics, 49; on discipline, 178; on evolution and race, 58; on governmentality, 21, 220n92; on "man-as-species," 49–50; on milieu, 8; on race, 17, 49–50; on security, 31, 178, 200; on sexuality, 19–20, 29
Fretwell, Erica, 75
Freud, Sigmund, 12, 93, 217n45; ancestral memories and, 221n141; on the body, 217n37; on repression, 80

Galton, Francis, 22; on eugenics, 90, 137, 176; on heredity, 29, 30, 177; legacy of, 24; on maternal impressions, 86, 87; modern heredity and, 240n14; nature v. nurture, 28; security and, 178
Gamble, Clarence, 172, 199, 239n1
Geddes, Patrick, 123
gender: as cultural, 32; development of, 206; labor and, 79, 228n45; origin of term, 219n72; race and, 17; social construction of, 206. *See also* sex; sex difference
genetics, 10, 173–174, 181; determinism and, 176; eugenics and, 185; heredity and, 184; Mendelian, 63, 167; security and, 179. *See also* heredity
Gilman, Charlotte Perkins, 26, 105; eugenics and, 231n19
Gish, Clay, 151–152
Godwin, William, 94
Gordon, Linda, 239n1
Gould, Stephen Jay, 39
Grant, Madison, 180, 241n28
Gray, Asa, 138, 144, 236n36, 236n38
Greenwood, Grace, 79
Grosz, Elizabeth, 144–145
Gruesz, Kirsten Silva, 92

Hall, G. Stanley, 126
Hall, Stuart, 157
Haller, John, Jr., 236n44
Hallock, Thomas, 38
Hamlin, Kimberly, 105
Harper, Frances, 5, 12–13, 32–33, 63, 72, 226n2, 229n87; black bodies in, 75; civilized bodies in, 96; evolutionary aesthetics of, 90, 91–92, 98–99; on heredity,

natural selection, 143–145, 222n2; Darwinian, 31, 46, 63, 95, 143; Lamarckian, 144–145

necropolitics, 15, 163–164

Negro Project, 172–173, 175, 198–200, 201; as genocidal, 173; as racist, 173. See also Du Bois, W. E. B.

Nelson, Claudia, 235n18, 238n117

Nelson, Dana, 38

neo-Lamarckians: on intelligent selection, 36; on sexual deviance, 62; social reform and, 179–181; women's bodies and, 102. See also American School of Evolution; Cope, Edward Drinker

nervous system, 123–124; civilized, 47–48, 65, 101, 103–104, 109; environment and, 4, 51; impressibility and, 7–9, 15, 21, 110–111, 113–115, 124–126; vagina as, 100–104

neuroplasticity, 211, 244n12

new materialisms, 25–27, 221n119; race and, 26; vitality and, 212

New York Foundling, 237n61; emigration program of, 152–153; pinned notes of, 152–153, 153, 154, 155

New-York Historical Society Archives, 152, 237n61

Ngai, Sianne, 14

Noble, Marianne, 85

Nyong'o, Tavia, 11, 81, 228n61

Oken, Lorenz, 78

Olmsted, Frederick Law, 150

Olmsted, John, 150

Olson, Joel, 188

On the Origin of Species (Darwin), 138, 142, 235n19

orifices: bifurcated body and, 108; civilization and, 132; civilized bodies and, 119; governmentality of, 132–133; hierarchy of, 120, 122. See also vagina

orphanages, 140

orphanhood: biopolitics of, 159; commodity fetish and, 161; in sentimental literature, 141–142, 157

orphan labor: profitability of, 157; settler colonialism and, 161. See also Emigration Plan

orphans, 134; literature of, 157–161

Orphan Train, The (Harris), 170

orphan trains. See Emigration Plan

Osborn, Henry Fairfield, 65, 183–184, 243n89; neo-Lamarckism and, 183

Packard, Spring, Jr., 36, 60; on scientific knowledge, 64

pain: blackness and, 75, 78; erotics of, 85; impressibility and, 75; Lamarckian evolution and, 46–47, 53–53

palimpsests: body as, 117, 161; civilization and, 97; as model for race, 12–13, 19, 33–34, 66, 71, 90, 191, 208

Passing of the Great Race, The (Grant), 180, 241n28

Peirce, Charles, 63

pharmacopornopower, 23, 24, 220n105

Phelps, Elizabeth Stuart, 79, 100

Planned Parenthood, 201; Negro Project of, 198–201

plasticity, 11, 24–25; of African Americans, 72; biological, 23–24, 136–137; of biological material, 212; in feminist theory, 4; heredity and, 146, 171; impressibility and, 123, 129; neuroplasticity, 211, 244n12; plasticity/determinism duality, 25; politics of, 5; of whiteness, 141–142

Plato, 41–42

polygenesis, 39, 50, 58, 180, 222n1, 236n44; in Darwinian evolution, 145, 237n45

population: biopolitics of, 3, 15, 86, 139; biopower and, 6, 174; evolutionary theory and, 31, 191; impressibility and, 6–10, 33, 45, 96, 110, 207; impression and, 48–49; Malthus on, 8–9, 94–96; race and, 69, 207–208; regulation of, 76; sentimental ontology of, 9; sex and, 69, 207–208; shared sensation and, 92

porosity: in feminist theory, 4; of the liberal subject, 103; racialization and, 25, 27

Powell, John Wesley, 51–52

Pratt, Richard Henry, 161, 238n90; genocidal logic of, 163–164

Preciado, Paul B., 24, 220n105

primitivism: African Americans and, 62, 84; desire and, 84; women's suffrage and, 62

primitivity: of the body, 56; of Irish youth, 142; masturbation and, 113; Native bodies and, 165; penetrability and, 44–45; race and, 58; sexuality and, 113–114; unimpressibility and, 41, 109

prostitutes, sentimental narratives of, 148–149

pseudoscience, 220n94; sentimentalism as, 180

Puar, Jasbir K., 13, 15, 29, 217n46; on biopolitics, 226n6; on homosexuality, 30

queer of color theory, 17
queer theory, heteronormativity in, 29

race: American School of Evolution and, 51, 55; as biological concept, 11, 175–176; as biopolitical category, 33–34; biopower and, 13, 66, 125–126, 204; birth control and, 174, 195, 200; capitalism and, 204; civilization and, 16, 96, 174; the civilized and, 12, 13; colonialism and, 204; as cultural, 31–32, 175–176, 191–192, 203, 205, 244n1; determinist notions of, 11–12, 31, 41, 93, 145, 204, 217n40; difference and, 71; environmentalism and, 10; evolution and, 105, 191; Foucault on, 17, 49–50; gender and, 17; heredity and, 88–90, 179, 202; impressibility and, 5, 13, 36, 41, 50, 55, 66; labor and, 14; language and, 145; Malthus on, 96; neoliberalism and, 205, 244n1; ontology of, 11; palimpsestic model of, 12–13, 19, 33–34, 66, 71, 90, 191, 208; performativity and, 219n83; population and, 69, 207–208; primitivity and, 58; reproduction and, 29; sensorial discipline and, 19; sentiment and, 36; sentimental biopower and, 4; sex and, 219n71; sex difference and, 17, 30, 59; as social construction, 10–11, 15, 188, 203, 205–206, 244n5; time and, 57–58; "true womanhood" and, 17; unimpressibility and, 13–14; the vagina and, 108–109

race science, homosexuality and, 30
Races of the Old World, A Manual of Ethnology (Brace), 145
Race Traits and Tendencies of the American Negro, The (Hoffman), 187

racial difference, 145; biopower and, 12, 60; evolution and, 208; impressibility and, 53,

101; malleability and, 146; nation and, 36; sex difference and, 105

racial formation, as palimpsestic process, 93–94, 96

racialization: affect and, 212, 218n49; biophilanthropy and, 164; biopower and, 164; environment and, 145; of Native bodies, 55; porosity and, 25, 27; sex difference and, 208–209; temporality of, 58; of touch, 79; vitality and, 25, 27

racism: biological determinism and, 11; evolutionary theory and, 50; variability of species and, 50. *See also* eugenics; race

Reed, Adolph, Jr., 192

representation, black uplift and, 89

reproduction, 37, 41; of civilized bodies, 111; as disability, 60; Du Bois and, 195–196, 201; heredity and, 28–29; heterosexuality and, 31, 182; impressibility and, 88–90; liberation and, 194–198; poverty and, 201; race and, 29; regeneration and, 29; sentimental ethic of, 160–161; sex and, 29

repulsion, 80–82

respectability: biopower and, 71; erotics of, 85; politics of, 81–82, 85, 194, 226n9, 228n61; shame and, 81

Rheinberger, Hans-Jörg, 29

Riskin, Jessica, 222n8; on sentimental empiricism, 40

Roberts, Dorothy, 174, 240n3, 240n9

Rollins, Alice Wellington, 160

Rose, Nikolas, 23–24, 217n28

Rusert, Britt, 89

Russett, Cynthia Eagle, 144, 231n12

Sacks, Oliver, 97–98

Sanborn, Geoffrey, 82

Sanchez-Eppler, Karen, 156

Sanger, Margaret, 105, 172, 182, 199; on African American reproduction, 197; birth control and, 182, 196; eugenic rhetoric and, 172, 182, 241n35; on sexual pleasure, 182; on women's self-determination, 182. *See also* birth control; Negro Project; Planned Parenthood

science: as anti-sentimental, 38; professionalization of, 38–39, 64; sentimentalism and, 5, 38, 64, 184; sympathy, 104

Seitler, Dana, 217n45, 231n19
sensation, 6; biopower and, 166; discourse of, 47; as palimpsestic, 98
senses, 77–79. *See also* sensorial discipline; sight; touch
sensibility, 7, 51; the civilized and, 16; defined, 40; discourses of, 10, 37–39, 47; empiricism and, 39; impressibility and, 40; touch and, 78
sensorial discipline, 18, 162; race and, 19
sentiment, 6, 48, 216n15; biopolitical function of, 96; biopower and, 36, 49, 219n80; defined, 40, 217n30, 222n8; as disciplinary technology, 55–56, 65, 70; as epistemology, 56; evolution of, 55–58; heredity and, 22; as male, 60; as ontology, 56; as women's provenance, 19. *See also* sentimentalism
sentimental biopower, 3–4, 6; antecedents of, 41–42; child welfare and, 33, 138, 140; Lamarck and, 48; population and, 3; racial difference and, 12; racial hierarchy and, 204; as regulatory technology, 207; sensorial discipline and, 166, 207; sex difference and, 12. *See also* biopower
sentimentalism: as affectation, 183–184; of American School of Evolution, 183–184; as biopolitical technology, 70; biopolitics and, 227n29; biopower and, 2, 75; black women writers and, 68; the body and, 3, 4–5, 20; capitalism and, 20; chrono-biopolitics of, 216n12; as disciplinary technology, 71, 176; discourses of, 37, 38, 59, 68, 181; emotional worth and, 184; as empirical knowledge, 180, 182, 187; as enervating force, 215n5; epistemology of, 38, 40, 63–64, 66, 176, 180, 184, 186–189, 202; eugenics and, 168, 176, 180–181; evolutionary aesthetics of, 90–93; feeling, aesthetics of, 38; ideology of, 215n5; impressibility and, 181; liberal democracy and, 2; ontology of, 3; as pseudoscience, 180; race science and, 40; as regulatory technology, 9–10, 18, 76, 85; as scientific discourse, 64; scientific epistemology and, 184; scientific practice and, 5, 38; state power and, 20; sympathy and, 2; time and, 3, 18, 57; visual culture and,

215n5. *See also* sentiment; sentimental politics of life
sentimentality: civilization and, 102; the civilized and, 16; as female, 60; sex and, 36; touch and, 102
sentimental literature, 184; biophilanthropy and, 156; child migration in, 160–161; domestic labor in, 159–160; as feminine, 188; orphanhood in, 141–142, 157; reproduction, ethic of, 160–161
sentimental politics of life, 4–5, 17–22, 28, 33–34; affect, regulation of, 103; animacy hierarchy of, 160; biopower and, 14; biosecurity and, 185; black feminist biopolitics and, 70; child migrants and, 135–136; civilized bodies and, 117; eugenics and, 146; genetics and, 173–174; habit, progressive power of, 36; heredity and, 104; labor and, 138; legacy of, 203; population and, 104; security biopower and, 188; self-discipline in, 104, 122; sexuality, regulation of, 117; sympathy and, 104. *See also* sentimental biopower; sentimentalism
settler colonialism, 24, 45; biophilanthropy and, 136, 164–165; capitalism and, 170; Emigration Plan and, 147; genocide and, 164–165; Lamarckism and, 144; Locke and, 45, 222n39; orphan labor and, 147, 161; whiteness and, 238n96
sex: as biopolitical category, 33–34; biopower and, 13, 125–126; civilized bodies and, 108, 110; as palimpsestic, 208; population and, 69, 207–208; race and, 219n71; whiteness and, 24. *See also* gender
sex difference, 60–61, 233n85; African Americans and, 88; American School of Evolution and, 59, 64–65; biopolitics of, 17, 69, 110; civilization and, 16, 114–115, 219n72; of civilized bodies, 16, 59, 117–119; consolidation of, 103, 231n12; discourse of, 16–17, 108; heredity and, 17; impressibility and, 16, 41, 101, 208; labor and, 128; of liberal subjects, 103; nation and, 36; nationality and, 16; race and, 17, 30, 59; racial difference and, 105; racialization and, 208–209; sentimental biopower and, 4; whiteness and, 209; women's rights and, 133. *See also* gender